THE LAST ROMANTIC

The Last Romantic

* * A LIFE * * OF MAX EASTMAN

William L. O'Neill

New York
OXFORD UNIVERSITY PRESS
1978

Copyright © 1978 by William L. O'Neill

Library of Congress Cataloging in Publication Data

O'Neill, William L
    The last romantic: a life of Max Eastman.

    Bibliography: p.
    Includes index.
    1. Eastman, Max, 1883–1969—Biography. 2. Authors,
American—20th century—Biography. 3. Editors—
United States—Biography.
PS3509.A752Z8   818'.5'209   78-249
ISBN 0-19-502405-2

Printed in the United States of America

For Ivan Dee

Preface

I did not know Max Eastman well. He was eighty years old when we first met, and I was twenty-eight, a difference in ages that could not be overcome entirely. I saw Max only four times, but two of these involved visits of several days each at his home on Martha's Vineyard. It was in the course of lengthy talks there that I formed the personal impressions reflected in this book. We also corresponded frequently when I was editing my anthology of his magazine, the *Masses*. To my regret we did not exchange political views. The fault is mine, as I took Max to be more conservative than he was, and so made unnecessary efforts to avoid friction. All the same he did drop political remarks, some of which I jotted down. Long afterward when I looked at these notes it became clear that in his final years Max had largely abandoned ideology. He was liberal on some matters and conservative on others, but not a member of either camp.

This book arises from deep affection and respect for Max, and my feeling that his best work has been neglected or undervalued. But it is not personal, nor have I relied much on interviews with friends and surviving relatives. Partly this is because I am not a good interviewer, partly because no one remains alive who was close to Max in the early years of his life for which the evidence is thinnest and most in need of augmentation. His later years are exceptionally well documented, and so I have found answers to most of my questions in libraries. Almost everything here is based on primary sources, chiefly Max's own books and papers.

Two important considerations shaped the design of this book. The first is my opinion that what we need most today is a reconsideration of Max's public life, and especially of his relation to what might be called the social history of ideas. Max was always best known as a celebrity, and among those who remember him he is still thought of mainly in that way. But he was a working intellectual all his life, with an excellent background in philosophy and the classics. For many years he was a distinguished social and political critic, an aspect of his life that is often forgotten or ignored. He was also a great memoirist, though only scholars seem to have recognized this. He was a master of the essay. Accordingly, it is the writer and not the man in whom I am most interested, though as the one cannot be understood without reference to the other I have included substantial information about his private life.

There is a second reason, or group of reasons, why I have made ideas rather than experience the focus. Although it is my professional judgment that has governed the choice, I am by profession an historian, not a biographer, more at home with abstractions than with people. Naturally I would prefer to work from strength. Then, too, Max's autobiography is immense and detailed, freeing me from the need to go over finely matters covered at length by him. The main reason, however, for not going more deeply into Max's inner life is that too many of the crucial documents are unavailable. There are revealing love letters to and from Max in the Lilly Library of Indiana University. These have been closed to scholars, and though I have read enough of them to generalize about Max's sex life, I am not allowed to employ them directly. Yvette Eastman, Max's widow, has in her possession family and personal papers which she has also restricted. When these are opened it should be possible to write an intimate study of Max, and possibly even of the complex relations between him and his remarkable mother and sister. At present, however, it makes no sense to dwell on matters for which we have little evidence but expectations of a great deal to come. At several points I have offered a Freudian explanation for the most puzzling aspects of Max's life. This has not been done because I have an expert knowledge of, or even much faith in, psychoanalysis. But there were contradictions in Max that cannot be understood in terms of the rule of reason. As they seem to yield to a classic Freudian diagnosis I have felt obliged to draw the obvious conclusions, but do so tentatively, aware of my ignorance, and in anticipation of a day when all the papers will be opened, thus permitting more accuracy and sophistication than now.

Meanwhile, we must make the best of what we have, which is actually quite a lot. Our sense of the inner man has to be uncertain, but of the public man we can speak with confidence. His career is a matter of record that future discoveries are unlikely to change. Yet the whole of that record has never been thoroughly inspected before. Historical figures do not usually improve on close examination. I think Eastman does, and hope the reader will agree.

Edison, New Jersey
March, 1978   WILLIAM L. O'NEILL

Acknowledgments

First I am indebted to Yvette Eastman, Max's widow, for permission to use his papers at the Lilly Library, and some of the Eastman family documents in her possession, which are identified in my notes as the Vineyard MSS. This is, however, in no sense an authorized biography, and Mrs. Eastman disagrees sharply with my assessment of Max. Mariejo Eastman, the widow of Max's son Daniel, generously shared her experiences with me. Samuel Eastman, Max's nephew, did the same. David J. Fischer clarified the Eastman-Rolland exchange for me. Wayne Cooper told me about his contacts with Max, and gave me the benefit of his detailed knowledge of Claude McKay. Jack Alan Robbins had some informative conversations with Max which he summarized for me. Alan Wald criticized my remarks on Trotsky. Joseph Slater gave me his impressions of Max, and access to his Eastman letters. Neil R. Joy kindly loaned me a copy of his unpublished article on the Eastman-Hemingway fight. Blanche Wiesen Cook, who has a special interest in Crystal Eastman, and who admires the family as I do, has been helpful and encouraging. Sheldon Meyer and Victoria Bijur of Oxford University Press have been a pleasure to work with. My agent Georges Borchardt has been a tower of strength throughout. I thank all of the above for easing my task.

I am very grateful to Rutgers University for a research fellowship that allowed me a year's leave to write this book. The American Philosophical Society helped with travel funds, which extended much further than one would suppose, thanks to the hospitality of friends.

My thanks go to Yvette Eastman, Katherine Olstein, Ginny and Tom Schornhorst, and Mr. and Mrs. Joseph Slater.

I thank the Lilly Library of Indiana University for permission to use and quote from the large body of Eastman papers in its possession. The collection is divided as follows: the Max Eastman MSS, the Eliena Eastman MSS, the Anstice Ford Eastman MSS, the Claude McKay MSS, and the Leon Trotsky MSS. Several letters from Max are in the vast Upton Sinclair MSS. I am particularly grateful to the splendid staff of the Lilly, notably Virginia Mauck, who catalogued the papers, and Wilma Etnier and Harriet Castrataro. Quotations from the Oswald Garrison Villard and John Reed papers are by permission of the Houghton Library of Harvard University. Quotations from the V. F. Calverton Papers are by permission of the Manuscripts and Archives Division, the New York Public Library Astor, Lenox and Tilden Foundations. The photographs which appear here were taken from the Pictures Collection of the New York Public Library. I am indebted to Louis M. Starr, Director of the Oral History Research Office of Columbia University, for permission to quote from "The Reminiscences of John Spargo" and "The Reminiscences of Max Shachtman," both copyrighted 1975; to Elena Wilson for permission to quote from unpublished letters, and to Mrs. Wilson and Farrar, Straus & Giroux for permission to quote from *Letters on Literature and Politics* by Edmund Wilson, Selected and edited by Elena Wilson, Introduction by Daniel Aaron, Foreword by Leon Edel, copyright 1957, 1973, 1974, 1977 by Elena Wilson, Executrix of the Estate of Edmund Wilson; from *Classics and Commercials* by Edmund Wilson, copyright 1940 by Edmund Wilson; and from *To the Finland Station* by Edmund Wilson, copyright 1940 by Edmund Wilson; to Harper & Row for permission to quote from *The Gulag Archipelago* 1918–1956 by Aleksandr I. Solzhenitsyn, Translated from the Russian by Thomas P. Whitney, Copyright 1973 by Aleksandr I. Solzhenitsyn, English language translation copyright 1973, 1974 by Harper & Row, Publishers, Inc. I thank the following individuals for permission to quote from their unpublished letters: William F. Buckley, Jr.; Leon Edel; Margaret Halsey; DeWitt Wallace.

It has given me much happiness to dedicate this work to my friend Ivan Dee, a great bookman.

Contents

Introduction

In 1918 Max Eastman was one of the most famous and influential radicals in America. His magazine the *Liberator* raised a lone voice against the suppression of liberty at home during World War I and the Red Scare that followed, spoke in aid of Soviet Russia, upheld women's rights, called for a social revolution. Twice the government indicted Eastman and his associates under the dreaded Espionage Acts. Twice the result was a hung jury, thanks especially to Max, the star of both trials and chief spokesman for the defense. He was thirty-six years old at the time, tall, startlingly handsome, a speaker who could rouse mass meetings or hold unfriendly jurors spellbound. Once he was nearly lynched for speaking against the war, a tribute to his effectiveness. Charlie Chaplin, then at the peak of his fame, paid Max another kind of compliment in saying he had "the essence of all art—restraint." Beautiful women fell at his feet, and often into his bed. He had already written four books, including his little classic, *Enjoyment of Poetry*.

He would visit Soviet Russia in the twenties and become Trotsky's first American disciple, also his English translator and literary agent. Max defended Bolshevism for eighteen years, yet was the only American writer Josef Stalin ever attacked by name. Once he knocked down Ernest Hemingway—or possibly vice versa. He wrote a total of twenty-six books, including five of poetry and one of fiction, made five major translations from the Russian, and edited two anthologies and a movie. Edmund Wilson said that Max's best books have "a clarity and terseness of form, an intellectual edge, which it would be hard to match elsewhere today in the American literature of ideas." Yet when Max died in 1969 few people knew who he was, and fewer still remember him today.

This is the public's loss, for Max led a remarkable life from the time he first set foot on the streets of New York in 1907. He studied philosophy at Columbia University and life in Greenwich Village. In 1912 he became editor of the *Masses,* a socialist monthly of art and opinion. The time was right for a witty and beautiful magazine with revolutionary aspirations, and Max made the most of it. As a result he became wildly popular among literary and left-wing people. The capitalist system failed to give way as Max had expected, but there was a moral and cultural revolution that did succeed, and Max was in the thick of it. This meant, on the one hand, campaigning for particular reforms such as birth control and woman suffrage, while on the other building a liberated climate of opinion. Free love of course; but free expression was wanted, too. Thanks to Max Eastman, Isadora Duncan, Margaret Sanger, Emma Goldman, Sherwood Anderson, thousands of agitators, anarchists, artists, the free souls and free thinkers of Greenwich Village, among others, the fight for personal freedom was largely won, and surprisingly soon. The "greening" of America in the sixties was an outgrowth of this earlier and better revolution, not a new invention of the young in 1967 as often claimed. Most essential personal freedoms, including freedom from Victorian sexual taboos, were secured in the early years of this century. Max's principal contribution to individual liberty was made even before America went to war in 1917.

The war made Max a hero, though not because he coveted martyrdom. Hiding from lynch mobs was a sport he failed to relish. Unlike most Socialists, however, and millions of other Americans who were against the war, Max was in a position to do something about it; indeed, was morally obliged to take action regardless of the risk. When his magazine was suppressed he promptly started another. He was in great demand as a speaker, first against American intervention, later on behalf of the new Soviet government, which he admired without restraint. His appearances at mass meetings, and government efforts to imprison him, made Max's name practically a household word. Max did not shrink from the limelight. He needed admiration and acclaim and was unhappy without them. Yet, perhaps because both his parents were ministers, Max was not comfortable with success. At the close of 1921, when his influence and reputation were greatest, Max left for

Europe. During the five years he was gone his glory faded, never to be restored.

Even had he known the price in advance, Max would still have paid it, and not just out of stubbornness. His twenty-one months in Russia determined his future. Russia was his greatest adventure, and explaining communism to the world became the great mission of his life. Soviet Russia brought out the best in him as a man and an intellectual, and the worst, too. It was on account of Russia that he ruined himself politically, alienating radicals and liberals alike. Events in Russia finally led him to abandon political beliefs held for over a quarter-century.

Max's progression from far left to far right was by no means unusual. On William Buckley's *Natural Review* he would find himself surrounded by former Communists. But it was typical of Max that he was almost the only one who had never been a Stalinist. The overwhelming majority of Americans who became Communists or communist sympathizers did so after Stalin came to power. But Max had favored Trotsky from the start and so was always critical of the Soviet government after 1924, even when he was most infatuated with Bolshevism. It was also typical that although Max became in a real sense the first American Trotskyist—from 1924 to about 1928 he was a party of one—he never joined Trotsky's movement. Max was a lone wolf and could not run in packs, no matter how small or distinguished.

When Max returned to America early in 1927, he found himself isolated politically for the first time. To most Americans he was a Communist, an exponent of Bolshevism since the Russian Revolution. But to most radicals he was in disgrace for having sided with the left opposition against Stalin and released documents harmful to the regime—notably "Lenin's Testament," warning the party to beware of Stalin. Not a single one of Max's numerous former friends and political allies in the American Left supported Trotsky. Max's position became even more difficult in the 1930s when many liberals and intellectuals became excited over Russia. Only a handful of independent writers —Edmund Wilson, Sidney Hook, V. F. Calverton—shared Max's increasingly negative view of the Soviet Union, appearing with him in V. F. Calverton's *Modern Monthly.*

The tide of history was running his way just the same. While liberals acclaimed Russia as a model of social and economic justice, Max kept piling up evidence to the contrary. In 1939 when Moscow betrayed the anti-fascists by signing a pact with Berlin, opening the way for Germany's invasion of Poland and World War II, Max was prepared. Within a year he woul.d bring out two big books, his most penetrating and finished critiques of Soviet politics and ideology. In *Stalin's Russia and the Crisis of Socialism* he reviewed Soviet history, exposed the Moscow Purge Trials as fraudulent, and disproved Russian claims to social and economic virtue. In *Marxism: Is It Science?* Max showed that it was not. These books especially, fruits of more than twenty years of meditation and experience, led Edmund Wilson to put Max in the front rank of contributors to the literature of ideas. Max now seemed destined to become a revered figure in journalism's higher strata, alongside Wilson and Walter Lippmann and very few others.

As before, Max contrived to diminish his reputation. He wrote an article for the *Reader's Digest* called "Socialism Does Not Gibe with Human Nature," branding himself as a Philistine twice over, and then joined the *Digest*'s group of contributing editors. In later years he sang the praises of capitalism, denounced the government repeatedly for being soft on communism, and aligned himself with Senator Joseph R. McCarthy in the worst days of the post-war witchhunt. This was unforgiveable, and Max was not forgiven. Few took him seriously after this except conservatives. Yet Max was an unconvincing conservative, as Buckley has pointed out. In the end he broke with the National Review. As a militant atheist he could not stand its religious flavor. It seemed to him unwise to link anti-communism with Christianity in a world where Christians were heavily outnumbered. Other doubts arose. At his death Max identified himself with no political faction or creed.

Such a life, marked by paradox and contradiction, raises many questions for which answers must at least be attempted. Why was Max so self-destructive professionally and politically? How could someone who believed fanatically in personal freedom, who hated bullies and deceivers, speak on behalf of Joe McCarthy? How could a man embrace in old age so much of what he had opposed when young? Why was Max so often out of step with his times and his peers? Since he viewed poetry as the highest form of expression and despised journalism, why did he write so much for magazines?

Beyond the personal are broader issues concerning the individual's relation to history. Although the revolution in morals he contributed to as a young man succeeded, most of the causes he fought for either failed or were compromised. Socialism lost in America, while its victory in Russia produced the opposite of what Max desired. An ardent interventionist in 1941, Max saw the war he favored lead to enormous gains by his enemies. Anti-communism succeeded in America, but at great cost to his personal standing and to the cause itself. The means used seemed in retrospect so unsavoury that anti-communism was discredited. Memory has been lost of why it was advocated by highly responsible people.

As leader, spokesman, or participant Max did not play a decisive role in any of these struggles. History would have turned out the same without him. Neither this fact, nor the failure or ambiguity of his causes makes his life any the less interesting or important. From individuals who court popularity we can learn only part of the story. It is people who go against the grain from whom we get the rest. Eastman was most admired when he was least original, in the wonderful Progressive era when Victorian culture fell apart and nothing seemed impossible, and during World War I when millions agreed with him that intervention was mistaken. He was most perceptive and also most heroic during the 1930s when hardly anyone listened to him, or cared in the least to know his unwelcome revelations. And this was conspicuously true of those who in theory attached the greatest weight to reason, openmindedness, and the rules of evidence. Marxists naturally abused him, but liberals and intellectuals did too. This tells us much about the life of the mind and the warping of progressive values in those bitter years.

America's journey through the first half of this century was too immense for any one man to experience or understand completely. But few intellectuals had a broader scope or were more involved in crucial issues and events over this long period than Max. His career sheds light on matters once thought important, and on others that still are. Max was not a great man in the usual sense. He did not always make the best use of his talents and sometimes seemed, especially to himself, to have "never done or been any definite thing." He did, however, lead a great life. This is a record of it.

It might seem fatuous to speak of him as the last of our romantics: but there are no others left who knew the real meaning of the word "joy," and who left that feeling in the hearts of those who knew him.

Leon Edel of Max Eastman

THE LAST ROMANTIC

CHAPTER ONE

Youth

1883–1912

Max Eastman was not Jewish, despite his name, Jewish first wife, radical enthusiasms, and graduate training at Columbia University. His ancestors were New Englanders, and Max, though born in New York state, was at least an honorary Yankee. Max was lucky to be anything, since he came into the world by accident. His mother had three children already and did not want Max, or "any more of the experience which produced me. My coming meant the end of my parents' physical relations and the beginning of a series of calamities that well-nigh broke up our whole family. Little could have been said in justification of my solemn-eyed arrival on the basis of existing data. And yet I made good and lived to hear my mother use me as an argument against birth control."[1]

Like Max's Grandfather Eastman, both his parents, Samuel and Annis Ford Eastman, were ministers. Max's father had caught pneumonia while on active duty during the Civil War and suffered from ill health for many years afterward, or claimed to. Max was suspicious of this, implying that father malingered. Samuel's condition meant that for years the burden of family support had to be assumed by his wife. This was not quite so onerous as might be supposed. At a time when woman's place was in the home, Annis had defied her father and gone to study theology at Oberlin College, where she met Samuel. When ill health obliged him to give up his profession, Annis became the first woman in New York state to be ordained a Congregational minister. Her career was much more successful than Samuel's, even after he resumed preaching.

Max described his father as distant, silent, passive, self-absorbed, isolated from the rest of the family. A very brief chapter on him in Max's autobiography is called "My Sainted Father." The point of this becomes evident when we learn that Max hated saintliness, piety, and genteel goodness. Although Annis was good, too, she was not pious and had other redeeming merits, being humorous, demonstrative, ambitious, capable, and open-minded. In one book Max called her his "first great companion." Samuel and Annis were married in 1875 and two years later had their first child, Morgan, who was followed by Anstice Ford (1878), Crystal (1881), and Max on January 4, 1883.

Though unwanted, Max was not unloved. His mother, and Crystal, too, lavished affection on him. Even so, Max believed that his childhood was blighted, partly because his conception marked the end of sexual relations between his parents, and by the tragic death of his oldest brother Morgan in 1884. Morgan's birth had improved the Eastmans' marriage. Like many middle-class Victorian girls, Annis had known nothing about sex. Marriage to Samuel relieved her ignorance but accomplished little else. Morgan was to her the first reward for having intercourse, and his sudden death of scarlet fever was catastrophic. Morgan's death resulted in what Max called "The Shadow in My Soul." For a year his mother was physically ill, and thereafter subject to deep depressions. Max felt that his own sickly, frightened childhood stemmed at least in part from her. "I imbibed that irrational emotion which engulfed so much of my early life and upon which my gradually emerging equilibrium, my gestures of courage, my wonderful days of delight, all indeed that I am . . . float rather precariously and on a shallow keel."[2]

The history of his youth, which occupies much of *Enjoyment of Living,* is in considerable measure a story of frights and fears, eased only by the attentions of his mother and sister and his love of nature. After Annis recovered physically from Morgan's death, Samuel, who had only one good lung, declined. She then went to work, and Samuel bought a farm, which delighted Max. He could not be sent to school until he was eight years old because of his "night terrors," feelings that in some way were heightened by the prospect of education. Fortunately he could indulge his passion for animals, the reverse side, he wrote later, of his fear of people. Even after the farm was sold in 1891, the year following Annis' ordination, the family lived in a small town. Though his professional life was always associated with New York, Max would never like cities. As an adult he managed to spend a surprising amount of time outside them.

Max did eventually go to school. He remained shy, fearful, and backward in most areas, unlike his brother and sister. Anstice (later called Ford and later still Peter) was a brash, impetuous boy, a Tom Sawyer-like figure whom beatings could not tame or dismay. He was also a good student, graduating from high school at the age of thirteen, a year younger than Max would be when he entered high school.* Crystal, too, was a good student, full of life and fun. Max always considered her one of the most vital, confident, outgoing individuals he knew. The social and academic successes of brother and sister did nothing to bolster Max's self-esteem, which was further undermined when his mother was called to become assistant pastor at Elmira's Park Church.

This was an honor because the pastor was Thomas K. Beecher. One of many famous Beechers, Thomas was second to none in force of character and liberality. Under his direction the Park Church was a nationally known center of progressive, non-denominational Christianity. Annis Ford Eastman earned her place in this rare institution by working her way up the clerical ladder, first as an unordained pastor, then as a licensed minister, and finally as a notable preacher in an age when oratory was much admired. The high point in her career before going to Elmira was an invitation to speak at the World's Congress of Religions in Chicago during the Columbian exposition of 1893.

Her success was remarkable, considering the time and the field, one in which women seldom achieved distinction. Max attributed her prominence to self-possession and a thrilling voice. Sermons were grim in those days, but the Reverend Eastman's were not. Joy and growth were the central features of her belief, Max wrote, and of her role as mother too. She taught her children to be individualists with excellent results. She also passed on to Max her sense of humor. From one of

---

* A psychiatrist who has studied the lives of one thousand eminent men in Western history born after 1600 believes that their place in the order of birth was crucial. "The later son usually occupies a lower position in the family pecking order, 'the kid brother,' 'the baby of the family,' or if the first son is brilliant academically— 'the slow one,' are the less illustrious labels affixed to him. Even though in years to come he might catch up to and surpass his elder brother, the achievement did not occur early enough to become a permanent part of his self-image. For this reason, the later son tends to have a chronic sense of inferiority. . . ." This describes Max perfectly. See Irving D. Harris, "The Psychologies of Presidents," *History of Childhood Quarterly* (Winter, 1975), p. 341.

her letters to Crystal Max took this description of a service: "Mr. Mac-Naughton, our fat tenor, got up and yelled to some angels ever bright and fair to take him into their care. He yelled it over and over again, but they never took a bit of notice so far as I could see."[3] Their household was run along feminist lines, with all the children sharing all the chores. Crystal was probably the only middle-class girl in Elmira accustomed to cleaning stables.

Annis flourished in Elmira, so much so that when Thomas Beecher died the congregation elected the Eastmans to replace him as co-pastors—though Mrs. Eastman seems to have been more equal than her husband. She gradually changed the orientation of Park Church from Trinitarian to Unitarian without, so far as Max knew, anyone objecting. And she continued to grow. In the last year of her life she did four bold new things according to Max: she learned to preach without a prepared text; she learned to swim a little; she consulted a psychoanalyst (A. A. Brill, one of the first to practice in America); and she decided to leave the ministry. This was the product of long-standing religious doubts. Unlike Samuel, Annis had a skeptical, inquiring mind, and by 1910, strengthened by attendance at Harvard summer sessions taught by the great philosopher William James and others, she had resolved to become an educator and reformer. This was prevented by her death on October 22 of that year at the age of fifty-nine. Her strong personality and accomplishments were almost too much for Max. He admired her extravagantly, at the same time blaming her for raising him to be a "mama's boy" and making him neurotic. It was her success that obliged Max to leave the countryside, his first love, and move to Elmira where Max was frequently unhappy.

Yet, if one had to live in a town there was none better than Elmira, he always felt. Mark Twain belonged to the Park Church on account of his wife's family, the Langdon's, who were prominent members. Annis was chosen to give the sermon at Twain's death, and though prevented by illness from delivering it, wrote the text that was read by her husband. One of Max's best essays is "Mark Twain's Elmira." It defends Elmira against the attack made on it by Van Wyck Brooks. In *The Ordeal of Mark Twain* (1920) Brooks argued that Twain never fulfilled himself as an artist because of the repressive influence of middle-class America in general, and his wife Olivia in particular. On the contrary, Max insisted, the Langdons were brave and independent. Mr. and Mrs. Langdon had led the abolitionists, who in 1846 split off from a Presbyterian congregation to form the Park Church. They sheltered escaped slaves, gave money to abolition, and entertained William Lloyd Garrison, Wendell Phillips, Frederick Douglass, and other controversial leaders.

Their spiritual guide was Thomas Beecher, the first minister of their rebellious congregation. He, too, was an abolitionist and preached, Max wrote, no doctrine "but the fatherhood of God and the brotherhood of man."[4] Beecher dressed in work clothes and served his parishioners not only as pastor but also as carpenter, paper-hanger, mechanic, and the like. For forty years he set the town clock. Lyman Beecher, his father, had been for prohibition and against abolition, feminism, and all other religions but his own. Thomas endorsed practically everything his father disliked, including pocket pool and beer. He kept his own mug in a favorite saloon. "Beecher and his church," wrote Max, "were regarded a moral ulcer eating up the harvest of the gospel throughout the whole Chemung and Susquehanna valleys."[5]

When Beecher's congregation grew so large that it had to meet in a local theater, scandalizing the godly, Beecher was expelled from the local ministerial union. But Jervis Langdon backed him; so, too, did Samuel Clemens, who had not yet become celebrated as Mark Twain. He wrote in the *Elmira Advertiser* that the world must be astounded to know "that a little congress of congregationless clergymen, of whom it never heard before, have crushed a famous Beecher and reduced his audiences from fifteen hundred down to fourteen hundred and seventy-five in one fell blow."[6] Beecher raised $65,000, and the Langdons gave a like sum to build Park Church, which extended through an entire city block, was the largest church in the region, and, Max guessed, the most progressive in the country. There Beecher had space for parlors, a free public library, pool and billiard tables, a dancing hall, a playroom, and other facilities rarely found in churches then.

Mrs. Beecher was remarkable, too. Max said she had a New England conscience, a Greek sense of beauty, and her own sense of fun. One of her letters to Max when he was in college survives and is charmingly illustrated with drawings of herself and the people she was writing about.[7] A granddaughter of Noah Webster, she had invented a rag "Beecher doll" that earned considerable sums for charity. Sculptor and cartoonist, a lover of Emerson, William Morris, and science, Julia bobbed her hair in 1857, more than a half-century in advance of the fashion.

From this Max concluded that the Park Church group had gen-

erated a progressive atmosphere that, far from repressing Twain, actually liberated him. Here Max went too far. Mrs. Langdon was narrower
than he realized. When Samuel Clemens was courting her daughter she
resisted the match. Writing to a friend, she questioned the sincerity of
his reformation. Jervis Langdon was less petty than his wife, but at the
same time less scrupulous than Max thought. He was, by local standards, a coal baron and in a hard age made his money the hard way.
Langdon was a big man all the same. The letters of reference that Mrs.
Langdon demanded Clemens produce were inadequate. Langdon
asked Clemens if he had a friend in the world. "Apparently not" was
the answer. Then Langdon said, "I'll be your friend myself. Take the
girl. I know you better than they do."[8] So Livy Langdon and Samuel
Clemens were married, at no cost to Mark Twain's art, according to his
biographer, Justin Kaplan. When Clemens and his collaborator Charles
Dudley Warner penned their bitter novel *The Gilded Age,* "both wives
were involved with its composition throughout; they were clearly the
final arbiters. All this puts in a different light the familiar claim that
Livy and her circle exerted an influence on Mark Twain that was genteel to the point of emasculation."[9]

Max embroidered his account of life in Elmira, but was otherwise
not too wide of the mark. Elmira was no Athens, but it must have
looked that way to an impressionable boy fresh from the country. Max
would be grateful all his life for the liberal and cultivated influence of
the Park Church group. To know Thomas Beecher, to meet Mark
Twain, whom he never stopped admiring, was no small thing. Yet the
Elmira experience, like the relation with Annis, had its drawbacks, too.
He missed rural life. Not long after moving to Elmira, Max wrote (in a
clear, childish hand quite unlike the illegible scrawl of later years) his
beloved Grandfather Eastman to say that school was all right, he was
collecting stamps, and adored his Irish setter, who "is lying by my side
helping me write this letter." Everyone was well. "I have several boy
friends here and I manage to have a pretty good time, though I am not
in the country where I belong."[10] Moving in such relatively exalted
circles as those of the brilliant Beechers and the rich Langdons made
him feel even more inferior. Max was proud of Annis, but also
ashamed that his mother was a Reverend. To be a child of one minister
was bad enough; two such parents were intolerable. While still a child
he rebelled against the moral atmosphere surrounding even this best of
churches. In an early essay on "The Ignominy of Being Good" he

recalled winning a blue ribbon for good conduct when he was nine years old, which so embarrassed him that Max wore his coat inside out to conceal the odious symbol.*

Max was happiest as a youth during the summers, when his family vacationed at local lakes. In 1896 his father bought a farm in Glenora, New York, by Lake Seneca. Until he was twenty-seven Max spent every summer on it. Cherith Farm was located 400 feet above this beautiful, spring-fed lake, and summers there, filled with swimming, boating, play, and parties, helped make up for the social and psychological anxieties he experienced the rest of the time. Sex, his greatest problem, as we shall see, was the exception to this rule. Girls, lightly dressed by winter standards, were more enticing than ever, and yet still beyond his reach. In his twenties he was especially bothered by Ruth Pickering, a beautiful girl ten years younger than himself, whom he had known since she was a child. Even so, Cherith Farm, with its agreeable mixture of work and play, was what Max always thought of as his real home. The Eastmans were part of a summer colony that shared tasks cooperatively among themselves. Life in Glenora was rather like living in a commune of congenial adults and playful children. In middle age Max would recreate the idyllic summers of his childhood on Martha's Vineyard—even to the point of building a house high above the water, like Cherith Farm.

* * *

In 1898 with sixteen other boys, all from rich families he was sure, Max left home to complete his secondary education at Mercersburg Academy, a respectable preparatory school in Pennsylvania. There he learned for the first time that he had a brain. This belated discovery was important because he still felt deficient in other ways—physically, socially, emotionally. The chance to achieve distinction, even in so lowly a field (to a schoolboy) as schoolwork, inspired him to earn the highest average grade, a 99, ever achieved by a student at the Academy. For this he was made valedictorian of the class of 1900 and gave, as his headmaster later recalled, one of the three best valedictories in memory.[11] More satisfying to Max was the general merriment aroused by his Class Prophecy. It was the greatest moment of his young life. "I felt

---

* In the article Max argued that pallid Christian saints had irreparably damaged the whole concept of virtue. His readers were urged to cultivate the moral heroism of ancient Greece. *Atlantic Monthly* (January, 1911), pp. 131–34.

that I was a boy among boys, and would be a man among men, and I
cared about nothing else in the world."[12]

Max would never become a man's man in the sense of liking male
society best. But he did finally as a college student break through the
wall that kept him from relating comfortably to his peers. He had
wanted to go to Princeton as his brother had, but was offered a scholarship to Williams College by a family friend. Since Crystal was already at
Vassar, the Eastmans could not let this chance pass by. It was probably
just as well. Williams students were not rich enough to intimidate Max,
who seems to have gotten over his feeling of social inferiority at college.
He joined a fraternity and made close male friends, something he had
not done before. At college he smoked (without inhaling) and drank to
excess at least once, he tells us proudly. Max even managed to get on
social probation one semester, a thrilling experience for the child of
ministers.

If Ralph Erskine, a close college friend, is any judge, Max was popular. Erskine remembered Max nearly three decades later as having
been a better speaker, runner, shot-putter, stone thrower, and javelin
caster (and dodger too; in their private Olympic games they used to
hurl javelins at each other) than himself. He could still remember
Max's power of concentration, how Max could sit down with *"Faust* or
Antigone fifteen minutes before the class, although the room might be a
bedlam of men, and then give the most beautiful translation of the
hour."[13] Though determined not to lead his class as at Mercersburg, he
did enough work to complete an excellent classical education. The ancient Greeks he studied at college set the standard by which he judged
men ever after.

Though good for Max in other ways, Williams was of no help in
his struggle against rising sexual appetites, nor were his parents, themselves a big part of the problem. An incident tells the story. Once Anstice persuaded Crystal to join him and another boy in a childish sex
game. They removed their clothes and explored each other's bodies.
When their gentle mother learned of this, she stripped him naked and
beat the story out of him. When their saintly father got home, he drove
home the lesson by whipping Anstice until the blood flowed. Encouraged by this, Max became more and more neurotic about sex to
the point of becoming physically ill during his junior year at Williams.
On the face of it, his problem was simple enough. Max was filled with
sexual passions that early and powerful conditioning prevented him

from expressing. Max was attractive to girls, but could not take advantage of this. When he was only seventeen Anstice wrote of a girl they knew that she was "probably in love with you like all the rest. But I doubt if you get the [unintelligible] unless you just go over and take it."[14] That was, of course, the sticking point. Unlike his brother, Max could not just go over and take what Anstice wanted for him, and what he desired himself.

The crisis arose when he fell in love; secret embraces were followed by remorse and vows to sin no more. The experience ended when Max came down with a mysterious fever. Three weeks in the college infirmary left him with a pain in the lumbar region of his back. Because of it he would be a semi-invalid for the next five years. In his memoirs Max attributed this extreme reaction to his mother's influence. "It is hard in the best of conditions for a mama's boy to give his heart to a girl. For one whose mother was both gentle and heroic, both intellectual and tenderly maternal, both a haven in the world and a brave sailor against it, it is doubly hard."[15]

Depression, debt, and his back ailment combined to keep Max out of college the following year. He remained in low spirits much of the time, to his mother's distress. She wrote his brother saying that Max was very down. She wished Anstice were nearby to cheer Max up. "Crystal is doing her best for him, she is more and more an angel of light to us all."[16] Crystal's best was pretty good. Max did return to Williams the following year, wearing a back brace, and had a busy and successful time. Despite the necessity of resting for half of each day, he became seriously interested in his studies and graduated with several prizes. His mother said of Max then, "he is not very strong, but so lovely that we all lean upon him and look to him for our best inspirations."[17]

Max spent the next year and a half, from the middle of 1905 to the end of 1906, seeking a cure. It was partly to obtain this delay between college and life that his bad back existed, Max was later to think. He needed time to chart his future. Max liked to write poetry and was a good student. He abhorred the ministry and had no wish to teach. Eastmans did not go into business. This left Max with no prospective occupation, hence his bad back. A later incident suggests a better explanation. In 1914 Max would submit to psychoanalysis briefly. Dr. Smith Ely Jelliffe, one of the first American Freudians, diagnosed Max's case in this fashion:

You weren't quite aware of the Oedipus situation, the hostility to the father working itself out in prejudiced radicalism. You were tied up also in a complex situation with your sister which made relations with your wife uncomfortable. There was a sister-identification, and through that identification a fundamental narcissistic cathexis or investment.

Dr. A. A. Brill agreed: "I think you have a strong mother-fixation. Your pattern is that you want to get away from mother and yet be with her."[18]

Max rejected these opinions, both at the time and later. He was not sick, merely confused, in need of common sense and not a lot of mumbo jumbo about narcissistic cathexis. If, however, we accept the judgments of two experienced analysts, a pattern emerges. In the autobiography Max seldom mentions his father, except in passing. The warmest passage concerning Samuel arises from the fact that one July Max found himself alone at Glenora with his father, whose merits then became more evident. To celebrate this discovery Max composed a sonnet in father's honor, which is included in *Enjoyment of Living*. The verse says that when the sun rises it finds an unidentified man working in his garden. This is the nearest thing to an outburst of filial piety or affection in the memoirs. Describing his father's death, Max notes Samuel's good qualities perfunctorily, and then explains that, absorbed as he was with events in Russia, Samuel's death could not affect him. This is the same excuse used later to justify his lack of feeling when brother Anstice dies. So much for his rivals in the fight for mother's love.

What we see here, then, was probably the consequences of an unresolved Oedipal situation. Father, who stands between Max and mother, must be destroyed. But at the same time the aftermath of total victory, union with mother, is unthinkable, so father must be born again. Having rejected his biological father Max was to spend much of his adult life looking for substitutes. Periodically he would find one, but even the father-figure is a rival and so must be eliminated. Again and again Max would be drawn to a Dewey or a Freud or a Trotsky. Always they would be found to have feet of clay, obliging Max, however reluctantly, to overthrow them with his pen. By the same token Max would never, except possibly once, be really close to another man. Having failed to resolve the Oedipal crisis, he saw all men anywhere near his own age as potential rivals.

Max's dealings with women were affected even more, inasmuch as they were substitutes for mother. He had to have intercourse with them and triumph over father; he could not have intercourse with them because that would be incestuous. On the one hand he lusted after women, on the other he was terrified of sex, a contradiction leading in the first instance to nightmares, childhood phobias, and the like, and then in college, when sexual feelings became stronger, to physical immobility. This was the inner logic dictating the exterior symptoms. But the solution was worse than the problem, giving rise to fears of permanent invalidism. Max determined not to accept this condition. Once the serious nature of his ailment became clear he began to look for help. Various alleged healers and quack nostrums had no effect. A New Thought sanitarium directed mental waves at him in vain. He was finally treated successfully by Dr. John George Gehring of Bethel, Maine.

Gehring was a medical doctor untrained in psychology, still less in psychoanalysis, then virtually unknown in America, but he was one of the first American physicians to believe that certain physical problems were rooted in the mind. After several weeks of interviews beginning in October of 1906, Gehring put Eastman on a regime during which he was to engage in physical activity for only five minutes an hour. Each week the period of activity was increased by another five minutes. For some three months Eastman was absolved by Gehring of all responsibility except to his health. At the end of it Max was convinced, as Gehring intended, that his illness could be overcome by self-discipline. Later Eastman tried to explain Gehring's approach in the *Atlantic Monthly* without much luck. He described the work of physicians like Gehring (with no mention of his own cure) as resting on the Law of Suggestion formulated by a French doctor in 1866. Max argued that it was soundly based on psychological and physiological principles, but failed to be convincing. All the article proves is that Max did not understand what had been happening to him.[19]

Because it was directed only at symptoms, Gehring's treatment was not a cure. Max's back improved, but his psychic dilemma did not. He realized this to a degree, and speculated later that the right kind of psychoanalyst might have helped him more. The short shrift he gave Jelliffe makes this seem unlikely. Max intended to cure himself, and in a way managed to do so. As we shall see, Max resolved the problem of how to have sex without commiting incest by going with many women. He would have scores, possibly hundreds, of sexual contacts in his long life, but seldom if ever complete intimacy. This strategy worked in that it allowed Max to have an active sex life without becoming disabled. It also saved him from homosexuality, which often results when a boy has a passive father and dominating mother. But like Gehring's treatment it left the Oedipal situation unresolved. In important ways Max would never grow up.

This failure expressed itself not only in personal relationships, it strongly influenced his career as well. Max would know success, but not how to live with it. He hungered for approval and recognition, for the usual reasons and because they showed he was not the disgusting sort of person who might violate the ultimate taboo. Max had to win to show he was not worthless, and had to lose because he was, or rather thought he was. Because Max did not fully approve of himself, he could not allow himself to be successful beyond a certain point. Thus he developed the habit of turning victory into defeat. And yet his arrested development, if we may call it that, had a positive side. He never acquired certain adult traits, sexual fidelity and a sense of irony, for example. By the same token he retained youthful qualities of value, an open and direct character, boyish enthusiasms, the wise-child aspect many saw in him. Probably also Max's creative energy was nourished by the part of him that stayed forever young. Max's cure, began by Dr. Gehring but carried on by himself, was a good one so far as it went. Because of it he would live boldly as an adult, welcoming new experiences, writing and traveling as he pleased. Through his own efforts the frightened, sickly boy became in later years courageous and productive. One cannot ask much more from any therapy than this.

* * *

Max's immediate problem in 1906 was where to go and what to do after his back improved. An obvious solution presented itself. Crystal was now living in New York. Joining her there would mean confronting his fear of cities head on, thus taking another step on the road to mental health. At the same time Max could count on Crystal, who already knew almost everyone worth knowing, to ease his way. She was exceedingly attractive, like Max, and in the same way, having the big Eastman frame and the strong Eastman features. The black poet Claude McKay called her the most beautiful white woman he ever knew. She also had the Eastman brains. Almost half a century after meeting her, John Spargo, an ex-socialist writer who detested Max, remembered Crystal as a "superb creature" who could have modeled for the "perfect American woman." Wherever you met her, Spargo continued, "she was the most intelligent person in the room."[20] After graduating from Vassar in 1903 Crystal had taken a master's degree in sociology from Columbia, and a law degree from New York University in 1907. She would go on to write *Work Accidents and the Law* (1910), while serving from 1909 to 1911 as secretary and only female member of the New York State Employer's Liability Commission. Crystal was a feminist and radical before Max, who followed in her train.

At this time New York was rapidly becoming not just the trading capital of America but the center of its social, cultural, and intellectual life as well. The muckraking era was far advanced, though Max missed it by not reading popular magazines. More to the point, New York was filling up with anarchists, socialists, feminists, and reformers of every kind. Max didn't know this either. He had graduated from college without ever hearing of Karl Marx or the class struggle. But he was ripe for conversion. Max had already become an internationalist, as shown by his first published essay, "Patriotism a Primitive Ideal."[21] "And I had a millennial yearning for a more free and equal, more friendly and more truth-loving society than the one I woke up in. I wanted it to be 'more like a parish.' I wanted it to strive after noble and real ideals instead of after wealth, elegance, and respectability."[22] His moral heroes were St. Francis and Tolstoy. His economics instructor was Thorstein Veblen, whose *Theory of the Leisure Class* made a great impression and eventually helped lead Max to socialism. He did not, however, as a college student have much hope that society would be reformed. "I wish I believed," he wrote in his notebook then, "in the second coming of Christ!"[23]

When Max got off the train in New York in January 1907 at the age of twenty-four, he was still unfinished. For years to come he would have to rest often, and his back would hurt in times of stress. He had much to learn about contemporary life. But Max had determined to be a writer, and as his fears receded he was able to bring his talents to bear on larger targets than school and college had provided. He had already developed the clear, lucid prose style that would always be his literary trademark. He had begun to compose poetry. An accomplished speaker, Max was soon to gain further poise and confidence and in time a reputation for oratory. And he was extremely good looking, which helped enormously.

Max came to Greenwich Village, where Crystal lived, just before it became famous. It was not so busy as most neighborhoods, for its streets had been laid out diagonally to the axis of Manhattan before the island's grid plan was established in 1811 This made travel to the Village a little more difficult, as did the lack of a subway, which did not reach there until 1917. In 1910 when the last tenement was built, the lower Village had a population that was 80 per cent foreign born or of foreign parentage, most of whom worked in lofts and industrial buildings. The combination of relative isolation and low rents made Greenwich Village attractive to artists and intellectuals, especially after 1912, when industry began moving out, taking many of the working class families with it.[24]

By accident Max came to Greenwich Village at the right time. He acquired an occupation in the same way. Through a friend of Crystal's, he was introduced to John Dewey, who needed someone to teach "The Principles of Science" in his Department of Philosophy and Psychology at Columbia University. Max knew little philosophy and less science, but Dewey was satisfied that he wished to learn about them, which was the main thing. Luckily Max was a quick study, for in a few years' time he would be teaching logic, aesthetics, and the history of philosophy, among other subjects, while completing the requirements for a doctorate in philosophy. Despite its casual hiring practices, Columbia had a brilliant faculty and was far ahead of Williams. Dewey himself cared deeply about social issues. His philosophy of instrumentalism, which judged an idea in terms of its practical results, was meant for activists. So was the work of James Harvey Robinson, who studied history not only for its own sake, but to discover its effects upon the present. Max also came in contact with, among others, J. McKeen Cattell, the first experimental psychologist in America.

Columbia benefited Max in obvious ways. Intellectually it brought him up to date. Max saw Dewey often, dining with him weekly for his first two years at Columbia. He was allowed to teach as he pleased, and was treated almost as an equal by his professors. Dewey, whose prose style was almost impenetrable, even asked Max to edit some of his writings. Max let down posterity by failing to do so. Most importantly, as his lecture notes show, Max learned to translate complex philosophies into language understandable by lay persons. This would be of great value to him when he encountered Karl Marx.

On the other hand, Max also acquired at Columbia views, sometimes contrary to those of his teachers, that were to prove harmful. One was a reverence for science, another a contempt for philosophy. Max never intended to make a career of philosophy, and prolonged exposure to it did not change his mind. His lecture notes on the history of philosophy, although they contain statements of admiration for such as John Stuart Mill, depict modern philosophy as useful mainly for "overthrowing scholastic dogmatism." It was desirable only to the extent that it advanced "the science of nature and society, by understanding the hypothetical method or process of it, and by adding results or valid matters."[25] That is to say, philosophy was worthwhile only to the extent that it was scientific, which, for the most part, it was not, Max felt—going against Dewey who believed it was. Max had shown little interest in science before entering Columbia. Afterward it became an obsession, almost a religion, for which Columbia must take a share of the blame—though in fairness it must be said that a great many people who had never been to Columbia shared Max's excessive optimism. Their belief in science as the answer to all human problems would make them, like him, particularly susceptible to Marxism in later years.

Philosophy became to Max either a joke or a menace. It was a menace when taken seriously, as in Soviet Russia. Otherwise, it provided Max with opportunities for humor. He once reviewed a group of books by philosophers at a time when Henri Bergson was highly regarded. Max wrote: "I like Bergson's Absolute Reality better than any other Absolute Reality in the whole of philosophy, but I agree with James that there isn't one anywhere outside of philosophy." He made fun of James as well, for bothering to write a book proving that the universe was pluralistic when every sensible person knew this already. "Could you, I ask myself, even supposing you had the genius, be brilliant and passionate about so obvious a thing? Well you could if you had spent enough time breathing in 'academic metaphysics.'" Every person of good judgment was now immune to the disease of metaphysics, Max believed, thanks to James himself. "James offered the world immunity from that disease, forever. He died, as you might say, to save us. For his passing from science to philosophy was a kind of death."[26] If so, James died in vain, for before long the Russian Revolution would breathe a violent new life into metaphysics. But Max was wrong about James, whose power and brilliance and humanity made him the pride of American philosophy.

Max could get along without philosophy, so his contempt for it, though unreasonable, was not fatal. His error was to replace it with a particular view of science that owed nothing to Professor Cattell. At a time when most psychologists held that the correct way to study behavior was to read books, Cattell insisted upon laboratory work. Max ignored this example and continued to believe that one learned psychology by reading books. What he did acquire at Columbia, aided by Dewey's example, was the habit of calling this practice science. So common was the failing in those days that no one noticed. For years Max got away with claiming the authority of science while neglecting the substance. One of his earliest essays is typical. Its subject was poetry, and Max proclaimed that "to my mind a psychological analysis of the material of literary art furnishes the only sound basis for the study of it, and it is with this end in view that I approach the old question of the nature of poetry." After this brave start Max fell back on literary rather than scientific declarations. "Poetry is thought clothed in its own form; prose is thought clothed in the forms of words." "Language is poetry, and prose is withered language." He ended with this line: "Not the definition but the existence of poetry is a mystery. Poetry marries the seen with the unseen world, but we have not guessed the nature of this union."[27]

Max made a lifetime vow to be "scientific" rather than "literary" in approaching life and literature. Yet in this and later essays, science would frequently be called on but seldom applied. Not until it was too late did Eastman see the problem, and then only partially. Writing on Dewey many years after having been his student, Max recalled that Dewey tried to restrain him from "transferring the conceptual apparatus of the physical sciences to social and psychological problems where the subject matter is so much more mixed-up and undelimited."[28] Max seems never to have realized that his parallel effort to apply psychology to literature was equally mistaken. His religion of science, acquired perhaps at the hands of Dr. Gehring, and confirmed by his graduate education, would never cease to cripple Max. The wonder is that he did so well despite it.

*   *   *

The gap between Max's inner and outer selves remained considerable during his Columbia years and for some time afterward. He continued to have back pains and difficulties with women, producing those fears of impotence that so often are its cause. In other respects his position improved. In 1910 he passed the oral examination for his Ph.D with flying colors and had his dissertation on Plato accepted by Dewey. He did not file it nor take his doctorate, because it cost $30 to have the necessary printed copy of the thesis made and also so he could thumb his nose at the higher degree system. As he never intended to make a career of teaching, this was an expansive but not expensive gesture. He still had difficulty getting published, but he began to attract notice as a friend of woman suffrage. Max had been a feminist since infancy. In an early speech he recalled: "Why, my sister and I used to hold feminist meetings out on the roof of our barn eighteen or twenty years ago. She would solemnly vow that she would never put on long dresses or do up her hair as long as she lived. And I would solemnly agree to accept her on those conditions and be true to her for life."[29]

By 1909 Max was sufficiently well known that his rash proposal to found a Men's League for Woman Suffrage received newspaper attention. Unknown to him, Anna Howard Shaw, president of the National American Woman Suffrage Association, had already asked Oswald Garrison Villard, noted liberal and publisher of the *New York Evening Post,* to take such a step. It was agreed that Villard and Rabbi Stephen Wise, the great reformer, would head the League if Max, as secretary-treasurer, did the work. In theory there was not to be much of this, for the main function of the League was simply to enlist as many prominent names as possible. This would give status to a cause that was still considered by many to be as absurd as it was obnoxious. In this the League succeeded, showing that equal suffrage was advocated by others besides the silly women who were thought to be behind it. The League also solved Max's immediate problem of how to make a living. He had decided that his life should be divided into three activities: creative and scientific writing; earning a living; aiding humanity. He was already writing poems and essays; now he found in the League a way to bring in money and benefit society at the same time. Soon he was receiving as much as fifty dollars an appearance, about what a laborer might earn in a month. Lecturing, and not just on suffrage, thus became a resource he could always draw on as needed.

Max had joined the cause at a time when woman suffrage was in the doldrums. This contrasted with England, where the militant suffragettes were constantly making news. Their Women's Social and Political Union, led by Christabel Pankhurst and her equally amazing mother Emmeline, was staging illegal protests, and, if arrested, its members were going on hunger strikes. These and other violent tactics rocked England, but left America unmoved. Few states had granted votes to women by 1909, and the NAWSA, America's only national suffrage organization, was flagging under Dr. Shaw, who spoke effectively but could not lead or organize. New York was the exception. Feminism was rising there, as it would nationally some years later, and Max and Crystal were rising with it.

From 1908 until 1914, when the cause began to prosper outside New York, Max spoke frequently on equal rights for women. Some of his speeches and essays were defensive, efforts at repulsing attacks on woman suffrage. Thus, in the *Atlantic Monthly,* Max opposed the notion that popular democracy had failed. Many people, alarmed by exposés of political corruption and the growing number of foreign-born voters, were calling for a more restricted suffrage and the rule of intellect. Max tried to show that universal suffrage was both desirable and scientific. This last remained obscure. But Max argued skillfully that critics were confusing intellect with education. There was, he maintained, such a thing as social intelligence, "that intelligence which results from a free, sympathetic inter-communication of all kinds of people."[30] Equality of citizenship fostered this sympathy and communication and could be justified by them alone. In any case, he went on, "democracy does not aim to produce a government as complete and regular and satisfying to the cultivated mind as possible; it aims to produce a government somewhat loose and dirty, in which citizens are great as individuals."[31]

In a widely circulated address he dismissed the idea, put forward by Theodore Roosevelt's organ *The Outlook,* that there should be a referendum among women to see if they wanted the vote. This was plainly undemocratic, Max observed. The main principle of a democratic government "does not allow that a majority shall decide whether or not a minority may have the privilege of voting; it demands that everyone shall be guaranteed the privilege of voting, and after that—and not until after that—the vote of a majority shall rule."[32] Eastman pointed out that neither Roosevelt nor Emma Goldman, the anarchist leader, considered woman suffrage important. They were wrong, he insisted, for many reasons, but especially because full citizenship would mean giving woman the right to be somebody. Roosevelt did not think woman suffrage important because, as a politician, people who did not vote did not matter. Given the vote, Max believed, women would matter.

Max varied his arguments to suit the occasion; however, he always came back to his basic position, which was that women should have the vote because it would make them better persons. Max thought that suffragists reversed the natural order of things in claiming that once women had the vote they would immediately reform society. This implied that votelessness had done them no harm. But Max held that keeping women out of politics had in fact stunted their growth. They needed the vote to achieve their full human stature, after which they could become reformers.[33]

An ardent democrat in these speeches, Max was a moralist even more. In one of his most popular talks, he called for equal citizenship to redress the balance between men and women, and attacked the condescension shown women by the "average man of affairs":

> And when he tries to make up for it with a great deal of sentimental adoration, he makes it only the more foolish. For to worship that which is held inferior in power and wisdom because it excels in innocence of the actual world, is the old and sure way to falsify your moral sentiments. We hear today a great deal of protest against that "double standard of morality," which allows men, but not women, to be vicious, without loss of standing. The roots of that evil lie in this false attitude. When we have abolished that double standard of morality which allows the ideal woman to be ignorant and silly, we shall see the disappearance of that double standard which allows her husband to be profligate and self-centered. When we have less innocence and more virtue in women, we shall have less vice and more virtue in men.[34]

Later, when Max came to think that chastity was not a virtue, this passage would need amending, but only in detail. Whatever Max believed in, he always felt that both sexes should have it equally.

* * *

Poised and confident in public, Max was still troubled privately. Back pains came and went. He remained unhappily celibate. Max fell in love every summer with the same girl, Ruth Pickering, to no effect. He had an unconsummated romance with Inez Milholland, a beautiful young suffragist, lawyer, and orator, who was Max's counterpart in the movement. He believed there was a public demand that they fall in love. Both made the required effort, but it came to nothing. Their attempt at union was based more on theory and peer group pressure than any real attraction. Instead she married Eugen Boissevain, for a time Max's closest friend. Inez died in 1916 at the age of thirty from a combination of pernicious anemia and exhaustion brought on by a suffrage campaign in the West. Feminists considered her a martyr, as perhaps she was.

Max suffered a far more grievous loss on October 22, 1910, when his mother died of a cerebral hemorrhage, the family curse. His mother's death, Max wrote in the autobiography, was like losing the gravity that held his parts together. She was also his source of energy, Max believed. On returning to New York after the funeral, he found her last letter to him, the end of a twelve-year correspondence that "had been pouring a stream of zest and vitality into my languid nerves." His mother knew no rest. Even her melancholy was active. "Only as I look back now, after years of blind wandering and blundering among loves, do I realize that this was the essential thing my mother gave me. This was the quality I most needed in a woman friend." [35]

Max and Crystal were with Annis when she died, attended the memorial service, and then fell apart. Although living together at the time they spoke little of their sorrow. Far from bringing them closer together, their mother's death, in Max's words, seemed "to increase my strong resistance to intimacy" with Crystal. She did not know of his acute sexual anxieties, he thought, despite having shared quarters with Max for years. He did not know that after Annis died Crystal went to Dr. Brill, hoping he would ease her unsuitable passion for Wallace Benedict, an amiable young insurance agent who apparently was the first man to rouse her sexually. In other respects he was poorly suited to Crystal, having the wrong occupation, no social conscience, and a home distant from New York. Before taking the plunge and moving to Milwaukee with Benedict, Crystal fell ill, as well she might, and returned to Elmira where she wrote Max a revealing letter:

> Getting back to New York and living with you was the hope I fed my drooping spirits on—not Milwaukee and the married state. Your suggestion that if I can't stand it, you'll know it's not for you, gives me a humorous courage. Perhaps after we've both experimented around a few years, we may end up living together again. [36]

Neither Crystal nor Max wished to marry, yet both did so on successive days in May, a half-year after their mother's death. In one way this made a kind of sense. Annis had figured powerfully not just in their childhood but in their adult lives as well. She corresponded frequently with both, encouraging them and supporting them at every step. Her feminism was the root of theirs, her religious doubts the sanction for their unbelief. Their radicalism arose from her social conscience. Faced with such a loss, each would naturally reach out for consolation.

Yet they did not reach out to each other. Instead they took an opposite course, marrying in haste and, as soon became clear, unwisely. Crystal's choice was plainly absurd. It was hard, even for her, to see Crystal living in Milwaukee as the wife of an insurance agent. She might as well have joined a circus, so remote was marriage to Benedict from her real concerns. Max's decision was not so obviously foolish, though in the long run just as wrong. These misalliances could not have resulted from grief alone. Annis, Crystal, and Max were sides of the same triangle, linked to each other in complex ways. Max recognized that his mother was a source of his difficulty, though he only touched the surface of their relationship in calling himself a mama's boy. Despite Jelliffe's analysis, he never admitted that Crystal was involved, too. If not siblings they could have been lovers. An entry in Crystal's journal made during her junior year at Vassar shows this. She had been reading a novel and wrote to herself that one fictional character was typically male:

> . . . clever, powerful selfish and animal to a great extent. Almost all men are like him in a lack of finesse—except Max. I can't believe Max is that way. I don't believe there is a feeling in the world too refined and imagined for him to appreciate. But it's that very quality in him that I have thought makes him like a girl. He wouldn't like it, but I think its the highest compliment you can pay a man to say that he has the fineness of feeling and sympathy of a woman. . . . If I ever marry a man he must be like Max in those qualities.[37]

Max's descriptions of Crystal suggest similar feelings. Florence Deshon, his first great love, was attractive to him because she seemed "utterly beautiful, and yet possessing the qualities of mind and feeling I adore."[38] These are the same traits displayed by Crystal. There is even a certain physical resemblance between the two dark-haired, bold-featured, handsome women. Crystal and Max can live innocently together while mother is alive because she forms the third side of their triangle even when absent. But with mother's death the triangle collapses, raising, on some buried but deeply-felt level, the spectre of incest. Hence the rush into marriages, which, however awkward, save Max and Crystal from a worse fate.

Max's closest female friend at this point was Ida Rauh, a beautiful and intelligent Jewish woman with a private income, whom Max had known since first coming to New York. She was rebelling against her bourgeois family and explained the class struggle to him so clearly, Max tells us, that he became a Socialist. Max would have joined the party in any case, for his reading and experiences alike were drawing him to the Left. But the actual moment of conversion took place with Ida, binding them more firmly together. This need not have resulted in matrimony. Eastman was against marriage in principle, like so many of his radical friends. He and Ida moved in the same bohemian circles, where marriage was viewed as backward, and probably a capitalist plot to enslave women. But an almost conscious need to replace mother, and the unconscious importance of escaping sister, overcame his scruples. Max's resistance collapsed when Ida offered to pay the cost of a trip to Europe. Because it would simplify matters for them to travel as man and wife, marriage seemed in order, or so Max rationalized this foolish act at the time. On May 4, 1911, when he was twenty-eight, Max and Ida were married by a Justice of the Peace in Patterson, New Jersey. There was no wedding ring—the start of an Eastman tradition.

Max realized his error almost at once. He had marched up the gangplank of the ship that was to take them to Europe feeling like a "mature and responsible adult." He awoke the next morning seized with terror. "I had lost, in marrying Ida, my irrational joy in life. I had lost my religion [that is, his pagan freedom], I had committed—irrevocably, it seemed to me—the Folly of Growing Up."[39] He would know this fear, caused by the threat of permanent intimacy with a woman, again in his life, but this was the worst of his post-Gehring crises. His backache returned. He was attacked by hives, indigestion, sleepiness, and all manner of afflictions. Their entire three months abroad was, for Max, a mixture of panic and pain, relieved by periods of boredom.

Another vacation in Elmira during the summer of 1911 improved Max's spirits but not his circumstances. He should not have married at all, and especially not Ida. Unlike his affectionate mother and sister, Ida was never one to shower people, even her husband, with compliments and attentions. Yet these were necessary to Max's well-being. She was given to periods of indolence and so could not pour vitality into Max's languid nerves as he thought essential. And whereas he remained productive despite his maladies, it seemed to him that Ida never finished anything. Max tried to pretend he was still free by writing Ida's maiden name above his own on their mailbox. Though Lucy Stone had retained her own name after marriage fifty-six years earlier, the practice was still uncommon enough to bring a newspaper reporter to their door. In hopes of avoiding sensation they confided in him. The result was a sensational story which quoted Ida as saying, "Our attitude toward the marriage service is that we went through with it; then we can say afterward we don't believe in it. It was with us a placating of convention because if we had gone counter to the convention it would have been too much of a bother for the gain."[40] This indiscretion caused them much trouble.* Max was widely condemned in Elmira for degrading the sacrament of matrimony. Worse still, the newspaper

---

* It brought some hate mail too, an example of which Max kept. This anonymous doggerel was dated September 13¿ 1912.

> I am the little Abraham,
> My mommer is Miss Rauh,
> And I'm the little Leah
> That makes to you her bow!
>
> And I'm the little Solomon
> My mommer is Miss Rauh,
> And I'm the little Rachel
> That makes to you her bow.
>
> Our popper has another name
> That's not at all like that
> And so we have no name at all,
> Just pulls one from a hat!
>
> But we've drawn our Mommer's famous nose
> And our Popper says his "charm,"
> So to be the No Name Series
> It can't *do us no* harm!

In addition Max received by his count one thousand "defamatory" letters that a private detective found had been written by an insane person. (Max Eastman to Oswald Garrison Villard, June 11, 1913, Villard MSS.)

story was untrue, a description of how radicals were supposed to regard marriage, not of their actual union. Ida had been quoted accurately, but did not mean what she said. According to Max she was sinking into domesticity and monogamy and carrying him down with her, finishing the job, as he saw it, by giving birth to a son, Daniel, on September 6, 1912.

* * *

Max's career prospered despite marital woes. The Men's League for Woman Suffrage grew, and Max's reputation with it. He was doing well as a lecturer. Max and Ida had bit parts in a film, "Votes for Women," starring Jane Addams and Anna Howard Shaw. He was beginning to establish himself as a man of letters, writing essays and book reviews for such leading monthlies as the *North American Review* and the *Atlantic*. He contributed to professional journals of philosophy and psychology, and in 1912 had a long poem published in the *Twentieth Century*.[41] That same year Max joined the Socialist party, altering his life forever.

Ever since the depression of the nineties ended, an appetite for change had been developing in America. Now it was at its greatest. During the five-year period ending in 1917, the "first years of our own time," Henry F. May calls them in his classic study, *The End of American Innocence,* the country would boil and bubble, confounding traditionalists in every sphere. Politically this meant attacks on boss rule, campaigns for direct democracy, the secret ballot, popular election of U.S. senators, the regulation of utilities, fair taxation, and much else. Social reformers were establishing settlement houses in immigrant wards, fighting against child labor, building playgrounds, demanding services for the poor. Jane Addams, who embodied the struggle for social justice, became one of the best-known women in the world through her eloquent appeals to conscience. Reform politicians and social workers came together in 1912 to form the Progressive party, whose platform embraced an extraordinary range of cures for what ailed the nation. "We stand at Armageddon and we battle for the Lord," Theodore Roosevelt had told his supporters. Their convention was more like a revival meeting than a political rally, especially when they sang "John Brown's Body" and the "Battle Hymn of the Republic." The Progressives lost, moral enthusiasm having its limits even in 1912. Historians have since pointed out that many proposed reforms were self-serving or misguided or inadequate. All the same, politics had become exciting and involved real issues after decades of squabbling between the major parties over patronage and little else. At the very least, reformers put an end to the nineteenth-century habit of saying that government could do nothing without disturbing the natural order of things, which was unthinkable.

1912 was a banner year for radicals, perhaps the best ever. In Lawrence, Massachusetts the revolutionary Industrial Workers of the World led a coalition of male, female, and child textile workers, immigrants from a score of countries, the skilled and the unskilled alike, to victory, despite language barriers, police brutality, and employer bloody-mindedness. No one except the Wobblies themselves believed such a thing to be possible. Eugene V. Debs was the Socialist candidate for president again. In 1900 he had received about 95,000 votes. This year he would win close to 900,000. There were a thousand Socialist officeholders scattered around the country, including mayors of medium-sized cities and, at different times, two members of Congress. Where the Progressives had failed, Socialists were still rising.

The arts, too, were being transformed. Isadora Duncan was laying the groundwork for modern dance and alarming moralists with her scanty garments and flagrant love affairs. John Sloan and other painters were challenging the formalism of the Academy with their vivid, sometimes socially conscious work. Theodore Dreiser's powerful, gritty novels made genteel fiction obsolete. In that year of wonders 1912 Harriet Monroe founded *Poetry,* which would introduce modernism to American readers. Ezra Pound appeared in the first issue and T. S. Eliot a few years later. It seemed, in the much quoted words of John Butler Yeats, a visitor from Ireland, as if the fiddles were tuning up all over America. Young Van Wyck Brooks put the thought another way in the title of his important book, *America's Coming of Age* (1915).

Greenwich Village was the ideal place to experience all this. Its resident population of radicals, social workers, reformers, and artists made it irresistible to the young, the free, the talented. All that was self-consciously new in American culture—the "new woman," the "new morality," the "new art"—could be found there. On one level Greenwich Village was becoming a showcase of the cultural revolution, on another it led the movement, serving as headquarters to what Henry May has called the Innocent Rebellion.[42] Here were the liberated intellectuals who believed, as May puts it, that "life transcends thought." Here also were the anarchists Emma Goldman and Hippolyte Havel. Big Bill

Haywood, one-eyed leader of the IWW, was no stranger to the Village. Poets abounded. Whether anarchist, socialist, or aesthete, each had the same mission. Hutchins Hapgood expressed it when he told Mabel Dodge, "I consider it my first duty to undermine subtly the foundations of the community." Hapgood was older than most rebels, with a family and a suburban home, or he would not have qualified the remark. Flamboyance, not subtlety, was the Village trademark. Villagers dressed outrageously by the standards of the day. Women bobbed their hair, wore sandals, peasant skirts, and worse. Men had soft-collared shirts and sometimes went without a hat, leaving themselves practically naked. They voted Socialist, if at all, admired revolutionaries, painted their apartments black. Villagers practiced free speech, free love, and contraception. They liked to eat at Polly Holladay's famous restaurant, where Hippolyte Havel might call them "bourgeois pigs" while waiting on their table. Afterward they could go upstairs to the Liberal Club, where all points of view found expression.[43]

This diversity and vitality enabled Mabel Dodge to establish her famous salon. She was a wealthy and seductive woman who in 1912, of course, acquired an apartment on Fifth Avenue near Washington Square. In her white drawing room she could entertain a hundred people. Readers of her huge autobiography, which set records for self-indulgence, find it hard to understand why talented people were willing to attend her weekly gatherings. Lavish hospitality was one reason. Other rich women were not much interested in showering low-income writers, artists, and agitators with masses of food and drink. Once a few celebrities were delivered to Mabel by Hutchins Hapgood, it became chic to be seen in her apartment. This does not explain why John Reed, who had plenty of choices, became her lover, or why Hapgood, a journalist who had ability and an immense circle of acquaintances, enjoyed her company so much.

One night she sponsored a memorable debate featuring representatives of the only movements Villagers cared about. Emma Goldman, her great colleague Alexander Berkman, and her lover Ben Reitman spoke for anarchism. The IWW's syndicalism was upheld by Haywood, Carlo Tresca, the Wobbly poet, and Elizabeth Gurley Flynn, the IWW's celebrated Rebel Girl. William English Walling, a prominent intellectual, and young Walter Lippmann, who was already distinguished, upheld socialism. The evening was not considered one of her most triumphant. Yet the fact that Mabel could bring together leading spokespersons from all three movements was itself newsworthy and enhanced her reputation. Margaret Sanger promoted birth control in Mabel's drawing room. Many Villagers first heard of psychoanalysis at one of her evenings. Max, who disliked Mabel, was proud of resisting her "witchlike fascination," and opposed salons on principle, admitted her success. "Many famous salons have been established by women of wit or beauty; Mabel's was the only one ever established by pure will power. And it was no second-rate salon; everybody in the ferment of ideas could be found there. . . ."[44]

Elegant and affected, Mabel was bound to annoy Max. But one incident in particular turned him against her. From an anthropologist, Mabel had learned of peyote and staged a ceremony during which the guests chewed this hallucinogenic substance in the Indian manner. Max and Ida left early for home and bed, to be awakened hours later by a pounding on their door. It was one of the guests, a young woman of precarious sanity who had been pushed over into madness by the drug. They administered a sedative and returned her to Mabel's, where she was staying. They found that Hapgood and other guests had either passed out or were behaving oddly. Mabel was fine, having only pretended to take the drug, Max believed. This experience confirmed Max's low opinion of Mabel, though her career as a hostess was not impaired by it, and may have benefited. It was, after all, another remarkable evening.

Many aspects of Village life were silly or trivial. Max especially disliked the arty pretensions of rank-and-file Villagers, their studiedly bohemian dress, a tendency to embrace the new for its own sake. Just the same, his Village, upon whose memory countless boutiques and real estate ventures would be erected, was a real place where men and women of real talent lived and worked together in numbers never equaled since. A genuine community with its own customs and institutions, it was also part of a nation-wide revolt against formalism in life and thought. Floyd Dell called the Village a moral health resort, but the cultural revolution of Greenwich Village was not provincial. Where the Village led, millions would soon follow. In August of 1912 Max entered the absolute center of this Innocent Rebellion. While vacationing he received a letter, written with a brush and signed by John Sloan, Art Young, Louis Untermeyer, and five other artists and writers. The complete text was as follows: "You are elected editor of *The Masses*. No pay." It was his call to glory.

CHAPTER TWO

Starting Out

1912–1916

The tale which follows tells how a poet and philosophic moralist, with a special distaste for economics, politics, and journalism, became known to the public as a journalist campaigning for a political idea based primarily on economics.

Enjoyment of Living

Eastman was most famous during and just after World War I, but the basis of his reputation was laid during his five years as editor of the *Masses.* Max felt that the *Liberator,* which succeeded it, was a better magazine because more sharply focused, disciplined, and purposeful. Even so the *Masses* was handsomer, with a broader scope and gayer spirit. Though not yet assembled, the elements of a brilliant magazine lay to hand when Max took over. Greenwich Village was filled with rebellious youth. Almost every artist and writer appeared to favor socialism. This created possibilities for radical journalism that the *Masses* under its founder Piet Vlag had failed to grasp. Vlag was a Dutchman mainly interested in consumer cooperatives, as was his chief backer Rufus W. Weeks, vice-president of the New York Life Insurance Company. Consumer cooperatives, though worthy, did not make hearts sing nor spirits overflow. Vlag's *Masses* was as flat and earnest as the rest of the socialist press, which reached unsurpassed levels of dullness. The illustrators were typical commercial artists of the period, given to drawings of brawny workers and ragged children. Their style was what would later be called socialist realism, adulterated with kitsch. No one was interested in such a magazine, and in 1912 it ran out of money.

The pre-Eastman *Masses* did have one major asset. At forty-six Art

Young was an established cartoonist, master of the powerful, dark line, a passionate enemy of wealth.[1] As capitalist publications were not overly interested in an artist, no matter how good, whose favorite target was capitalism, Young never had much money. During the *Masses* era he supported himself as a Washington cartoonist for the socialist *Metropolitan* magazine. Young loved the *Masses,* even under Vlag, because in lieu of cash it gave him absolute freedom. Young was short and round, a jolly, outgoing man with a wreath of silver hair, usually veiled by cigar smoke. He was so well-liked that in later years, when he could not earn a living, Young's friends gladly supported him. It was Young who launched Max's editorial career. They met at a dinner for Jack London and found they agreed it would be good to have a magazine equal to the best European satirical reviews. Young nominated Eastman to be the *Masses'* savior, and read to its editors a humorous article by Max on how he had founded the Men's League for Woman Suffrage. Unlikely as it seems, this convinced them that Max was just the person to rescue a bankrupt magazine of unpopular opinions.

Why the staff writers and artists imagined Eastman could save the *Masses* is a mystery. Max had never run anything, or raised money, or been an editor or journalist. His suffrage league existed mainly on paper. None of the *Masses* group except Young knew him personally, though some had read him on equal suffrage. Perhaps he looked right: young, handsome, quietly assured. No matter how nervous he was, Max always made a serene impression. Accounts of him in those years speak of him as being not just relaxed but utterly boneless. Everyone remembered him as being draped over pieces of furniture. Were there not pictures to the contrary, we would have to think of him as a person who managed to reach the age of thirty-five without ever standing upright or sitting erect. Whatever their reasons, the editors had made a good move. Eastman fitted the job exactly. He had a practical turn of mind, unlike the owner-editors. He also had, it turned out, a gift for raising money that was as valuable as it was unexpected. Eastman quickly learned that, if the magazine was to come out on time, the notion that it was a working collective would have to be abandoned—at least by him. It remained cooperative in theory, but in reality, as his assistant Floyd Dell put it, the *Masses* was a practical dictatorship based on persuasion rather than force. Says Dell, Eastman could "talk anybody into doing anything."[2]

At first Max agreed to put out only a single issue, that of December

1912. The staff remained the same, except for the addition of Eastman and John Sloan, but the magazine was transformed. Instead of its usual bulky design, the cover had a graceful drawing of a clown by Charles A. Winter. Max's editorial column was headed "Knowledge and Revolution," a title he would use for years. In it he switched the magazine's politics from right to left-wing socialism without apologies. He endorsed the IWW's Lawrence strike and other controversial labor actions. Also, though he felt no one noticed, he pledged the magazine to experimentalism as opposed to dogma, even radical dogma. "By Knowledge, when it is spelled by a capital, we mean experimental knowledge—a free investigation of the developing facts and a continuous re-testing of the theories which pertain to the end we have in view. The end we have in view is an economic and social revolution."[3] This was his first shot in a war against right-wing timidity and left-wing dogmatism which would last for more than a quarter-century.

The unique qualities of the *Masses* did not evolve gradually but appeared fully grown in Max's first issue. Three things made the *Masses* special: it was for revolution, not reform; it was a rebellion against commercial journalism by commercial journalists; it was beautifully designed. The first was Max's doing, though the staff went along. The second was a genuinely collective act by professionals who felt that their best work was rejected by the moneymaking press. The elegant format was John Sloan's achievement.

Sloan was a painter of rare talent.[4] Born in Philadelphia in 1871, he studied art there under the influential Robert Henri. Sloan moved to New York in 1904, as Henri and other friends had done. Most supported themselves by teaching or producing commercial art, and the biggest markets for both were there. Four years later Sloan appeared in a group show with Henri and six other painters, who accordingly became known as The Eight. Many of their paintings were harsh and realistic, a far cry from the stylized academy art of the day. Art Young later dubbed them the Ashcan School because of this. But though the show was popular and Sloan's reputation increased, he did not gain financially. Sloan was forty-two years old before he sold his first painting. He never made much from art, working as a teacher most of the time. His personal life was difficult, too, for his wife Dolly, to whom Sloan was devoted, suffered from alcoholism. Like many artists in this period he was a Socialist, eager to give his talent to the cause. He twice ran for office on the Socialist ticket, campaigning on street corners as was then expected. On the *Masses* he found a better way to make his politics felt. Next to Eastman no one contributed more to its success, or cared for it more obsessively. In Eastman's absence Sloan could bring out the magazine himself, once sending Max for his approval a tiny model he had made of the current issue, with each drawing parodied in miniature.

Max set editorial policy, preserved the peace, and found money to keep the magazine afloat. Inez Milholland showed him the way by introducing Max to Mrs. O.H.P. Belmont, an extremely rich feminist. She gave him $2,000, obliging a conservative southern dinner guest to add another thousand. Thus they became benefactors of a periodical dedicated to the overthrow of their class. Max had vowed to quit after six months if the magazine was not self-supporting. But though it never paid its way, the six months turned into five years, and would have gone on longer still had the war not intervened. Max hated soliciting funds and resented the job's other demands on his time. But he relished making up the magazine, which combined, he said, "the infantine delight of cutting out paperdolls or keeping a scrapbook with the adult satisfaction of fooling yourself into thinking you are molding public opinion."[5] Then, too, the *Masses* quickly attracted a remarkably talented band of contributors for whom Max felt responsible.*

They were lively and independent, so Max could not rule them with a heavy hand. As contributors were not paid, the illusion of collective management had to be sustained. This was accomplished by open editorial meetings held monthly at which, people liked to think, the current issue was made up. Submissions were criticized and sometimes voted on. Picture captions were suggested and revised. Sloan was an especially tart judge, advising one artist that "there is only one thing left for you to do, pull off one of your socks and try with your feet." Another time Floyd Dell set off an outburst when, after reading a poem, he called for a show of hands. At this Hippolyte Havel cried out, "Voting! Voting on Poetry! Poetry's something from the soul! You can't vote on poetry!" Dell raised the flag of reason, observing mildly that

---

*Writers and poets included Witter Bynner, William Rose Benét, Carl Sandburg, Harry Kemp, Susan Glaspell, Franklin P. Adams, Arturo Giovannitti, Sherwood Anderson, James Oppenheim, Mabel Dodge, Vachel Lindsay, Amy Lowell, William Carlos Williams, Randolph Bourne, Babette Deutsch, Romain Rolland, Bertrand Russell. Maxim Gorky. Artists included Arthur B. Davies, Boardman Robinson, Jo Davidson, Stuart Davis, Glenn O. Coleman, George Bellows, Robert Minor.

decisions had to be made, and asking if Havel and the other anarchists who worked on Emma Goldman's *Mother Earth* did not make decisions also. Yes, Havel answered grandly, but we don't abide by them. Much as he objected to anarchism, Eastman secretly agreed. He, too, thought that poetry was from the soul, and did not abide by decisions made at these meetings when he thought them wrong.

Besides serving the myth of collective management, editorial gatherings promoted cohesion. The *Masses* was not so much a publishing venture as a movement, even for some a way of life. The contributors, few of whom were prosperous, gave their work to it because they believed in what the *Masses* stood for. They needed in return to see each other as a group, strengthen common ties, manifest their loyalty. Editorial meetings aided this, as did the *Masses* balls. These began as a fund-raising device but became a Village institution. A search for suitable premises led to the discovery of Webster Hall on Eleventh Street. The owner, who kept a saloon next door, let them have it for free, once he was assured by Floyd Dell that they would work up a tremendous thirst.

The first ball was such a hit that others followed. Dell to the contrary, *Masses* people were not heavy drinkers. Dancing was the chief entertainment, followed by costume watching. Someone was inspired to make the admission charge one dollar for those in costume and two dollars for those without. This resulted in a profusion of sheiks, cavewomen, circus dancers, and the like, frequently showing, for the times, generous amounts of flesh. For reasons of economy as well as titillation, hula skirts, ballet costumes, and ragged beggars' garments were favored. Harry Kemp, the "tramp poet" (after whom a street in Provincetown is named), showed the right spirit in donning a white robe decorated with small, hand-painted lions. Rounded off with a tin scimitar and helmet derived from a wash basin, this outfit enabled him to pass as an Assyrian king. And so the social and moral revolution of the era went forward.

The *Masses* broke all the rules of publishing. Where commercial magazines liked sentimental and romantic stories, the *Masses* ran heavily to realism or even the grotesque. One story was about two men who supported themselves by eating live rats in public.[6] John Reed turned up with a story he had written about a prostitute that his employer, the *American Magazine,* would not print. This was, Max later recalled, the first sign that there was a body of creative literature unsuited to money-making publications that the *Masses* could promote.

Reed was born in 1887, a vintage year for *Masses* editors, to a middle-class family in Oregon.[7] He attended Harvard College, where he was a writer and editor for the humorous *Lampoon* and the literary *Harvard Monthly*. He was also the manager of music clubs, a poet, and a student in the famous composition course of Charles Townsend Copeland. This did not mean that Reed was an aesthete. In college he organized an eating club notorious for its sophomoric practical jokes. Reed got into fistfights and was captain of the water polo team, delighting in the brutality and lack of rules that characterized the sport. After graduation he worked on a cattle boat in order to see Europe. Ambitious and talented, he was drawn to New York, where Lincoln Steffens, the famous muckraker, hired him to work on the *American*. Within a year Reed's articles and short stories had appeared also in *Collier's*, the *Saturday Evening Post*, the *Forum*, and the *Century*, all important magazines. Reed plunged into bohemian life as he had college life, rooming for a time in a sort of commune at 42 Washington Square, with some college friends and Steffens, whose protégé he had become. Reed's poem, "The Day in Bohemia," celebrates his Village experience.

> But nobody questions your morals,
> And nobody asks for the rent,
> There's no one to pry if we're tight, you and I,
>   or demand how our evenings are spent.
> The furniture's ancient but plenty, the linen is spotless and fair,
> O life is a joy to a broth of a boy
> At Forty-Two Washington Square![8]

Reed was noted for his youthful exuberance. Lincoln Steffens called him a "beautiful boy"; Van Wyck Brooks would later describe him as the "wonder boy of Greenwich Village." Floyd Dell saw him as "our marvelous boy." Big, handsome (Max was alone in being reminded of a potato by Reed's face), he seemed like a force of nature, charging recklessly through each day, searching out new experience, always ready for a party or a fight. He acted as if he knew that his life would be too short to waste a moment of it. In Reed's case, boyish did not mean frivolous. Soon after joining the *Masses* he went to Paterson, New Jersey, where the IWW had organized a silk strike. He was arrested and spent four days in jail, which completed his education. Thereafter he was to specialize in strikes and revolutions. On leaving jail he wrote "War in Paterson" for the June 1913 issue of the *Masses*, a landmark in the history of radical journalism. Next he organized a vast pageant of silk workers in Madison Square Garden, decorated for the event with the giant red letters IWW, a sign so dangerous that the police tried to turn it off. Reed then left for Europe with Mabel Dodge. Soon after this interlude, he was in Mexico with Pancho Villa, sending stories and reports of the revolution to the *Masses* and to the *Metropolitan,* which was paying his bills. These items, published later as *Insurgent Mexico,* made Reed famous. At the age of twenty-seven he was the subject of an article by Walter Lippmann in the *New Republic,* "Legendary John Reed," written partly with tongue in cheek, but out of grudging respect as well.

John Reed, Jack to his friends, was invaluable to the *Masses.* He gave it much of his best reporting. He stood with Max and the left-wing editors against pure aestheticism on the one hand and mere reformism on the other. Max took credit for Reed's political education, thinking he had saved Jack from the pernicious teachings of Lincoln Steffens. This was going too far. The *Masses* itself was a school for socialism, and Jack learned his lessons well; too well Max was later to think. Reed went on to become a Communist functionary, something Max in his wildest moments never dreamed of doing.

The *Masses* is best known today for its art work, which ranged from huge, powerful two-page illustrations down to Arthur B. Davies's pretty nudes. The cartoons were always underlined by brief, often witty captions, though whole paragraphs of dialogue were usual in commercial magazines. The artists had insisted on this "revolution." It made the *Masses* bold and beautiful and the *New Yorker,* which later adopted the style, wealthy. Three types of artists appeared in the magazine. Least valuable were the commercial illustrators, who had started the magazine but were loyal Socialists and could not be gotten rid of. More valuable were the fine artists, the Ashcan painters, and others, like Sloan's protégé Stuart Davis, who fell outside the category.

Davis, who later changed his style and became a forerunner of pop art, liked to draw cartoons of "happy darkies." As few whites at the time found racial stereotyping offensive, a number of these appeared in the *Masses.* At least one reader was angered by them, notifying Max that "your pictures of the colored people . . . would depress the negroes themselves and confirm the whites in their contemptuous and scornful attitude." This was true, and Max's reply lacked conviction. He said that Davis "portrays the colored people he sees with exactly the same cruelty of truth with which he portrays the whites. He is so far removed from any motive in the matter but that of art, that he cannot understand such a protest . . . at all."[9] Here Max spoke more for himself than Davis. Max personally was above reproach on racial issues. One of his first editorials in the *Masses* dealt with a recent wave of Southern lynchings. "There is no more awful thing in this country than the problem here revealed. It is the only problem of democracy that nobody offers an ultimate solution of." In the absence of democratic remedies he suggested that blacks arm themselves and fight back. "We believe there will be less innocent blood and less misery spread over the history of the next century if the black citizens arise and demand respect in the name of power than there will be if they continue to be niggers [that is to say, servile], and accept the counsel of those of their own race who advise them to be niggers."[10] In advocating black power Max was far ahead of his time. But he was very much of his time in liking racial and ethnic humor and seeing nothing harmful in it. Accordingly, in its early years the *Masses* depicted blacks in traditionally demeaning ways. Long afterward Max admitted that Davis went beyond this. "I remember rejecting with disgust a viciously anti-Negro picture of his."[11] Even in those days, however, while publicly rejecting the charge of bias, Max seems privately to have accepted it. Once he understood that caricaturing blacks injured them, the *Masses* stopped doing so. It became more sensitive to the color question and ran many pro-black, anti-racist items. In a bigoted age this made the *Masses* unique.

Davis notwithstanding, contributing artists were almost always socially conscious. Even Davis was to a degree, for appearing in the magazine constituted a political act. The Ashcan artists were especially valuable because their style was so well suited to propaganda. A picture such as that by George Bellows in the July 1913 issue showing a crowd of poor city children trying to swim and sun themselves by a city river full of shipping needed no words at all to make the point, even though in this case the point was underlined beautifully with the caption "Splinter Beach." In their time the Ashcan artists had real authority, which they conferred upon the *Masses*. It was a great loss to radical aesthetics that changing fashions made them obsolete. This process began as early as 1913 when the famed Armory Show introduced avant-garde European art to Americans. John Sloan seemed not to realize what this meant, dashing off a good-natured caricature of cubism in response. But his colleague Jerome Meyers knew that Arthur B. Davies, the show's main organizer, "had unlocked the door to foreign art and thrown the key away—more than ever we had become provincials."[12] Their school would not survive the advent of modernism.

A third category of *Masses* artists were the newspaper cartoonists. This group included men with very different styles. Art Young had a fine literary as well as graphic imagination. His idiom was based on the art of woodcuts, and though stiff this was well suited to his formal allegories. Robert Minor, in contrast, developed a brilliant, epic style for the *Masses* that combined, in the words of one authority, "simplicity, directness of line, and a sense of motion and conflict." However much they differed, *Masses* artists had this in common, according to Harvey Swados. They "respected each other's intentions even when they did not care for the finished product; they were, each in his own fashion, against commercialized glamor and easy sentimentality, and they were all committed to struggling against those of their own comrades who wished to reduce their work in size or insisted on captions beneath their pictures."[13] As we shall see, this was a struggle they sometimes lost.

The *Masses* published an enormous amount of verse because so many of the writers considered themselves poets; falsely in most cases, posterity has in its unkind way decreed. The fiction has worn rather better, thanks to Floyd Dell especially. Like Reed he was born in 1887, but to a poor midwestern family.[14] Though he failed to complete high school, Dell had a good self-education, aided by the family's residence during his teens in Davenport, Iowa, the most cultivated city for many miles around. There he met local intellectuals who would themselves go on to have interesting careers, including George Cram Cook, Susan Glaspell, and Harry Hansen. He became a Socialist under the influence of Davenport's party branch, and a newspaper reporter. Like ambitious youngsters everywhere, he dreamed of wider opportunities and in 1908 moved to Chicago, capital of the heartland in cultural matters as in other things. The Chicago Renaissance was just beginning, and Dell promoted it as associate editor of the *Friday Literary Review,* a supplement of the *Chicago Evening Post,* and then, in 1911 at the age of twenty-five, as the editor in charge. Dell thus found himself at the center of Chicago's lively group of writers, which then included Harriet Monroe, Vachel Lindsay, Carl Sandburg, Edgar Lee Masters, Alfred Kreymborg, Maxwell Bodenheim, and Ben Hecht. He was one of the first to discover Sherwood Anderson, who called the younger Dell his literary father.

Despite an unsuccessful marriage, Floyd was happy in Chicago. There he lived the free bohemian life undreamed of in Iowa. He knew all the best writers and as editor of the *Friday Review* was himself slightly famous. He had his first real love affairs in Chicago, and wrote his first book *Women as World Builders* (1913). But when the owner forced unwanted changes on the *Review* Floyd resigned, leaving Chicago in October 1913 with no regrets. New York was calling him. An aspiring artist and free spirit, destiny compelled him to live in Greenwich Village. And with his proven editorial skills it was inevitable that the *Masses* would seek him out once he had arrived. In December he joined the tiny paid staff, acquiring soon the title of managing editor. The theory was that Floyd would prepare the dummy, leaving Max's morning free for writing, and part of his own day as well. This tidy division of time and labor frequently broke down, but the choice of Floyd as, in his own words, Max's "faithful lieutenant," was a happy one all the same. A broadly gifted man of letters, he had a particular talent that astonished Max. Floyd could sit down in a roaring press room and compose a verse or paragraph that would fit precisely any gap in the dummy. He served as a literary editor, too, contributing pieces of his own and recruiting others. Thanks to him, several of Anderson's best *Winesburg* stories appeared first in the *Masses*. Floyd also managed during these years to write, direct, and act in plays at the Liberal Club and the Provincetown Playhouse, be psychoanalyzed, write two books, parts of a novel, and stories, poems, and occasional pieces without number.

Floyd looked more like a poet than anyone else on the magazine. He was pale and slender, with a high forehead and well-modeled features. Though by no means promiscuous, he shared the current enthusiasm for sexual affairs, and was considered the foremost proponent of free love in the whole of Greenwich Village. When he married again in 1919, and worse still, announced that he believed in marriage on principle, people were shocked. His disciple Joseph Freeman said it was almost as if William Z. Foster, a Syndicalist and later Communist leader, had come out in favor of the profit system. Dell never understood this reaction and in old age denied that it had existed. Floyd was wrong here, but rightly remembered his own opinions at the time. Even before reaching New York, he had written a friend: "My experiences in marriage and in love, have left me believing in them more thoroughly than ever I did before."[15] But the facts did not matter. Villagers wanted a romantic figure to embody the new morality. Dell was selected for this position by popular demand. As he was an exceptionally nice man, the choice was a good one, even if based on false assumptions.

*   *   *

According to Dell the *Masses* stood for "fun, truth, beauty, realism, freedom, peace, feminism, revolution." It was against militarism, capitalism, organized religion, stuffiness. Irving Howe said of it: "For a brief time . . . the *Masses* became the rallying center—as sometimes also a combination of Circus, nursery, and boxing ring—for almost everything that was then alive and irreverent in American culture."[16] Though best remembered for its lighter side, the magazine could be serious, too. The political reporting of John Reed, Max's best essays, and those of William English Walling and some others were intended to promote class struggle, a fight they all believed would end in victory for the workers. A declaration of principles ran at the masthead. It was suggested by Reed but written by Eastman, whose policy it described.

> THIS MAGAZINE IS OWNED AND PUBLISHED COOPERA-
> TIVELY BY ITS EDITORS. IT HAS NO DIVIDENDS TO PAY,
> AND NOBODY IS TRYING TO MAKE MONEY OUT OF IT. A
> REVOLUTIONARY AND NOT A REFORM MAGAZINE: A MAG-
> AZINE WITH A SENSE OF HUMOR AND NO RESPECT FOR
> THE RESPECTABLE: FRANK, ARROGANT, IMPERTINENT,
> SEARCHING FOR TRUE CAUSES: A MAGAZINE DIRECTED
> AGAINST RIGIDITY AND DOGMA WHEREVER IT IS FOUND:
> PRINTING WHAT IS TOO NAKED OR TRUE FOR A MONEY-
> MAKING PRESS: A MAGAZINE WHOSE FINAL POLICY IS TO
> DO AS IT PLEASES AND CONCILIATE NOBODY, NOT EVEN
> ITS READERS—THERE IS A FIELD FOR THIS PUBLICATION
> IN AMERICA.

The *Masses* aimed to promote both art and the revolution, which in those days everyone thought went together. As Harvey Swados put it, "the style with which the two were held in tension testified not only to an openness that was virtually to disappear from our cultural and political life, but also to the way in which Max Eastman exemplified and celebrated a largeness of spirit in both areas that has also become foreign to us, to our considerable disadvantage."[17]

There was indeed a place for the *Masses* in America, but only just.

It had about 5,000 subscribers and sold as many more through news-stands in its early days. Max built sales up to 15,000 and even as many as 25,000 at times. Yet while no one received a regular salary except Eastman and Dell, and all the contributions were free, the magazine was expensive to print and always lost money. To be self-supporting, it needed a wide audience that it never got, despite, and possibly even because of, considerable notoriety. The adage that any publicity is good publicity did not hold here. The magazine was often under fire. Circulation did not rise in consequence as would happen today. Max's first issue attracted unfavorable comment because of an Art Young cartoon likening publishers to prostitutes. Oswald Garrison Villard told Eastman it was "vulgar beyond anything I have ever seen in an American magazine."[18] Later, when Young depicted the Associated Press poisoning a reservoir labeled "truth," he and Eastman were indicted for libel. After two years and much publicity the suit was dropped. This moral victory did not lead to a flood of new subscriptions.[19] Neither did the revelation that Columbia's bookstore would not sell it, nor the university library subscribe to it, because of the *Masses'* treatment of religion. Getting barred from Canada seems not to have helped. Being raided by John S. Summer, Anthony Comstock's successor as head of the New York Society for the Suppression of Vice, made no apparent difference either. Nor did sales rise when Merrill Rogers, the business manager, was arrested and the September 1916 *Masses* confiscated for advertising August Forel's pioneering work, *The Sex Question,* which was considered indelicate.[20]

The *Masses* was too intellectual to be popular, and too irreverent to win a broad following among Socialists, who had their pieties, too. Earnest Socialists were always complaining to Eastman. George Bernard Shaw sent Max a long letter in 1914 urging caution and good taste. Shaw took exception to its anti-clericalism and the advertisements for books on sex. His motto was, "if you want to preserve real freedom, you cannot be too fastidious." Shaw accused Max of "admitting vulgar and ignorant stuff because it was blasphemous, and coarse and carnal work because it was scandalous."[21] The magazine did not pander to left-wing sex fiends as Shaw appeared to think. But it gave offense because most Socialists were as prudish as Shaw, if only to avoid association with free love, of which they were very afraid. As eros had no place in their movement, neither did the *Masses.*

Eastman met these charges variously. To Upton Sinclair he ex-

plained that items found objectionable were not vile, nor inspired by
"an indiscriminate habit of rebellion." "If you knew how much continual resistance I have put up to what you call a Greenwich Village atmosphere, from the very start, you would be satisfied upon that point."[22]
Resisting Village artiness and bohemianism was a sacred duty to Max.
He would not let them compromise the *Masses'* politics. At the same
time he knew that one could not build a great radical magazine with
propaganda alone. Years later, he wrote Reed's widow to say that, while
the *Masses* had differed from Greenwich Village art magazines in having "a revolutionary and fundamentally Marxian policy," it differed
from other socialist magazines in rejecting "the idea of having a propaganda note, or even the remotest suggestion of it, in everything that
was published."[23] The magazine would be revolutionary but bold and
beautiful as well. When Norman Thomas protested against having his
name appear in a peace statement, saying that the magazine angered
more readers by its sexual frankness than it persuaded with anti-war
propaganda, Max was firm. "We would strengthen our propaganda
value by toning down our expression of life. But it isn't just political
propaganda, it *is* life to which the venture is primarily dedicated. I can't
help it. That is deeper in me than the desire to be useful."[24]

   This distinction seldom applied. Nearly everything in the *Masses*
seemed useful to Max one way or another, especially if erotic. He had
rebelled against sexual constraint in theory before learning to do so in
practice. To him nude drawings, articles on birth control, even the advertisements for sexual guidebooks that Shaw complained of, were important. Max was proud of this service. Half a century later he still felt
that "these books were invaluable, and of revolutionary import in the
lives of women—American and English women especially. It's regretta-
ble that they were needed, but they were—desperately."[25] Given his
background, Max could not fail to identify with victims of sexual ignorance and repression. No one would champion their interests with
more conviction.

   Yet it was religion, not sex, that caused the greatest trouble. Shaw
might see the *Masses* as recklessly sensual, but Max and his peers took a
romantic view of sex and would not have, even if the Censors had
allowed it, published anything obscene. Religion was another matter.
To them Christ was at best "Comrade Jesus," a labor orgnizer in ancient Palestine, while the Church was the evil that lived on after the
good had been interred with his bones. When not attacking organized

religion they liked to rewrite the Bible. One such effort in January 1916, called "A Ballad," portrayed Joseph as a man who generously saved Mary from becoming an unwed mother. It aroused many protests, some from freethinkers, who argued that it would offend others. One friend wrote Max that by printing it he had "slaughtered a most beautiful ideal" and caused "unspeakable offense to the religiously inclined." Though Max was slow to anger in those days, this was too much. He replied that the writer had told him that her family, though not religious, had recently had a child christened anyway, or, as Max put it:

> . . . initiated with hypocritical sacrament into a solemn and monumental lie. This is what I call irreligious. I do not know that it "shocks" me. It makes me angry and contemptuous. Childhood and Truth at least ought to be sacred. But the trouble with all you kind friends who preach to me, is that you are never heroically and affirmatively declared for truth. You are serious, but you are not serious enough. And you are gay, but you are not gay enough. The world will never get its rebirth from you.[26]

"A Ballad" got the *Masses* barred from New York subway newsstands, which were controlled by the firm of Ward and Gow. A state senate committee was then investigating the subway system, so the *Masses* and its friends were given a chance to state their case in public. John Dewey testified that the *Masses* was not obscene, as did the Reverend Percy Stickney Grant, despite his feeling that "A Ballad" was in poor taste. Abraham Cahan, editor of the Jewish Daily Forward, was nostalgically reminded of his native Russia by this act of censorship. "It almost makes me homesick," he testified humorously.[27] Floyd Dell was not amused. He told reporters: "It seems that the holy mantle of Anthony Comstock has fallen upon the shoulders of Ward and Gow."[28] Lincoln Steffens reported that Mr. Ward had expelled the magazine from his newsstands because it offended his religion. But Ward was not a hard man. If the *Masses* came to resemble the *Atlantic Monthly*, he would think about relenting. As this seemed a fate worse than bankruptcy, the *Masses* decided to remain itself.

Because it was anti-modernist, the *Masses* is seldom valued by custodians of high culture today. Both its art work and creative writing were pre-modernist, naturally at first, deliberately later. The founders had learned their craft at a time when modernism was unfashionable or unknown. After it began to flourish, *Masses* contributors kept on working as before. Arthur B. Davies, a principal organizer of the 1913 Armory Show, helped introduced modern art to America, but his style was not affected by it. Floyd Dell was one of the first American critics to recognize the talent of Ezra Pound. Dell rejected most avant-garde poetry just the same. In 1914 he complained to an old friend that "about nine-tenths of the new art, in painting, sculpture, and poetry seems to me to have no aesthetic values at all."[29] A few years later Dell was surprised to find that the youngest villagers were coming to regard the *Masses* as a citadel of old-fogyism in the arts. Though shocked at this, Dell was unmoved. He would always dislike modernism and "the incoherent and semi-mystical thinking that accompanied it."[30] For the *Masses* group as a whole the acceptably new did not include free verse, cubism, or any avant-garde school of importance. Today this counts against them. People take it for granted that political radicals have a duty to embrace all that is radical in the arts. Actually, as Reed Whittemore points out, this seldom happens. To the contrary, "journalists and the radical activists have not in general been sympathetic to modernism but have favored traditional literary forms even as they set about to destroy other traditions."[31]

The *Masses* political writings have not always fared well either, for even poorer reasons. One scholar has dismissed Max's editorials as "a kind of formalized ritual of identification, which was got through in haste before the playful and discursive activities of the magazine could begin."[32] In fact the chief editors and many readers took their politics very seriously indeed. Joseph Freeman, then a student a Columbia and later an active Communist, testified that he and his left-wing friends considered the *Masses* to be their real university. This showed excellent judgement, for the articles and editorials of Eastman, Jack Reed, William English Walling, Frank Bohn of the IWW, and some others were always good and sometimes penetrating in the extreme. Reed's accounts of the Paterson strike, the Mexican Revolution, the Progressive party convention of 1916, to name only a few, are among the best things of their kind ever written by anyone. When he wanted to, which was not often enough, Eastman could produce great journalism also. He did feel like it after the Ludlow Massacre. This atrocity was committed by state militiamen while breaking a strike against the Rockefeller-owned Colorado Coal and Iron Company. In the course of it they set the strikers' tent colony afire, suffocating twelve women and children.

Infuriated workers then destroyed a quantity of mine machinery. Eastman went to Colorado after this and reported his feelings to the *Masses:*

> I think the palest lover of "peace" after viewing the flattened ruins of
> that little colony of homes, the open death-hole, the shattered bed-
> steads, the stoves, the household trinkets broken and black—and the
> larks still singing over them in the sun—the most bloodless would
> find joy in going up the valleys to feed his eyesight upon tangles of
> gigantic machinery and ashes that had been the operating capital of
> the mines. It is no retribution, it is no remedy, but it proves that the
> power and the courage of action is here.[33]

To a monthly magazine, essays are as important as topical pieces,
perhaps more so. Accordingly, the *Masses* had a regular column by
Walling, usually devoted to socialist activities abroad. It reviewed a
large number of difficult or noteworthy books, not only radical works
but studies in the new history and social sciences. Bohn and other
radical intellectuals appeared often in the *Masses*. For a time after the
New Review, a journal of left-wing thought, ran out of cash it appeared
as a separate section in the *Masses*. The magazine tolerated a broad
range of opinion but not an indifference to politics. This was made
clear by the famous artists' revolt. In 1916 a group of artists protested
against the editors' habit of desecrating their work by adding captions
to it. As this was always done cleverly and with taste, some suspected
the real complaint was against Eastman's strong editorial hand. With
the aid of mild, lovable Art Young, who said, "anybody who doesn't
believe in a socialist policy, so far as I go, can get out," the rebels were
soundly beaten.[34] Sloan, Davis, Maurice Becker, and Robert Carlton
Brown, a writer, resigned. They were missed, Sloan especially, but the
magazine had enough depth in every position to get along very well
without them. Afterward, everyone had a clearer sense of what their
venture was all about.

Not surprisingly, the dominant voice on the *Masses* was Eastman's.
Almost every issue had one or more editorials by him, and sometimes
other pieces, too. In them Max explained as systematically as he could
the intellectual basis for radical action. To the extent that he had a
guide, it was Karl Marx. Eastman considered himself a scientific socialist but had doubts as to whether Marx, for all his usefulness, qualified.
Thus he used Marxist ideas while seldom identifying their author. His
aim, as Joseph Slater put it, was to resist dogma and rigidity, to make of

Marxism "an instrument and not a faith."[35] He thought the concept of class struggle was particularly important and often used it as a litmus test of radical sincerity. Their refusal to embrace it demonstrated, so far as Max was concerned, the weakness of what he (privately) called the "sentimental rebels," meaning Steffens, Hutchins Hapgood, Clarence Darrow, and other essentially liberal people who were friendly to radicalism but not friendly enough. Max was unfair to Darrow, a one-man justice department to the poor and oppressed. Lincoln Steffens was another matter. Max once said that the *Masses* did not preach brotherhood because the capitalists did not practice it.[36] Steffens annoyed him greatly by trying, at one point, to make capitalists practice the golden rule. This was folly to Max, who with most Socialists thought it obvious that the rich had no intention of giving up their privileges, which would have to be taken from them by the workers. At socialist meetings he was clear about the method involved, though still without mentioning Marx by name.

> But it so happens that there has never in the history of the world, been but one thorough-going and highly scientific attempt made to think out a plan by which the worker can be secured the whole product of his work—and that is the plan of having a democratic state take over the land that is used for production and the machinery of the greater productive and distributive enterprises and administer them not on a wage system, but on a system of returning the profits to those who produce them.[37]

Anarchists did support the class struggle and believed in seizing the means of production, but their dogmatism and, as he saw it, backwardness irritated Max. Circumstances sometimes obliged him to appear with anarchists and defend their rights, which was even more irritating. He felt they were not entitled to use the word "revolution" because it was "for me defined and consecrated to the uses of science." He thought anarchists had a literary infatuation with the idea of revolt. They had no taste for experimental science, only a passion for "rather undiscriminating hurrah."[38] Anarchists were both obsolete and naive in his view, and never more so than when it came to assassination:

> I do not mean to imply that killing is peculiarly the anarchist method. A great many anarchists do not believe in it and a great many who are not anarchists do. But the practice of individual praise and blame, the old-fashioned business of evangelism (of which assassination is

perhaps only an extreme instance) seems to be the essence of their method, and it belongs almost as properly to the past as their philosophy.[39]

Max was certain that when the revolution arrived anarchists would not lead it. Subsequently he would turn a blind eye to Lenin's suppression of the anarchists, having made the same judgment years before.

As a revolutionary Max had to admire the Industrial Workers of the World. The Wobblies were tough talkers. They liked to scare employers by reviewing the merits of dynamite as a strike weapon. They were tough in practice, too, real activists, not armchair radicals, like so many Eastman knew. Wobblies got out in the field, organized immigarants, migrant workers, women, the unskilled, toilers, who it was believed in those days could not be organized. Wobblies had their flaws. They did not vote or bargain collectively, so even when they won strikes the gains were never permanent. All the same, they were the first real revolutionaries in American history, anti-capitalist to the bone. Max chided those socialists who insisted that only their method of political action was valid, defending direct action as practiced by the Wobblies. "So far from being opposed to each other, political action and direct action always have and always will accompany each other."[40] If this made him appear to condone sabotage, which in the public mind was associated, usually falsely, with the IWW, Max did not care. In Joseph Slater's words he "was to preach action as relentlessly as Piet Vlag had preached cooperation."[41]

As a socialist Max naturally favored political action, but unlike many he did not think it a sufficient means for revolution. Economic power would be needed, too, and this was what the IWW could provide. Disliking Max's position, orthodox socialists tried to ignore it. The *Call,* a socialist daily newspaper in New York, once reported an IWW rally without mentioning that he was a principal speaker.[42] Max returned the sentiment. He was loyal to socialism, not to the Socialist party. After the 1916 elections, when the party's vote had fallen by one-third and membership by half since reaching peaks in 1912, Eastman wrote that this setback was good for the party because "an element of doubt has been injected into minds heretofore paralyzed with certitude. And this in itself is a corrective of the chief fault of the party. Scientific thinking requires the power to suspend judgment, and that power has been habitually renounced as an automatic part of the act of becoming a party member." The party was in the habit of ignoring unpleasant or unwanted facts, and this "theological automatism" was the main cause of its failure to progress. "The number of people who are willing to sell out their intelligence to a formula is very large. But the number of liberty-loving people who will sell out to a Socialist formula is not large."

Recent events proved this, and it was now time for the party to abandon dogma for the sake of growth. To this end it must keep in mind that "a political party ought to represent, not a certain kind of knowledge, but a certain economic interest. It ought to take in all the people who *agree in something concrete and immediate*. The American Socialist Party includes only people who agree in *understanding something remote and ultimate*. It is not a party of the working-class: it is a party of the theory of the working-class." Worse still, the theory was European. No great number of American workers would ever accept so alien and difficult a system, Max believed. He concluded, in words that explain his later defection from it, "the Socialist party will never become the party of the labor struggle until it subordinates the idea and builds around the will. And if the Socialist party does not become the party of the labor struggle, another and wiser party will take its place." [43]

Max here was not interested in the other reasons why socialism was failing: the popularity of middle-class ideas; the lack of class consciousness among workers, divided as they were between foreign and native born, and further segregated by race, religion, nationality and sex. Nor did he dwell on the numerous prejudices aroused when people from different and often conflicting traditions were thrown together. In Europe, socialism in each country was based on common backgrounds, the proletariat having as a rule the same language, religion, and heritage. Workers in America lacked these bonds, which made organizing them difficult for trade unionists and Socialists alike. But so far as it went, this was a brilliant critique of the Socialist party's theory and practice. As might be expected, Socialists paid it little mind. No one listens to Cassandra until it is too late.

Max's problem, as revealed by his unfinished essay, "Towards Liberty: The Method of Progress," is that he could see flaws in all existing radical doctrines, but not how to repair or replace them. He believed that intellectuals could advance the class struggle, if "they have trained their intellectuality in the art of instrumental thinking, when they have learned how to hold themselves in doubt, and have foresworn absolutely in all active situations the static love of an idea." [44] Beyond this he was uncertain. Even so, Max's political essays and editorials in the *Masses* foreshadow his political history during the next quarter of a century, his period of greatest accomplishment as an intellectual. They indicate why he was so quick to hail the Russian Revolution, and to fall under the spell of Lenin, who embodied that combination of theory and will that Americans seemed to lack. They explain also why he was to remain critical of Marxism even while professing it. Thanks to Dewey, Eastman was an instrumentalist before he became radical, and that orientation was to remain with him. When he became a Leninist in 1918, it was for instrumental reasons, the October Revolution having, as it were, established the cash value of Marx's ideas. But even then, as we shall see, he continued to reject crucial Marxist teachings, and he admired Lenin precisely because it seemed to Eastman that in practice Lenin had shown himself able to discard theories that in principle he was wedded to. In short, Lenin would be most attractive to Eastman when he was least Marxist. Throughout his radical career Eastman would owe more to Dewey than to Marx.

In Eastman's writing before 1918 we see him fighting dogma, defending science and experimental thought, exalting liberty, deploring the obstacles, concrete and theoretical, to it. Both his Marxism, such as it was, and his anti-Marxism are here in embryo. So, too, in clearer ways were the basic values he would cling to all his life. In these years he was most open-minded and responsive to new ideas and events. Despite his prejudices against religion, anarchism, and progressivism, Eastman was broadly sympathetic, intellectually generous, and flexible as he would never be again. When he grew older, Max would speak with more authority, paying for this with loss of suppleness. The great irony of Max's life is not that the enemy of capitalism became a friend of it, or that the radical Socialist became anti-Socialist and anti-Communist. Rather it is that the champion of free inquiry, experimentation, and instrumentalism became a dogmatist—the very figure of what as a young man he had most abhored.

* * *

Occupied though he was with socialist issues, Max did not forget his earliest cause, feminism, nor birth control, which was related to it. He criticized the Socialist party for not recognizing that the woman question was "equal in importance" to any other. Though committed in principle to sexual equality, American Socialists were behaving "like every other group of sexually selfish men." To Max they stood for sex equality," not fightingly as they stood for masculine democracy, because they felt the great possibility and the great principle, but passively and tamely, because it had been written into their platforms by greater men than they." He asked why feminists were more active in England than the United States, and, like de Tocqueville before him, wondered if it was not because Americans worried more about social respectability than people in older countries.[45] Max continued to urge woman suffrage in the same terms as before, claiming that women needed it to become fully developed persons. He kept insisting that when women enjoyed the same right as men to be happy, both sexes would have more fun.[46] When President Wilson advised a convention of suffragists to be patient, Max remarked that if these women had been voters Wilson would have gone to them not to lecture but to please. "The courtesy of a man to a woman is a lovely and beautiful thing, but for real working reliability it can't compare at all to the courtesy of a politician to his constitutents."[47] It was such observations that inspired a letter to the *New York Times* accusing Max and other suffragists of being dyspeptic. The writer suggested they seek relief through hard work—preferably far from New York City.[48]

Max strongly supported birth control, which was even more unpopular than woman suffrage and possibly more important. This was why the work of Margaret Sanger was so vital, as Eastman realized even when provoked by her methods. Discussing her magazine, the *Woman Rebel,* Max complained that it was shrill, negative, and offensive to reasonable people. "Like the *Anarchist Almanac,* the *Woman Rebel* seems to give a little more strength to the business of shocking the Bourgeoisie than the Bourgeoisie really are worth." He applauded her all the same for doing great work and risking jail. "And if the virtue that holds heroes up to these sticking points must needs be united with the fault of a rather unconvincing excitedness and intolerance—all right, we will hail the virtue and call it a bargain at the price."[49] In this spirit Eastman spoke, wrote, and raised money to further Sanger's work.

Max also gave her sensible advice when she was indicted for twelve articles that had appeared in the *Woman Rebel.* One of them defended the right of assassination, the others birth control—though without describing contraceptive techniques, which would have been illegal. On January 5, 1916, she issued a statement entitled "To My Friends and Comrades," saying the district attorney was willing to make a deal. If she pleaded guilty, he would see that she got off lightly. Sanger wrote that she "refused to do this because the whole issue is not one of mistake, whereby getting into jail or keeping out of jail is of importance, but the issue involved is to raise the entire question of birth control out of the gutter of obscenity and into the light of human understanding." Eastman failed to see the point. He spoke to her personally and then wrote to say he agreed with her lawyer. Sanger could plead guilty and still attack the law that kept her from promoting contraception. Eastman saw this as more useful than courting martyrdom. He was against her going to jail for the sake of articles that had avoided the crucial issue. Even if she pleaded innocent and won her case, nothing would be gained, since the law forbidding the spread of contraceptive information was not involved.

Eastman begged Sanger to examine her conscience. "I think if you would once write a definite and clear statement of the reason why you are risking this wonderful chance to go ahead with your work for human liberty, you would see that it is no reason at all. At least, it has to do only with the salvation of your own self and not of the world." [50] Though the government did not press charges against Sanger, this incident is revealing just the same. Max wanted the best for her, and he understood that to be staying at liberty without loss of principle. He would want the same thing for himself in a few years when he was indicted under the Espionage Act.

Most enemies of birth control were conservative, but there was a left-wing opposition to it as well. Some radicals argued with Max that birth control was a mere palliative designed to make the workers more content with their poverty, less likely to rebel. Max did not subscribe to the doctrine that the worse things got the better it was for revolutionaries. Some matters were too important to be put off. Regardless of whether a society was just or unjust, the "bearing and rearing of children should always be a deliberate, and therefore a responsible act." [51] Max favored revolution, but not at any price. For this reason, though he was to work hard at it, he would make a poor Bolshevik.

* * *

Editing and raising money for the *Masses* took up much time, too much Max was to feel later, as did lecturing. Yet he still managed to write creatively, thus meeting the requirements of his tripartite life plan. In April 1913 Max's reputation soared with the publication of *Enjoyment of*

Poetry. Many years and many volumes later, he was to remember it as the easiest of his books to write. "I was more convinced that I was a wonder then than ever again." [52] It was also the most durable of his works, going through printing after printing for the rest of his life. Max felt that he had accomplished several things in the book. No one before him had explained metaphor, he was certain, nor had anyone applied psychology to literature.

As we saw, Max was deeply prejudiced against literary approaches to literature, even when employing them. In his introduction to *Enjoyment of Poetry* Max declared firmly "that a study of books must be either science—that is the chemistry and physics of their make-up, and the psychology of their author and its readers—or else history, an account of the general conditions and consequences of their production." [53] Max's book was not history, nor was it science, though he and Dewey shared the delusion that it was. Dewey praised it for containing "good sense, wise philosophy and correct psychology," thereby erring twice. [54] Max had an interesting approach to poetry, but it owed little to philosophy or psychology. The most engaging and commented on of his ideas was the distinction Max drew between what he saw as the two types of people in the world. Some, he wrote, were "chiefly occupied with attaining ends, and some with receiving experiences." The difference was between a practical and a poetic approach to life. Children, for example, were not task-oriented, lived in the present, and therefore were poetic by nature. This was scarcely scientific research, and yet it had a certain truth. The result of such speculation was a delightful book that could be read with pleasure by any literate person.

As would be his custom Eastman sent many copies of *Enjoyment of Poetry* to friends and authorities, receiving many warm notes in return. Walter Lippmann wrote "I love you for it. I love it being so much more than a book about something else; it's the revelation of a very vivid and loving human being." Walter Weyl, with Lippmann and Herbert Croly, a founder of the *New Republic,* called it "vivid, penetrating, true—charming. It is delightfully unpedantic." Bliss Perry, a leading academic critic, found "your discussion fresh and keen, and most stimulating to a jaded expounder of such subjects." [55] The notices were as good. Max was commended by the stately *North American Review* for writing both imaginatively and logically. The *New York Times* hailed the book twice, first in a regular review and then later as one of its hundred best books of the year. To the *Times* it was "a clever book, which holds out the possibility that he may yet accomplish a great deal for American literary criticism . . . a fine effort to free poetry from what he conceives to be schools and to reveal it wherever it exists on the lips of children and savages and in the rude hopes of the unlettered, as well as in the poetry of Keats and Christina Rossetti."[56] Long afterward Maxwell Perkins, Scribner's legendary editor, told Eastman how much *Enjoyment of Poetry* had meant to him: "I had only been here two or three years when it came and up to then we had had dreary lists, and I was feeling quite dreary about publishing. That was the first book that made it seem like the business that I had thought it was."[57]

Max's pleasure at this response did not last long. A few months after *Enjoyment* appeared his first book of poetry, *Child of the Amazons,* was published and fell flat. In the memoirs he says that only Vida Scudder, a friend of Crystal's who taught literature at Vassar, wrote favorably of it, and then in the *Survey,* a magazine for social workers and reformers.[58] Things were not so desperate as Max remembered. The *New York Times* was kind. It disliked the title poem, a long allegory about the woman movement whose main character vaguely resembled Inez Milholland. The work seemed "too argumentatitive to be art, and too sketchy to be argument." But some of the other poems, especially "At the Aquarium," earned praise. "Here we see what Mr. Eastman can do when he knows precisely where he stands. Perhaps it was scarcely to his discredit to fail in the more ambitious poem, for no one will get a firm grip on the woman problem of the twentieth century before the twenty-first, anyway, and maybe not then. Our safety as poets—and sociologists as well—lies in recognizing the fact."[59] This was small consolation. Eastman wanted to be a great poet. The limp response to *Child of the Amazons* broke his fragile confidence. "It deterred me from cultivating myself as a poet. It confirmed me in the habit of writing poetry only when an emotion took such romantic hold of me that I had to."[60] In later years he would mourn his lost vocation more deeply than he did at the time. In 1913 he was too busy to dress in black. Love awaited him, and unsought fame as well.

CHAPTER THREE

Love and War

1914–1917

Despite success Max remained unhappy, especially about his marriage. He had not lost his desire for sexual adventures, while Ida, her contacts with bohemia notwithstanding, took the usual view that married people should love only one another. For Max this was not so much ridiculous as impossible. In desperation he turned to psychoanalysis. Still unknown to most people, it had been growing in prestige among intellectuals, especially since Freud's visit to the United States in 1909. Max's analyst was Smith Ely Jelliffe, an early convert to Freudianism. Jelliffe knew many artists and bohemians and was the obvious choice. Max saw him for a few months in the winter and spring of 1914, but nothing much happened. Jelliffe talked too much and arrived at the wrong diagnosis. As we saw, he believed Max was still trapped in the Oedipal situation. Though it was probably true, Max rejected this explanation out of hand. However, he was quick to see Freud's importance as a thinker. Freud's ideas helped to account for the baffling failure of human beings to stay on the path of reason and self-interest. After studying Freud, the job of introducing psychoanalysis to laymen was assumed by Max. In two articles for the slick magazine *Everybody's* he described such conceptions as repression, the unconscious, and wish-fulfillment in dreams, in greatly simplified terms.[1] One expert says these articles did "for the general public what reviewers and special writers for the *Nation* and the *New Republic* were doing for the educated layman, what the men and women of Greenwich Village and Mabel Dodge Sterne's circle were doing for the intellectuals and the artists." "I first learned of psychoanalysis in a magazine article by Max Eastman,"

Edmund Wilson wrote.[2] Max would lean heavily on Freud in his pioneering study *Marx, Lenin, and the Science of Revolution* (1926).

If psychoanalysis was a false start on the road to health for Max, he did move forward in 1914 by confronting Ida with his need for privacy and breathing space. When they got back to Greenwich Village after summer vacation, he took a room for himself as a retreat. Later he bought a small house on Mt. Airy Road in Croton-on-Hudson. In 1915 and for years afterward the area was at least semi-rural. There Max could be in the country where he belonged, he had written as a child. Yet it was close to his work in the city, and a place where other radicals located, making it rich in friendship as well. He would have some of his happiest times and do much of his best work in Croton. That house was his first real home as an adult, remaining so for over a quarter-century.

Distance eased the strain but did not solve his marital problem. He went on agonizing over it until late in 1916 when a new friend, Eugen Boissevain, took him in hand. Boissevain was a Dutch businessman who became the first male friend Max ever confided in, and possibly the last. After the death of his wife, Inez Milholland, Boissevain took an apartment in New York and invited Max to share it. This was not a casual offer. He knew from Crystal that Max's marriage was foundering. Crystal was back in New York, having divorced her first husband and married an Englishman named Walter Fuller, whose three sisters toured America singing English folksongs.

Ida took the point. Staying in his own room, or in Croton, was one thing; living all the time with someone else, even a male friend, was another. She told Max that if he joined Boissevain they were finished. He agreed, and in fear and trembling walked out on his little family. It took, he said, "more courage than anything else I ever did." He was miserable at first, depressed by failure, burdened, one would like to think, by guilt at abandoning his infant son. But soon hope returned, and with it a sense of freedom. His upward movement was helped along by Rosalind Fuller, one of his new sisters-in-law. Crystal sent Rosalind over to see how Max was getting on. They were soon lovers, and after that Max was very well indeed. Rosalind gave Max his first uncomplicated sexual experience, opening the way for a lifetime of erotic abandon. He was properly grateful for this. They would always be friends, as sometimes happened between Max and his lovers.[3] Soon Max fell in love with another girl, Florence Deshon, an actress he met at a *Masses* Ball in December 1916. Thus, the final chapter of *Enjoyment of Living* is called "My Life Begins."

* * *

As Max's life began, that of the world he had grown up in was ending. The Great War, as it used to be called before standards rose, shocked everyone:

> Like all my radical friends I had mistaken for final reality the comparative paradise that prevailed in America at the turn of the century. Notwithstanding Ludlow Massacres and bomb warfare in the structural steel industry, it was a protected little historic moment of peace and progress we grew up in. We were children reared in a kindergarten, and now the real thing was coming. History was resuming its bloody course.[4]

Few at the time thought the Great War would have such awful consequences, or even take place at all. Industrialization was supposed to have rendered another long war impossible, both because of the damage that would result and on account of the new interdependence of national economies.

Many radicals believed that the Second International, or at least class-conscious workers, would prevent war. Modern warfare required popular consent, which Socialists liked to think would be withheld. Instead, the European Socialist parties supported their warring governments, exploding the fiction of a unified international proletariat. This was appalling and unexpected, though not to Eastman. After fighting broke out, he said in the *Masses* that it was obvious European socialism could not prevent war. The German Social Democratic party, greatest of all left political organizations, had voted for huge military taxes before the war, showing how it would act once hostilities commenced. What could be expected of the weaker parties elsewhere? "When socialism is strong enough to combat capitalism, then it will be strong enough to combat capitalism's wars."[5]

At first Max was not dismayed by the conflict, for he thought it would advance democracy and the interests of working people by wiping out German autocracy. "It is for Germany, more than for the Allies, that we want the Kaiser's defeat." In the short run labor would suffer. But over time the war would ruin the governing classes of many nations, free the proletariat to rebel, and show workers they had more

in common with each other than with their masters.[6] In view of the
slaughter to come this seems cold-hearted. But though he wrote care-
lessly of Europe being reduced to a shambles, Max had no more idea
than anyone else how long the war would last, or how many millions
would become casualties. As the war grew more frightful, Eastman
would take it with greater seriousness. In the event, Max's prophecies
were at least half right. The war disappointed him by failing to inter-
nationalize the proletariat. It did destroy both Kaiser and Tsar on
schedule, creating opportunities for the democratization of Germany
and Russia—though of course they were lost. It strengthened the hand
of Socialist parties in most countries, for the ruling classes were discredited, as Max had said they would be. The difference was one of
degree. Capitalism, except in Russia, wobbled but did not fall. Even so,
as prophets are notoriously wrong, this was a good batting average.

The war did not affect Max personally for several years. In 1915
he went to Europe for a two-month investigation, learning almost nothing. Instead of a brilliant essay, such as he had written about the Ludlow Massacre, he produced "The Uninteresting War."[7] It explained
how boring the struggle was, an absurd thesis arising from Max's frame
of mind and his inability to reach the front. Max predicted, correctly
again, that if the war went on much longer the English would have to
introduce conscription. Otherwise, he had little to say. Though Ida was
not with him on this visit, it was as sterile as the last—except for a vivid
poem Max wrote after seeing photographs of war casualties, "At the
Red Cross Hospital." It was not much to show for two months spent in
a world turned upside down.

*   *   *

Max published two books in 1916. Both were collections of essays suggested to him by commercial publishers. *Journalism vs. Art* struck a false
note. Max had vowed that writing would be to him a sacred act un-
soiled by the profit motive. He regarded commercial journalism as
worse than prostitution. In this book, a work of journalism published to
make money, he deplored the effects of commercialism. While trying
to walk both sides of the street he denied that doing so was possible. "A
man is either living or earning his living. He is never doing these two
things, purely, at once."[8] *Journalism vs. Art* seems to make his point,
though more by example than force of argument.

Max confessed that he knew writing for money was sordid and

degrading because he himself had once sunk so low as to commit an act of journalism. Needing money to go to Europe, he wrote a magazine article to order. Afterward friends told him that it was not of high quality, only well written. The reference is to his articles on psychoanalysis. *Everybody's* aimed for popularity, so Max's articles were tailored to meet that need. This proved to him that "the whole commercial magazine system is, in fact, bent upon the spiritual ruin of talented young people with a beautiful ambition." [9] Though he wrote here with tongue in cheek, Max believed it to be true. It was why he did not become a professional journalist until forced to by necessity almost a quarter-century later.

In the end, Max's prejudice against journalism would keep him from making the best use of his talents on a regular basis. When in top form he was as good a reporter as Jack Reed, as intelligent about politics as Walter Lippmann. He was a natural essayist, as journalists ought to be. After his death a friend observed that "the world lost a great political journalist when Max went in for art and philosophy." [10] Max resisted this truth, maintaining that what he did on the *Masses* was not journalism, and in any case only temporary. Though his finest political books would blend current history with the higher journalism, he did not follow them up. Even when on the *Reader's Digest* payroll he called himself a "literary artist." Max preferred the illusion of purity to fame and possibly fortune in the role he seemed designed for. Edmund Wilson would call himself a journalist, and prove that it was not incompatible with honor and intelligence. Max would learn nothing from this example. Fortunately, having common sense, Max did not carry prejudice to extremes. He practiced journalism as little as possible, but as required, so his life was not a failure. The same cannot be said of *Journalism vs. Art*.

His other book in 1916, *Understanding Germany*, stands up better. In his autobiography Max made light of it, saying that most of the essays had already been published elsewhere first, and, anyway, he knew little about Germany. In his preface to the book Max wrote that the title essay was unimportant because anyone not driven insane by newspapers could have written it. Both comments miss the point, which was that most writers and intellectuals had lost their minds when it came to Germany. That Eastman did not made him indispensable. He argued that both sides were behaving poorly, though only Germany got blamed. Germany had violated the neutral rights of Belgium; England those of Greece by marching Serbian troops through it without permission. There was little moral difference between the German U-boat campaign and the British blockade of Germany, which killed invisibly. Max had come to think, as President Wilson would for a moment, that Germany's defeat would be undesirable. It would mean not the democratization of Germany but another war brought on by "injured self-esteem." Max wanted what Wilson would later call a peace without victory, or, as Max put it, "equable failure." He could not know at the time how right he was. Europe needed a negotiated settlement at the earliest possible date. The lack of it gave rise first to communism, then to fascism and nazism, products of the moral and physical destruction brought on by protracted war.

Orthodox Socialists thought the war resulted from clashing imperialisms. Max disagreed, believing that it stemmed from patriotism which he took to be inherent in mankind, having its roots in the natural human traits of pugnacity and gregariousness, or the "herd-instinct." He held that patriotism would always be a source of war so long as it was narrowly defined. Max did not side with those liberals, pacifists, and others who held that people's attitudes could be changed, thus making war unlikely. What he hoped was that nationalism could be subsumed in some kind of international union that would create a larger allegiance—as the American's loyalty to his state had been submerged in a greater loyalty to the United States. This was, as Max put it, "The Only Way To End War."[11]

In a speech Max called patriotism infantile, leading the *New York Times* to refute him editorially, praising love of country, mother, college, while omitting, for some reason, Nanny, Rover, and the tooth fairy.[12] The *Times* review of his book was more sympathetic, apparently because Max thought it better at present to establish a federation of bourgeois states than to reorganize the Socialist International—though he wanted that, too.[13] Francis Hackett, literary editor of the *New Republic,* complained not so much about Max's ideas, which he opposed, as the way they were put. He found *Understanding Germany* to be "extraordinarily smug and condescending and bland." Eastman was too distant from the passions involved. He wrote of the war as if it were "happening on Jupiter."[14] Hackett had a point. Eastman's style was cool by nature. At a time when millions were dying, something warmer might seem called for. Yet, as so many Americans, including Hackett, were losing control of their feelings, Eastman's way made sense. Emotionalism would lead America into war and result in a bad peace. If Eastman and his friends had been listened to, this would not have happened. Arturo Giovannitti, Eastman's least critical admirer, said he should get the Nobel Peace Prize for his essay "The Only Way To End War."[15] This was less absurd than might be supposed. Theodore Roosevelt, a militarist, racist, and imperialist, had won the prize. Measured against him, Eastman was positively Tolstoyan. The contrast was spelled out in a memorable Boardman Robinson cartoon, "Max Eastman Expounding Pacifism to a Winner of the Nobel Peace Prize." It shows a relaxed Eastman addressing T. R., who is having a fit.[16]

Strictly speaking, Max was not a pacifist. He believed in taking up arms for a good cause, such as the revolution. In opposing American entry he tried to be educational rather than demagogic. He spoke often on "The Religion of Patriotism" which, he said,

> combines the strongest possible appeal to altruism, the appeal of infant memories with the strongest possible appeal to egoism, the chance to behold ourselves enlarged and clothed in public splendor. In patriotism we have both the emotion of losing ourselves, which has been celebrated by the saints in all ages, and the emotion of magnifying ourselves so large that there is no possible danger of our getting lost, which is more enjoyable if not so celebrated.[17]

Though this is almost professorial, Max was greatly in demand at antiwar rallies. War protestors must have been more patient then, or possibly more cerebral. Max's approach would have failed utterly in the 1960s when militants liked to get to the name-calling right away. This decline is to be expected. As wars become more outrageous, so also will war-resisters.

The failure of socialism to prevent war, while no surprise, convinced Max that militarism had to be fought before war broke, as then it was too late. To his mind the war had not discredited socialism, only the Second International. War "destroys the business of moral recrimination, it destroys the ideal of evangelical regeneration under capitalism, and makes the socialist mode of procedure look supremely sensible."[18] However, those socialists who thought the war provided them with easy answers were wrong. Max felt that to them a handful of slogans was food enough for thought: " 'Thou shalt damn the capitalist class with all thy heart and with all thy mind and with all thy strength; and thou shalt love the proletariat as thyself.' Upon these two commandments hang all the law and the prophets," Eastman mockingly observed. He thought their religious attachment to socialism was the opposite of what changing times demanded. "Wisdom must be won and conquered afresh every morning. I would rather get the spirit of that truth into the Socialist party than half a million new members." He asked those whose habit it was "to dismiss every problem that arrives with a sentence from *Das Kapital* or *The Communist Manifesto,* to let this overwhelming thing which seems to have befallen in spite of and against the economic interests of everybody concerned shock them a little as it shocks the natural heart of man, and make them bend down humbly to the task of examining its character and decide what stand we ought to take." [19]

Slogans were inadequate to the crisis, as were references to treasured ideas dimly understood. Hard thought was needed, but action, too, even if that meant siding with Woodrow Wilson. Max had been impressed by Wilson when they shared a speakers' platform in 1912, and he was more impressed when Wilson kept, as it seemed, America out of war. In the summer of 1916 Max and other representatives of the American Union Against Militarism spoke with the President. The Union had been organized by Crystal, and, though it was small, some prominent reformers, such as Amos Pinchot and the settlement leader Lillian Wald, were members, giving the AUAM strength beyond its size. Wilson handled them beautifully, Max was forced to admit. The President "throughout the interview always referred to the Union Against Militarism as though he were a member of it. The whole interview became in his hands a friendly and harmonious discussion of how 'we' could meet the difficulties of a national defense without the risks of militarism." [20] Socialist doctrine held that one capitalist politician was much like another. Max disagreed. As he saw it, Theodore Roosevelt's motto was "Americanism and Preparedness," while Wilson stood for "International Action and Preparedness," an important difference.

Only months before intervention Max still believed that Wilson was less likely to enter the war than his opponents and was, therefore, a de facto ally of the working class. Max urged Socialists to support Wilson and "the capitalist governments in their new motion toward internationalism, because they will get there before we will." [21] Max testified against intervention before a congressional committee in January 1917. In March he met again with Wilson, though the President was less reassuring than before. Yet even after war was declared in April, Max let

Wilson off the hook. Though the world was not going to be made safe for democracy, as was now being claimed, Wilson at least invoked it. And he still might make a decent peace. "Wait and see" was the proper attitude.[22]

In the last days of American neutrality Max indicated what his position would be when the country went to war. At a mass meeting in Detroit, he called for armed neutrality and renewed efforts to mediate an armistice. He asked, as Wilson had earlier, for a peace without victory. He pointed to the Russian revolution and the socialist votes against the most recent German war budget as evidence that Europe was sick of fighting. It would be tragic to let this chance go by. He insisted that American entry did not of itself guarantee the realization of democratic war aims. Who favored intervention?

> It is Elihu Root and Joseph Choate and half a hundred others of the most notorious and astute defenders of class-rule and special privilege this country has memory of. They can be seen any day foregathering in the windows of the Union League Club on Fifth Avenue and consecrating to the service of their country the last full measure of conversation.[23]

Max and Randolph Bourne and other critics of intervention saw that, as it was championed by the most reactionary elements of the community, it could not result in a progressive crusade as liberals were claiming. And they saw that by entering the war America was making a negotiated peace unlikely, thereby embittering Germany and sowing the seeds of another great disaster. When the country went to war, Max would stand his ground. His persistence had no relation to a taste for losing causes. He had joined the Socialist party in 1912 not as a rebellious gesture but because he thought the cause would prevail. By the same token, even after war was declared, it seemed to Max that the opposition still had a chance. Millions had not changed their minds— radicals, absolute pacifists, German-Americans, Irish-Americans who were praying for England's defeat, immigrants from the Austro-Hungarian Empire, believers in the tradition of non-interference in European affairs. If intervention had been voted on by the electorate it might very well have lost.

Yet the war's unpopularity was misleading. It was because so many opposed the war that resistance had to be crushed. A few dissenters could be let off easily or ignored, as during World War II. In 1917 this was considered unsafe, so the law of the jungle reigned. Espionage Acts were passed making it a crime to do anything that displeased the government. Conscientious objectors were put into the military's hands. Most were bullied, beaten, or tortured into accepting some form of military service. Thousands were jailed for having wrong opinions. Many more lost their jobs or were mobbed, molested, or lynched. Some were made to kiss the flag, which was considered humiliating. The German language was no longer taught in schools nor German music played. Sauerkraut became "liberty cabbage" for the duration. Eugene V. Debs lost his freedom, thus giving substance to his famous charge that, "while there is a soul in prison, I am not free." The first casualty of the war for democracy, as radicals tirelessly remarked, was democracy itself.[24]

Despite the risks, Max kept advocating peace, notably at a giant rally in Madison Square Garden organized by the People's Council. In theory the Council was a broad coalition of anti-war groups. In practice, most of the work was done by a few people—Crystal, of course; Margaret Lane of the Woman's Peace party; Scott Nearing; Norman Thomas, then head of the Fellowship of Reconciliation, a Christian peace organization; Louis Lochner, who had organized Henry Ford's much ridiculed Peace Ship voyage in 1915; and a handful of young women. Max's speech at the rally was especially well received. He called for support of the peace proposals made by the new democratic government of Russia headed by Kerensky, and attacked the terror at home. "There is no use making the world safe for democracy if there is to be no democracy left in the world. There is no use waging a war for liberty if every liberty we have must be abolished in order to wage war."[25] That hot night in the Garden was a turning point for Max. He had toured the country before, speaking on poetry, humor, and the *Masses'* need for money. Now, sponsored by the People's Council, he would do so again, jeopardizing his life and liberty.

Max was better known outside New York for his lectures than for his magazine. In the past he had gotten much attention by offending respectable opinion. President Van Hise would not let him speak on the University of Wisconsin campus. Ministers in Detroit denounced him as an infidel. Such incidents assured him full houses. Promoting the Russian peace plan was another matter. The houses were even fuller but the pressure was intense. Everywhere he spoke policemen and government agents made themselves conspicuous. He spoke without incident to a tense crowd of 5,000 Chicagoans. But in Fargo, North Dakota, his luck ran out. Soldiers from a local training camp were given special passes to attend his meeting, which they broke up. Max was nearly lynched and had to be smuggled out of town on the floor of an automobile. This could not fail to make an impression on him. He saw now that opposition to the war was futile. Though millions were against it, the government and the mob had stopped their mouths.

The fate of the *Masses* reinforced this lesson. As Floyd Dell says, the magazine had risen to the challenge. The *Masses* became "against that war background, a thing of more vivid beauty. Pictures and poetry poured in—as if this were the last spark of civilization left in America. And with an incredible joyousness, the spirit of man laughed and sang in its pages. It is strange to look through the files. So much humor, sweetness, happiness is there! A few of us could be sane in a mad world."[26]

Masses people knew what the war was from its first day. A Maurice Becker drawing in the September 1914 issue spoke for all of them. A naked man is prancing amidst ruins, bomb in one hand, torch in the other. Underneath is the caption: "Whom the Gods Would Destroy They First Make Mad." In July 1916 Boardman Robinson showed a firing squad, made up of soldiers from both sides, executing Jesus Christ. It was captioned "The Deserter." Robinson also illustrated the *Masses* position on preparedness, as rearmament was called before intervention. A distraught man is pointing toward Europe, which smokes away behind him. He is identified as a preparedness advocate and says, "If we don't prepare as they did, it'll happen to us." Robert Minor's statement on militarism is a classic. His picture in the July 1916 issue was of a headless giant who stands before an army medical examiner. The doctor says, "At last a perfect soldier."

After war was declared, the artists became, if anything, bolder. In the June 1917 issue a drawing by R. Kempf shows Death embracing three naked women, who represent the major warring powers. They are standing in a pool of liquid, out of which several hands extend. "Come on in America, the Blood's fine," says Death. In October 1917 a picture by Henry J. Glintenkamp required no caption at all. Death is shown measuring a naked young man, who stands before rows of coffins. Glintenkamp was indicted by the Justice Department for this, along with Eastman, Reed, and others. Reed offended by reprinting a newspaper article about shell shock, with the addition of his own head-line: "Knit a Strait-Jacket for Your Soldier Boy."

Reed also wrote the strongest indictment of government policy to appear in the *Masses*. His essay capped a long chain of anti-war pieces, including contributions by himself and Eastman and, among others, William English Walling, before he succumbed to nationalism, Amos Pinchot, and even Mabel Dodge. In "One Solid Month of Liberty," written for the September 1917 issue, Reed called the roll of mournful events. Emma Goldman and Alexander Berkman had been sent to prison; eighteen periodicals, the *Masses* among them, had been denied mailing rights; a socialist parade had been mobbed in Boston; there was a bloody race riot in East St. Louis; hundreds of striking miners were kidnapped at gunpoint in Bisbee, Arizona, and dumped out of trains in the desert. Suffrage pickets were mobbed in Washington and then arrested and jailed. It was, Reed said at the beginning and end of his essay, "the blackest month for freemen our generation has known."

As the war meant police-state tactics, lynch law, and the suppres-sion of dissent, it doomed the *Masses*. To accomplish this, a version of Catch-22 was employed. The August 1917 issue was delayed by court order. Postal authorities then announced that, having failed to appear on schedule, the *Masses* was no longer a periodical as defined by law. Its second-class mailing privileges were thereupon revoked. Judge Augustus Hand expressed the public mood in upholding this technical-ity. In his opinion the *Masses* was "not attacking a mere party program or executive policy, but is seeking to undermine those means which the nation has adopted to protect the people of the United States and civili-zation as well."[27] So perished this threat to world order. The *Masses*' last issue was dated November–December. The age of lyrical leftism had ended.

By this time, as it happened, strangling the *Masses* was no longer necessary. On August 24, 1917, President Wilson in a letter to the Pope began outlining what would become his Fourteen Points for a just and democratic peace. In the October *Masses* Eastman endorsed them. This dismayed his radical friends without saving the magazine. In response to a direct appeal Wilson thanked Max for praising his letter to the Pope, but added that in wartime things must be regarded as dangerous that in peacetime would seem quite innocent.[28] So much for the *Masses* and Eastman, too. He would soon be indicted under the Espionage Act.

Max remained healthy through all this, sustained by the love of Florence Deshon and exciting news from Russia. The Kerensky government was faced with social revolution: "What makes us rub our eyes at Russia is the way all our theories are proving true. Nothing else could give us this crazy feeling of surprise. One by one the facts fall out exactly as they were predicted by Marx and Engels and the philosophers of syndicalism." Eastman was especially thrilled by the new Soviet, which he described as a "Parliament of proletarian deputies, entirely unofficial politically—a body like the American Federation of Labor convention with a majority of I.W.W.'s."[29] Just as Marx had foretold, workers were seizing the means of production. Even if the Russian experiment failed, Eastman wrote, "it has established us and made us sure. A working class will yet own the tools with which it works, and an industrial parliament will govern the operative affairs of men." He added a postscript to this, saying that events in Russia seemed too good to be true but were not. He had just talked to Lincoln Steffens, who had seen the future working in Russia. Steffens assured Eastman that there "the Mob rules," and well at that.[30] One might suppose that having had a taste of mob rule in South Dakota, his joy at this news might be a little confined. Such was not the case. Socialist mobs and capitalist mobs seemed to have nothing in common. So began Eastman's long obsession with Soviet Russia, and his embrace of the double standard of morality on which for many years it rested.

Though heartening, the rising level of violence in Russia did not solve Max's problems at home. The division in socialist ranks was especially troublesome. Everyone expected that people like Theodore Roosevelt would rant and rail at the peace movement. He was half-crazed on the subject, regarding even President Wilson as yellow and a slacker. Surprisingly, the pro-war socialists were as bad. Walling, John Spargo, Algie Simons, and other right-wing intellectuals slandered their former comrades, in extreme cases asking that they be shot. This was Roosevelt's solution, too. Even so, Max still pressed for unity. When Upton Sinclair quit the party because it went on record against the war, Max called for moderation: "If this magazine has contributed anything to social revolutionary philosophy in America, its contribution has been a resolute opposition to bigotry and dogmatic thinking of all kinds. It has insisted upon the recognition of variety and change in the facts, and the need for pliancy in the theories of the revolution." He urged his fellows to take a liberal view of the pro-war Socialists, who were mistaken rather than criminal.

Sinclair's error, Max pointed out, was to think that by joining the war effort he had bound the Allies to accept his terms for peace. This was a common delusion among pro-war intellectuals, who in their enthusiasm failed to notice that the Allies had their own war aims, which were not necessarily liberal and progressive. Though Sinclair was wrong, Max concluded, "we are not, thank God—a church. And disagreement is not heresy and resignation is not apostasy. And I, for my part, have faith enough in the underlying motives of the pro-war Socialists, and the anti-war Socialists, to believe they will most of them be working together along the main highway of industrial liberation as soon as the present turmoil of passions and opinions is past."[31] In this he was mistaken. Lacking fanaticism himself, Max was a poor judge of it in others. He saw that there was a case to be made on both sides of the peace issue but underestimated the depth of feelings aroused and the rapid movement of events. The war and its consequences would destroy the Socialist party, leaving Max without a political home. He would never, except briefly, have another.

CHAPTER FOUR

Defiant Years

1918–1922

Eastman divided his life into two parts. The first was dominated by his struggle to overcome neurotic fears and the physical ailments they produced. In his notebook Max wrote that his life began in 1917 because "I had won my long war of independence; I had accomplished the feat of confiding in a friend; I had faced loneliness without melancholy; I had outlived that bashfulness which deprived me of the joys of adolescence; I had fallen wholeheartedly in love."[1] This was the truth of his inner life. Insofar as he ever would, Max had conquered the psychic diseases of his childhood and youth and was ready at last for that enjoyment of living which had eluded him during his first thirty-three years.

Eastman's outer, public life did not change so dramatically, even with the founding of his new magazine, the *Liberator,* in 1918. The *Masses* had made him known among radicals and intellectuals. His still growing legend would be an important part of the *Liberator*'s capital. In 1918 at the age of thirty-five Eastman was almost as famous as he would ever be. To his many admirers he was already, as Joseph Freeman would write a bit later, godlike, "because it seems to me that he is very much like Apollo must have been both in appearance and in temper. In him you have wisdom without timidity, strength without insolence, and beauty without vanity."[2] Max was better looking than in his twenties. Then his features were too large for his narrow face. Now it had filled out so that all the parts were in harmony. Years of lecturing had polished him to the point where Robert Hallowell, the treasurer of the *New Republic,* could write Crystal that a speech of Eastman's was "the best I have ever heard, or hope to hear. I never dreamed that such a combination of wit, grace, charm, simplicity and substance could be put into the spoken word."[3]

* * *

Eastman's personal life during the *Liberator* years was described by him at length in *Love and Revolution*. Although he lost some friends, like everyone in the anti-war movement, he gained new ones, including Charlie Chaplin, whom he met during a speaking tour in 1919. Chaplin was then the world's most popular entertainer, but Max had been in the news also. His "hands-off Russia" lectures in that violently anti-Communist year became notorious. In Cleveland Max and Crystal were forced to hide in a closet to escape vigilantes. In Los Angeles the auditorium where Eastman spoke was ringed with policemen. Chaplin came anyway and later told Max that he had the essence of all art, "restraint." Mutual admiration cemented their friendship, which lasted until political differences arose in the 1930s.[4]

Max's love life was equally exciting. It was dominated in this period by the actress Florence Deshon, and their affair set the pattern for Eastman's later romances. At first he was completely in love. Their time together, stolen from two thriving careers, was precious to them both. But, as with Ida Rauh, there came a day (in August 1918) when for no apparent reason Eastman suddenly lost interest. The relationship which moments before had seemed idyllic was now confining, even scary. He sought to hide his change of heart from Florence, and they were together off and on for several more years—though both had other lovers as well. For a time Florence shuttled between Eastman and Chaplin and, according to Max, once became pregnant by Chaplin. The fetus died in her womb, and she contracted a nearly fatal case of blood poisoning, from which, following an operation, Max nursed her back to health. This incident changed nothing. Their romance could not survive his diminished ardor, her angry outbursts, and the strains of radically different careers. After many false stops their affair came to an end in 1921, though they went on seeing each other socially.

In February of 1922, just before Eastman's journey to Russia, Florence was found unconscious in her gas-filled room. Max learned she was dying while at a play and rushed to the hospital, where he gave Florence a blood transfusion to no avail. While the coroner ruled it an accidental death, so many of their friends believed she had killed herself on account of Max that the *New York Times* did a story on it. A reporter contacted Eastman while he was still virtually in shock. Max strongly denied the charge:

> I am sure her death was accidental. There was no reason in the world why she should take her life, and no letters seem to have been found or received to indicate that she did. She was healthy and happy when I last saw her on Thursday afternoon [she died that night], and we had an engagement for the theater on Saturday. Please do not question me any more about it.[5]

Privately Max was not so sure. Perhaps she did kill herself, though not from unrequited love. After a promising start her career had flopped unbearably. Marie Howe, an old friend, agreed with this diagnosis. She wrote: "No love affair could ever kill our beautiful Florence. You know and I know that she could always rise above her emotions. They never conquered her, she conquered them. But with pride lost she could not face the world."[6]

Though more highly charged than any other, this affair was typical. In deserting Ida Rauh, Max had broken with his past history of miserable shyness and frustrated desires. He had also abandoned monogamy. Even when deeply in love with Florence, he still went with other women, notably Lisa Duncan of Isadora's celebrated troup.[7] He would have many lovers thereafter, usually on his own terms. These were not binding ties or exclusive relations. A woman could have fun with Max, but no future. A saving grace was that Max avoided sexism. He believed in a single standard of immorality and expected his lovers and mates to enjoy the same sexual freedom he did—whether they wanted to or not.

* * *

In these years Max was making love and working at politics as never before. In 1918 alone he founded the *Liberator,* stood trial twice for conspiring to obstruct the draft, and published a volume of poems asserting that art came before politics. In his introduction to *Colors of Life* Max said that the world-wide struggle for freedom

> has always occupied my thoughts, and often my energies, and yet I have never identified myself with it or found my undivided being there. I have found that rather in individual experience, and in those

moments of energetic idleness when the life of universal nature
seemed to come to its bloom of realization in my consciousness.[8]

Critics did not agree that as between art and politics he had made
the right personal choice. Reviewing *Colors of Life* Harriet Monroe,
whose magazine *Poetry* was the advance guard of modernism, said of
Max that "in politics and social ethics he is a radical; but shocked conservatives must take refuge in some sacred corner of one's being, and
in his case the muse presided with draped and decorous dignity."[9] This
was not the first time Max had been accused of poetic stodgyness. Two
years earlier he reviewed a book about poetry approvingly, despite its
being only literary criticism and not science. *The Lyric* was good even so
because it attacked free verse, the medium of lazy poets, Max declared.[10] This was simply terrible, according to Waldo Frank, an editor
of *Seven Arts* in which the review appeared. Frank was so exercised that
he lost his composure. Max was charged with "a treacherous conservatism." "He is emotionally so at home in the chants of conformity, in the
rhythm of barbarity, in the era of the tom-tom that a form of poetry
projecting man's individual revolt and society's coherent heterogeneity
disturbs him." The day of rhyme and meter was over, despite Max's affection for them. "A new dawn has been breaking these few hundred
years—the dawn of a more complex and self-conscious freedom. And it
is now finding its materialization in the arts. It is unbelievable that Max
Eastman, of all men, should be even fractionally against it."[11] Astound-
ing as it seemed to Frank, Eastman was against modernism not fractionally but with his whole heart. It would be his undoing one day.

Monroe and Frank were still in the minority, so *Colors of Life* had
its fans. Vachel Lindsay enjoyed it—or at least the "fraternal thrill" of
receiving a copy. Floyd Dell compared Max, whose taste he shared,
with those "eternally restless spirits of the late Renaissance."[12] Most who
disliked the poems were not in the avant-garde. The *Nation* said they
were self-indulgent. Louis Untermeyer, who admired Eastman's prose,
said the sonnets were a "bit dissicated," and the lyrics "strangely
cool."[13] Arturo Giovannitti sprang to the defense. He considered Max
a great poet, the only one writing in English "who sees and feels beauty
with a Greek eye and Latin nerves," whatever that meant. Untermeyer
replied that Max's "flavorless verse" seemed to him "the result of a
desire to write rather than a burning need to create."[14] Except for
"Lot's Wife" (1942) Max would go on writing the same sort of verse

and getting the same responses for the rest of his life. Fickleness was not his problem, except in matters of the heart.

*   *   *

Max continued to think of himself as a scientist, offering *The Sense of Humor* in 1921 as evidence. Humor was one of his oldest and most successful lecture topics. He was certain it had never been studied scientifically before. Max insisted on supplying this lack, despite George Bernard Shaw's warning that there "is no more dangerous literary symptom than a temptation to write about wit and humor. It indicates the total loss of both."[15] Shaw was right. *The Sense of Humor* is a dull book, though noted scientists did not mind this. They praised it highly, encouraging Max's delusion that he, too, was a scientist. G. Stanley Hall, a distinguished but unreadable psychologist, told Max that it made a recent article of his on "The Psychology of Fun" obsolete. Dewey wrote that the book was "a quite extraordinary work in combination of real scientific study and artistic presentation."[16] Other scientists felt the same, though it is hard to see why as Max drew on the usual literary sources. Maybe they appreciated having a man of letters over-value science as much as they did. These two books enabled Max to go on thinking of himself as a scientist and, with more reason, a poet too. Both books enhanced his legend by showing that the philosopher-prince of the anti-war movement, the John Barrymore of radical letters, had mastered science and art as well.

*   *   *

The Eastman legend owed much to accident. Events had made him a leader despite himself, of the *Masses* group first and then of the anti-war movement. Max did not hold office in it, but he was one of its best speakers, and, as others were jailed or silenced, his voice became more important. A magazine was needed, too, and Eastman was the logical choice to found it. He was still at liberty in 1918. Most contributors to the *Masses* were eager to press on. And Max had exclusive rights to Jack Reed's dispatches from Russia. On November 7, 1917, Reed cabled Max that he had seen the storming of the Winter Palace. Reed's stories had a high market value. Their worth to radicals desperate for knowledge of the real situation in Russia was even greater. These elements combined, Eastmen would later say, to make the *Liberator* an "historic necessity."

Though physically similar to it, the *Liberator* would be a very different magazine from the *Masses*. The lyrical Left was dead, a victim of repression at home and revolution abroad. The old light-hearted optimism was gone as well, having been replaced in some cases by the Marxist faith that history worked inevitably toward radical ends. In his first editorial Max showed the effects of Russia's Soviet revolution: "The world is in the rapids. The possibilities of change in this day are beyond all imagining. We must unite our hands and voices to make the end of this war the beginning of an age of freedom and happiness for mankind." [17]

Where the *Masses'* policy was "to do as it pleases and conciliate nobody," the *Liberator* saw compromise as essential. There was a place for defiant gesturing, but not in the *Liberator*. If it was to guide the Left its first duty was survival. To that end it supported the war aims of both America and Soviet Russia, in an ultimately vain effort to make them seem identical. Though narrower than the *Masses,* it still believed in socialism, the independence of women, racial equality, and birth control. The *Liberator* was owned outright by Max and Crystal. There would be no pretense of collective policy-making as with the *Masses*. The cast of characters was much the same early on. The first issue, dated March 1918, listed among others Howard Brubaker, Hugo Gellert, Arturo Giovannitti, Robert Minor, John Reed, Boardman Robinson, Louis Untermeyer, and Art Young as contributing editors. The cover was by Gellert, and the issue had Eastman's poem "Isadora Duncan," another by Untermeyer, and book reviews by Dell and his young assistant Dorothy Day, future head of the Catholic Worker Movement. Here John Reed began his classic history of the Bolshevik Revolution.

More than anything else Max wished to influence America's Russian policy. Hence he spoke well editorially of President Wilson and Secretary of War Newton D. Baker, an eminent progressive. Partly this was a matter of necessity, partly of conviction. Though some wanted the *Liberator* to fire a broadside at the government and go down with all flags flying like the *Masses,* this was not Max's way. He had tried hard to save the *Masses,* which had not been destroyed by inflexible devotion to principle. Max wanted to gain the government's ear, and this meant taking a soft line on certain issues, no matter how dear they were to radicals. Then, too, he agreed with Wilson on the need for a collective peace-keeping organization, a capitalist one being better than none at all. "If the world falls into peace, exhausted, without having ac-

complished this, it will be a sad peace—a peace without victory indeed."[18] Even the Bolsheviks, he noted, were calling for a federated
republic of Europe.

Max still thought highly of Wilson. Despite his warmongering, the
President appeared to retain that combination of intellect and action
Eastman most admired. In an early *Liberator* Max wrote that he "seems
to me to bring into statesmanship some of the same things that Bergson
and William James and John Dewey have brought into philosophy—a
sense of the reality of time and the creative character of change."[19]
Wilson's early response to the Bolsheviks justified this enthusiasm. He
sent a message of friendship to the "Republic of Labor Unions" in Russia and freed several hundred imprisoned conscientious objectors. Wilson's peace proposals, the celebrated Fourteen Points, were much to
Eastman's taste, calling as they did for freedom of the seas, reduction
of armaments, and other good things including national self-deter-
mination in Europe and German withdrawal from Russia.

Like most of Eastman's heroes, Wilson proved on close inspection
to be defective. By the fall of 1918 he was making one mistake after
another. He failed to recognize the Soviet government. Worse still,
American troops accompanied the Allied forces that landed at Archan-
gel in September. The Siberian intervention followed. In thus joining
the anti-Bolshevik front Wilson demonstrated to Eastman's satisfaction
that he was only "another detached political idealist who undertook to
utter great and terrible promises, [but] was nevertheless compelled to
act in accordance with the economic interests of those who possess the
world." Max even turned against Wilson's prose, ridiculing it at considerable length. So readers learned that Wilson was not Bergsonian or
Jamesian after all, simply more clever than other tools of the proper-
tied class.[20]

The *Liberator*'s brief flirtation with Wilson and respectability had
no effect beyond making radicals angry. John Reed quit the editorial
board in September 1918, declaring that he would not be responsible
for a magazine that existed on the Postmaster General's sufferance.
Eastman replied that the editors felt it their obligation to keep the magazine alive regardless. "Personally I envy you the power to cast loose
when not only a good deal of the dramatic beauty, but also the glamour
of abstract moral principle has gone out of our venture, and it remains
for us merely the most effective and therefore the right thing to do."[21]
Loftiness concealed hurt feelings. Max and Crystal assumed that Reed's

gesture would be taken as a slap at their policy of compromise. Reed assured Eastman that there was no personal ill will involved.[22] His contributions to the *Liberator* after resigning were, if anything, more frequent than before. It was a tempest in a teapot but wounding even so. Max derived only slight comfort from the knowledge that in this respect he was a better Bolshevik than Jack. In resigning Reed put principle above expediency, which ran counter to the spirit of Leninism.

* * *

The *Liberator* was important—its circulation reached a peak of 60,000—but it did not cover Max with glory as did the two *Masses* trials. Though one would not know it from reading the brief accounts of them in the *New York Times,* both were significant. There was a martyr school of thought on the Left which held that everyone should go to prison. True believers of this doctrine, especially those not in jail, looked down on the *Masses* group for selfishly trying to remain among them. But most radicals were glad that Eastman and company made a fight of it. However encouraging the news from Russia might be, American leftists were still oppressed, without strong leaders, headquarters, or even much to read. They needed some victories, however small; this was where the *Masses* came in.

Then as now radicals adopted different courtroom styles and strategies. Wobblies sometimes offered no defense at all to show contempt for an unjust system that would convict them anyway. Others, like Debs, used their trials chiefly to propagandize. The *Masses* group hoped to spread the good word but also to stay out of jail. This seemed unlikely, as the government seldom failed to win under the Espionage Acts. Seven editors and contributors were indicted for conspiring to obstruct recruitment and other vile deeds. They were Eastman, Dell, Reed, Young, Merrill Rogers, and H. J. Glintenkamp, who fled to Mexico rather than stand trial. The indictment of Josephine Bell, author of a poem mourning the arrest of Emma Goldman and Alexander Berkman, was dismissed after the court learned that she did not know any of her alleged co-conspirators. Though conspiracy was a vague and elastic charge, there was still some feeling that it required a person to have met the other plotters. As Reed was still in Russia, this left four defendants to face an outraged government and a hostile public, further aggravated by bad war news. In April 1918 when the trial began, Germany's last great offensive, the Hindenburg drive, was pushing the

Allies back in France. Liberty bonds were sold outside the courthouse while bands played patriotic airs. This did not seem like the right atmosphere in which to be tried for disloyalty.

Nor did the jury's beliefs inspire confidence. When quizzed, most prospective jurors said they were against socialism and pacifism but would nobly rise above these feelings and give a fair verdict. Defense counsel protested but had no answer to Judge Augustus Hand's question as to whether a jury could be found anywhere in the country that did not share these prejudices.[23] On the plus side, Judge Hand, though he had helped kill the *Masses,* behaved correctly. The accused had a defense fund and two able attorneys. Morris Hillquit, a leader of the Socialist party's right wing, was, according to Dell, "cool, unshakable, resourceful, with a tremendous dynamic quality behind the relentless workings of a keenly logical mind."[24] Dudley Field Malone was an ardent Democrat and friend of President Wilson, who had made him Collector of the Port of New York. When the trial began, Malone was out of favor. He had resigned his Collectorship to protest the jailing and mistreatment of suffragists picketing the White House, among whom was his sweetheart, Doris Stevens. Though a Democrat, Malone was "a man of the most warmhearted devotion to principle, gifted with passionate and eloquent speech, and with a remarkable power of synthetic argument."[25]

The defendants were their own best asset. Eastman was tall, gorgeous, articulate, winning. Dell had a shy charm and fluency. Portly Art Young was lovable. Even the prosecutor, Earl Barnes, liked them. He called Max "one of the brainiest men of our time." Dell was "a writer of exquisite English . . . Young a cartoonist of national reputation, a friend of Congressmen . . . I could cry when I think of the position in which this undoubtedly fine personal character finds himself today."[26] No one noticed Rogers except when he jumped to attention, which he did each time the national anthem was played outside the courthouse. Everyone else had to follow suit until Judge Hand put an end to these patriotic displays. The trial seems to have been unaffected by Eastman and Dell's change of heart. They had opposed intervention but now favored the war effort, as it relieved German pressure on the Soviets. When drafted, Floyd Dell reported for duty and was briefly a soldier until news of his horrid crimes against the state became known. Young remained opposed to war in principle, but good-naturedly. After testifying that he had not meant to obstruct recruiting with his cartoons, Young fell asleep. Malone told a defendant to keep Young awake at least until he reached jail. On regaining consciousness, he dashed off a sketch of himself slumbering, entitled, "Art Young on Trial for His Life."[27]

Newspapers saw Max as the trial's key figure, often calling it the Eastman trial. So did the government, who kept him on the stand for three of the trial's nine days. Max evaded numerous attempts by Barnes to force disloyal admissions and made his chief points: that the war aims of both Russia and the United States were much the same, that CO's should be better treated, as was happening, and that the real question was not did the *Masses* group conspire to prevent the draft but would there be free speech and a free press in wartime. Most jurors seemed to think not, but two (according to the *New York Times,* the *Liberator* believed three) voted to acquit, so the trial ended with a hung jury.

At the victory dinner Max observed that the martyr school was angry with him for not going to jail. Others felt he would go to jail anyway, as a second trial was scheduled. To both groups "I should extend my apologies, and the apologies of my attorneys, for having put me in this lukewarm and humiliating position." Still and all, "we neglected to conspire to obstruct recruitment and enlistment. We neglected to commit the crime and we will have to take the blame for it."[28] For his part Hillquit had no doubts or reservations, not even mock ones. The trial had gone wonderfully, and never more so than when Max was on the stand:

> and when quietly, honestly and courageously, at the same time with compelling force he drove home every argument he had made in the *Masses* or in public speeches during those troublous days after we entered the war, when he advocated his right, our right, to think and to speak—and when finally he became so convincing that even half of those jurors, hostile as they were, were won over, and the crowd in the courtroom that had come to scoff remained, as it were, to pray, then I could see that trials of this kind, if continued long enough, if they forced their way into the papers, will be about the only medium of education for the American public.[29]

Years later, when they were political enemies, Hillquit still believed this. In his memoirs he said that Eastman was the "ring leader," "star witness," and "mastermind" of the trial. Hillquit was proud that the defendants had not traded on the fact that they now supported the war but fought the case "on the principles involved."[30] Though Max had a few critics, Hillquit's feelings seem to have been widely shared by radicals. After the first trial the Socialist party of New York County nominated Eastman to run for Congress from the Eleventh District (Staten Island).[31]

The second trial was another personal triumph for Max. Though the war news was much better in October the defendants (now including Reed, "the Bolshevik agitator," as the *New York Times* called him) were even less sanguine than before. They had been lucky once and could not expect good fortune a second time. Their old attorneys were not available, and the lawyer they did have was unwell. Eastman had to organize the defense himself. The trial was short, lasting only five days (because of the lawyer shortage, Max believed) and ended with another hung jury. "The great factor in our victory," wrote John Reed, "was Max Eastman's three-hour summing up. Standing there, with the attitude and attributes of intellectual eminence, young, good-looking, he was the typical champion of ideals—ideals which he made to seem the ideals of every real American." Prosecutor Barnes had tried to show that the Bolsheviks were German agents. "But Max boldly took up the Russian question and made it part of our defense. The jury was held tense by his eloquence; the Judge listened with all his energy. In the court room there was utter silence. After it was all over the District Attorney himself congratulated Max."[32] Years later a practicing attorney wrote Eastman to say that as a youngster he attended the trial. "I still have the notes which I made at the time of the summation which you made on your own behalf to the jury. In the course of many appearances in Court since, I have listened to a great many summations, but I fail to remember one which impressed me more with clarity of expression, ease, succinctness and a masterly grasp of the facts."[33]

Max's speech was remarkable for its casualness. In an age of courtroom theatrics he did not strive for rhetorical effect. Eastman meant to win over the jurors, if that was possible, conversationally. He assumed the jury's good will but made no concessions to gain it. He admitted that the *Masses* had indeed opposed American entry, and in "extremely vigorous and sometimes extravagant language." This was, he explained, the same language employed by the magazine for five years, not a new idiom whipped up by conspirators to defy the law. Max also defended Soviet Russia, though in theory it was not on trial. The Red issue having been introduced anyway, Max was glad of the chance to argue that Russia was not in a state of anarchy as the press would have Americans believe, but was starting "a cooperative system of production, in which human brotherhood and not a reign of terror" will prevail.[34] Max admitted the need for sensible restrictions on speech during a national emergency. He was not a "bigoted or fanatical advocate of mere abstract principle" on the point. His objection was to government excesses that violated the Constitution and the traditions of a free people. Though he now supported the war effort for the sake of Russia and a Russian-style peace, he insisted that the *Masses* had been within the law when it opposed American entry and conscription. As before, several jurors agreed.

Luck apart, Max was the deciding element in both trials as captain of the defense team and chief spokesman for it. His summation in the second trial was widely circulated in pamphlet form. Max was fast becoming, as a reporter would soon say, "probably the most influential radical in the United States."[35] At a time when radicals were discouraged, divided, oppressed, and, when indicted, nearly always convicted, getting two hung juries was quite a trick. Earl Barnes recognized this and explained why the government would not indict the group again. There was no reason to suppose a third trial would end differently. In any event, the war was over, and all the defendants were native-born Americans. So much for equal justice.[36]

In the fall of 1918, when his own future was still undecided, Max covered the trial of Eugene Debs in Cleveland. After the first *Masses* trial Eastman had said, "I know the truth is usually unpopular and often persecuted, but I do not belong with those who try to be unpopular and invite prosecution with the idea that this will prove they are true."[37] Yet he respected Debs's decision to force the government's hand and join his imprisoned socialist colleagues. Eastman, who was seldom moved by oratory, was deeply affected by Debs's conduct at the trial and wrote about it feelingly. Debs loved the article, writing Max that it was "a beautiful, artistic, masterly piece of work." If the trial was remembered at all he was sure it would be because of Max's chronicle:

It is my good fortune to be seen through the eyes of great souled Max Eastman, eyes which magnify the good qualities they see in a comrade and are blind to all else.

You are truly a beautiful comrade. The thought of you is elevat-

ing to me. You have not a trace of the petty or ignoble in your nature. I loved you the moment I looked into your smiling eyes. I did
not know why then; I do now.[38]

Max was so touched by this that he kept the letter private. He appears
not to have printed or even alluded to it in any of his published writings, not even his autobiography, which detractors have claimed is a
monument to his egotism.

In 1919 when the Red Scare was most intense and thousands were
jailed or deported because suspected of disloyalty, Max was brave to
the point of recklessness. At a mass meeting in Madison Square Garden, where he shared the platform with such future leaders of the
Communist party as Charles E. Ruthenberg and Benjamin Gitlow, Max
called for a "dictatorship of the proletariat in the United States." And
he made headlines by reading a secret cable from the acting head of
the State Department to Secretary Lansing in Paris asking for money
under the table so that the Siberian Railway could go on transporting
counter-revolutionaries.[39] Eastman said this proved that President Wilson was "waging a private war against Soviet Russia." Acting Secretary
Polk admitted the cable was genuine, but claimed that the version Max
read was garbled. He asked for an investigation to discover the leak's
source. The *New York Times* demanded that existing laws against sub-
version be applied more vigorously, and that those responsible for
making the cable public be dealt with "sternly and remorselessly."[40]
Max was saved from remorseless prosecution by Dudley Field Malone
who advised him to announce that he possessed other documents of a
similar nature. Eastman made the implied threat and the government
took no action against him. This seemed to prove Malone's theory that
the government was more afraid of the cables, which Max had gotten
from an anonymous person claiming to belong to military intelligence,
than of letting Eastman go free. It also made them too valuable to
waste so Max gave the cables to Oswald Garrison Villard who printed
them in the *Nation*. Later Villard told Max that publishing these documents had forced Wilson out of Russia.[41] This went too far. Wilson's
Russian policy was failing all by itself. Even so, it felt good to have hastened the process, if only a little.

The entire period from 1912 to 1922 was a golden age for Max,
but the very best years were 1917, 1918, and 1919. Eastman did not
spend all this time being heroic. The public events were only incidents

in a busy life filled with writing, love affairs, friendship, travel, and meetings with celebrities. Yet it was these incidents that made him the Byron of the Left. Though glamorous, this role was less a blessing than a curse. It was what people would always want him to be. To an extraordinary and unfair degree the balance of his career would be judged in terms of its legendary beginning. His best books were as yet unwritten; his bravest acts still to be performed. But Max would never again be so loved and esteemed as in the days of his golden youth.

CHAPTER FIVE

Political Writings

1918–1922

Also in 1921 the arrests of members of all non-Bolshevik parties were expanded and systematized. In fact, all Russia's political parties had been buried except the victorious one. (Oh, do not dig a grave for someone else!) And so that the dissolution of these parties would be irreversible, it was necessary that their members should disintegrate and their physical bodies too.

The Gulag Archipelago

Max used the *Liberator* much as he had the *Masses* to back socialism's left wing. In 1918 it seemed to be gaining strength, and Eastman applauded its platform as a "blue-print of revolutionary reconstruction. It is the work of able and technically trained minds. It is a platform to stop the mouth of those who tell us 'we have nothing constructive to offer.' " But Socialists still needed to identify with and support the Soviet government as "unmistakable evidence that our socialism is scientific and not Utopian."[1] Max thought the Socialist party would hang together and be revolutionary. These were false hopes, based more on events in Russia than in the United States. Though the party could still win votes (Hillquit got 145,000 when he ran for mayor of New York in 1917), most were cast not for socialism but against the war.

By 1919 a majority of Socialists belonged to foreign language federations dominated by Russian immigrants, unintended beneficiaries of the October Revolution. Foreign-born socialists rejected American leaders in favor of the Communist Third International. When the International ordered left Socialists to attack the pro-war, right-wing Socialists, the foreign-language federations complied, though in America, unlike Europe, right-wingers had opposed the war. Moscow instructed class-conscious militants to ready themselves for the fall of capitalism, and the federations did so, even though American capitalism obstinately refused to fail. Their obedience to irrelevant Comintern directives obliged Socialist party leaders to expel the foreign-language federations, who took with them perhaps 70,000 members, leaving only some 40,000 in the old Socialist party. As a minority cannot expel a majority and survive, this meant the end of socialism in America. Membership dwindled rapidly, and thereafter the party existed mainly as a vehicle for Norman Thomas.

Dissension turned what was to be one socialist convention in the fall of 1919 into three. Max covered these Chicago meetings, striving as always in those days to be constructive and find a common ground for the Left to stand on. Despite himself he could not praise the regular Socialist party convention. He was sorry for its leaders, Hillquit and Victor Berger and the rest. They had run big risks during the war, only to be brushed aside by radicals afterward. Their convention was a kind of rump parliament, especially after they expelled the English-speaking remnants of the old left wing. The most Eastman could say of the socialist old guard was that its morals were all right, implying that everything else was wrong.

Max identified with the expelled English-speaking left wingers, while deploring their revivalist tendencies. They organized their own convention and "were always singing and shouting and feeling that the true faith was about to be restored in their hearts and homes."[2] John Reed and Benjamin Gitlow got them to accept "a program of hard-headed, revolutionary science" just the same. This faction became known as the Communist Labor party to distinguish it from the communism of the foreign-language federations.

Though he admired their intelligence and discipline, the foreign Communist leaders did not appeal to Max. There was "something a little childish, a little sophomoric, in all this exaggerated statesmanship. I saw in the flesh that academic and rather wordy self-importance that has characterized the official literature of the Left Wing and made it get so much on my nerves." These men seemed to him not so much Bolshevistic as caricatures of Bolshevism. "The heads of the Slavic Socialist Machine are in a mood for the organization of a Russian Bolshevik church, with more interest in expelling heretics than winning converts."[3] It seemed to him poor strategy to "start the American

Communist Party with a mixture of theological zeal, machine politics, and nationalistic egoism in control."[4]

The tendencies Max observed in Chicago became more pronounced. Revivalist emotions could not make up for lack of numbers so the Communist Labor party, which Max wanted to see become the nucleus of a real revolutionary movement, faded away. The other Communists, whom Max had hoped would adjust to the realities of American life, became even more dogmatic and conspiratorial. Some Communists gloried in playing cat and mouse with federal agents and boasted of having the only underground Communist organization in the world, as if that were some kind of distinction. The Comintern was disruptive. Its head, Grigory Zinoviev, sent an order to America laying down unacceptable conditions for reunification with the Socialist party, one of which called for Hillquit's expulsion. Whereupon Eugene Debs, who was a leftist and supported the Soviet Union, said that "to commit the party to the International program . . . would kill the party."[5]

As Max expected so much from it, he was slow to admit the Comintern's imperfections. When Hillquit complained of Zinoviev's high-handedness, Eastman said that, having thrown everyone he disagreed with out of the Socialist party, Hillquit was in no position to cry about his fate. Anyway, the Bolsheviks were not dogmatic and did not control the International as Hillquit and others charged.[6]

Robert Dell, a liberal English journalist who sympathized with the Bolsheviks but not with their handling of the International, was less easy to ignore. His letter published in the *Liberator* issue of May 1921 insisted that the Bolsheviks took a religious view of politics, as was shown by the twenty-one conditions they laid down for membership in the Third International. Moscow's demand for total obedience was "shattering European Socialism and dividing the proletariat." Dell felt that "if the proletariat is merely going to exchange one form of economic slavery for another, it is hardly worth while to have the trouble and inconvenience of a revolution."[7] These complaints, which Max would echo years later, touched a nerve. Of course there was always the danger that communism might degenerate into religion, Max conceded. Servility should be discouraged. Russian domination of the International, now visible to Max, was unwise. Being scientific did not make Communists infallible.

Yet he insisted that the larger policy of the Comintern made sense. The left wings of socialist parties everywhere should be joined with sympathetic leftists of all persuasions to form a truly revolutionary movement. Anyway, Dell and other English intellectuals undervalued economic justice, which of itself excused a multitude of sins: "The most rigid political tyranny conceivable, if it accomplished the elimination of wage-slavery and continued would produce wealth, would increase the amount of liberty so much that the very sides of the earth would heave with relief."[8] Eastman had been to the Lower East Side of Manhattan and knew what real poverty was. Like many radicals he was prepared to see much sacrificed to its abolition, including political democracy if necessary. Democracy was a luxury the starving could not afford. By eliminating want, even at the expense of political rights, real liberty would increase. Keenly aware of the injustices taking place under democratic rule, radicals did not see that without it there could be no justice at all. It would take Max years to realize this.

While glorifying communism in principle, by the fall of 1921 Max was disgusted with the actual Communists around him who seemed more interested in factional fights and underground theatrics than in building a genuine movement. He had also come to feel that the Comintern's policy of breaking with everyone who disputed the party line, which he had once defended, was mistaken. It had been formed at a heady moment when capitalism seemed about to collapse. There was, perhaps, some excuse for thinking this in a year of savage labor disputes such as 1919 had been. In the Roaring Twenties it made no sense. Yet American Communists insisted on a degree of discipline suitable for combat. They spoke of a "white terror and exaggerated it";

> They were making conditions as bad in reality as well as in their imagination, instead of trying to revive the opportunities that formerly existed here for a fundamental revolutionary propaganda. They have formed an elaborate conspiratorial organization excellently adapted to promote treasonable and seditious enterprises, although they have no such enterprises on foot.[9]

Communists were proud of being invisible, but "it is not so much the ruthlessness of the American capitalists as the romanticism of the American communists, which accounts for their being underground. They enjoy disciplining the devotees of a rebellion, but educating the workers for the revolution is a less interesting task, and they are not fulfilling it."

There had always been two sides to Lenin's policy, Max believed.

One was loyalty to revolutionary truth, the other loyalty to the workers—something no underground organization could display:

> It was thanks to the infantile disease of "leftism"—not at that time identified—that the Left Wing Movement lost the Socialist Party in Chicago. It lost the Socialist Party and failed to form a Communist Party. It formed two half parties, or half-dead parties—one of them stagnant with complacence over its own theological perfection, and the other not sure of itself to act. And it is thanks to this disease that these two parties in their amalgamation have produced little more than a lively underground debating society.[10]

The task now was to form a legal party and discard the "pure and perfect theologians of Bolshevism" who were only interested in a "secret brotherhood of revolutionary saints." In their way they were as bad as the "sentimental socialists," and equally irrelevant.

The article was suggested to Max by Jim Cannon, a communist leader who was struggling to achieve unity. In December 1921 the surface Communists joined with his Worker's party, though factionalism continued until 1928 when Stalin put an end to it. Eastman never joined any of the Communist parties, factions, or tendencies—though he took a Worker's party card to the Soviet Union for identification purposes. He was not an organization man or willing to take orders. This alone would have kept him out of the Communist movement, even were it less peculiar.

* * *

Aptness and clarity, Max's hallmarks as a political writer in those years, deserted him when the question arose as to how artists and intellectuals should behave politically. In 1919 the French writer Romain Rolland tried to enlist the *Liberator*. Rolland was then at the peak of his fame, having won the Nobel Prize for literature and great moral prestige as a result of his anti-war activities. Moreover, Rolland was familiar with the *Masses,* as shown by his article "Voix Libres D'Amerique" (1917) which praised Max and his colleagues knowledgeably and at length. Rolland asked Max to sign a "Declaration of Independence of the Mind" that was supposed to reunite the "workers of the mind" in all countries.[11] Even though Rolland complimented his poetry, Max refused to sign the statement, not out of affection for disunity but because he thought the appeal was sentimental and elitist. It glorified intellect while neglecting the class struggle. This was not the way to build a better world. Nor was Max taken with Henri Barbusse's effort a year later to affiliate the *Liberator* with his Clarté group. Barbusse had persuaded many famous writers—Anatole France, Thomas Hardy, Upton Sinclair, H. G. Wells, Shaw—to endorse Clarté, whose aim was to harness intellect to the pursuit of justice and other worthy goals. Max did not like the term "intellectual," which to him signified priggishness. He disapproved of the popular habit of "sneering at real thoughtfulness," but felt it was his duty as an American to resist intellectual bombast. The thought of allying with a group that called itself the "International of Thought" made him queasy. As a Marxist he could not endorse a manifesto that described history as "a conflict of beliefs and abstract ideals" and asserted that intellectuals, rather than the masses, would win the struggle for international peace and liberty.

Max's experience with the pro-war socialist intellectuals had convinced him that such people could not be trusted. In the next crisis "the humanitarian intellectuals will function up to the critical point as obscurers of the issue and when the critical moment comes they will function as apostles of compromise and apologists of the masters."[12] Their shameful past required intellectuals to form, not grandiose movements like Clarté, but rather a "penitential order, retiring into a convent in sack-cloth and ashes, resolved that if they can not help the working class in its struggle, they will at least cease to corrupt and water its vigor with misleading and obscure idealistic notions."[13] Clarté was recruiting both radical and moderate intellectuals. Accordingly it would either "split in two at the first active effort it makes, or making no active effort will expire with a long sigh like any pious and impractical intention."

This seems clear enough, but Barbusse was moving left and so the issue did not die. Clarté forced out moderates and soon felt itself able to lend useful intellectual and educational support to communism. Some American radicals agreed with this role. Mike Gold said of himself and others on the *Liberator* that "we want to be the Gorkis and Lunacharskys, rather than the Lenins and Trotskys of the revolution in America."[14] Yet Max still refused to join Clarté, offering various unconvincing reasons. The *Liberator* had to propagandize during the war, but now that the radical press was coming back it no longer needed to. Then again, it was not the proper role of writers and artists to hand out political advice as Clarté wanted. Instead they should "cultivate the poetry, but keep the poetry true to the science of revolution—to give life and laughter and passion and adventure in speculation, without ever clouding or ignoring any point that is vital to the theory and practice of communism."[15] People could not understand this Delphic formula, so Max tried again. Some readers, he noted, had taken "too absolutely the distinction I made last month between poetic and practical, or scientific service to the revolution." He had not meant the distinction to seem absolute. Art Young was always running for the New York State Senate. Robert Minor "sweated his talents away" on propaganda. "It is only in so far as they distinguish themselves from the regular propagandists that I maintain these people must use poetic, or some similar word, instead of intellectual to describe what they are."[16]*

Joe Freeman deduced from Max's essays that the artist should take orders from the party.[17] Van Wyck Brooks felt that Max was trivializing the role of artists in the social struggle. Writing in a little magazine, the *Freeman,* Brooks said that Max viewed art "as a gay little handmaiden that delights in trimming the beard and warming the slippers of a certain grim, strenuous giant whose name is Science and whose business is revolution."[18] Both conclusions were plausible. Max thought it was an excellent idea that Anatole France, who had taken the wrong stand on World War I, should join the Communist party and thus obtain "the guidance of science." This supported Freeman's view. On the other hand, Max himself did not become a party member. Was it because he was right on the war, or was already scientific, or, as Brooks suspected, that he did not think art and intellect had much to offer the revolution? Brooks was probably correct. Max accepted Brooks's claim that artists could inspire revolutionaries, but denied that they could themselves practice "revolutionary education." There was a line between art and the science of revolution that could not be crossed.

Max tried to ease the blow by saying that in separating art from the revolution he was not belittling it:

* In France the debate was more sharply focused than here. Rolland had disagreed with the Clarté group as early as 1919. By 1921 the differences between them were so great that an angry polemic resulted, stretching into 1923. Barbusse took a rigidly Bolshevik position, asserting that Marxism was an exact science and communism its expression in practice. This was close to Eastman's view. Rolland insisted on complete liberty of conscience, attacking Barbusse for narrow sectarianism and blindness to the evils of police-state rule. He favored the proletariat only as it respected truth and humanity. "There are no class privileges," said Rolland, "either high or low, in the face of supreme human values." As a Bolshevik sympathizer Max could not agree with this, except in his heart. See David James Fisher, "The Rolland-Barbusse Debate," *Survey* (Spring–Summer, 1974), pp. 121–59.

Oh how foolish it is to try to justify poetry and art on the ground of their service to the revolution. They are but life realizing itself utterly, and only by appeal to the value of life's realization can the revolution be justified. Be a little more pagan, Comrade Brooks, and a little more recklessly proud of your trade. It has a value that no "movement" can justify, no theory dim, no regime and no practical mandate ever create or destroy. It belongs with and enriches the source of all values—the living of life.[19]

The reasoning here, if it can be called that, was based less on logic than on experience. Max always believed in the primacy of art even when most political. On the *Masses* both had worked nicely together. War and revolution gave him pause for thought. He had seen art betray itself for patriotic reasons. He met revolutionaries. On some level, far below the surface of his mind, a question was being asked. What would be the climate for art if these fanatics were running things? Conscious doubts were pushed back by his certainty that in Soviet Russia everything was better managed. Unconsciously Max was already beginning to protect himself. His rigid distinction between art and revolution made little sense if taken at face value. It annoyed all his friends, who were thirsting to strike a great blow for liberty in their capacities as artists and intellectuals. There was a hidden purpose here just the same. When he broke with the Communists, it would be—their inhumanity aside—as much as anything because they regimented art. It was the fear of this, not quite spelled out or fully realized, that led Max to distinguish so sharply between art and revolution even before he went to Russia. False though this distinction might have been, it protected him against Marxist sophistry. He would never fall for party double-talk about the social responsibility of artists. Others would have to explain how in suppressing art the Soviets were advancing it.

*   *   *

The *Liberator* could still be amusing, though less often than the *Masses*. Playfulness remained a matter of conviction, except to Mike Gold, who was coming to see levity as distracting, maybe even counter-revolutionary. He had taken to wearing dirty shirts and spitting on the floor as expressions of solidarity with the proletariat. Comrade Gold, Floyd Dell was forced to report, "tells us that we are a lot of poor aesthetes, and that our habit of sitting around talking about ideas disgusts him." Dell believed Gold was missing the point, which was that the poor should have the same opportunities as middle-class people to be aesthetic and intellectual. It was romantic of Gold to carry on about hard work, to fall down "in prayerful awe before Steam and Steel and Mother Earth, and Mud, and Noise and such things."[20] Dell seemed to think the good society would not put intellectuals into ditches but take the workers out. He didn't say who would dig ditches under this dispensation, and surely did not care. Lyrical leftists always believed that if an idea was sound little details could be ignored. In the event, Gold was not amused. He went on advocating mud, and throwing it, too. He would become famous in the Red Decade as a literary assassin for the Communist party.

Though an extreme case, Gold was the wave of the future. Revolution was no longer a laughing matter. Even Max was getting grim. As capitalism was still going strong in America, Max's mind turned inevitably toward Soviet Russia, which he had adored from the start. He became a Leninist the minute he knew who Lenin was, supporting the imprisonment. of opposition leaders without really knowing or caring what it was they were against.[21] Lenin's "Program Address to the Soviets" affected Max more than any political statement delivered in his lifetime. Even before reading it, he knew that Lenin was Plato's ideal statesman come to life, an expert in economics, politics, and social psychology; altruistic, a concrete thinker, iron-willed.[22] The Program Address was further proof that, by comparison with the "temperamental rebel" of Bohemia, Lenin was a "Christ of Science." That Lenin endorsed the Taylor system of scientific management was additional evidence of his pragmatic temper, wrote Max, not knowing that Taylorism, which made factory work simple and repetitive, was detested by laboring men. Eastman was with Lenin on almost every point including the dictatorship of the proletariat, which Max took to be the dictatorship of the majority—forgetting that most Russians were peasants. There were dangers, Max admitted, but Lenin minimized them by stressing dialogue, self-discipline, and worker participation in management and the Soviets. Best of all, Lenin was a "democrat by nature," said Eastman, not noticing the elitism and arrogance in Lenin's concept of the vanguard party. Lenin could be hard when necessity required, but this was tempered by "the warm sympathy, the fatherly, or teacherly, human understanding of Lenin's heart."[23] Though not so certain in later years about the composition of Lenin's heart, Max never repudiated this snap judgement. "Lenin did excell all Marxists, and it seems to me most consecrated men of any faith in combining inflexibility of purposes with fluidity of plan. And he was selfless enough to do this without moral confusion." Max stood by his poem about Lenin written during the first world war, which hailed Lenin's many virtues and "conquering purpose."[24]

Where Max went wrong, as he later recognized, was in ascribing to Lenin all of his own beliefs. Wanting Lenin to be open-minded, Max wrote in 1920 that "I have never seen a sign in any speech or writing of Lenin that he regarded the Marxian theory as anything other than a scientific hypothesis in process of verification."[25] That Max knew of no evidence to the contrary proved exactly nothing, since he did not yet read Russian and had as much access to Lenin's philosophy as he did to Lenin's heart. Ignorance allowed Max to indulge in flights of fancy. Lenin reminded him "of my teacher in philosophy, John Dewey." It seemed as though "the instrumental theory of knowledge was at last actively understood."[26]

Marx and Engels, it now turned out, were pragmatists, too. They had decided, Max wrote, that "instead of being pious evangelical nincompoops they would be efficient revolutionary engineers."[27] As a result, "their theory of the evolution of capitalism and the proletarian revolution . . . has survived every test and observation and has held true in very minute detail. . . . It is the one thing that has ever happened in the political sciences comparable to the confirmations of the hypotheses of Copernicus and Kepler and Newton in the physical sciences."[28] It followed then that the Bolsheviks as students of Marx had to be "learned and painstaking scientists of human nature and human history" and "specialists in the science of revolution."[29] At long last all the guesswork had been taken out of politics.

Max tried his best to resemble the Bolsheviks. If they repressed unwanted opinions, so would he. When an advertisement for an anti-Bolshevik book by the former Socialist John Spargo was submitted to the *Liberator,* Max rejected it, explaining to Fremont Older, liberal editor of the *San Francisco Call,* that the magazine was not wedded to any one principle, even that of free speech. "Our loyalty is not to abstract ideals, our loyalty is to concrete purposes."[30] After being teased by the press, for no one had complained of censorship more loudly during the war than he, Max became even more Leninist. There was no free speech in this country he asserted. Given the power he would suppress obnoxious capitalist newspapers, and if they felt like it they would do the same to the *Liberator*.[31]

Max said this because he didn't know what real repression was. Though savage, the recent Red Scare was a piece of cake by Soviet standards. The "insects" Lenin was purging included not just counter-revolutionaries but whole classes of people such as "malingering workers, parasites," and "saboteurs who call themselves intellectuals." Solzhenitsyn writes that

> the people in the local zemstov self-governing bodies in the provinces were, of course, insects. People in the cooperative movement were also insects, as were all owners of their own homes. There were not a few insects among the teachers in the gymnasiums. The church parish councils were made up almost exclusively of insects, and it was insects, of course, who sang in the church choirs. All priests were insects—and monks and nuns even more so. And all those Tolstoyans who, when they undertook to serve the Soviet government on, for example, the railroads, refused to sign the required oath to defend the Soviet government with *gun* in hand showed themselves to be insects too. . . . The railroads were particularly important, for there were indeed many insects hidden beneath railroad uniforms, and they had to be *rooted out* and some of them *slapped down*. And telegraphers, for some reason, were, for the most part, inveterate insects who had no sympathy for the Soviets. Nor could you say a good word about Vikzhel, The All-Russian Executive Committee of the Union of Railroad Workers, nor about the other trade unions, which were often filled with insects hostile to the working class.[32]

Rage at injustice in America was another reason behind Max's Leninism. When, following the wartime persecutions and the Red Scare the *New Republic* declared that "freedom of speech and a respect for the due process of law are among the fundamentals of true Americanism," Max exploded. In America, he charged, people were sentenced to years of imprisonment for statements that in Europe would cost them at most a few months. Every major European state had more freedom of speech than America. "We are not distinguished by freedom, but by the sanctimoniousness with which we institute the grossest forms of tyranny."[33] It was laughable to speak of due process in a country where so little effort was made to control mobs, private gunmen, and vigilantes. In the previous year six whites and seventy-two blacks had been lynched. The mayor of Omaha had nearly been killed by a mob when he attempted to save a lynching victim. This being so, "what chance have the obscure, the destitute, those who are without influential friends?"

Nothing upset him more than the deportation to Russia (or rather to Finland, as officially Russia did not exist) of Emma Goldman, Alexander Berkman, and 247 other aliens accused of being anarchists or Communists. They were packed off on an old troopship, the "Buford," at the end of 1919. Families were broken up, and before the ship sailed distraught wives, sweethearts, mothers, and sisters attacked the ferry building leading to an immigration station where the men were confined. Some of these women were "not only thus left homeless and destitute, but they were left without any plan or prospect of ever meeting their husbands again. They tore at the gates and broke the windows of the ferry station in the agony of grief and despair. Whether the government that committed this atrocious thing, or the press that laughed at it as an "anarchist riot" is the more contemptible it is hard to say." [34]

Max would not have been human if such events had failed to make him angry. Yet they were stripping him of a unique asset, the ability to understand both sides of the class struggle. William E. Bohn of the *New Leader* once recalled how different Max had been from other socialist speakers during the Progressive era:

> Genially he would lean against his chair and launch into a gay and careless, seemingly pointless disquisition on us and the world. Instantly tension would be eased. We would begin to see ourselves, and also our enemies, the reactionaries, in an illuminating golden haze which tended to reduce our virtues and their vices. Doctrinaire rigidities began to loosen, the world, as it is, began to take shape. And the clarification was as easy, as natural, as good-humored as the blowing of breeze on a summer day. [35]

This trait, to which Max owed much of his influence, was another casualty of the war and Red Scare.

With alienation came loss of judgment. Max needed Soviet Russia to be better than it was and so found it easy to dismiss criticisms whatever their source. In 1919 Robert Minor, Eastman's friend, Croton neighbor, and collaborator, left Russia after a nine-month stay. He then attacked Lenin and the Bolsheviks in the *New York World*. What else could you expect from an anarchist was Max's response:

Anarchism is a natural philosophy for artists. It is literary, not scientific—an emotional evangel, not a practical movement of men. With the spirit of the 18th century libertarians, who never saw industrial capitalism, the anarchists still think that human freedom can be achieved through the mere negation of restraint. They have no appreciation of the terrific problem of organization involved in revolutionizing the entire world.[36]

Max had never expected that the revolution would be completely satisfying. Years earlier he had predicted that, when it came, "there will be great evils and wastefulness and graft and scandal and vituperation—and something to kick about all the time, just as there is today. There will be no millenium."[37] Accordingly, Max had little patience with those who found Soviet Russia to be imperfect. In any case Minor soon changed his mind. In the October 1920 issue of the *Liberator* he withdrew all his objections to the Soviets and announced that Lenin was a scientist.[38] Minor was soon completely cured of anarchism and its enfeebling dreams of liberty. He joined the Communist party and became a lifelong Stalinist.

Secretary of State Lansing was even less of a problem. When his department issued a report saying there was no democracy in Russia, Max replied: "In the old days, when he didn't know what socialism is, Mr. Lansing and his kind used to tell us, 'You can't change human nature.' I don't see how he can blame us now if we are compelled to establish socialism without changing it."[39] This was clever though completely beside the point. Max considered himself far above Secretary Lansing, who was a rather dreadful man. But two decades later Max himself would write a widely denounced article for the *Reader's Digest* called "Socialism Does Not Gibe with Human Nature." It is one of the infamies of life, for radicals especially, that we tend when older to become what we despised when young.

Bertrand Russell was not so easily passed off. A world-famous philosopher and heroic member of the English peace movement compelled respect. He had supported the Bolshevik revolution at first, giving it a cautious endorsement in the *Liberator*.[40] But after a visit to Soviet Russia he rejected Bolshevism, saying that "kindliness and tolerance" were worth more than any creed. In articles for the *Nation* Russell deplored Communist fanaticism, the creation of a new aristocracy of party leaders, and the human cost of revolution. Lenin was "too opinionated and narrowly orthodox. His strength comes, I imagine, from his honesty, courage, and unwavering faith—religious faith in the Marxian gospel."[41] In the *New Republic* Russell attacked the theory as well as the practice of Marxism, for the one disproved the other. By their conduct Bolsheviks had exposed the fallacies of Marx. He concluded: "I am compelled to reject Bolshevism for two reasons: First because the price mankind must pay to achieve communism by Bolshevik methods is too terrible; and secondly, because even after paying the price, I do not believe the result would be what the Bolsheviks profess to desire."[42]

As Russell was both brilliant and right, answering him posed a problem. Max was too honest to deny his representations, striking instead at the attitudes behind them. Russell, Max argued, wanted the Reds to be philosophic, democratic, and soft. But Eastman was glad they were efficient and scientific, "an aristocracy of brains and talent."[43] Bolsheviks were Nietzschean free spirits, not Christian saints. Russell suffered from the Christian habit of idealizing the weak and ineffectual. He was offended by Soviet Russia because it resembled Plato's Republic, which was why Max admired it.

The *New York Times,* having gotten over the Red Scare, was amused by this. It jovially suggested that the *Liberator*'s editors wanted to be seen as "terrible persons" because their "revolutionary self-esteem" had been gravely wounded by the government's failure to imprison them during the war. Thus they missed no opportunities to be ferocious "despite innate predilections for gentility." The *Times* was only half-right. They had fought to stay out of jail and were not ashamed of this. But admiration for Bolshevism was pulling them in a direction contrary to their natural instincts, Eastman most of all. He was not bloodthirsty, and so his efforts at it struck a false note, even a comic one. Eastman's view, said the *Times,* was that we "must be ready to cut all the throats in the world, our own included, rather than let revealed truth, which has been entrusted to ourselves alone, be rejected by a world which does not accept our authority. To such iron minds as these—and Mr. Eastman intimates that he can be just as ruthless as anybody, though so far as the public knows his ferocity has hitherto been entirely academic—Russell's retreat toward 'kindliness and tolerance' is beneath contempt."[44] Though Russia was a dictatorship of the party elite, the "process of transubstantiation by which any small number of hard persons with machine guns becomes the Proletariat offers no obstacle to the true believer." Plato, Eastman, and Field Marshall Ludendorff shared the same confidence in an "aristocracy of the able":

> And the pretences of the oligarchs are supported by a religion which may or may not be supported by the lower classes. These latter have it shoved down their throats, whether they like it or not. A priestly caste, possessing the power, controlling the wealth and teaching that the divine scheme of things so ordains—most of the ancient races of the East lived under such a system for a period which perhaps includes the greater part of the history of human culture; if Bolshevism prevails, we shall all come back to it."[45]

One day Max would agree.

In 1921 Henry W. Alsberg, who as foreign correspondent of the *Nation* had supported Bolshevism for three years, turned against it. The Soviet government, he announced, was neither revolutionary nor communist, but, rather, "dogmatic, bureaucratic, corrupt, tyrannical, doctrinaire, contemptuous of personality." Since Alsberg was not a capitalist lackey, Max only patronized him. "The liberal humanitarians," he explained, "all carry about in their hearts a little ideal of utopia, which has no relation whatever to their practical efforts to pass reform bills and keep working girls out of jail." Now and then a humanitarian falls into a real revolution, "and he is stirred and upturned to the bottom of his soul, and cries out, 'My God, it is heaven! I won't have to worry about working girls any more!'" But, Max continued, if this well-meaning person stays long enough, he discovers that revolutionary leaders are still dealing with the same imperfect humans as before. Then the liberal becomes disillusioned, because he understands only the revolutionary idea and not the revolutionary method. He compares the revolution, not with the outside world, but with his notion of the perfect state and, not surprisingly, finds the revolution wanting. So much for the "petit-bourgeois liberal" and his search for the "celestial revolution."[46] In a few years Max would find himself being dismissed in the same easy way.

*　*　*

Max was armored against the truth not only by enthusiasm but by bad reporting. In 1920 the *New Republic* noted that between 1917 and 1919 the *Times* had reported on ninety-one occasions that the Bolsheviks were about to be overthrown. It had announced that Lenin and Trotsky had fled the country four times, that Lenin was in prison three times, and that he was dead once.[47] Max had every reason to doubt capitalist reports from Russia. Jack Reed, the only person who might have been able to set Max straight, was dead. Later there would be controversy over Reed's position just before his death in Moscow of typhus on October 17, 1920. His widow, Louise Bryant, would claim that he had become disillusioned and meant to give up party work on returning to America.[48] Max could not know this. Louise Bryant wrote him after Reed's death but made no mention that he had changed his mind.[49] So far as Max knew, Reed died a hero of the Soviet Union, having been buried in the Kremlin with full honors.

Of all his political friends Eastman probably liked Reed the best. And he trusted Reed's judgment more than others. One of Reed's poems, "A Dedication to Max Eastman," shows their close relationship, as does Eastman's "To John Reed," which first appeared in the February 1921 issue of the *Liberator*. Eastman was proud of Reed's place in the social struggle. At a memorial meeting he acclaimed Reed as a member of the intelligentsia who was "uniquely distinguished among the members of that class by the fact that he possessed a great intelligence."[50] Max praised Reed for giving his all to the revolution, yet it seems clear that some part of him thought Reed gave away too much. In the memorial speech Max said that Reed was a poet who "chose to make a great poem of his life." Max had chosen to make his life not a poem but a pleasure. Eastman's dedication to the revolution was real and intense. Unlike Reed's it was not complete. Even when most fanatical, Eastman knew there was more to life than politics. This was his salvation.

Reed's last contribution to the *Liberator* was upbeat as always, thus confirming Max's views. Even so, it offered an important clue to the future of Russia. The article, which appeared posthumously, noted that "the majority of the working class vanguard who made the October Revolution are dead." The cream of the proletariat, the most intelligent, loyal, and selfless activists had been wiped out not just once but, Reed estimated, no fewer than eleven times. Each crisis brought forth a new vanguard, which in turn was killed off, leaving "an ever and ever greater proportion of unintelligent, unskilled, un-class-conscious workers, boys, old men, half peasants fresh from the villages. And still the revolutionists spring up. This is the test and the justification of the Revolution."[51] Without realizing it Reed was describing not the glory of the revolution but its death. Such losses could not be made up. In the hands of lesser men the gains of the revolution would fade away.

* * *

If anything, negative reports from Russia made Eastman all the more eager to see communism at first hand. Russia had been calling him ever since the October Revolution. At first he was too busy with love affairs, humor, the trials, speech-making, and most of all the *Liberator*. As before, Max imagined that he could run a magazine without actually doing much work. But even with Crystal's help, editing the country's most important left-wing periodical took time. When she left for England with her husband early in 1921 the work became more difficult still. Max took leaves of absence, and Dell, Joseph Freeman, Mike Gold, Claude McKay, and Robert Minor helped bring out the magazine. But it remained burdensome, and increasingly so as the tide of radical enthusiasm ebbed. By 1921, when the Left was in ruins, the *Liberator*'s mission seemed unclear. The last straw for Max came when business manager E. F. Mylius absconded with the cash reserve of $4,500. Mylius was a strange character. Ten years before he had been jailed in England for libeling King George V, which ensured him a warm welcome in Greenwich Village. He also was the author of a pamphlet entitled "The Socialization of Money," an ambition he put into practice at the *Liberator*'s expense. Mylius added insult to injury by writing the *Times* that he had only borrowed the money, following the example of Max and Crystal. Eastman replied that the *Liberator* had advanced money to contributing editors, recording such transactions in the books. Mylius simply stole all the magazine's cash and then lost it in the stock market.[52] The *Times* was delighted by this, but the humor in the situation escaped Max.[53] If he stayed with the magazine he would have to go fund-raising again. Though he was good at it, the job disgusted him. Eastman abandoned the *Liberator* instead, appointing Gold and McKay co-editors, with the stipulation that, if they failed, it was not to be sold commercially but given to the Worker's (Communist) party. This was done in 1924.

In casually handing over the *Liberator* Eastman was giving up more than he realized. While he would later regret the time lavished on both his magazines, they were vital parts of his legend. In letting go of the *Liberator* Max felt free at last after nine years of bondage to radical journalism. But he was also being deprived of his position as America's best known and most influential left-wing editor. His magazines had helped Max acquire celebrity and even a sort of power. Freedom from the *Liberator* meant for Max the end of that part of his life when he was most famous, most admired, and best able to influence opinion.

If Max was losing more than he knew, going to Russia involved taking on more than he could have guessed. Russia would be, as he expected, a great adventure. But it would cost Eastman most of his old friends on the Left and plunge him into struggles far more painful than anything he had seen yet. One way or another Russia would shape the rest of his life. Max had called Jack Reed a "great boy." In a sense this was true of himself as well. At the age of thirty-nine, when most men are settled in life, Max was still boyish, plunging romantically into Russia with no fixed plans and hardly any money. He was after excitement and hoping, as he said half-seriously at the time, to find out if what he had been writing about Russia was true. He would learn that it was not, and in doing so leave youth and glory behind him. Eastman believed that he had matured in 1919 when he discovered love and life, but the Soviets had much to teach him about evil and death. Russia would sink the iron in him, and he would never throw it off.

CHAPTER SIX

The Great Adventure

1922–1928

Among subsequent generations, a picture has evolved of the twenties as a kind of holiday of totally unlimited freedom. In this book we shall encounter people who viewed the twenties quite differently.

The Gulag Archipelago

When Eastman sailed for Europe in 1922, he expected to find in Russia a band of social engineers rationally employing the scientific principles of Marxism. This misconception, which he shared with other western supporters of Bolshevism, arose partly from self-delusion, mainly from lack of knowledge. Like most American radicals, Max saw Russia's revolution in terms of the *Communist Manifesto* issued during the liberal revolutions of 1848. Max had closed his mind to the negative reports of liberals, anarchists, and conservatives. Instead he listened to Lincoln Steffens, who after several days in Russia announced that he had seen the future and it worked. Max expected some brutality and muddle, but as a Westerner he could not understand how their unique history had shaped the Bolsheviks.

In western Europe and the United States Marxism had resulted in democratic parliamentary movements up until World War I. Revolutionary in theory, they practiced moderation. By contrast, Russian Marxists had been forced to compete with terrorists on the Left while enduring persecution from the Right. This made them hard, as did years of exile and imprisonment. The Bolshevik wing of Russian Marxism under Lenin became a disciplined and authoritarian movement that employed violence in Russia and quarreled violently with rival movements abroad. When given their chance by the first Russian revolution, the Bolsheviks tore down the very government that set them free. They fought a bloody civil war and established both socialism and the police-state thought necessary to maintain it. Lenin understood the dictatorship of the proletariat, which had been foreseen by Marx, to mean the dictatorship of an elite group of professional revolutionaries like himself. Believing that history was on his side, he led the Bolsheviks to victory over rival Marxists (who were called Mensheviks, ever afterward a term of abuse on the Left), Social Revolutionaries who represented the peasantry, anarchists, White Guardists loyal to the old regime, invading Allied armies, and diverse nationalities of the old Russian Empire who wanted independence (except for the Poles, the Finns, and the Balts who gained or were given their freedom). This was a great achievement. The costs in morality and humanity were greater still.

Eastman could not know that terror had been institutionalized and the Gulag Archipelago established. He could not guess the implications of single-party rule. He did know that the Bolsheviks had performed miracles of sacrifice and dedication. He realized, too, that Lenin embodied qualities he most admired—decisiveness coupled with flexibility, a practical turn of mind, a distrust of intellectuals combined with great intellect. There were things Max was ignorant of—that Lenin wasn't a pragmatist but a devoted if not always faithful Marxist, that corruption and cruelty were built into his regime. History had made the Bolsheviks suspicious, tyrannical, and doctrinaire. Eastman was slow to see this.[1]

Eastman's illusions were strengthened by the time and manner of his entry into Russia. He did not go there directly but first attended an international conference in Genoa, where twenty-nine nations had assembled at the call of Prime Minister Lloyd George of Great Britain to solve all the world's problems. Soviet Russia's delegation was, Max thought, by far the most impressive. Soviet Commissar for Foreign Affairs Chicherin seemed the conference's star, poised, articulate, logical, scholarly. "Here indeed," Eastman wrote in his memoirs, "was a foreign minister from Utopia." He was struck by others as well, especially Christian Rakovsky, a most unusual Bolshevik. Georges Haupt calls him "Bulgarian by birth, Romanian by nationality, French by education and Russian by his relations, feelings and culture."[2]

It took Max four months to get from Italy to Russia. He dallied in France with Edna St. Vincent Millay and other friends, met Anatole France, attended an artists-and-models orgy in Paris, and spent a gloomy evening with Henri Barbusse, made dismal by Barbusse's funereal manner rather than any political disagreement. Also in Paris Eastman met Josephine Herbst and Albert Rhys Williams, with whom he traveled to Moscow. Williams had been in Moscow during the October Revolution and was captivated by it forever, which made him a good companion at the time and a bad enemy later. Entering the first Russian train station, Eastman was impressed by the contrast between Soviet citizens and the dull, worried people he had seen in France and Germany:

> What I found was a land brimful of people and a people brimful of energy. Many of them, to be sure, were dressed in rags. Indeed, a very large number looked as though they had just stepped out of a meal bag—or what is nearer the truth, had just stepped into one. But even the poorest looked healthy and had plump cheeks and a surprising vigor of movement.[3]

This vibrant condition arose not, as Max thought, from progress toward socialism but rather the opposite. War Communism, the policy of abolishing private property and forcing peasants to deliver grain to the cities, had failed. Peasants rebelled and hoarded foodstuffs. Technicians, managers, and experts who had survived laid low, fearing that visibility would lead to destruction. National income fell to one-third of what it had been in 1913. Iron foundries were producing one-fortieth as much as before. Cities and towns were depopulated. Moscow shrank to half its former size, Petrograd to a third. The food ration in cities was two ounces of bread and a few potatoes a day. Unemployment soared.

In desperation Lenin decreed that War Communism was only a temporary measure, though he had considered it permanent, and announced the New Economic Program, which he privately hoped would be temporary. The NEP replaced the era of chaos and amateurism with a workable mixed economy. The state owned the banks and heavy industry. Light industry was in private hands. Peasants had to pay a grain tax but could sell on the open market. Though repugnant to left Communists, the NEP pleased most Russians. It revived the economy, rehabilitated the petty bourgeois to a degree, satisfied the peasants, and even the Communist right wing, who saw the NEP as a smart tactical move permitting future advances toward socialism.

Eastman arrived in Moscow during this brief, happy moment in Soviet history. The people were grateful for peace and bread. Non-Communist oppositionists were dead, imprisoned, or silent. The writers, politicians and intellectuals he did meet were Communists or sympathizers and thus free to speak out with little fear of reprisal. As the editor of a pro-Soviet magazine, Eastman was allowed to do as he pleased in Russia, and had access to high party leaders. They nourished his favorable opinions.

Few letters from this period appear to have survived, but Max described it at length in *Love and Revolution*. The essentials of his account are supported by his later close and well-documented relations with Trotsky and the Left opposition. Max first went to Yalta from Moscow, where he made love to a girl who taught him Russian—this being the only way to learn a language, he believed. Max returned to Moscow for the Fourth Congress of the Communist International, riding on a special train from Moscow to Petrograd with Communist party leaders and impressing them, so he says, with his new fluency in Russian. Trotsky agreed to let Eastman write a biography of him, which Max worked on during the winter of 1923–24. He read Russian classics and studied Marxism seriously for the first time.

Max took up with Eliena Krylenko, impressed by her playfulness, vivacity, agile, muscular body, and free spirit. She was, he said, the gayest person he had ever known and a skilled cook, painter, poet, and dancer. As with Florence Deshon, Max blew hot and cold. Sometimes he lived with Eliena, other times he craved isolation. When their affair became serious, he went into the customary panic. What he called his "demon" returned, bringing with it nameless terrors, nightmares, a fear of insanity, rapid heartbeats, and other alarming symptoms. A Russian doctor prescribed sedatives and advised placing an ice pack over the heart when it raced. Though lacking in depth, this analysis had the great merit of doing the patient no harm—another stroke of the Eastman luck. Where medicine failed, Eliena succeeded, nursing him back to mental health.

Max's admiration for the Bolshevik captains remained high, though he disliked the way they ran the Comintern, handling foreign radicals like children. He complained to Trotsky about this and was told, "in general we treat each of them according to what he deserves."

He attended the Twelfth Congress of the Communist Party in 1923, the first held without Lenin, and, not knowing of the power struggle going on in secret, he thought it was quiet and businesslike, with issues being fought out on their merits. Further travel and wider experience raised doubts in Eastman's mind, but they remained small at first. He was surprised to learn from factory workers that union leaders were appointed by the party, not elected. Even so, his few articles for the *Liberator* gave nothing away. One was prompted by a letter from home lacking in enthusiasm for the USSR. This reminded Max, he wrote, of his duty to spread the truth, which he had lost sight of as a result of living "in this land where intelligence reigns and simple human good will." Americans critical of Russia were "lyrical socialists," whereas the Soviets themselves continued to be "practical engineers of history." He defended the NEP as a necessary retreat, while endorsing Trotsky's concept of the permanent revolution. There was no need to be gloomy. "If the proletariat in a 'hopeless minority' can accomplish the political and military wonders that have been accomplished in Russia, then the proletariat in western Europe and America can accomplish all that we have expected of it."[4] The final outcome of Russia's experiment was uncertain, Max admitted, but early results were encouraging.

Eastman's first doubts were, he tells us, products of study rather than observation. Reading Marxist tracts made him wonder if Lenin and other top men were really instrumentalists as he had been claiming. This suspicion was not evident in his last essays for the *Liberator*, panegyrics inspired by Lenin's death early in 1924. Called "The Wisdom of Lenin," these two articles repeated again the sentiments of "A Statesman of the New Order," which he had written in 1918. Lenin remained the most adult figure in world history, "a master of the Mechanics of History," and the "first man who ever consciously and in a profound sense made history."[5] He had mastered the art of staying with the crowd, while at the same time advocating revolution. This was "after the science of Marxism, the primary source of his power."

Max still accepted the official version of recent events. In speaking of the Social Revolutionaries who had been crushed, Max said that Lenin only wanted them to give up their roles as populist intellectuals and become Marxian engineers—which would have come as news to all concerned. Max was on firmer ground in noting that a basic difference was that the Socialist Revolutionaries had a broad peasant base, whereas Bolshevik strength was in the much smaller working class.

Though he failed to draw the moral, this meant that the dictatorship of the proletariat was not the dictatorship of the majority, as he had earlier claimed. At this point his argument begins to collapse. Superficially, Eastman's views are the same as in 1918. What was missing now in 1924 was a conviction sufficiently strong to overcome his want of evidence or logic or both. Did Westerners worry about the lack of democracy in Soviet Russia? How silly of them, Max explained, there was nothing to fear, nobody in the USSR gave the slightest thought to it, regardless of what camp they were in. Did Westerners find it hypocritical or worse to call the dictatorship of the Communist party a dictatorship of the proletariat? "There is so little hypocrisy about it, and it has lain so long and so solidly at the bottom of the whole development of Russian Marxism, that Bolsheviks are entirely unaware of the necessity of commenting upon it."[6] As rebuttals go, these were pretty thin. That no one he knew in Russia was concerned about the absence of democracy and the dictatorship of the party meant exactly nothing. It was as if the question of poverty in America had been dismissed on the ground that rich people were not alarmed. Keeping the faith was getting to be uphill work.

Eastman's breaking point was the Thirteenth Party Congress which met on May 23, 1924, to deal with such matters as who would rule now that Lenin was dead, and whether there should be worker control of industry. Max sat next to Krylenko in the front row of this Congress had learned that it was packed with followers of Stalin, Zinoviev, and Kamenev. He saw Trotsky, after Lenin the ablest Bolshevik, publicly humiliated. He heard grown men debate over whether the party was infallible (Trotsky said it was, Stalin and Zinoviev that it wasn't). This made the idea of leaving Russia seem attractive. Max agreed to take with him a package of documents supporting the program for worker democracy that he took to be the central issue. With the wisdom of hindsight he would call this effort pitiful. What he and the budding left opposition did not realize at the time was that by centralizing all power in the party, and all the party's power in its bureaucracy, Lenin had unwittingly made Stalin his heir. The job of party secretary, once purely administrative, became in Stalin's hands the chief source of real authority. Backed by the hundreds of thousands of place-holders appointed by or responsible to him, Stalin was already in command.

Leaving Russia in 1924 with Eliena was a complicated task made possible only with the aid of the diplomat Maxim Litvinov, for whom

Eliena worked. Max's passport had expired, and western Europe did not want him, for he was classed as a dangerous radical. Litvinov solved this problem by appointing Max to the staff of a Soviet delegation that was visiting London in the summer. Two difficulties remained. The secret police would not let Eliena go until she signed a document committing her to work for the GPU abroad. Litvinov told her to sign and forget it. Finally, even if Max did get a passport, Eliena could not live in the West unless married to him, since Soviet passports were not yet valid. All else having failed, Max submitted to marriage.

Eastman accepted this fate with all the gracelessness at his command. It was a marriage of convenience only, he insisted. According to him, Eliena promised in advance that he could go on making love to other women. This seems likely, for one cannot imagine him marrying again without some such understanding. The service was minimal, consisting of Max alone in a registry office, except for two witnesses, while Eliena packed their bags. To everyone's surprise, Eastman's most of all no doubt, the marriage lasted a lifetime.

*   *   *

In leaving Russia Max escaped one set of worries only to gain another. He had been working on a novel, his biography of Trotsky, and a study of Marxism. It was his plan to have a good time in France and also complete his books. As so often in his life, politics intervened. At the urging of French oppositionists, especially Boris Souvarine, he agreed to write a true account of the struggle for power in Russia. It was published as *Since Lenin Died* in London during May of 1925. The book faithfully reflected the view of the left opposition, with which Max identified completely. It was almost an official document, having been secretly approved by Christian Rakovsky, who was in Paris when Max finished the manuscript. In it Max explained that he had delayed releasing this information for fear of injuring the revolution, but events were making further hesitation unwise. Max described how Trotsky had been out-maneuvered by Stalin. In large measure he thought this was Trotsky's own fault for failing to take Lenin's offices when Lenin offered them and by not making a public fight when attacked by the party leadership.

The newsworthy part of *Since Lenin Died* was its quotations from what became known as Lenin's Testament, in which the dying leader warned against Stalin and made Trotsky his successor. In additon Max described the fight over Worker's Democracy, which he believed western Communists did not understand. It was a program designed by Trotsky and the opposition to break Stalin's machine and establish party democracy. Max believed the confusion arose because Stalin, Zinoviev, and Kamenev paid lip service to Worker's Democracy while secretly opposing it. As a concept it was too attractive to denounce but too dangerous to allow. Party bureaucrats had to resist the application of Worker's Democracy because the transfer of initiative to the party as a whole meant Trotsky's return to power on account of his "superior moral and intellectual revolutionary greatness."[7]

While critical of Trotsky's inept leadership, Max described the party heads' abuse of power. Stalin and Zinoviev lied and threatened. Bukharin falsified history, charging that Trotsky had always been a Left Communist (then a term of opprobrium), while others wrote articles proving he was really a Menshevik, that is, a right oppositionist. Trotsky's supporters were purged from their position in the party, the army, and the universities. As Max saw it, there was now only one aristocracy in Soviet Russia, that of the Old Bolsheviks, whose claim to office was based on length of service. In attacking them, Trotsky was also attacking the seniority system. To discredit Trotsky and save the system, they had to show he was never really a part of it, hence the rewriting of history that was to become a permanent feature of Soviet life to Eastman's surprise.

Max further believed that many Soviet leaders had become rudderless and fearful without Lenin to guide them. This explained the rise of Zinoviev, "a notoriously timid man." Assaulting Trotsky made them feel, all other evidence to the contrary, that they were still "very bold and ruthless and revolutionary—very Bolshevik."[8] Trotsky, on the other hand, was a genuine revolutionary and better still a pragmatist. To Trotsky, Marxism did not consist of "learning by heart a set of dogmas that are true in the abstract, and then making automatic and universal inferences from them."[9] Max would learn differently in time, but for the moment he still believed in revolutionary engineers, though they seem to have narrowed down to two men—one of whom was dead.

Eastman's account of events in Soviet Russia was the best-informed and factually accurate statement available. Its faults, such as exaggerating differences over principle between the factions, resulted not so much from partisanship as from lack of information and perspective.

Eastman, like Jack Reed and others, misunderstood the meaning of the Civil War. Bolshevik rule had first been based on the democratic Soviets. But the Soviets became casualties of the very struggle that was supposed to preserve them. When Lenin's government claimed to rule on the basis of the Soviets, it was actually deriving its legitimacy from itself. The dictatorship of the proletariat, real when there was a proletariat, came to mean only the dictatorship of the party. A second factor that Max was not then alive to resulted from banning opposition outside the party. As Issac Deutscher, Trotsky's biographer, put it, the Communists "did not realize that they could not ban all controversy outside their ranks and keep it alive within their ranks: they could not abolish democratic rights for society at large and preserve those rights for themselves alone. The single-party system was a contradiction in terms: the single party of itself could not remain a party in the accepted sense. Its inner life was bound to shrink and wither."[10] When the party tried to cleanse itself of careerists and the like in 1921 by expelling some 200,000 it stifled criticism and debate among the survivors. Trotsky himself contributed to this atmosphere by prosecuting the Social Revolutionaries and criticizing a reform movement, the Worker's opposition, when it first appeared, not because of disagreement with it but on the ground that opposition as such was wrong. When he went into opposition himself it was too late to restore party democracy.

Max knew that in publishing *Since Lenin Died* he was exposing himself, but he underestimated the danger. That the truth was on his side seemed armor enough. A friend who admired the book warned him that it "will be hated by all the 'orthodox' communists, and cried up by the enemy."[11] Max was still surprised when the party press fell on his book. The English *Worker's Weekly* called its review "Since Eastman Lies." It was reprinted by the American *Worker's Monthly,* which charged that Max was never a real Communist, only a Greenwich Villager. This would become standard, as would the magazine's charge that *Since Lenin Died* was "intended to preface a military attack on the Soviets."[12]

Worse was to come. In a statement printed all over the world Trotsky disavowed Eastman's book and their relationship.[13] He was a virtual prisoner and had little choice in the matter. Eastman felt betrayed anyway. Except for other oppositionists, even those who had some knowledge of Soviet affairs thought Max was in the wrong. Lincoln Steffens was typical. On the one hand, he wrote Max, *"Since Lenin Died* cleared up the whole situation." On the other, Max shouldn't have printed it:

> The machine, as we used to call it—has to be supported, even as against Trotsky. It is liberalism to resent the injustice done to Trotsky, it is liberalism to feel as strongly as you do, I think, the crookedness of the methods of the red terror, which we have learned to understand.

Whatever happened, nothing "must jar our perfect loyalty to the Party and its leaders."[14]

Steffens had known Max and Crystal for years and meant well. Though he was not a Socialist, they all moved in the same left-wing, Greenwich Village circles and were on the same side of most disputed questions. Like Eastman and many other intellectuals of the period, Steffens made a cult of science. From the beginning, he had doubts about democracy. In *The Shame of the Cities* (1904), his famous muckraking book, Steffens argued that boss rule came about because people were too weak or lazy for self-government. Steffens also discovered that corrupt government resulted not just from bad politicians but from bad businessmen as well. The entire system was faulty and ought to be scrapped. He was open-minded on what should replace it, so long as the new culture was scientific. Thus for a time he would admire the new capitalism of America in the 1920s, and Italian fascism, too. Unlike most liberals, however, Steffens became an instant fan of Bolshevism for the same reasons as Eastman. He too saw it as scientific and instrumental.

The difference between them was that Max never thought that the complete abandonment of truth and morality would result in a good society, whereas Steffens did. Accordingly Steffens could write smugly to Max of how "we have learned to understand" the crooked methods of the Red terror, and seem truly puzzled as to why, he would write later, Max "did not really understand the Russian Revolution."[15] Eastman, in turn, failed to see why knowing the worst about Soviet Russia had no effect on Steffens. When Eastman's instincts told him there was something wrong in Russia, he trusted his feelings and followed, if slowly and torturously, where they led. Steffens had the same feelings but decided they were at fault rather than anything in the Soviet Union. To a surprising degree this has not been held against him. One reason is that Steffens was in his personal relations warm, generous, good-natured, and tolerant. These qualities, together with good writing and delightful paradoxes, would help make *The Autobiography of Lincoln Steffens* (1931) a best-seller at the time and a favorite of historians. Even Christopher Lasch, Steffens's sharpest critic, cannot resist the old man's charm. Lasch recognizes that justifying mass murder and tyranny, as Steffens does in this letter to Eastman, and would do more often in the 1930s, might seem callous. But Steffens errs in such a nice way, with so much tolerance and intellectual modesty, that his choice of Stalinism is described as "morally more attractive than the choice made by the anti-Communist liberals in the aftermath of the Second World War."[16] Steffens has that effect on people, even after death. One can see why when he was alive Max found it hard to be as angry at Steffens as the circumstances warranted. All the same it depressed Max to see old friends criticizing him for *Since Lenin Died,* especially when they knew what it said was true.

Max got good notices in the capitalist press as expected. The *Nation* and *Athenaeum,* a respected English weekly, marveled that "this despotic junta should have succeeded in imposing itself upon simpleminded Communists in other countries as the first Worker's Republic. We hope that Mr. Eastman's book, as well as Trotsky's own works, will be widely read among those who entertain this strange illusion." The *New York Times Book Review* ran a favorable review on its front page, the only time an Eastman book would get there.[17] Earlier, however, the *Times* had touched a tender nerve editorially. It ran a news story summarizing *Since Lenin Died* and then remarked that Stalin had the edge over Trotsky because he was only carrying Leninism to its logical conclusion. "The last man in the world to criticize this pragmatic philosophy is Mr. Eastman, who some years ago declared that he owed no allegience to abstract principles, but only to the proletarian cause, and that any methods which promoted the victory of proletarianism are justified."[18] Henry Alsberg, the journalist whose liberalism Max had earlier deplored in the *Liberator,* saw this, too. He pointed out what were at the time Max's two weakest political views. The first was that as a sympathizer bound to support Communist unity Max had to make it seem as if not Trotsky but his enemies were the factionalists disrupting party unity. The second was Eastman's previous endorsement of the party's right to silence non-Communist opponents. Eastman had told Alsberg in the winter of 1923 that suppressing its critics was necessary to pre-

serve the dictatorship of the proletariat. Accordingly, Eastman "should
not complain if the dictatorship grows narrower and is applied to his
own group." Alsberg predicted accurately that "unless he exercises
some agility Comrade Eastman will shortly find himself on the outside
of the fence looking wistfully in, surrounded by a lot of people whom
only a short time ago he would have characterized as 'bourgeois-
minded,' 'pseudo-revolutionists.' "[19]

Max's position immediately after *Since Lenin Died* came out was ambiguous. To the bourgeois world he was still a Communist. Party
members were angry with him, but as his criticism was not fully developed and as the left opposition outside Russia hadn't jelled, he was not
yet an official class enemy. He could visit the Soviet embassy in Paris,
but was not allowed to use its library. Communist opinion was still
divided, the memory of past heroics canceling out present infamy to a
degree. All the same, he could be criticized now in ways not possible
earlier. This was shown by the publication in 1925 of *May Days,* an anthology of poetry from the *Masses* and *Liberator* edited by Genevieve
Taggard.

Taggard was a poet Max had discovered and made love to when
he was running the *Liberator* and going with many women.[20] When she
asked for permission to edit a book of poetry from the magazine, Eastman agreed, thinking they were still friends. Though he didn't know it,
Taggard was still furious with him for having been untrue. She seems
also to have sensed his political vulnerability. *May Days* contains many
of Eastman's poems, but the preface accuses him of having sold out in
the first *Masses* trial to avoid imprisonment. Worse still, she quoted a
statement he had made at the trial that was so embarrassing Max had
forgotten it. Along with everyone else he had been standing up whenever the national anthem was played outside the courthouse. The prosecutor then asked him how he could do this in light of his documented
contempt for patriotic rituals. This was a trap. If Max stood by his
previous opinion, standing for the anthem would be exposed as an
empty gesture, which it was. To repudiate the opinion would be dis-
honest, but not provably so. He took the latter course, saying that
American boys dying for liberty in France had altered his feelings. This
was so shameful in his eyes that he promptly lost all memory of the incident.

Taggard knew what would hurt him most and went for the jugu-
lar. She printed the offending statement and wrote that a "revolu-

tionary leader does not purchase immunity from jail by repudiating his revolutionary opinions."[21] On reading the preface to *May Days* which first appeared in the *Nation,* Max wrote her an emotional letter of complaint. She had been waiting for such a chance and made the most of it. Ignoring his accusations she got directly to the point, which was that Max had evoked in her "a passion you could not possibly fulfill."[22] An appeal to her publisher, Horace Liveright, was equally futile. He found nothing in the book that Max (or Floyd Dell, who was also smeared) could object to. Describing the preface accurately as "a dastardly attack on my reputation, dictated by personal spite," Max tried to establish that he had never made a statement about American boys dying for liberty, even though it appeared in the trial transcript.[23] Max was wrong here, as he admitted years later by including the passage in his memoirs. But he was right to tell Taggard that the main line of defense could not have been based on such an approach, for if so "we would have been acquitted by the jury, and condemned without quarter by our political friends."[24] All his efforts were in vain. Taggard added insult to injury, explaining to Max that the whole thing had been for his own good. "People over here think the article has revived your reputation, and given your life work great significance. In fact it has occured to nobody that you would not like it!"[25] This showed what came of mixing sex with politics.

No doubt to Taggard's surpise, *May Days* did Eastman little if any harm. Reviewers passed over the accusations, remembering instead the golden age, so recently ended, so completely lost, that made the book possible.[26] This was true even of Mike Gold, the future Mickey Spillane of radical letters. Gold detested the poetry, written by people "searching for Beauty, that cheap, cowardly modern substitute by religion-tainted poets for the word God."[27] He disliked Max's poetry, too, for its "mood of weakness, helplessness, indecision." But Gold was still loyal to Eastman. Thinking of how it had been in the old days, he wrote of Eastman: "I was one of those who esteemed his intellect this side of idolatry." Eastman and Dell, too, he regretted to say, lacked political acumen. Just the same, they "were the best teachers youth could have found during those years. I say this as one who was given his intellectual impetus in life by the *Masses,* and who can never be grateful enough to its memory." In 1926 Gold founded a magazine of his own, called, for obvious reasons, the *New Masses,* and asked Eastman to be a contributing editor. Even so, Max's credit among Communists and sympathizers was about used up. It was Taggard, not Gold, who read the tea leaves right.

Max was still working for the cause. His projected full-length biography of Trotsky fell through, but in 1925 he published what material he did have as *Leon Trotsky: Portrait of a Youth.* In this book Marx is still the founder of a "science of historic engineering." Trotsky does not come off as well, for Eastman had taken his measure:

> What Trotsky lacks is a sense of the feelings of the other man. When Trotsky triumphs, it always has a triumphant look. When Lenin triumphed, it was just the truth and nobody was disturbed. Trotsky is too full of himself . . . too full of his own will and passion to orient himself tactfully in a group. For that reason, while he is great as a commander and inspirer—and also as a political intelligence—he is not great as a leader of men."

Leon Trotsky did not set any sales records, but won praise from the *Book-man, Dial,* the *New York Herald Tribune,* and John Maynard Keynes for being intelligent, well-written, and even temperate.[28]

The next year, 1926, Max tried to strike a harder blow for the left opposition. He was told that in October a direct, public challenge to Stalin would be made in the USSR. Max's job was to support the demonstrations by releasing the full text of Lenin's Testament, which had been smuggled to Souvarine in Paris. Eastman sold publication rights and an introductory article of his own to the *New York Times.* The gist of Lenin's Testament was distributed to papers around the world by a French news agency. Eastman's article brought *Since Lenin Died* up to date. It explained that Stalin's power was such that "the Bolshevik State is ceasing to be in any real sense of the word a workers and peasants government."[29] The Dictatorship of the Proletariat had become the Dictatorship of the Secretariat. The party apparatus, sustained by the GPU, could now do as it pleased. Trotsky remained the last hope for proletarian democracy.

The result was another fiasco. The same issue of the *Times* that carried his story on the front page had a companion feature written by Walter Duranty announcing the opposition's total defeat. Unknown to Max, the October protest had been led by Zinoviev and other former allies of Stalin, sometimes called the right opposition. Thinking them too conservative and unreliable, Trotsky did not cooperate. He shared in the general humiliation when they were defeated just the same. As before, the losers had to confess their sins and disown their foreign supporters, including Eastman.[30] The *New York Times* was not displeased. It liked the NEP and gave Stalin credit for helping the peasants. Stalin still seemed to it more conservative than the fiery Trotsky, hence more desirable. Duranty confirmed that Stalin was a pragmatist, and blandly maintained that the urban proletariat continued to rule.[31]

* * *

Much of the confusion about Soviet Russia between the wars arose from the *Times'* belief that Stalin was a practical man who got things done, and from its curious faith in Walter Duranty. He was an Enlishman sent to Moscow by the *Times* to improve its early, notoriously bad coverage of Soviet affairs. He did so, earning the undying loyalty of his superiors. From his stories and his autobiography, published in 1935, it is difficult to tell where Duranty's true sympathies lay. There is no question of his self-interest, however, which was not to get thrown out of Russia. This he accomplished brilliantly. Duranty's artful distortions and omissions enabled him to spend many years in Russia and made him a world-famous reporter. Given the *Times'* prestige he was probably of more value to Stalin than the entire American Communist party and all its works.

On February 7, 1922, not long after he took up his position, Duranty reported that the Cheka had been abolished and "a measure of civil rights and freedom not greatly diffrent from those enjoyed in America, France, or England is promised to Russians and foreigners alike, and I venture to say that no one who behaves himself has any more to fear from the 'Gay Pay Oox' [GPU] than the average American citizen has from the department of Justice."[32] Nine years later in a think piece on Stalin we find Duranty comparing the Kremlin to Tammany Hall and saying that Stalin had created a bureaucracy which "he is now powerless to stop and scarcely can control."[33] The function of this particular piece of nonsense is clear. To remain credible in the West, Duranty had to be critical sometimes. As Stalin could not be blamed when things went wrong, there had to be a scapegoat. The Soviet bureaucracy met this need perfectly, being at once inefficient, amorphous, unpopular, and yet invulnerable. It was the safest of all possible targets.

When the first Five Year Plan was well underway, Duranty wrote that "the whole purpose of the plan is to make a nation of eager, conscious workers out of a nation that was a lump of sodden driven slaves."[34] As slave-driving was the principal means used to achieve this commendable goal, the point here remains obscure—except no doubt to Duranty, who chose his words carefully for the sake of maximum obfuscation. He outdid himself; when reporting on the purges he asked rhetorically if kulaks, engineers, and other class enemies were being killed? The anwer was "of course not—they must be 'liquidated' or melted in the hot fire of exile and into the proletarian mass."[35] That is to say, liquidation did not mean death as the casual visitor to police cellar or labor camp might suppose, but rather purification through exile and hard work.

Duranty's account of agricultural collectivization, a process stretching over several years and involving the death of millions of peasants through deliberate starvation, imprisonment, exile, and often gunfire, was masterly. First he reported that there were food shortages, but made no mention of starvation; then in 1933 he attributed these shortages to the work of traitors in the Communist party, plus mismanagement and muddle. He accepted official accounts showing that crop failures resulted from conspiracies on the part of counter-revolutionary agronomists. It was true, he admitted, that the Kremlin had to be severe, but it was cruel only to be kind, for in the end collectivization triumphed and grain production rose. Thus he explained away millions of peasant deaths and the ruin of Soviet agriculture.

In his autobiography—cynically entitled *I Write as I Please*—Duranty confessed that he should have had more sympathy for the victims of collectivization and the Five Year Plan. But his heart was lightened by the knowledge that these programs had been successful. "Their cost in blood and tears and other terms of human suffering has been prodigious, but I am not prepared to say that it is unjustified." Soviet plans had their harsh side, but some plan was better than no plan. Anyway, "I cannot escape the conclusion that this period [1921 to 1935] has been a heroic chapter in the life of Humanity."[36] A man who could find heroism in mass murder and the brutalization of an entire people was someone to reckon with. Of all western reporters in Soviet Russia, Duranty was the most successful. The lesson here was not lost on other correspondents, many of whom followed his example.*

* * *

*One who did not was Malcolm Muggeridge, a young newspaper correspondent in Moscow during the early 1930s. He tells us that Duranty followed the official Soviet line even more slavishly than Louis Fischer, and was often held up to other reporters by Ou-

Trotsky's second betrayal of him ended Max's career as a political activist. He would go on speaking and writing about politics and do political translations, but he was through with the business of politics. He was through with Marxism, too, except as a critic. His forthcoming book on the science of revolution seemed to him more important than ever after Trotsky's fall, but he feared no one would read it. The trouble, as Max now realized, was that few had an interest in serious works on Marxism except Communists and fellow travelers whose minds were set against him. *Marx, Lenin, and the Science of Revolution,* published in England in 1926 and in America two years later, was not newsworthy as *Since Lenin Died* had been and attracted little notice. This was too bad, for Eastman had written an unusual book. It avoided the traditional subjects of Marxist scholarship such as the labor theory of value. Nor did Eastman argue that the failure of socialism in Russia disproved the theories of Marx, or that Marxism was a false science of prophecy, which were, or would become, staples. Instead, as John P. Diggins points out, he began by asking two basic questions: "how did Marx come to know what he knew, and how do we know that it is true."[37] These were philosophical questions, but Eastman would not neglect psychology. With Freud's help he wanted to disclose the unconscious motivations behind Marxism.

Eastman believed Marx suffered from Hegelian idealism, that is, the concept of an absolute and divine mind of which the motions of the material world are an alien reflection. Marx was cured of this, but in developing his own system of ideas Marx retained Hegel's dialectic, and his psychology. Marx does not say that ideas are products of the central nervous system because then thought becomes subject to study by biology and physiology rather than logic, and it will be found, Eastman says, that brain motions are not logical, still less dialectical. Once logic is seen not as factual account of what thought is but rather as a set of rules, "which men have made for the better employment of their thoughts," Marxist psychology collapses. This is because Hegel's psychology assumes that truth can be gained through pure reason. According to Eastman, Marx had claimed to have turned Hegel right side

mansky, the censor, as an inspiring example. Some correspondents believed this was because the Soviets were blackmailing Duranty. Muggeridge thought the basic reason was Duranty's love of power, arising perhaps from his small stature and having lost a leg. "Duranty was a little browbeaten boy looking up admiringly at a big bully." Malcolm Muggeridge, *Chronicles of Wasted Time: The Green Stick* (New York, 1973), p. 256.

up by making matter rather than mind the basis of dialectical materialism. Eastman disagreed, believing that the dialectic remained more mystical than scientific because it placed logic above biology and physiology
as a means of finding truth.

Marx and Engels thought they had escaped the false side of Hege-
lianism, but, Eastman wrote, they never did. Instead they declared personal desires—the inevitability of revolution, the dialectic—to be facts, a
process Eastman called animism. This failure to ground Marxism in
human realities continued under Lenin. What passed for psychology in
the Soviet Union was merely a search for the dialectic in states of consciousness. The result was not scientific socialism but a "socialist religion." Eastman did not like Marx's *Capital,* which to him "combines
the principal vices of the classical German philosophy with the principal vices of the classical British economy."[38] But it was the dialectic
that seemed to him the worst part of Marx's legacy. In his view Lenin,
"perhaps the most effective political thinker in history," believed that
his own thought was dialectic, which helped him not because he really
thought dialectically—that was impossible—but paradoxically because it
freed him to do what had to be done. "Believing in dialectic thinking is
a method by which having made false intellectual assumptions about
the nature of thought, you can escape from them, and win back your
freedom to use thought as it was meant to be used."[39] Eastman called
dialectic thinking Lenin's intellectual declaration of independence. "It
was a metaphysical contraption by which he managed to defend his
right to use thought naturally, in spite of an unnatural conception of
what thoughts are."[40] This talent was not passed on to Lenin's heirs,
hence their dogmatism.

The second part of Eastman's book, called "The Science of Revolutionary Engineering," purports to show how Marxism, cleansed of its
mystical or animistic elements, could still be useful to radicals. So puri-
fied, "Marxism as a practical science redefines the existing mechanism
of society from the standpoint of the ends produced by the utopian socialists; it redefines those ends from the standpoint of the facts of economics; and it points out the method of procedure by which it will be
possible to take a real step from the existing situation in the direction
of the desired ends."[41] Eastman was still a Leninist and so once again
defended Lenin's abolition of the non-Communist Left. As Diggins has
said, this shows the limits of Eastman's analysis. He was as yet unaware
that Lenin "divorced the democratic means and ends of Marxism from

the authoritarian methods of the Bolshevik Party, thereby severing the 'unity of theory and practice' and making power and success the standard for political action."[42] Eastman slighted the democratic basis of Marxism and the totalitarian results of Leninism. He did not see the equation "Marx plus Lenin equals Weber, that is bureaucracy and managerialism." Nor did he realize the danger that "Lenin minus Marx equals Mussolini, that is, revolution for revolution's sake." But Eastman had

> written the earliest and most penetrating critique of Marxist philosophy in the English language, with the possible exception of Bertrand Russell's. He had gone beyond Russell in subjecting Marxism to a psychological analysis based on Freudian insights. Moreover, Eastman was perhaps the first writer in the Western world to draw a critical distinction between the ideas of Marx and the actions of Lenin that would make a case for the October Revolution to infuriate both Bolsheviks and Mensheviks. Many of the philosophical issues he raised remain worthy of attention after a half-century of debate and revisionism.[43]

This achievement did him no personal good. In taking the Marx out of Marxism, he alienated most Communists not already opposed to him, without winning favor among non-Marxist radicals. He did receive some encouragement on he Left, but it was slight to begin with and lessened as the thrust of his argument became apparent. Samuel D. Schmalhausen applauded his independence but urged him to forego metaphysics and get down to his proper duty "of becoming the leader of the younger generation of revolutionary radicals whose one deep need is a leadership like his, at once courageous and far seeing."[44] However, Max was determined not to allow leadership to be thrust upon him again. In any case, Schmalhausen was boring and had no influence. Eastman was encouraged by Oscar H. Swede, a member of the prestigious Marxist Institute for Social Research in Frankfurt, Germany, who thanked him for showing that Lenin "did the right things but did them for the wrong reasons."[45] The letter ended, "it will intrigue you to know that a colleague to whom I mentioned your book said 'Ah, yes.' Just a journalist!' " This was a prejudice Max never overcame.

Lincoln Steffens wrote Max an odd letter praising *The Science of Revolution*. He knew from having talked with the great man that it was exactly the kind of book Lenin wanted to see written. Steffens felt that

Eastman was showing how a "cleaning out of the Bunk will help, not hurt the Socialist state to get on to Communism without a state." A little later came this astonishing remark: "I am feeling now that I can be a disciple of yours, with a preference for working among the Mensheviks of America and England. I believe your critique will save Socialism, as it should help Soviet Russia, unless the state and their state religion has already got them."[46] This fit of honesty soon passed, thanks probably to his much younger wife Ella Winter, who loved all things Soviet. The way was still clear for Steffens to become the grand old man of Stalinist letters.

Communist reactions to the book were predictable. Bertram Wolfe, who had not yet seen the light, devoted two articles to showing that *The Science of Revolution* came from the "White-Guard rumor-factory." Scott Nearing regretted that Max was wasting his time on such things.[47] Walter Duranty, strange to say, had a use for the book. In a news story he remarked that "many observers of the Russian experiment have agreed with the thesis put forward in Max Eastman's book on Marx and Lenin that the chief danger to the revolutionary party is isolation from the masses and bureaucratism."[48] This was the last time anything good about Max came out of Russia.

Almost all the favorable notices stemmed from liberal or social democratic sources. H. G. Wells sent Max a card praising his "very important" book.[49] John Strachey, who would become a famous literary Stalinist in the thirties, thought *The Science of Revolution* was Max's best book yet, "a careful and intensely illuminating description of how this fundamental defect in Marxism has warped, crippled and distorted the revolutionary movement ever since his day."[50] Strachey believed Eastman's book showed the superior merits of the British Labour Party, a conclusion that Eastman the revolutionary must have found obnoxious. The *Manchester Guardian* said that it was an "interesting and subjective" book. The *Economist* called it "thoughtful and lucid," of equal value to the curious and the faithful.[51]

The book was intelligently received at home. Malcolm McComb in the *Journal of Philosophy,* while noting accurately that the second part was not as good as the first, said Eastman had successfully used pragmatism to clarify and criticize Marx. He doubted the wisdom of trying to psychoanalyze Marx, which Max had attempted. Robert Bruere liked the book also, though he had similar reservations. Having shown Marx's unconscious motivations, he asked, might not Eastman discover his own radicalism to be "a vestigial Freudian wish?"[52] Other reviewers acclaimed Eastman's book as a "devastating attack on orthodox Marxism, from the standpoint of instrumental thinking," a "beautiful piece of work," and more.[53]

Simeon Strunsky liked the book but put his finger on the flaw in Eastman's central metaphor. He saw that Lenin's policy of "short turns" was no different from the habit of changing their minds common to American politicians. Many reviewers admired Eastman's representation of Lenin as an engineer. Looked at closely, however, it made no sense. "It is a queer kind of engineer who now thinks his bridge will be finished in six months and now thinks it might take as much as fifty years. An actual bridge built on the 'short turns' principle would be an odd structure. It would head out on arches from the opposite bank, then turn to one side and become cantilever, then run a couple of hundred yards backward as a suspension . . . and so on." Furthermore, if Lenin's short turns were so admirable, what was wrong with Stalin's? He was now for the peasant, now against him, now allowing private trade, now abolishing it. "Stalin, the practical man, would seem to be working in the best Leninist tradition."[54] This was such a common view that Eastman would soon try to correct it. In his next book he would write that Leninism had come to mean "discipline, centralized authority, obedience within the party, and practical craftiness, skillful maneuvering," and similar traits.[55] The imputation was false because in Lenin these disagreeable qualities were counterbalanced by honesty and realism. Max insisted there was a difference between Lenin's flexibility and Stalin's opportunism. Most non-believers went on doubting this.

If Eastman had studied the criticisms cited here, he would have saved himself much time and trouble. Though he used Freudian concepts more skillfully in *The Science of Revolution* than anywhere else, they still posed a danger to him. While exposing the unconscious motivations of Marx and others, he denied his own. They were moved by unrecognized forces, he by common sense. As Strunsky pointed out, his engineer analogy was equally unsafe. Opportunism was still opportunism whatever one chose to call it. Making revolutions was not and could never be a science. Eastman paid no attention to these corrections. He was the very model of David Riesman's inner-directed man who sails a straight course regardless of the weather.

Politics
and Literature

1924–1934

Eastman's physical absence from America partly explains his isolation. In *Love and Revolution* Max says he first began to sense he was out of touch with things when F. Scott Fitzgerald, who read it in manuscript, treated his novel *Venture* as a historical document. Until then Max thought he was writing about a proletarian revolution still going on in America. Fitzgerald also read T. S. Eliot's *The Waste Land* to Max. Eastman could not understand the poem and momentarily felt "dismay, the gropingly cosmic dismay that afflicts you when, keenly and for the first moment, you realize that your time is past, the generation you belong to has been laid away, your life and opinions are history." [1]

These feelings did not last, as Max was having too much fun in France. *Venture* was coming along nicely. Eliena was a social success. One day when Max was away, she wrote him from the Riviera that Fitzgerald had told her, "When you smile, everybody smiles. . . . When you come into the room, the room is lighted." Zelda thought so too. "Too bad he was drunk. I wish I could believe that he and Zelda really think so." [2] They probably did, for Eliena was cheerful and attractive and made many friends among the expatriates.

Max returned to America after a five-year absence in 1927. His public statements combined praise of Bolshevism with support for Trotsky. [3] This made him a Communist in the eyes of most people, but a renegade to the militant Left. "In revolutionary circles where I had moved so confidently, shining with no reflected light, I was extinct."[4] None of his radical friends supported Trotsky. The *New Masses* would not print his political articles, so he resigned from its Executive Board on January 27, 1928. For a time Max was the sole American Trotskyist, a party of one in a country where a decade earlier thousands had thrilled to his oratory. His books were not selling either. He blamed his publishers, as writers always do, but they were not at fault. In the 1920s only Communists were interested in books about Communism, and they would not read Eastman. So it was back to the lecture circuit again.

Max was disappointed at the response to his novel *Venture,* though some critics liked it. Fitzgerald told him again that it was "beautifully written and it tells me so much about what are to me the dim days 1910–1917 that formed so many people of the liberal side in the generation just ahead of me and mine. You make it all very real and vivid— nothing so sane on that terribly difficult subject—for it was after all a creed, a faith, in the purest and most helpless sense, has ever been written."[5] Oswald Garrison Villard found "much that was beautiful and moving" in it. Mabel Dodge liked it, too, no doubt because the main character, Joe Hancock, had a love affair with someone very much like herself, as Jack Reed had in real life. The *Times* called *Venture* a novel of ideas that was "extremely well written" and "extremely well characterized."[6]

Max was not satisfied. Others besides Fitzgerald had the same distressing tendency to see his book as a period piece. No one noticed the structure of the novel as Max had conceived it. He had written the book, he later recalled, in the shape of a capital T. The stem had his youthful hero go to college, live in Greenwich Village, and reach out to life. Then Joe Hancock "broke through" this bohemian phase, realizing that a choice must be made between plutocracy and revolution, the two arms at the top of his T. *Venture* was a talky novel. Plutocracy, represented by a character modeled on E. W. Scripps, the publishing magnate, had pages and pages of dialogue. So did the Wobblies, who embodied "the heart of contemporary reality," so far as Max was concerned. In his study of radical fiction, Walter Rideout said that *Venture* had the "verbal bounce so characteristic of the twenties," but that even in 1927 it must have seemed to deal with a "past and more golden age." He judged that it came out "ten years after its proper time."[7]

In the summer of 1928 Crystal died. She had spent years in England, and they had not been reunited for long, which made the blow more terrible. Like Jack Reed, her kidneys had been damaged in childhood and were giving out. In August 1927, when she learned of her husband's sudden death of a brain hemorrhage, she herself was already dying. Her physicians held out false hopes and for months she went from healer to healer desperately seeking a cure. Finally, resigned to death, she expired in her older brother's home in Erie, Pennsylvania. The next day Max drove to Glenora, "our real home," as he had done after his mother's death. He seems never to have gone there again. The last tie with his childhood was broken.

Eastman meant to write about Crystal at length sometime but never did, probably because his loss always remained painful. In *Love and Revolution,* published thirty-six years after her death, he contented himself with quoting from Freda Kirchwey's tribute to Crystal in the *Nation.* Kirchwey wrote that Crystal's religion was her faith in the triumph of freedom and decent human relationships. "Her strength, her beauty, her vitality and enthusiasm, her rich and compelling personality—these she threw with reckless vigor into every cause that promised a finer life to the world." She was "to thousands of young women and young men a symbol of what the free woman might be." [8] Crystal was the best of a great generation of women, combining feminism, socialism, and pacifism with common sense and charm. She could not be spared, least of all by Max who took advice from no one else. He would miss her throughout his life.

*   *   *

Lecturing was Max's bread and butter, but though good at it he found the platform to be a strain, especially as he grew older. He was always looking for other ways to make a living and at one point aspired to become literary editor of the *Nation,* which was absurd. He had lost the tact and patience of his salad days. He did not read much contemporary literature, and what he did read he didn't like. He was soon to become a notorious critic of modernism. Eastman told Oswald Garrison Villard that he could establish in the *Nation* "a real standard of scientific book criticism." [9] Luckily for both of them, the job was not vacant.

So long as Villard controlled it, Max appeared more frequently in the *Nation* than anywhere else. Villard was an old-fashioned liberal and, though often in disagreement with Max, would publish him just the same, unlike Max's radical acquaintances on the *New Masses.* There was a moral here that Max chose not to see. It was underlined early in 1928 when the *Nation* published an editorial on the exiling of Trotsky and thirty other oppositionists. Eastman had made available to the *Nation* a long letter written by Adolphe Joffe of Trotsky's faction, who was sick and discouraged and committed suicide after writing it.[10] The *Nation* agreed editorially with Joffe's view that Russia was entering a phase resembling the French Termidor: "This is an extreme opinion, but it is difficult after reading his letter to doubt that in a sense Stalin does represent the conservative tendency ever to be associated with excessive personal power, and that Trotsky has defended the original principles and purposes of the Bolshevik Party."[11] It criticized western Communists for following Stalin in defiance of this fact.

Albert Rhys Williams, who had traveled in Russia with Eastman, Joe Freeman, who had worshipped him as a young man, and Kenneth Durant, wrote Villard accusing Max of tampering with the Joffee letter and of being a "hireling" of the opposition. Max denied being on anyone's payroll, saying Williams had been a correspondent for *Izvestia* while Freeman and Durant worked for *Tass*. They replied in kind.[12] Though carried out in private, this exchange was a harbinger of things to come. In the future Max would repeatedly have his character attacked for political reasons, especially when he was right. This tactic worked partly because in the Red Decade liberal readers had no desire to know the truth about Soviet Russia, partly because liberal magazine editors would not print Eastman, or if they did, stacked the cards against him. Old liberals such as Villard believed that in a free market good ideas would drive out the bad. Villard's successor, Freda Kirchwey, and other totalitarian liberals of the thirties preferred to play it safe. They rigged the market to insure that bad ideas, such as Eastman's, would fail.

Max kept on fighting for a long time just the same. By 1928 the Soviet opposition was down to about a thousand members. The leaders were mostly in jail or exile. Scruples about party unity, hopes that Stalin would hang himself, the possibility of new alliances, of rousing the masses, were all gone. Having nothing more to lose, the left opposition asked Eastman to publish its program and related documents. Despite the previous betrayals, Max agreed, translating and editing them into a book called *The Real Situation in Russia*. Max was still faithful to the truth about Soviet Russia, and to Trotsky inasmuch as he embodied it. Max would spend countless hours translating and publicizing

Trotsky's work, earning in return little money and less gratitude. Trotsky sent him a letter of apology for disowning *Since Lenin Died.* That was about all. Though he did not realize it, this was to Eastman's advantage. Owing Trotsky nothing, he felt no compulsion to join the Trotskyist movement, thus retaining his freedom of action.

Max's introduction to *The Real Situation in Russia* shows that he had as yet no quarrel with the opposition. Trotsky and his followers still stood for "scientific thinking." The enemies of progress continued to be NEPmen (tolerated small businessmen), Kulaks (successful peasants), and the state bureaucracy. The Stalinists were political gangsters who used revolutionary language to conceal reactionary acts. As in America, Max pointed out, everything deplorable was wrapped in the national flag and justified in the name of liberty and democracy. Stalin had created a new, or as Eastman said, "artificial," class of bureaucrats loyal not to Marxism or Leninism but to Stalin and their own privileges. These facts had to be told even if nobody was listening:

> The world-wide vulgarization of Marxism, its transformation into a system of catch-words for keeping up political lies and official optimisms, holding the bottoms of bureaucrats in their firm seats, and covering up from the masses of mankind the real truth of history and their future will soon be complete. No man of intellectual ardor and integrity can reconcile himself to this process of debasement.[13]

The book inspired another attack by Albert Rhys Williams, this time in public. Like so many American Stalinists, Williams has been forgotten by history. Once a minister in a working class section of Boston, he had turned to journalism and was in Petrograd when the October Revolution took place. The result was a firsthand account, *Through the Russian Revolution* (1921), and several other books on Soviet affairs. Communism replaced the church in his affections, and Williams spent the balance of his life lying about Russia with great conviction. Williams began his review of *The Real Situation in Russia* with this statement: "Fundamental to any understanding of the real situation in Russia is the fact that Communist Party policies are not determined by a few score leaders, but by the hundreds of thousands of members."[14] Having with his pen restored party democracy, Williams then discussed the views of twenty communist party members he knew intimately from having lived in their small town on the Volga for fourteen months. They rejected the left opposition because it was unsympathetic to peasants, said Williams, which was true. A program imposed on the peasants was out of the question because it would mean "the army in the villages, sabotage and hatred of the Communist regime. It would mean the dissipation of loyalty and confidence built up by seven years of tireless labor."[15] This was true also, as forced collectivization would soon make evident. After dismissing Trotsky for wanting what Stalin was actually to obtain, Williams reached the heart of his argument. If conditions in Soviet Russia were as bad as Trotsky and Eastman claimed, Russian Communists "have been hoodwinked and tricked . . . or craven, cowering, and browbeaten, they lack ordinary backbone and courage to rise up in protest. . . . The party that wrought the greatest revolution in history, the party that fought through a decade of war, famine, blockade, now become a crowd of dupes or cowards! Is it possible that anyone believes that this is the real situation in Russia?"[16] Though this was the real situation in Russia, Williams was correct: no one believed it.

Max did not let this nonsense go by. In a letter to the *Nation* he said there was not and never had been any democracy in the Bolshevik party because Lenin was against it. Anyway, the revolutionary party Williams admired no longer existed. According to *Pravda* old Bolsheviks constituted only 1.4 per cent of the Russian Communist party in 1927. Williams countered that he knew better than Eastman because of having spent five years listening to Russian peasants while Eastman was living it up in France and Greenwich Village. Eastman only became an oppositionist because he was overcome with greed, Williams charged, greatly exaggerating the willingness of capitalists to pay for left-wing criticisms of Soviet Russia. Now feeling rather put upon (he scrawled "Oh Hell" across Eastman's letter of January 26, 1929, asking for more space), Villard allowed Eastman the last word. In his final statement Max went over familiar ground before ending with a rather technical discussion of the opposition platform that most *Nation* readers must have found incomprehensible.[17]

Eastman's problem was that Stalin was beginning to enjoy the favor of Communists and non-Communists alike. Thus the *New York Herald Tribune* reviewer compared Trotsky's *The Real Situation* with a recent work by Stalin on Leninism and came down on Stalin's side. Trotsky was shrill and defensive, Stalin the responsible man of affairs. Unlike Trotsky, Stalin "does seem to show a certain reasonableness called for in Russia's present stage and lacking in Trotzky's fiery protests." Stalin seemed milder, too. Trotsky only objected to terror when it was used against him and seemed determined, so the reviewer thought, to make it

> a more or less normal and permanent political weapon as long as any considerable portion of humanity thinks differently from him. Isn't it possible that after all these years of intense preoccupation with theories which, after all, a very considerable portion of humanity does not accept, this brilliant, if somewhat erratic, mind has gone just a bit "cuckoo?" What sort of a world, actually, does he picture in his own mind, or what have Russians and the rest of us to look forward to, if his expressed theories are literally carried out? Must Russia look forward to a government of materialistic scholasticism tempered by assassination as a perpetual thing?[18]

The *New York Times* reviewer did not think Trotsky had lost his marbles but otherwise agreed with this. J. B. S. Hardman in the *New Republic* had no preference for one leader over another. He did take the general view that having employed terror himself Trotsky was on weak ground in protesting Stalin's use of it.[19]

The Real Situation in Russia was not completely without effect. It helped split the American Communist party. Max Shachtman read the book and had his fears confirmed. He, Jim Cannon, and other left Communists were soon expelled from the party after hearings during which the manager of the party bookstore testified that Shachtman had ordered a copy of the offending work from him. Shachtman and Cannon then visited Max, raising his hopes. He was no longer the only oppositionist in America. Better still, Trotsky's new partisans were "real party people" who, Shachtman recalled many years later, "might have an influence over the Communist party militants such as he could never hope to exercise."[20] Eastman turned over his share of the royalties from *The Real Situation* to them. It amounted to only a few hundred dollars but, as they were penniless, was "most welcome."

This was encouraging but did not shake the prevalent view of Stalin as the more reasonable and desirable Russian leader. Nor could Max and Trotsky's other defenders keep Stalin from getting credit for what seemed attractive in Russia. People kept coming back with good news, including even John Dewey, as shown by his book *Impressions of Soviet Russia* (1929). On visiting the Soviet Union in 1928, Dewey saw Leningrad teeming with energy. The streets were safe, the museums full of peasants. Soviet education was exciting. Dewey didn't like the Comintern and its policies, but thought Russia was the most interesting experiment in the world. Who was to be believed, the losers in a power struggle or the Deweys, Williams, Freemans, and others who announced the birth of a nobler and more humane future? To ask the question is to answer it.

While radicals faulted Max for going too far in his criticism of Soviet Russia, his real error was in stopping short. He dwelt too much on the left opposition, too little on oppressed non-Communists, who were both more numerous and more innocent. The opposition did, after all, try to have Stalin removed. Most victims were not threats to the regime at all. A clue to later events was the Shakhty trial in 1928. As purges go it wasn't much, having only fifty-three defendants and fifty-six witnesses. But it was the first important show trial of the Stalin era and received much publicity. The charge was that a group of engineers in the Donetz coal basin had sabotaged production. No evidence was introduced against them, and no one seems to have found this surprising. Key defendants had been broken in advance and confessed as required. Solzhenitsyn says of this trial:

> On the threshold of the classless society, we were at last capable of realizing *the conflictless trial*—a reflection of the absence of inner conflict in our social structure—in which not only the judge and the prosecutor but also the defense lawyers and the defendants themselves would strive collectively to achieve their common purpose.[21]

The trial lasted from May 18 to July 15, 1928, and was, according to Eugene Lyons who covered it, a "Roman Circus." Spontaneous demonstrations of workers and peasants took place regularly, during which justice, that is to say death to the defendants, was called for. The prosecutor was Max's brother-in-law, "Krylenko the man-hunter" Lyons called him. It strained "one's nerves and credulity watching men writhe under Krylenko's whip."[22] Louise Bryant, who had seen Krylenko at work in happier days, said he had the "ardour of 'Bill' Sunday." He was given more credit than any other man for turning the Russian army red. She herself once saw him win over an entire armored car regiment with one speech. Though her aim was to glorify the Bolsheviks, Bryant could not keep herself from saying the truth about Krylenko. "He is a violent little person," she wrote.[23] Walter Duranty thought Krylenko was one of the greatest speakers he had ever heard: "in Krylenko there is terrific passion, but it is restrained. He glows incandescent, but it is with a cold flame. He is a bewildering compact of fire and ice."[24] As usual Duranty worked both sides of the street before ending up on Stalin's. On the one hand, the only evidence in the trial was the testimony of "self-confessed scoundrels." On the other, Soviet prosecutors made a good case even so. The *Nation* congratulated Duranty for his shifty reporting, agreeing that many of the accused must have been guilty. Anyway, it was a test of strength. Failure to convict, the *Nation* wrote innocently as if such a thing were possible, would have weakened government control of basic industries: "That so many [defendants] were let off with moderate sentences is to the credit of the judge and the public defender. If some were unjustly convicted, it is not to be wondered at. No German accused of espionage in America in wartime ever faced a more hostile public or a more bitter prosecution."[25] In other words, the defendants were probably guilty, but even if innocent they had to be convicted for the sake of building socialism. And, in any case, American justice was equally bad. This was the voice of the Popular Front before there was a Popular Front. Max seems to have ignored the Shakhty trial, probably because no Communists were indicted. Like other leftists, he was short-sighted. It would not take Stalin long to prove that what worked against non-Communists would work as well against the faithful.

*   *   *

While defending Trotsky, Eastman was also trying to influence him. He knew Trotsky wouldn't agree with *The Science of Revolution,* but still hoped to make some kind of impression. He wanted Trotsky to understand that "my attempt was to make a *revolutionary* revision of" Marxism. Eastman's aim was not simply to reject or replace Marx, but only "to clear out of this revolutionary science the last vestiges of the influence of Marx's bourgeois philosophy teacher. It is the only form in which Marxism will ever take root in the Anglo-Saxon intelligence—of that I feel sure."[26]

Trotsky was not interested in the Anglo-Saxon intelligence and refused to look at Eastman's book. Eastman took issue with his reasoning: "You say that you don't know any case in the last 30 years in which anyone has opposed the philosophy of dialectical materialism without going to ruin politically as a revolutionist. The answer to that is that only one (genetic) science has come into being since Marxism reached its full development, and that is psychology."[27] Eastman did not consider himself a backslider and implored Trotsky not to class him with Boris Souvarine, who was so far to the right, Max admitted, that he believed the cure to what ailed Russia was democracy!

Eastman insisted that determinism was not a scientific doctrine but an article of faith. This got him nowhere, for Trotsky believed that his own life showed it to be true. Max Shachtman once raised this issue with Trotsky, telling him that Eastman believed Marx had used "condition" and "determine" interchangeably, though they had different meanings. Certain conditions made socialism possible without guaranteeing its success. Trotsky replied that the revolution took place, as Marx had predicted, because "the point was reached where, of all the conditions for the socialist revolution created by capitalism, all of those necessary for the revolution were present. In other words, possibility turned into necessity, which is precisely what happens and must happen when *all* the conditions are at hand." One of those conditions was the presence of a trained and dedicated revolutionary like himself. "I am part of that inevitability," Trotsky said to Shachtman, "of that inevitable process."[28] There was no need for Trotsky to read Eastman. Unlike Trotsky, Max was not inevitable.

*   *   *

Max had little hope of changing Trotsky's mind, and came to expect shabby treatment from him. He disliked Trotsky as a person, serving the cause rather than the man. Young Sidney Hook, who attacked *The Science of Revolution* furiously, was another matter. It's difficult to tell why Hook set upon Eastman in the *Modern Quarterly*. He too was a Dewey student and therefore, perhaps, a rival sibling. Like Eastman, he had doubts about Marx, which, again like Eastman, he tried to ease by assertions of loyalty. For whatever reasons, he began his review by saying that Eastman had "bungled a great theme."[29] Eastman was philistine, facile, scholastic, anti-philosophical, journalistic, and a disciple of Freud whose theories "represent the crassest violation of scientific method." Then things got nasty. Eastman accused Hook of dishonesty.[30] Hook replied that Eastman was trying to deceive readers of the *Modern Quarterly* and showed how, in seeking to revise Marx, Eastman had in fact eliminated him. After jabs at Eastman's weak sense of logic and "characteristic bad taste," Hook declared that his own morals "need no defense against a man who has been found guilty time and again of systematically abusing texts and contexts to save his own face and discredit others."[31] Though the charge was false, the emotions were certainly genuine.

When not defaming each other, Hook and Eastman had much to say, but the arguments of both were flawed. Eastman did not understand revolutions or what was required to stage them. He wanted Marx to be as sensible as himself. Lewis Mumford disagreed. Commenting on the exchange he said Eastman was "badly muddled":

> What creates or at all events formulates the "goal of desire," which he acknowledges? surely not science but philosophy. And who puts this goal of desire before society? Not the engineer, but the prophet, whether as philosopher, as poet, as artist. The notion that the scientist and the engineer are capable of formulating a new social order is fantastic.[32]

Instrumentalism and revolution were incompatible. John Dewey could not be used to overthrow society; Karl Marx could not be made practical and up to date.

Like Eastman, Hook wanted to pragmatize Marx. His problem was that he wished also to save the dialectic, confusing, as John Diggins has said, objective reality with his personal desire. Hook was better at philosophy than Eastman, but Max had one big advantage. To him "history would remain a problem for which philosophy offered no solution."[33] Mankind would not save itself by reading Marx.

*   *   *

There was more to Eastman's life in the twenties than being rejected by Trotsky and mugged by Sidney Hook. He still reviewed poetry, winning the gratitude of Edna Millay for being among the few who liked her book of verse, *Buck in the Snow*.[34] Arturo Giovannitti remained friendly. He sent Eastman a long letter in 1929 telling Max that "I've always claimed—and I think I once wrote—that you were the re-embodiment of Lorenzo il Magnifico with less business ability, a bit more charm, and . . . immensely more passion . . . and that therefore you could start a new renaissance, and possibly a better one, all things being equal, whenever you wanted to."[35] There were moments when a detente with the Communists seemed possible. Once in 1929 Eliena ran into Joe Freeman on the street, and he was extremely warm, saying, in her words, that but for this "unfortunate situation in which you and

Trotsky got yourselves you would be now the center of the new intellectual movement of America, the God Almighty yourself of all the thinking radical youth."[36] After studying the first Five Year Plan Max was briefly "full of excitement about 'building socialism' in Russia. . . . I think this restored hope is one of the main reasons why I'm speaking so much better. I feel so much surer that I am right—that I was right all along. It is not so hard to walk out on a platform where these people haven't seen me for 8 or 10 years, and say 'Well, I told you so!—and here are the figures.' "[37]

Periods of optimism had to be short-lived. Conditions in Russia were going from bad to worse. Having balked at lesser evils in the 1920s, Max could not ignore the greater ones to come. He had been lonely when few cared about Soviet affairs. He would be lonelier still in the 1930s when Russia became fashionable.

* * *

Max began the thirties by ruining himself as a critic. He had started doing so as early as 1929 when he published an attack on modernist literature called "The Cult of Unintelligibility." Probably most of the world agreed with him that modernist writing was hard to understand. Millions agreed further that this was reprehensible. Those whose opinion mattered most did not. Critics, avant-garde writers, the best professors of literature were laboring to gain a high place for Yeats, Eliot, and the other masters of modernism. After years of struggle against philistines they had no patience for the negative views expressed in Eastman's book *The Literary Mind* (1931). He also annoyed them by attacking under a flag marked "science." Here he described science not as revolution, and sometimes not even psychology, but as "the persistent and skilled use of the mind and the stores of human knowledge about any problem."[38] This was baffling. Most people thought of science as having something to do with exact measurements, controls, tests, means of verification. If science was to mean only the intelligent application of knowledge, then not just Max but all the critics attacked in his book, from T. S. Eliot to Irving Babbitt, were scientists too, which was ridiculous.

Having destroyed science by accident, he set about wrecking philosophy by design. Max had never liked it because, he wrote, from a scientific standpoint philosophy "consists of jumping to conclusions." Dewey's work was no exception. His "tendency toward a philosophy of pragmatism is, like others of its kind, a tendency to jump to conclusions where no conclusion has been reached, and where the conclusion when it is reached will probably be less neat and simple than the one jumped to." Then came the thesis of Max's book: "You might sum it up by saying that science, having displaced magic and religion and abstract philosophy as a source of help and guidance, is now successfully attacking literature.' "[39] In the first nine pages of *The Literary Mind* Eastman managed to alienate almost every critic. Claiming that his opinions were scientific offended those few, such as I. A. Richards, who really were applying science to literature. Insisting that science had replaced literature as a source of moral authority antagonized many of the rest.

Worse was to follow. Max wanted to knock down what he regarded as the leading schools of criticism. One group were the modernists, including Tate, Pound, Eliot, Robert Graves, and Edith Sitwell, whom Max called neo-classicists. The other was humanism, an academic school of criticism led by Professors Irving Babbitt and Paul Elmer Moore. It was elitist, anti-Romantic, conservative, at war with the false gods of vulgar materialism, equalitarianism, and humanitarianism. Max condemned both groups in the same terms: "They are fighting for the right of literary men to talk loosely and yet be taken seriously in a scientific age."[40] Neo-classicists failed to communicate as a matter of principle. E.E. Cummings was unscientific. Joyce wasted his talent by being obscure. Gertrude Stein was awful. Edith Sitwell's poems had meaningless titles. Modernists had a few saving graces. They were not preachy or didactic. They offered in each poem "a moment of life, a rare, perfect, or intense moment," what Max called the "tendency toward pure poetry." This was good, but not good enough.

Max's literary dogmatism made him vulnerable to teasing, or at least the suspicion of it. Once he was invited to tea by James Joyce, who praised Max's essay "The Cult of Unintelligibility" even though he was a target of it. This was only just, Max seemed to feel. But he was startled when Joyce told him that there were the names of 500 rivers woven into "Anna Livia Plurabelle," a chapter of *Finnegans Wake*. Max could only find three-and-a-half, giving rise to fears that Joyce was putting him on. This seems likely, for it's hard to imagine him admiring Max's essay. Yet Joyce's claim was literally true. One scholar says that the chapter actually contains over 800 river names, thanks to the diligence of "colleagues, amanuenses, a grandchild, and houseguests; anyone who could feed the obsession."[41]

Max's obsession was clarity; hence his war on modernism. But he could fall short of it, too, especially when attacking members of the avant-garde. In *The Literary Mind* he first indicts them for not communicating, then he suggests they do, though badly. Next the problem becomes their failure to interpret. What they are supposed to interpret is far from evident, since he has already assigned all the big topics to science. To Max discourse fell into one of two categories: the scientific, which was concerned with life, and the poetic which wasn't. In his view poets had been "compelled to realize that as poets they don't know anything about life. That is not their business."[42] What their business was is not easy to determine. "Pure poetry is the pure effort to heighten consciousness; it is poetry spoken when a practical person would have nothing at all to say." Then again, "poetry represents the world as man discovers it and will always understand it, science as he must view it in order to make it over as he would like to have it."[43] The reader would never know that Max yearned to be another Homer or Milton. Having failed in this, he downgraded the competition. Max was utterly sincere. The flavor of sour grapes comes through even so.

He was as didactic about critics as about poets. There were no great critics any longer; no one had the stature of Samuel Johnson and Matthew Arnold. Living critics talked a lot but had little to say because social scientists monopolized their subjects. They pretended to be generalists but were only unskilled practitioners of loose talk and a "drag upon our civilization." Luckily salvation was at hand if only literary criticism became a branch of psychology, "the science which can alone define literature and explain its forms and mechanism in the more immediate relations in which they arise."[44]

The reviews were better than one might guess. Modernism alarmed all sorts of people. Max offered them relief. As an English reviewer put it, "Mr. Eastman justifies the view of the ordinary reader who is disturbed by modernist work and feels vaguely, as in crossword puzzles, that there's a catch in it."[45] Bernard Berenson agreed with Max, as did H.G. Wells and Sinclair Lewis, who hailed the book as a "swell corrective to the innumerable and pettily important fuzzy minded of today."[46] Even Clive Bell, a member of Virginia Woolf's Bloomsbury circle, wrote Max (from Bloomsbury) to say how much he "enjoyed and admired *The Literary Mind.*" It was "the best first aid for commencing authors . . . that has appeared in English in my time."[47] Haakon Chevalier, an unknown student of literature who became famous later as the contact man who tried to bring Robert Oppenheimer and Soviet Intelligence together, was enraptured. He wrote Eastman that *The Literary Mind* was "undoubtedly destined to mark a turning-point" of some kind. He confessed that his forthcoming study of Anatole France would have been a better book had he read Eastman's first.[48] Santayana was cool as usual. A former professor, he disapproved of Max's charge that the opinions of professors were designed to promote job security.[49]

Some readers liked Eastman's style, though not his principal ideas. An English reviewer was typical: "What thundering flashing hoofs, what devastating lance-thrusts, what a dust-up? To all the literary-minded who enjoy a one man show I recommend Mr. Eastman's first three chapters." Henry Hazlitt thought the book oversimplified, but "Mr. Eastman's brilliant polemics delight me immensely."[50] John Chamberlain, later a close political ally, wrote that *The Literary Mind* was an intelligent book, "but it is intelligent on almost every subject under the sun except the nature and purposes of literature." Like most critics he objected to Eastman's use of science: "What Mr. Eastman has done is to confuse the advance of science upon the mind of the reading public with the advance of science upon the territory occupied by literature itself." To Chamberlain, literature "has not given way to science; it has simply changed with science, for the poet is simply the reflected glory of his particular world."[51]

I. A. Richards, the English psychologist and critic, enjoyed Max's writing to a point: "What a pleasure it is to read a man who so evidently enjoys what he is doing, a writer with a swift feline grace of movement and at least the appearance of a punch." Even so, "Mr. Eastman is not a man of science; he is as much a man-of-letters, and suffers as much from the 'literary mind', as any of his opponents." Richard saw Eastman as a politician, "sadly divided in his loyalties to the Revolution and to a Science which he invokes distantly without practicing its discipline."[52] This hit the mark. So did Leon Whipple, writing in the *Survey* that Eastman's "science is that of the amateur who claims far more than any professional ever would. He overlooks the fact that science seems busily engaged in enlarging our ignorance, and so widening the field for literature which, as he says, has a perfect right to make guesses about the unknown."[53] The *New Yorker* rebuked Max for betraying his craft: "Let me say that you, a poet—you ought to be ashamed of yourself."[54]

These mixed reviews were deceptive. Over time critical opinions hardened. Frederick J. Hoffman writing in the 1950s expressed the official view that Eastman believed poetry "had lost its real function and should be banished from serious consideration."[55] This was dead wrong, but only a close student of Max's writings could know better, and in the fifties there were none. Another academician declared that Max's "philistine tastes would hardly allow him to entertain the idea of poetic complexity." To him Eastman's work was "but a parody of serious theorizing in this direction."[56] In a cranky attack on modernism Van Wyck Brooks grouped Eastman with other American writers who

> often expressed their contempt for writers, but seldom failed in respect for men of science; and, while he also respected science, he was often puzzled by the scorn that writers felt for their own trade. Max Eastman had written a book, *The Literary Mind,* for the sole purpose, its seemed, of expressing this scorn, while he could not say enough in praise of science.[57]

An essay of Allen Tate's, first published in 1940, says that Eastman "is a debater, not a critic, and he is plausible, because, like the toothpaste manufacturer, he offers his product in the name of science."[58] Lower than this Max could not fall.

In his memoirs, published more than three decades after *The Literary Mind,* Eastman stood by everything he had said in the book and betrayed no sense of why it was so disliked by the "vanguard literati." He took comfort from the applause he always got from scientists when writing in this vein, and dismissed his critics whom, it is clear, he had not read carefully. They had much to teach him, especially Alfred Kazin. *On Native Grounds,* Kazin's influential survey of contemporary American literature, put *The Literary Mind* in context:

> Eastman spoke not as a trained scientist, but as a lay brother in the scientific priesthood; in fact, as a literary critic speaking for the enemy. He "proved" nothing that had not been proved before, and he could not convince literary men jealous of their honor, not to say the vested interests of their profession. But his attack—in itself particularly unworthy of him and significantly a critic's *tour de force* full of the harsh wit and irascible intensity that were to be so characteristic of a new age of critical polemic—had a topical significance. By bringing to a head a general suspicion of the validity of criticism, Eastman leveled his attack upon its studies at a time when criticism had come to think of itself as a mediator between two worlds, as an exercise of intelligence that could help bring a new society into being.[59]

The book gave offense because it was a literary criticism posing as science, and because it attacked literary criticism as a serious and worthwhile endeavor just when critics had become most ambitious. Eastman left room for poetry in his scheme of things. He even allowed modernism a small claim to worth. But for literary criticism as then practiced (except by Richards) he had absolutely no use. This was unforgivable in an age of criticism, and Eastman was not forgiven for turning on his own kind, which they were however much he tried to disown them.

* * *

Eastman took a final shot at literature in 1934. *Art and the Life of Action* is a collection of speeches and essays, including perhaps the best single review he ever did, "Bull in the Afternoon," about which more later. In the title essay Max tried once again to pull his ideas on art and propaganda together. The result is more successful than *The Literary Mind* in that it is more of a piece. Yet so far as ideas go, the essay does not improve on the original except in one respect. When Eastman published *The Literary Mind,* there was no such thing as a Marxist criticism in America. In the three years since, intellectuals had developed a considerable interest both in Marxism and the Soviet approch to culture. *Art and the Life of Action* was most timely when it addressed these concerns.

Eastman felt that Communists and Fascists agreed that propaganda was the only function of art. The *New Masses* had recently sneered at the poet Archibald MacLeish for saying that in a free society poetry might be enjoyed for its own sake. To Eastman this was no more satisfactory than the opposite view, that art existed purely for its own sake. By insisting that all art be propaganda, the Soviets betrayed their ignorance of the theories of Marx and Lenin, let alone the scientific method. "It is for this reason . . . that the 'fellow travelers' of the revolution have been its only supreme artists. Every critic in Russia, so far as I know, concedes this fact but none draws the inference from it. Art is of its very nature the fellow traveler of a practical enterprise, and the more scientific the enterprise the more independent is the behavior of this traveller." [60]

Communists failed to distinguish between what had to be changed and what couldn't be. Thus religion and education were certainly alterable, but the multiplication table and the octave were best left alone. "If, however, you have not learned to call a purpose a purpose and a fact a fact, but think it is necessary to believe that something called the 'dialectic essence' of human life is engaged in, and consists of, a division into classes and a conflict between them, carrying with it the accomplishment of your purpose as a necessary result, then the changes entailed must, theoretically at least, extend to all important items of that life."[61] This was Soviet doctrine, and it led to such official statements as "in a class society there can be no neutral art" and Bukharin's claim to have discerned a "proletarian class approach to mathematics."

Eastman held that the "defining function of the artist is to cherish consciousness." Doing so was not incompatible with service to a cause. In fact much great art, he believed, didn't begin as such but was meant to serve other purposes. An example was Boardman Robinson, "whose political drawings in the old *Masses* and the *Liberator* were as fine as any graphic art in this country, but whose mural paintings, preoccupied with being rhythmic and harmonious, are less compelling even in harmony and rhythm."[62] Eastman was sure that art tended toward "lusciousness and rhetoric" when it consciously set out to be pure. It was best when absorbed with human experience. The revolution was a boon to artists only in the sense that it was great experience, hence potentially the stuff of great art. On the other hand, in the Russian revolution poetry in relation to other forms of literature declined in output by two-thirds, showing the demands made upon art by action. Despite this Eastman did not agree with Trotsky that the state should confer special advantages on artists. They must be entirely independent (except for counter-revolutionaries) if they are to do their best.

Because less ambitious than *The Literary Mind,* and surely also because Max's basic ideas were now familiar, *Art and the Life of Action* was not as broadly reviewed as its predecessor. It got good notices all the same. Selden Rodman, co-editor of *Common Sense,* an independent liberal monthly, thought the title essay showed Eastman to have a "truly human and embracing evaluation of life," even though it offended both Left and Right and so would not be widely appreciated except by posterity. Rodman was a better editor than prophet. V. F. Calverton, who edited the *Modern Monthly,* Eastman's most frequently used outlet in the thirties, called the book Max's finest and Max himself the "best essayist in America today." Ernest Sutherland Bates agreed, praising four of Max's pieces as among "the best American essays ever written." Henry Seidel Canby, editor of the *Saturday Review,* was even more pleased than usual: "I cannot do justice in a review to the acute reason-

Max Eastman Addressing a Protest Meeting in Union Square in 1912
Courtesy of the New York Public Library Picture Collection

Max Eastman in 1915
Courtesy of the New York Public Library Picture Collection

Max Eastman in 1939
Courtesy of the New York Public Library
Picture Collection

Max and Eliena Eastman in 1948
Wide World Photos, Inc.

Max Eastman in 1960
Courtesy of the New York Public Library Picture Collection

The Freedom of the Press
drawn by Art Young, December 1912

" 'I gorry, I'm tired!"
"There you go! YOU'RE tired! Here I be a-standin' over a hot stove all day,
an' you wurkin' in a nice cool sewer!"
drawn by Art Young, May 1913

Splinter Beach
drawn by George Bellows, July 1913

Army Medical Examiner: "At last a perfect soldier!"
drawn by Robert Minor, July 1916

Come on in, America, the Blood's Fine!
drawn by R. Kempf, June 1917

ing and vigorous imagery of this short but important contribution to straight thinking in the esthetic murk of this day. For those oppressed by the mystical, unscientific thinking of fascist and communist dictatorships more interested in the means than in the ends of living, it is a sharp sword stroke which cuts out the heart of argument." Santayana was almost complimentary: "I have devoured your little book almost at one sitting, and found it, I won't say the best of oats, but a most palatable and fresh and digestible kind of *hay*." [63] Pleasing this distinguished palate was not one of life's easier challenges. The wonder is that Max persisted.

Radical reviewers did not like being told that art and action could not be joined. Granville Hicks felt that in the end Max was defending art for its own sake. Hicks took an opposite view, agreeing with Bukharin and I. A. Richards that "a work of art changes us, and that it is necessary for the critic to ask what the change has been and whether it is desirable." [64] There was something to this. Max denied that he believed in art for art's sake but was unconvincing, as when denying that he was a pragmatist. Obed Brooks was another critic who thought Eastman's distinction between art and action was false. In evidence of this he cited Malraux's famous novel of revolution, *Man's Fate*. It was a great work not because it took a "correct," that is, pro-Communist view of the Chinese civil war of the 1920s, but because it prepared readers for action by increasing in them "the consciousness and necessities that Malraux had felt in the struggle he describes." [65] Babette Deutsch shared the general feeling that art and action were compatible, chiding Max for repeating himself. Eastman was fluent and learned, and it was a pity that "a lively intelligence should be wasted on matters of slight import and on a question to which the same intelligence has already applied itself quite thoroughly." [66]

Max's dogmatism and old-fashioned tastes ruined his reputation as a literary critic. His elevation of science at the expense of letters was fatal to *The Literary Mind. Art and the Life of Action* perished on account of his tiresome refusal to allow them anything in common. This mechanism had saved Max in Russia, armoring him against Soviet cant. But though it served no real purpose now, he clung to it anyway. Max could change political positions, though seldom and with great difficulty. His basic ideas on art and life were immutable. The cost to Eastman was heavy. His experience, his knowledge of Marxism and the Russian language made him better equipped than anyone in America to refute the claims of Marxist critics. In *Artists in Uniform,* as we shall see, he had already exposed the poisonous effect of Stalinism on Russian literature. Marxist criticism and Stalinist letters were his strong cards, but he played them badly. His comments on the one were brief and buried in an unpopular essay. He did not follow up on *Artists in Uniform.* Max could have been a star of left-wing cultural investigative reporting, the I. F. Stone of this field, which he had practically invented. Instead he gave his obsessions free rein, recklessly ignoring the consequences. Physically Max was self-protective and lived to a ripe old age. Professionally he could not keep himself from courting disaster.

CHAPTER EIGHT

The Red Decade Begins

1930–1934

In the old days Max had been famous and admired by leftists. They thought him a hero for risking prison and the wrath of mobs. In the thirties he would be infamous and disliked, though even more heroic. Then he had been borne up by praise and sustained by fellowship. Now he would stand alone, telling truths few wished to hear.

Max was still writing poetry. In 1931 he published *Kinds of Love,* a volume that included his most ambitious work to date, "Swamp Maple," which ran to sixty stanzas. It got good notices in the papers. William Rose Benét hailed "Swamp Maple" as evidence that Eastman was becoming a better poet. Genevieve Taggard, bucking the party line for once, said it reminded her of Keats.[1] Politics remained his chief interest just the same. After his first exchange with Sidney Hook he summed up his position as follows:

> The crisis consists in this: that Marxism in so far as it is a practical science of proletarian revolution has survived the changes in human thinking introduced by Darwin, has survived the decline of the philosopher and the ascendency of the engineer, has been verified by the success of Lenin's policy and party in the Russian Revolution. But Marxism as a system of philosophic belief about the inevitable dialectical development of human history has been eaten away and destroyed by these three things.

This led, Max believed, to a double irony: "Marx and Engels believed they were abandoning all philosophy when they were only inventing a new one; Lenin believed he was adhering to theirs, when he was really achieving their ambition to abandon all philosophy." Now it was necessary for socialism to escape these delusions and see Bolshevism for what it was, Marxism stripped of philosophy and converted "into a hard-headed technique for changing the social world."[2]

This continued to irritate the faithful. Some, like Hook, thought Eastman was wrong; others, like Arthur Calhoun, an American social historian, that it didn't matter. To Calhoun the content of Marxism was unimportant. All he wanted was for people to believe in its inevitable triumph.[3] This indifference to truth, seldom acknowledged publicly, was Eastman's biggest obstacle. He could have proven Marx mistaken on fifty counts and still been brushed aside. To believers, the success of Bolshevism established the rightness of Marx, whatever his actual errors.

Eastman's relations with Trotsky did not improve. He was still acting as an unpaid literary agent, still translating Trotsky into English, especially the monumental *History of the Russian Revolution*.[4] These translations did much to enhance Trotsky's literary reputation, as even be realized.* In 1934 the Trotskyist *New International* reprinted the letter Trotsky had written praising Max after he went into exile. It described Max as a revolutionary "of the John Reed type . . . whose entire conduct is proof of his ideals and political disinterestedness."[5] Yet at the same time Trotsky felt it his duty to denounce Max's errors of doctrine. In 1933 he sent the *Militant* a communication attacking Eastman's ideas once again. Max wrote him privately to see if he wanted their professional relationship to continue, which he did. Max then answered Trotsky in kind with an article of self-defense.

Trotsky had written the *Militant* that Eastman's critique of Marxism "does not differ in any way from the other varieties of petty bourgeois revisionism, beginning with Bernsteinism. . . ." Praising

---

* Indeed one expert feels that this work, of which he disapproves, was mainly responsible for the cult of Trotsky among intellectuals. "The *History of the Russian Revolution*—in the limpid, lucid translation by Max Eastman, beautifully printed, illustrated and boxed— preceded the English language publication of most other significant revolutionary memoirs . . . by at least a dozen years and cast its tricky shadow well past the self-deceiving 1930's."

Anatole Shub, "Never in the Running," *New York Times Book Review* (November 6, 1977), p. 12.

Eastman's loyalty to the Russian Revolution and skill as a translator, he dismissed the "Croton variety of revisionism" as "vulgar empiricism."[6] So far as Max was concerned, this polemic made his case. Trotsky replied to arguments with slogans. He still had not read *The Science of Revolution,* as shown by his reference to Bernsteinism, which Eastman had spent a chapter exposing. Eastman could not understand why Marxists behaved as if the very notion of "theoretical progress were a reactionary idea." Trotsky was not scientific but papal. The more "crack-brained" Marxists were even worse, preferring exorcism to reasoned debate. Despite everything, Trotsky was worth protecting. After writing this, Max corresponded with everyone he knew who had influence, trying vainly to get Trotsky an American visa.[7]

Sidney Hook, too, was still attacking Eastman, though with more sophistication than Trotsky. In 1933 he reviewed Eastman's anthology, *Karl Marx's Capital and Other Writings.* Hook admitted that Eastman's modernization of Marx had never been refuted. This was only because official Communists in America were so backward. The Communist party's "unskilled intellectuals" were defending the "mechanical Marxism of the Second International" with its "monism, reductive materialism and fatal theory of inevitability."[8] Worse yet, they argued that truth was independent of experience. "Is it any wonder that Marxists of this stripe cannot answer Eastman except with vituperation?" Their failings obliged Hook to undertake the chore.

Eastman's error, said Hook, came when he identified the philosophy of the Second International with that of Marx and Engels. Had Eastman begun with the *Communist Manifesto* or Engels's *Principles of Communism,* he would have "avoided the queer procedure of appealing from Marx drunk; the Hegalian metaphysician—to Marx sober—the revolutionary realist."[9] Furthermore, Eastman was attempting to "make of Marxism *nothing* but the science of revolutionary engineering." This was both false and dangerous, for the social engineer might be a Lenin, and then again maybe a Hitler. Engineering metaphors also blurred the crucial distinction between the "dictatorship over the proletariat" and the "dictatorship of the proletariat." They suggested, in fact, a dictatorship of experts as in the engineer fascism of technocracy." And Hook asked the vital question: what did Eastman mean by science?

In answering Hook Eastman ducked this question, but admitted that social engineering could go either way—though he didn't see this

as altering his case: "That Mussolini made some use of the Marxian historic understanding and enormous use of Lenin's practical applications
of it, although in a contrary direction, is obvious. This only makes education, agitation, propaganda, organization on our side, more important. It makes metaphysical optimism more risky. There is a genuine
hazard in this struggle and every simple man feels it. Why should those
who pretend to be wise deny it."[10] The stern note here did not result
from Hookian abuse. Hook's review was temperate, unlike earlier
blasts. But he had defended the dialectic again. This proved Hook was
still pushing an "animistic religion," which could not be allowed.

Despite a relatively promising start, the dialogue soon collapsed as
before. For obscure reasons Hook took Eastman's reply personally and
announced that "further discussion with Eastman about Marx is hopeless."[11] Eastman countered that Hook had plagiarized ten of his ideas
and then savaged the book they were stolen from. Hook denied everything and charged Eastman with misusing evidence. False gestures of
reconciliation had been made, Hook and Eastman agreed, differing
only in who was responsible.[12] V. F. Calverton, whose magazine was the
battleground, finally refused to print any more insults. He took the
blame for trying to bring the two together, having innocently given
each the impression that the other was trying to make up. There was
talk of arranging a debate between Hook and Eastman. Nothing came
of it, to John Dewey's relief. He had agreed to preside but feared a
bloodbath.[13]

Eastman was not one to let go easily. In 1933 Hook published
Toward the Understanding of Karl Marx, which Eastman attacked twice,
first in a review, then in *Art and the Life of Action.* Here Eastman poked
fun at Hook for trying to Deweyize Marx; to create, Eastman said, a
philosophy of "dialectical pragmatism." Both Marx and Dewey wanted
theoretical knowledge applied to concrete problems. This enabled
Hook to pretend that dialectical materialism and pragmatism were
much the same. Eastman explained why this would not wash:

> The essential difference between them is this: Marx accomplished
> that unification of objective knowledge with program-of-action by
> reading his revolutionary program-of-action as a "dialectic necessity"
> into the objective processes of history. He was a philosopher in the
> complete old-fashioned animistic sense of the term—namely, that he
> engaged his mind to prove that the external world, however "mate-
> rial" he might feel obliged to call it, was engaged in realizing his

ideals. Dewey lives in an age dominated by skeptical methods of empirical science, an age in which philosophy in this old sense is sadly out of fashion. He cannot combine objective knowledge with program-of-action by the simple device of reading his program into the objective process. But he reaches the same attitude of mind by a more subtle scheme. He declares that knowledge itself, no matter how "objective" it may appear, is and can be nothing but program-of-action. "The effective working of an idea and its truth," he says, "are the same thing—this working being neither the cause nor the evidence of truth but its nature."[14]

As he saw it, Marxism and pragmatism had similar motives but different beliefs. An obvious one was that, according to Marx, the philosopher must know for certain that his program-of-action will be realized. The follower of Dewey regards this "quest for certainty" as a survival of barbarism. Eastman said that Hook wanting to make Marx into a Deweyite had to eliminate from Marxism "the very central pillar of its temple of faith, the belief in 'historic determinism.' " According to Eastman, this was accomplished simply by asserting that Marx did not mean that Communism was inevitable, only possible, something that people might help realize by believing in it. This was all wrong. Hook wished that Marx had not said communism was inevitable, and so persuaded himself that Marx hadn't, though he had.

This did not exhaust Eastman's feelings about Hook, for he ended the war with a final forty-seven page pamphlet that he brought out himself, using the imprint "Polemic Publishers." Despite this light touch, "The Last Stand of Dialectic Materialism: A Study of Sidney Hook's Marxism" was a deadly serious recital of Eastman's grievances against Hook.[15] Almost no one appears to have read it. It relieved Eastman's feelings anyway, the main object no doubt. Eastman was satisfied that he had won the debate. Alfred Kazin thought otherwise, chiefly because Hook was "the most devastating logician the world would ever see." Even so, he felt Hook was on shaky ground, despite his verbal skills. Kazin was sure that Hook found Marxism to be "acceptably scientific, logical, experimental and naturalistic because he could not uphold anything that was not scientific, logical, experimental, and naturalistic."[16]

In Dewey's opinion they were both right. Each proved his points by choosing what he liked in Marx and ignoring the rest. But Dewey rejected Eastman's claim to be the only scientific student of Marx: "I'll content myself with saying that you don't apply your sceptical power to 'science' you are rather naive about actual method, if I may say so without being thought to be anti-scientific. In spite of all your assertions, your own position is philosophical. . . ." Just so. Finally, Dewey said, Eastman gave himself away "when [you] talk about 'finding out what *the* truth is.' "[17] Dewey was on the mark again. Eastman wanted to be open-minded but kept lapsing into dogmatism. Having once reached a conclusion, his inclination was to keep it for life.

Theodore B. Brameld, an independent leftist, agreed with Dewey. Both Hook and Eastman were right on some things, wrong on others. They were alike in advocating "an experimental, naturalistic approach to social experience." Both believed in the class struggle and sided with the proletariat. They differed in that Eastman felt strict Marxism was a poor guide to the good society; Hook believed that "the more we follow Marx the surer we shall be of achieving our proletarian goal."[18] East-man was right to criticize Hook for mistakenly trying to portray the dialectic as a tentative, problem-solving method when Marx clearly regarded it as the prime law of history and a guarantee that the class struggle would end in victory for the workers. Yet Brameld could not understand why Eastman minimized what was experimental in Marx when elsewhere Eastman admitted that Marx anticipated a "social engi-neering attitude." Eastman correctly accused Hook of "drastic revision-ism." He was "wrong in minimizing a methodology which Hook, on the other hand, exaggerates." Hook's *Toward the Understanding of Karl Marx* "is a study in contradictions because of its effort to reconcile Marxian absolutism with experimentalism and yet award the latter victory." Eastman, by the same token, "to the extent that he lauds Lenin as the emancipated social scientist . . . wishes away as a bad dream Lenin's conscientious defense of dialectic materialism." Even so, Brameld pre-ferred Eastman, whose

> treatment of Marx, at least is fairer than Hook's; for Eastman, al-though he admits the presence of scientific elements in Marx, and al-though he does not deny that Marxian absolutism might have a cer-tain value, chooses to reject rather than to cloak Marxism in taste with his own experimental temper. Hook's acceptance of it perpetuates not only the experimental elements of Marxism but lends covert sup-port to a doctrine the influence of which, because its absolutism is ingrained in the system as a whole, must differ even though surrepti-tiously from what Hook himself would wish.[19]

This was not the common opinion. Most independent leftists preferred Hook at the time, and probably still do. Though Eastman was the best of the early critics of Marxism, he was always out of fashion. Hook defended dialectical materialism in the early thirties when others were struggling to believe in it, turning against it only when they did. He was in harmony with his peers and so got the credit. Years later Irving Howe praised Hook for leading "the major battle against Stalinism as a force within intellectual life," forgetting Eastman, who got there first.[20] When Max was right it was usually at the wrong time. He has not been forgiven for this either.

* * *

Eastman's writings on Russia were to meet a similar fate, but the failure here was more serious. Americans seldom cared deeply about Marxism, no matter what they said. Eastman was correct when he warned Trotsky that Marxism taken straight would have little appeal for Anglo-Saxons. Even when diluted, as by Eastman, it offended the national palate. What drew Americans to communism was not the theory but its actual practice in Soviet Russia. Though America was rich, millions were out of work. Russia, though poor, found jobs for everyone. The American economy lurched and staggered, while in Russia, so it was believed, efficient planning smoothed things out. Russia paid lip service to noble ideals, while in this country it was obvious that high-mindedness had little chance against greed and bigotry. Hoover, and for years even Roosevelt, ignored fascism. Stalin did something about it. Few intellectuals knew the truth about Russian communism, fewer still were willing to disclose it when they did. The small number who had personally experienced Soviet life tended to ignore or excuse its defects, thinking that by doing so they were helping build socialism, maybe even stopping Hitler.

Max knew this feeling. For years he worried that his criticisms would blind people to what was good in Russia. His lectures through the early thirties reflected his hopes for the USSR more than his fears of Stalinism. In aid of this he even employed the dubious strategy of trying to make Communism seem homey. "The Russian Soul and Bolshevism," a lecture he began giving in 1929, assured audiences that the Bolsheviks were just plain folks like you and me, except that they had destroyed capitalism, reformed prisons, upgraded education, enhanced family life, and collectivized agriculture. Otherwise there were no differences.

To Max nothing was more admirable about Communists than their treatment of religion. "Religion and the Bolsheviks" was Max's answer to a campaign of prayer against Communism organized by the Pope. He first gave the lecture at Carnegie Hall in 1930. As Max explained it, the Soviet policy toward religion was simple and scientific. Church wealth had been confiscated. Priests could not enter politics, teach, or discuss religion outside of churches. All artificial supports having been removed the churches were obliged to stand or fall on their merits. That so many people failed to welcome this challenge showed their want of faith. "They are afraid that neither God nor the belief in God will stand this test."[21] Religion would fail in Russia, and deservedly. It was unscientific, clouded the mind, weakened the character, encouraged hypocrisy, and made people irresponsible by allowing them to think that a divine power watched over the world, "steering to good ends whatever evil things may come to pass in it."[22] He did not acknowledge, and possibly did not know, that the competition for minds and hearts was far from equal. Religion was deprived of artificial supports but atheism was not. Behind it stood the GPU, a powerful inducement to clear thinking on the religious question.

No Communist was happier about the Five Year Plan and collective farming than Max. Collectivization was "the biggest news since the October Revolution."[23] He had always regarded peasants as the skeleton in the closet of Marxism. Nationalizing industry and urban property made sense to workers who owned very little. Nationalizing land went against everything that peasants had always lived for. Max understood that, needing peasant support, Communists had been forced to create new freeholds during and after the civil war. He regretted it just the same. Max was overjoyed when agriculture was socialized, wiping out this embarrassment. A great many peasants were wiped out, too, which Max was slower to recognize. These progressive steps, as he then thought, made Stalinism easier to bear. "The usurpation of Stalin is discouraging in a small way," he rationalized to audiences, "the fact that this usurpation has not yet shaken or undermined the economic foundations of the proletarian regime is encouraging in a larger way."[24]

As with the Shakhty trial, Eastman's will to believe survived the "Industrial Party Trial" of 1930. The defendants were all high-ranking experts in Soviet industry, including the head of the Supreme Council of the National Economy, which administered most important industries, and the vice-chairman of the State Planning Commission known as Gosplan. As in the Shakhty trial, the charge was conspiring with western powers, Russian émigrés, and dissidents to destroy the Soviet system. Krylenko was the chief prosecutor again, and as usual there was no documentary evidence. All indictments were based on absurd confessions in obedience to tradition. Although only eight men were indicted, anywhere from 2,000 to 7,000 prominent engineers and technologists were arrested out of a total of about 10,000 Soviet engineers with higher education working in large-scale industry at the time. The leaders of Russian technology, most of them trained before the revolution and known as the "old specialists" or the "bourgeois specialists," were purged.

Most of them were technocrats in the Veblen sense. They believed engineers should be socially responsible and involved in major policy decisions. Most opposed the Five Year Plan, the hastiest, most brutal, and ill-conceived parts of it at least. Most sympathized with the right opposition, hence Stalin's desire to crush them.[25] A transcript of the trial was published by the Soviets in 1931, though there is no indication that Max read it. If he had he would have seen the frame-up easily enough. Solzhenitsyn says of the engineers:

> They were damned if they did and damned if they didn't. If they went forward, it was wrong, and if they went backward, it was wrong too. If they hurried, they were hurrying for the purpose of wrecking. If they moved methodically, it meant wrecking by slowing down tempos. If they were painstaking in developing some branch of industry, it was intentional delay, sabotage. And if they indulged in capricious leaps, their intention was to produce an imbalance for the purpose of wrecking. Using capital for repairs, improvement, or capital readiness was tying up capital funds. And if they allowed equipment to be used until it broke down, it was a diversionary action.[26]

This event, often called the Ramzin trial after its chief victim, gave the lie to claims that Soviet Russia was governed by science and rationality. If Eastman missed the point, so did other well wishers. Louis Fischer in the *Nation* simply took for granted that the engineers (and the agronomists in a related case) were plotting to restore capitalism. The *New Republic* had already perfected the distortion machine which would serve it so well in the thirties. It did seem unlikely, the magazine

admitted before the trial, that engineers would conspire to launch a
revolt in connection with invasions by Rumania, Poland, and France.
On the other hand, Russia had been invaded before. Readers were advised to suspend judgment. Afterward the trial was hailed as model of
socialist justice. All the accused reeked with guilt. Western charges that
the confessions were false and obtained by torture had "broken down
by the sheer weight of [their] implausiblity." Westerners claimed that
fictitious counter-revolutionary plots were part of the "necessary myth
of the revolution," but there was as "good or better reason to believe
that the repudiation of such stories is part of the necessary myth of
capitalism as expressed in the press of the Western world."[27] The reasoning here seemed to be that as Westerners wanted to believe the
worst about Soviet Russia, the worst did not exist.

When the stomachs of Russian sympathizers became irritated, a
little of this baby food set them right. Not so with Max. By 1933 he was
finding the truth all but impossible to resist. He stopped giving his lecture on "The Russian Soul and Bolshevism" just when the rising interest in Soviet affairs was making it highly profitable. He scheduled at
least one speech defending the Soviets in 1934 but canceled it. Traces
of the old faith remained. In 1933 he wrote an article on Technocracy,
a popular movement of the day that wanted to apply engineering principles to social problems. Eastman identified Technocracy with Marxism and endorsed it on that basis.[28] The next year he wrote an important essay for the *Modern Monthly* tallying the gains and losses of
socialism in Russia. The two great evils remained bigotry and bureau-
cratization. It would be a disaster if they were transplanted to other cultures as necessary parts of the socialist revolution: "They belong to the
socialist revolution as it has developed in a backward country, indoc-
trinated with a veritable medieval theology, and under the leadership
of a man of limited vision and feeling, uncompromising only in the
grasp for power." To Max this explained but did not excuse the failures of socialism in Russia. It was a laboratory, and the experiment
would be decisive: "If the soviet culture as it developed did not bear
out in essential ways the hopes predicated upon it, I should be ready to
abandon the idea of improving human society by guiding a revolution
toward socialism."[29]

Luckily, he thought at the time, this drastic step was not required.
The Soviets had proved there could be initiative under socialism, dis-
pelling the old maxim that without the profit motive people would not

work. As evidence he cited the Five Year Plan, not knowing how limited its success was, the importance of police terror to it, or that the incentives employed were much the same as under capitalism, leading toward income disparities that would become, relatively speaking, quite as great. Max was still thrilled by collective farming, though not with the means used to obtain it. Collectivization proved there was a socialist solution to agricultural problems. The methods used, what Max described as "sheer administrative orders backed up with military invasions, gunfire and executions and the deportation of whole populations in the manner of Ghengis Khan," only showed that Stalin was the wrong person to have in charge.[30] Max was behind the times, though less so than American Communists and fellow travelers. Russia already enjoyed the defects of capitalism—poverty, discrimination, the exploitation of labor, maldistribution of incomes—and none of the advantages—wealth, high productivity, personal freedom, adaptability. In savagery and contempt for human life it had no equals. Yet because the Soviets abolished private property, started the Five Year Plan, collectivized agriculture, and made many empty promises, all was forgiven them by Western sympathizers.

These were becoming more numerous, giving rise to mixed feelings on Eastman's part. He welcomed the testimony of reformers (he personally owned no fewer than thirty-five books by them) who were constantly reporting back from Russia with good news. At the same time Max distrusted them. Too many were "so surprised to find themselves convinced by an experiment of what they had hitherto dismissed as crazy and disreputable fanaticism, that they are quite ready and eager to be crazy and disreputable in its service."[31] Police-state tactics and the cult of the infallible leader filled them with religious enthusiasm.

The Comintern was even worse. Litvinov had recently announced that Russia would give up the revolutionary struggle and join with capitalist states for security purposes, a change foreshadowing the Popular Front. The *New York Times* hailed this as "marvelous in the eyes of the rest of the world." To the contrary, Max insisted, it was yet another betrayal of the international working class for the sake of Russian national interests. Russia would do anything to protect its borders. Soon, he predicted, "it will become obvious to all cool heads that the slogan socialism in one country meant "sabotage the international revolution" and "strike-breaking" on a world scale, means collaboration with the

Chiang Kai-Sheks, means non-resistance to the Hitlers and war against those who would fight them, means fascism triumphant throughout the western world." It called for no great wisdom in 1939 to predict the Stalin-Hitler pact and the war it made inevitable. Max did so in 1934.

By now Max was much closer to anti-communism than he realized. He thought the moral of his long essay was as follows:

> It may seem difficult to those whose participation in the revolutionary movement is new, and who do not realize the part played here by critical thinking, to support and defend the Soviets and yet at the same time criticise the Stalin bureaucracy and reject its international leadership. It requires a certain emotional equilibrium. It is the only course left open, however, to a thoughtful revolutionary with the courage to face the facts.[32]

In this he erred. Critical support was the only course open to someone like Trotsky who had staked everything on the October Revolution. For independents there was another way, as Eastman soon discovered.

*　*　*

Artists in Uniform brought Max close to a final break with communism. It began as a series in the *Modern Monthly,* his only regular outlet and the only magazine open to independent, left-wing anti-Stalinists in the early thirties. It was the creation of V. F. Calverton (real name, George Goetz; his friends called him George), who founded the magazine as a quarterly in 1923 when he was twenty-three years old. Calverton was a very nice man with an indiscriminate appetite for the new and radical, which he often misunderstood. Intellectually his reach exceeded his grasp, as can be seen in the numerous books written, edited, or co-authored by him on everything from morals to literature.[33]

Calverton wished his magazine to be catholic in spirit, like the old *Masses.* This was no longer possible. For publishing Eastman, Hook, and other apostates he was called a social fascist by the Soviet Journal *International Literature,* which laid down the law on cultural matters. This was a signal for American Communists to boycott Calverton. In appreciation Max joined the editorial board, as did Hook and later Edmund Wilson. Though he raised money for the *Modern Monthly* as well as contributing to it, Eastman's relation with Calverton was not an easy one. Ten years of getting his way on the *Masses* and the *Liberator* had not prepared him to take a back seat. More than once Eastman threat-

ened to resign from the board over editorial disputes. There was nowhere else for Max to go, so he didn't.[34] Commerical magazines seldom
printed his political essays. Calverton's home was one of the few places
where Eastman felt comfortable socially. The two were political allies,
of necessity if nothing else. In 1933 John Strachey, whose book *The
Coming Struggle for Power* was one of the great radical statements of the
thirties, visited the United States. Max tried to win him over to their
side but failed. He reported back to Calverton that Strachey had baldly
described himself as a Stalinist.[35] In 1937 Carleton Beals accompanied
the Dewey Commission which visited Mexico to determine if Trotsky
was guilty as charged by the Soviets. Beals questioned Trotsky so
roughly that Max got Calverton to drop him from the editorial board.[36]

When Max decided to expose Stalin's control of letters he naturally
turned to Calverton. He was inspired to do this by an anthology of Soviet writing edited by Joseph Freeman, Joshua Kunitz, and Louis Lozo-
wick. He did not object to the items in *Voices of October* (1930), which
had been gathered by Freeman during the 1920s when Soviet writers
enjoyed some freedom. What set Max off was the rapturous introduction hailing the progress of literature under socialism. Max wrote his
essay "Artists in Uniform" to dispute this claim. Its thesis was that in
Soviet Russia art was just another commodity like steel or tractors, and
judged by the same standards. Max described the Kharkov Congress of
November 1930, when artists and authors from twenty countries resolved "upon the the world-wide 'mass organization' of art and literature as 'weapons of the working class in its struggle for power.' " The
Congress's international secretary, after being presented with a red
army uniform, declared, "Pen in hand we are soldiers of the great invincible army of the international proletariat." The thought of writers, inkpots at the ready, charging off to battle amused Max but
also appalled him. Here was the union of art and action in its most
odious form. It was part of "the crude humiliation of arts and letters,
the obsequious and almost obscene lowering of the standards of the
creative mind of which that Kharkov Congress and the whole subsequent record of the International Union of Proletarian Writers form
a picture."[37]

The Kharkov delegates pledged to use art as a weapon in the class
struggle but never asked how this was to be done. They were told that
"every proletarian artist must be a dialectical materialist. The method
of creative art is the method of dialectic materialism." According to

Max, not "six creative artists in the world" knew what dialectic material-ism was, and fewer still had the slightest knowledge of the "dialectic method of artistic creation." This didn't matter much because two years later the International Organization Bureau set up by the Congress and manned, naturally, by Russians annulled "dialectic materialism" and declared "Socialist Realism" to be the true method of proletarian art. The *New Masses*, which had been represented at Kharkov, patiently adapted to the changing line. At one point its editors made the humil-iating admission that they had ignored the role of social fascist idea-logues like Eastman and Calverton, neglected the achievements of so-cialism in Russia, adopted an "empirical attitude" toward labor, and worse.

This proved to Max that "the 'cultural revolution' represented by these uniformed neophytes of the drillmaster priests of 'Marxism-Leninism-Stalinism' is a runt and rotten inside. Before these young men ever become revolutionists they will have to be rebels."[38] Max still had not quite gotten the point. In his youth, people became leftists because they were independent and freethinking. One became a Stalin-ist for the opposite reason. The party was a world of its own, complete with doctrines, institutions, recreations, even businesses. American Communists liked to appear as dissenters, but this was a false pose. In rejecting capitalism they embraced its opposite and hence were as se-cure as before, more so probably. Capitalism in those days expected people to look after themselves. The party was a little welfare state providing the inner circle with all that was needed—including even their ideas. Alienation was not rebellion, despite the likeness. To the faithful, party discipline was part of the attraction.

Independent leftists such as Eastman and Hook were especially troublesome to Communists precisely because their dissent was genu-ine. They protested injustice wherever they found it, even in the USSR. By doing so they exposed American communism for the servile thing it was, which members found intolerable. Eastman was the most vexing of all, partly because he knew Russian. The Soviets innocently pub-lished a great many documents that when read by unbelievers were ex-tremely damaging. The New York Public Library was rich in this mate-rial, and Eastman made good use of it, profiting from Soviet isolation and ignorance. Max gave special offense by muckraking Soviet culture, the pride of foreign Communists. The achievements of Eisenstein and

Russian writers were hailed as products of Russian socialism, though accomplished in spite of it. Max was determined to make this known.

Every informed person recognized the threat Eastman posed. Max Shachtman told him that "Mike Gold was seen, surrounded by copies of your articles, uttering low groans and running around on his belly eating grass in Washington Park while a compassionate mob looked on."[39] Joshua Kunitz, who had been uplifted at Kharkov and was the *New Masses'* authority on Russian literature, tried to strike back. Max had it all wrong, he insisted. "Revolutionary writers *are* soldiers of the great invincible army of the international proletariat, they are in that sense *artists in uniform,* with one purpose, one aim, one objective for which they are ready to fight, to go to jail, to die. And for the life of me I fail to see anything humorous in that."[40] The truth of the Kharkov Congress, suppressed of course by Max, was that it had been an anti-war meeting, since the artists and writers "present there knew of the forthcoming trial at which the plots of French and English imperialists to invade Russia would be exposed." Kunitz did not see that there was anything improper about organizing a meeting around evidence not yet introduced, in a trial still to be held, whose verdict, an American might suppose, could not be known. This was the Stalinist mind at work, evidence of the magnitude of Eastman's task.*

Max kept chopping away with further articles. "How Art Became a Class Weapon," written before Kunitz's attack, compared Trotsky's view of art with Stalin's.[41] "Stalin's Literary Inquisition" was partly in response to a second Kunitzian onslaught. Kunitz was still willing to be called an artist in uniform, claiming that it was Lenin, not Stalin, who had enlisted art in the class struggle. In 1905 Lenin had written, "Literature must become a part of the general proletarian movement, a cog in the vast unified socialist mechanism."[42] Though this would seem to support Eastman's charge that Russian artists were being run according to the principles of scientific management, Kunitz said no. The writers quoted by Max in aid of his thesis were members of a discredited clique. The very excellence of Soviet art proved that it was not being

---

* Eugene Lyons confirmed Max's view of the Kharkov Congress, adding that Mike Gold really wanted to be an American Commissar of Culture so as "to liquidate Heywood Broun, H. L. Mencken, and others who poked fun at Gold; to liquidate, particularly, those swinish writers and publishers who had never even heard of him." *Assignment in Utopia,* p. 333.

Fordized and Taylorized as Eastman claimed: "The truth is, there is no other country in the contemporary world where the arts are so vital, so earnest, where the creative artist, even the beginner, enjoys such prestige and security as in the Soviet Union."

To show the relation between art and life Kunitz described a moving encounter that the delegates to Kharkov had with Soviet workers, who indicted them for failing to give the "facts" an "artistic presentation." This was typical. In Kunitz's essays Soviet workers and peasants are forever correcting grateful artists. Kunitz denied that RAPP, the Soviet writers union, controled artists, pointing out that most did not belong to it. And he maintained that dialectic materialism had not been dropped in favor of socialist realism. It was more a matter of the truly dialectical artist naturally turning out to be a socialist realist. In any case, Eastman was not qualified to discuss Soviet literature because he was a petty bourgeois ecapist as shown by *The Literary Mind.*

Max replied by agreeing that only a few prominent writers belonged to RAPP, which was proof of their helplessness, since until April 23, 1932, RAPP had "an absolute dictatorship over the whole field of literary publication in the Soviet Union." Eastman then traced the history of RAPP from its origins in 1923, when a group of writers came together for the purpose of opposing Trotskyism in art and letters. From 1925 to 1932 this group dominated Russian literature, applying Stalinist methods to it. Then in 1932 it was decreed, in the Soviets' own words, that "all literary organizations, all magazines, all publishers, all critics, must firmly acquire this simple truth—that writers ought first of all to write books."[43] Freeman and company had brought out *Voices of October* during the period of RAPP's ascendency, a time when, according to the Soviets themselves, revolutionaries were not allowed even to discuss whether a work of literature possessed any merits beyond fidelity to the party line.

If the Kharkov congress was an anti-war meeting as Kunitz said, why did only one of the nineteen resolutions passed by it concern war, Max asked. This brought him to the "revolution" of April 23, 1932, when Stalin reversed himself, abolishing RAPP and its leader, a certain Auerbach. Louis Fischer then found himself free to tell the truth, which was that RAPP had persecuted and silenced all who failed to conform. Yet Fischer was free to denounce RAPP only because Stalin had eliminated it. Fischer hailed Stalin's role in "liberating" Soviet writers, forgetting that it was Stalin who originally enslaved them. What this quick turn in literature meant, said Max, was that Stalin's grasp was as firm as ever. Soviet writers were allowed to speak out only because Stalin knew that none of them would:

> The true character of this order, "Right-face, March!" to the "proletarian poets," is shown in the swift click of the heels and clock-work leg-spring with which it was obeyed. Stalin called off RAPP because he deemed it, for the present, safe to do so. His honest Bolshevik critics were all jailed, muzzled, mum or underground. Let Voronsky try to avail himself of this new decree to say a few words for the true views of Lenin; let Kosnovsky, from his solitary prison cell, try to creep into print with one of his classics of revolutionary journalism; let any daring young student-friend of Trotsky say one clear word in honest appraisal of Russia's greatest living historian, essayist and literary critic—you will see what kind of "creative freedom" this is!" [44]

Max's final article in this series was a case study of one novelist, Boris Pilnyak, whose literary lynching and subsequent confessions and apologies Eastman described at length. He chose Pilnyak because the writer was well known in the United States on account of a recent visit. In the course of it he was feted and escorted around the country by Joseph Freeman, complimented by Dreiser and Sinclair Lewis, and acclaimed by Mike Gold for exemplifying the "artistic conscience of Russian writers." His American triumph followed a period during which Pilnyak had been hounded to the point where he would say, do, and write anything if it would save his neck. He had managed to survive, temporarily as it turned out, only by degrading himself in ways Eastman was able to document.

Max expanded these offending articles, which were published as *Artists in Uniform*. This required Kunitz to go twice more unto the breach. Since in abolishing RAPP the Soviets had admitted to past abuses, Kunitz could not deny them. Instead he excused these outrages on the ground that "the arts, like the collective farms, the cooperatives, the factories, the scientific institutes, the planning commissions were honeycombed with saboteurs, plotters, and hidden enemies of the working class." [45] The existence of so many traitors might seem to cast doubt on the advantages resulting from communism. But Kunitz was oblivious to contradictions. According to him only a white guardist like Eastman would deny the glory that was Communist culture under Stalin, and the almost equally splendid triumphs of the cultural revolution in America. How could Eastman call this a "bloodless runt" when no fewer than forty-six distinguished artists and writers—including Kenneth Burke, Dos Passos, James Farrell, Freeman, Gold, Hicks, Langston Hughes—were part of it. The John Reed clubs, to which young Communist writers belonged, were wonderful also.

The *Daily Worker* despised *Artists in Uniform,* as did *Partisan Review,* then an organ of the Stalinist John Reed Clubs. It ran a statement by poor Pilnyak, who was marked for death, refuting Eastman's charges and citing the example of Max's hero Christian Rakovsky. He had just written that everyone should stop resisting Stalin and do as they were told.[46] *Partisan Review* followed this with an attack on Max by Leon Dennen, who had worked for the *Moscow Daily News* and was therefore privy to the innermost secrets of Russian literary life. He warmed to his task by accusing Max of having "disowned and discredited the anti-war articles" of John Reed during the second *Masses* trial. This was a remarkable statement inasmuch as Reed was present at the time and praised Eastman's defense unrestrainedly. Max claimed that the brilliant writer Issac Babel (also on Stalin's death list) had been muzzled by RAPP. Eastman was all wet, according to Dennen. Babel's problem was that he wrote slowly. RAPP had not been tyranical but enjoyed power because it captured "the imagination of the younger generation of Soviet writers."[47] RAPP was dissolved simply because, for undisclosed reasons, it had outlived its usefulness, and no doubt had stopped capturing the imagination of gifted youth yearning to write dialectically.

Max thought these attacks were instigated by Moscow, as *International Literature* had denounced Calverton and himself again after *Artists in Uniform* appeared. Calverton was described as the "official corruptor of the left intelligentsia, serving up . . . under the flag of Marxism, the most anti-Marxian, counter-revolutionary rubbish." In the delicate language of official communism Eastman was a "provincial old maid," a Menshevik, and a "superficial petty bourgeois intellectual" who wore the uniform of "bourgeois counter-revolution."[48] Eastman may have been wrong in believing that Moscow directly ordered American Communists to malign him. If so, it made no difference. They knew how to take a hint.

In his history of the Left, Daniel Bell wrote that "American cultural circles completely ignored Max Eastman's book, *Artists in Uniform*" when it appeared.[49] This was not quite true. The book was widely and, except by Communists, generally well reviewed. Selden Rodman of *Common Sense* disclosed that it had changed his mind. Before reading it he could see no point to attacking the Soviet state's control of letters. Even if true, the news of it would only detract from Soviet accomplishments, which too few Americans appreciated as it was. But after reading the "story of this servile adoration, of the Priesthood in the Holy Land, of the fate of the great writers in Russia, of the descent from the truly profound and lofty views of art held by the founders of communism," he thought otherwise. Max had helped explain why "the doctrinaire importation of religion has failed to catch on here."[50]

The *New York Times Book Review* said the book was written with "intelligence, insight and good common sense." The critic didn't like Max's Trotskyism or his "determinism" as expressed in *The Literary Mind*. He saw that Eastman had understated the degree of censorship and regimentation under Lenin, but Max had proven, especially in criticizing dialectical materialism, "that it is possible to endorse and even fight for a program of practical communism without a servile and uncritical adherence to scholastic interpretations of the Marxian Bible."[51]

In a long, thoughtful review William Harlan Hale blamed the willingness of American intellectuals to accept dictation from Moscow on the 1920s. Their "revolt" against art and intellect and their flight to Marxist simplicities arose from the intellectual, moral, and aesthetic confusions of the previous decade. It made Hale suspicious to see young poets hailing Verlaine one year and Marx the next. The suddeness of these changes he attributed to the years when ethical and artistic values had been "dissolved in the bitter solution of the new materialism and psychoanalysis." As he saw it, "romanticism had declined into nostalgia, religious belief into affectations such as Anglo-Catholicism; and even ordinary reality—what was left of it—was fast breaking asunder in the all-denying investigations of physical science." Finally the tension became unbearable and having "lost faith in their own individual ability to choose and act . . . they require a new faith in the ability of some great leader to choose and act for them. They prefer, that is, to surrender to a superman and trust in magic." Hale ignored facism and the great depression, which were important, too, but correctly drew the moral of Eastman's book: "When order is imposed on our lawless economic system, the greatest benefits which that would entail would be lost if the spiritual life were, at the same time put in chains, and the artists into uniform. If the intellectuals themselves do not fight for their independence and integrity, no one will."[52]

British journals were complimentary as usual. The *Spectator* said it was a book "that should be placed, on Christmas Eve, in the stocking of every bright-shirted Bolshevik in Bloomsbury." [53] The *Nation* unaccountably assigned Eastman's book to the right man—Carl Becker, a distinguished historian. Becker agreed with Eastman that Stalinists treated Marxism as a religion. He was struck by the fact that when Trotsky was exiled, the truth of his ideas and the wisdom of his program were never at issue. Becker agreed also with Eastman's criticism of Marxism as philosophy "in the very sense that Marx himself denounced philosophy." Becker disagreed with Eastman on two crucial points, beginning with the nature of science. Eastman's scientism was less pronounced in *Artists in Uniform* than usual. But Eastman did say that the world could be saved only by scientific method. He held that the choice for Americans was between science and "soviet ballyhoo," a tag much admired by critics. Becker doubted that scientific method, so useful in changing the physical world, was applicable to society. As he saw it, "the problem of changing the physical world differs profoundly from the problem of changing the social world: the physical world is indifferent to changes proposed or made, the social world is very much interested. Mr. Eastman knows this, without, I think, sufficiently allowing for it." [54] Any social experiment must be strongly affected not only by what the leaders, however scientific, think, but by the opinions of their followers as well. Russian leaders had found that a combination of force and ballyhoo worked best. Becker disagreed with Max both as to the nature of science and the usefulness of ballyhoo. He didn't think a revolution could be made solely on the basis of science as Max hoped. Some tub-thumping would always be required. "Nevertheless, I delight in Mr. Eastman's exposure of the ballyhoo, partly because he does such an honest good job of it, chiefly because I am convinced that man cannot better his lot in the long run by suppressing factual knowledge and critical intelligence in favor of any species of wish-fulfilling dogma." [55]

Babette Deutsch, whose association with Eastman's magazine had convinced book review editors of her competence to dicuss everything he wrote, was deeply troubled by *Artists in Uniform*. She knew that Max's indictment of Soviet cultural policies was accurate. But was it wise to say so? In writing such a book Max had created a "two-edged sword which could be used effectively by the enemies of the workers as well as by their friends." On the other hand, Eastman had made a real contribution by exposing the unscientific basis of Marxist thought. His exposé of the religious sectarianism of American Communists was valuable, too. Then again, "the fear is that he speaks either to those who will not listen or to the few who are in agreement with him, while some may overhear who are bound to misinterpret his message and turn it to purposes of their own. If the pen is mightier than the sword, it should be handled in no ambiguous fashion."[56] Deutsch could not bring herself to say that the truth should be suppressed for political reasons. Honesty was her problem, and Max's, too. Both would soon be getting off the communist bandwagon.

Deutsch's uncertainties and divided feelings were not typical. Most radicals and Soviet sympathizers thought either that Max lied, or that he was telling truths which, for political reasons, should not be revealed. Lincoln Steffens in a virtually incomprehensible review for the *New Republic* appeared to say that Eastman's charges were accurate but beside the point. What did it matter that artists were sacrificed in Russia? The main thing was that Russia's people were acting on the "scientific perception" that they must follow "one leader, one party, one plan," said Steffens from his home in Carmel, California, where, thanks to bourgeois democracy, the arts were entirely safe and no one had to follow any leader, party, or plan.[57]

Eastman knew that Steffens could hardly be held responsible for his actions, having become psychologically dependent on communism and Ella Winter, his fanatically pro-Soviet wife. Eastman told Calverton that Winter was "pushing the pen."[58] He guessed right. She had put Steffens up to the review out of hatred for Max who, she said, "is turning definitely into an enemy now. It is unbelievable that anyone could turn so bad."[59] Steffens's biographer defends his pro-Communist activities on the ground that Steffens sometimes failed to follow the party line. Then too, "despair and illness bred intermittent gullibility and desperate faith."[60] Ill health and the need to be loved explain a great deal. They still leave Steffens ready to see Russian artists exterminated if necessary for the sake of his political opinions. Eastman complained publicly that Steffens had ignored the issues raised by *Artists in Uniform,* which was true. He urged the *New Republic* as it moved left "to bring with it what is of enduring value in the tradition of liberalism, the effort toward a clear and clean confrontation of facts and ideas. It ought not to lend itself to the publicity manuevers of the Stalinists."[61]

The liberal tradition was not doing too well at the *New Republic.* Its editors had preceeded the Steffens review with a fairy tale about art by Matthew Josephson, who was fresh from Russia with good news for friends of literature:

> In Moscow I felt a special curiosity about the adjustment of the artist, the writer, the theatre worker, to life under the Soviets. Were they "artists in uniform," as is so often alleged? They seemed neither to suffer nor to have regrets. Many spoke to me of their work, work most often bound up with what we call "propaganda," with so much genuine enthusiasm and earnestness that the notion of their being coerced seemed more and more mythical. They themselves alluded good-humoredly to the legend of heavy-handed Bolsheviks standing over Russian artists with clubs as a typical bedtime story for the more or less grown-up children of the bourgeois.[62]

After these cheering assurances, Josephson had his spirits further raised by speeches on the Five Year Plan delivered by Stalin, Molotov, Kaganovitch, and others. He instantly recognized these talks for what they were, "a sustained dramatic literature of a high enough order." Josephson knew no Russian, a real advantage to one wishing to praise Soviet political speeches.

Both the *New Republic* and Steffens denied the charges in East-man's letter.[63] A pure love of truth was said to be their only motive. In fact the Josephson article had been written with no thought at all of Eastman's book. Seemingly Josephson had invented the phrase "artists in uniform" all by himself, placing it in quotation marks out of humil-ity. Knowing it would do no good, Max soldiered on regardless. As he told the *New Republic,* he had seen what a policy of "dignified silence" had done to Trotsky in Russia. Eastman would not make that mistake. Though the analogy was more than a little strained, Max's feelings were justifiable. *Artists in Uniform* was a true account, insofar as the truth could then be known, of the end of artistic freedom in Soviet Russia. It sold fewer than five hundred copies.

The book did not fail because poorly done. In strength, clarity, pace, and even feeling it was the best Max had yet written. The times were against it even so. Interest in Soviet affairs had risen greatly among literate people, but one-sidedly. Few people wanted to know more about misrule in Russia. The faithful denied there was any. Sym-pathizers who acknowledged flaws brushed them off. There was a double standard by which offenses in America aroused much indignation, while far greater crimes in the USSR were said to make no difference. By the early thirties Max was in an impossible position and the worst was still to come.

CHAPTER NINE

The Unmaking of a Socialist

1933–1940

Communists were not satisfied with attacking Eastman's present work. They wanted to rewrite his past, too, in the Soviet manner. Max was always being accused of having sold out during one or another of the *Masses'* trials. He was always being dismissed as a bohemian. Max was hypersensitive on this point, since, if the label stuck, no one had to take him seriously. And it was untrue, for though a great believer in free love and nude bathing, Max had always looked down on Greenwich Village bohemianism. He preferred to live in Croton near other serious radicals.

When Albert Parry's *Garrets and Pretenders,* a popular history of bohemianism, came out in 1933, Max naturally saw the hand of Moscow in it. This was unfair. Parry did say Max turned yellow during the *Masses* trials, offering as evidence the line about the flag that embarrassed Max to the point of amnesia. The charge had been made so often Parry doubtless believed it. Otherwise, he was complimentary. Parry loved the *Masses* and, if less excited by the *Liberator,* admitted that its compromises were necessary. The book was a far cry from being Red Propaganda, so far in fact that Joseph Freeman admonished Parry for his frivolity. A real history of Greenwich Village would make clear "why the *New Masses* cannot follow Albert Parry's advice to recapture the 'romantic moods' of the old *Masses.*"[1] Modern times required "firmness of purpose and clarity of thought," Freemen wrote, just as if the *New Masses* was not famous for hysteria and muddle.

In suspecting the worst of Parry Eastman was not being paranoid. Though Parry meant well, he was the exception among Eastman's critics. More typical was Bob Brown, who as Robert Carlton Brown contributed to the *Masses* until the artists' rebellion of 1916. In 1916 he wrote an article saying that the old *Masses* had flamed with rebellion until Max became the editor and poured cold water on it.[2] This reversed the true order of things for Vlag had believed in cooperation, Max in revolution. Brown used the big lie knowing that many more people had heard of the old *Masses* than had ever read it. Less silly, though still false, was Brown's charge that John Reed had resigned from the *Liberator* because it was insufficiently communistic. This also reversed the truth. Reed took his name off the masthead in protest against compromises that enabled the *Liberator* to stay alive despite government hostility. He showed himself to be less of a Bolshevik than Max, who sacrificed principle to expediency, following the example of Lenin.

Brown was still angry with Max for having forced his hand during the artists' revolt. Eastman probably should have ignored him, but in those days could not let any smear go by, however ridiculous. He wrote two long articles in the *Modern Monthly* striking back at Parry, Brown, and the *New Masses*. Max defended his personal freedom, much as Dell had done against Gold years before, as something that everyone ought to enjoy and revolutionists ought to promote. He defended his right to run magazines as he pleased on the ground that he solicited the money for them. This anti-Marxist, proprietorial view was rooted not in theory but experience. "Raising money is the most painful and devastating labor of soul that my ideals ever demanded of me, and it is needless to say that I did it for my ideals, not for Bob Brown's or Louis Untermeyer's, or George Bellows'."[3]

While he was in the right, Max's harsh tone was far from winning. It showed his fear of this tactic that misrepresented him to a new generation of radicals who did not remember his glory years. Even young Alfred Kazin, no friend of Stalinism, fell for it until he met Eastman:

I had always known of Max Eastman as a romantic poet and rebel, vaguely a male counterpart of Edna St. Vincent Millay, and was not prepared when I saw him in action at Calverton's parties for such a steady drumfire in behalf of science, scientific method, experimental naturalism and scientific engineering. When it came to poetry and art he sounded, in the phrase of the time, like a Technocrat.[4]

For all that he loved her poetry, Max could not afford comparisons with Edna Millay, whose image still was that of a madcap bohemian, or with others like her, hence the bitter articles in *Modern Monthly,* as also the "steady drumfire in behalf of science."

Short of turning Stalinist there was little Max could do to repair or prevent the harm done to his political reputation in the thirties. If he ignored the lies, they went unanswered. Counter-attacking made him seem unsympathetic to the better world that Communists and sympathizers thought they were building. Except for a few persons on the *Modern Monthly* there was no one to speak for Max. His position of critical support for the Soviets in a world divided between critics and supporters meant that every hand was raised against him. Max tried to sympathize with Soviet goals while remaining objective about the means used to reach them. This was difficult under the best of circumstances. When in addition you became a social leper, it is easy to see why the role found few takers. Max assumed it for a dozen years, which, for an independent, may have been a record.

Though moving away from them, Max still tried to rally support for jailed oppositionists in Russia. In 1933, before the great terror, this was not so obviously futile as we might think. It could still be supposed that Stalin would listen to reason, or at least the appeals of fellow travelers. But Eastman could not reach them. Sherwood Anderson wrote Max that he didn't understand Soviet politics well enough to sign any petitions. "It seems a shame they should have to spend so much energy hurting one another and being cruel, but Max, here I am a provincial, absorbed really in story-telling. How am I to know what is black and what is white? The whole thing leaves me terribly confused."[5] Anderson was straightforward, unlike Theodore Dreiser. When Max wrote Dreiser asking that he lend his name to a fund-raising effort on behalf of the left opposition, Dreiser waffled and then consulted Peter A Bogdanov, head of Amtorg, the Russian trading agency.[6] Dreiser's final answer was foreshadowed by his initial one: "It seems to me, whether badly managed or well managed, that it [Soviet Russia] is at least a set-up which should be preserved and fought for. If that means serious, and in some cases, seeming cruel sacrifices, it is, as we say, just too bad."

Not knowing that Drieser was seeking advice from the enemy, Max tried to persuade him that it was only because of the left opposition that Stalin had taken any progressive steps in recent years.[7] But Dreiser was listening to Bogdanov, who told him that siding with Eastman would put Dreiser in Trotsky's camp and "would be a great disappointment to your friends the world over."[8] So Dreiser informed Max that, while sympathetic to the plight of Trotsky's imprisoned followers, he could not do anything "that would in any way injure the position of Russia."[9] In his defense it must be said that Dreiser's political intelligence was such that by comparison Lincoln Steffens approached genius.

*   *   *

Though he was isolated and had no power, Eastman continued to annoy Stalinists. No one bought *Artists in Uniform;* it haunted the faithful just the same. This was evident at the first American Writers Congress in June 1935, which anticipated the Popular Front. For the previous seven years, known as the Third Period, it had been Comintern policy to make war upon democratic Socialists or "social fascists" on the theory that they were more dangerous to communism than real Fascists. In Germany while Hitler was attacking Social Democrats the Stalinists did, too. But when Hitler came to power he wiped out not only the Social Democrats but the Communists as well. This cast doubt on the reasoning behind the Third Period. Second thoughts in Moscow led to a new policy of forming broad anti-fascist coaltions. Ideological differences were passed over rather than sharpened as before. Yesterday's Social Fascist became today's Progressive, a fit companion in the struggle against reaction.

Literary communism reflected these turns. During the Third Period Stalinist writers were critical of all who did not follow the party line. Targets were plentiful, for its sectarian tactics prevented many sympathizers from joining the party or even fellow traveling. From 1930 to 1934, the worst years of the depression, the Communist party recruited 49,000 members of whom 33,000 promptly dropped out. A glance at the *New Masses* suggests why. It was constantly attacking non-Communists and potential literary allies, often scurrilously. To Mike Gold, who did most of the dirty work, the humanists were forerunners of fascism and "pansies" to boot. (Walter Pater, a nineteenth-century critic, "wrote like a fairy.") Thornton Wilder was just as bad. Archibald

MacLeish displayed symptoms of "the fascist unconscious." Despite Gold, writers moved to the left, but it was uphill work.

Things became much easier for literary leftists in 1935 when, as part of the turn toward the popular front, the party decided to liquidate the militant John Reeds clubs and enlist big names. The Writer's Congress showed this. The delegates were "reliable" writers, Communists and fellow travelers for the most part. But they took a soft line, avoiding the character assassinations of previous years. Those who could not be praised were not named. Max ceased being an enemy of mankind as before. Under the new dispensation he achieved non-personhood. The old strategy of admitting that Communist writers took orders was also abandoned, though reluctantly. When Mike Gold, "the best loved American revolutionary writer," was introduced, he got right to the point. "The charge has been made," by unknown fascists apparently, "that writers who ally themselves with the workers are artists in uniform. This charge is made by intellectuals who believe they do not wear a uniform—the uniform of the bourgeois. Well, we are proud of our role."[10] He was soon put straight by Moissaye J. Olgin, who explained that Soviet writers were free agents. He hailed the abolition of RAPP in 1932, an event made possible by the fact that "nearly every writer had admitted the correctness of the proletarian line." Thanks to the inspiration of Comrade Stalin, fresh triumphs of "Socialist realism" were being achieved daily without coercion. "The [Soviet] Congress emphasized the freedom of the individual writer." Russian writers were more determined than ever to create great art, as they were enjoined to do by collective farmers, workers, young Communists and other patrons of literature.

Matthew Josephson was again uplifted by the grand spectacle of Soviet letters in action. In his address to the Writers Congress he confessed to knowing little about Russia. He was sure it treated writers splendidly even so. Josephson was especially excited about a recent book by Russian writers celebrating the Bielnstroy Canal. It was a huge public works project utilizing thieves, saboteurs, and the like, many of whom were being rehabilitated, he was glad to report, thanks to social work by the GPU. The volume in question, written by Maxim Gorky and thirty-six others, is described by Solzhenitsyn as "the disgraceful book on the White Sea Canal, which was the first in Russian literature to glorify slave labor."[11] The Canal itself, a characteristic triumph of Stalinist planning, cost the lives of 100,000 people and by 1962 was practically unused.

Joseph Freeman told the writers congress that the magazine *Comrade* (1901) had not been a " 'Stalinist' plot to put American artists in uniform."[12] Later he gave a capsule history of the *Masses* without mentioning Eastman, copying all those Soviet histories that left out Trotsky. Granville Hicks, in a talk on Marxist criticism, recognized Eastman's role while minimizing it. "Max Eastman has as little understanding then as now of the nature of the creative process and the social role of literature."[13] This did not end the matter. The faithful could not resisting scratching where Eastman made them itch. As late as 1938 V. J. Jerome, cultural commissar of the American communist party, was still annoyed. At the party's national convention he said that "as party comrades we must be the first to demonstrate that it is not true what the Eastman's say, 'Artists in Uniform, crushing art out of creation.' On the contrary we have to demonstrate by our creations that we are the guardians of art."[14]

Party members had trouble deciding if they were artists in uniform bravely fighting fascism with their typewriters, which was clearly a good thing, or if they enjoyed artistic freedom, which was also a good thing. During the Popular Front era freedom usually got the nod. Some writers, movie writers especially, saved their uniforms just in case. Later events justified this precaution.

* * *

The treatment of him by communist writers explains Max's reaction to Granville Hicks's book on John Reed. It was the first biography of Reed and the most important, for Hicks gathered the documents on which subsequent works have depended. He and an assistant interviewd hundreds of people who had known Reed. Hicks was the nicest and most ethical of Communist writers. Max refused to cooperate with him anyway, telling Hicks that as a member of the "Stalin International" Hicks could not be objective. Eastman was mistaken. *John Reed: The Making of a Revolutionary* was a remarkably honest book. Hicks praised the *Masses* for having "the seriousness of strong convictions and the gayety of great hopes."[15] He presented, from Max's point of view, a fair account of the great artist revolt of 1916, saying that Reed gave Eastman his proxy vote because he knew that Eastman more than other editors cared about economic issues. Hicks even went against the party line in assigning Max some credit for the second *Masses* trial. "Eastman, in his eloquent summation of the defense, was far more outspoken than he had been in the spring, and made fewer concessions to the hysteria of the moment."[16] Hicks did not make Eastman out to be the central figure of both trials, which he was. Otherwise the book is hard to fault.

Max took issue with it just the same. Quibbles aside, the sticking point was Reed's frame of mind when he died. Hicks presented the official story, which was that, though Reed had quarreled with Zinoviev and resigned from the Comintern, he later rejoined it and died a loyal Communist. As it was not disputed by Louise Bryant, everyone accepted this version at the time. Years afterward Louise told Max that Reed had been shocked by the self-indulgence of Soviet bureaucrats and by Zinoviev's callous management of the Comintern.[17] Angelica Balabanoff, an oppositionist who had been Secretary of the Comintern and knew Reed well, supported Bryant. She believed Reed's disillusionment with Soviet rule hastened his death.[18] Hicks replied that he did not accept Louise Bryant's revised version because she had told different stories to different people. While recognizing that lack of evidence made for uncertainty, Hicks stood by his account.[19]

Eastman had the last word again, writing a long essay on Reed published in his *Heroes I Have Known* (1942), and reviewing the question of Reed's ideas at the end yet again in his memoirs. The real question, what Reed's politics would have been had he lived, was unanswerable. Because Eastman saw Reed as being much like himself, it followed that Reed, too, would have become disgusted and left the party. But Reed was an activist, unlike Max, and had given everything else up for party work. Militants did not abandon their dreams easily, so no one can say what Reed would have done. His was an unfinished life, which allows everyone to write their own ending to it. In the mid-thirties Hicks saw Reed as a disciplined revolutionary, while to Eastman he was an incipient oppositionist. In a 1975 review of yet another biography of Reed Andrew Kopkind, identified him with the "historical romance of revolution" and claimed that his "spiritual descendants are the racy revolutionary adventurers of Weatherland, the gadfly Guevarists, the rock-'n'-roll outlaws of a newer, more bitter Bohemia."[20] This is nonsense, but typical also. Reed's legend is easily turned to the service of all kinds of radicalism, however alien to his own.

Mabel Dodge, who had been Reed's lover, saw the problem clearly. Under the layers of goo was a sharp intelligence rarely employed. After reading Max's eassays on Reed, she informed him that he was using Reed "just as much as the others, as a tool to carve your own prejudices into a satisfactory form. Just as much as the insignificant Hicks, you use the innocent Reed as a proof of this and that. Of course I feel that anyone so lovable and so amorphous as he was is destined to be kicked back and forth like a football."[21] Naturally she was the only one who really understood Reed. Max answered that "you couldn't say the final word about Jack because Jack was a growing child. He changed so utterly that he was too earnest of political purpose for me, and I can be pretty earnest. . . . Also because not having political passions you don't understand their workings."[22] This was true. Mabel did not know Reed as a Communist and took no interest in politics. Still, she saw what Max was blind to. In protecting Reed's reputation Max was defending his own. This does not mean he was wrong, or that his concern for Reed's place in history was insincere. It does mean that Eastman had a personal stake in the matter quite as great as Hicks's.

Reed suffered twice by dying young and by dying politically intestate. Eastman outlived his legend, so his career is a matter of record. No one can invoke Eastman's name to justify Stalinism or terrorism or whatever, as still happens to Reed. Max should not have overreacted to Hicks's book as he did. It was better and fairer than he wanted to admit. But his willingness to defend Reed's good name calls for no apologies. Reed would have done the same had their positions been reversed. Both were deeply loyal to friends, a trait that when not destroyed by political opinions has a way of outliving them.

All the same, incidents such as this enabled people to dismiss Max. Even Edmund Wilson, who was moving in his direction, felt Max treated things too personally. When Babette Deutsch was upset by an Eastman attack on her translation of Pushkin, Wilson reassured her. She was not to worry about Eastman's review "because, unfortunately, he can't write about anything without appearing to make a personal issue of it, and people know and discount this."[23] Here Wilson was unjust, for Max had not exceeded the limits of fair play in his review. The worst thing he said of Deutsch was that she displayed a "crudely immature taste." This was not very nice, but a far cry from character assassination. Thanks to his endless polemics, it was now almost impossible for Max to criticize anyone without laying himself open to the charge of trafficking in personalities, as, of course, he sometimes did. Thus Max played into the hands of his enemies.

* * *

Even as he feuded with Stalinists, Max was enjoying the biggest popular success he would ever have as a writer. This arose from his interest in humor. Max had been dissatified with *The Sense of Humor* because it wasn't funny. In 1933 he agreed with his publisher friends Dick Simon and Max Schuster to do it over again with more jokes. The result was *Enjoyment of Laughter,* a widely and as a rule favorably reviewed book. Max said that he could only find one real criticism of it, and that by William Saroyan, who confessed later that he had reviewed the book without reading it.[24] As might be expected, Eastman had not made a thorough search for bad reviews. Louis Kronenberger panned it in the *New Republic.* Wolcott Gibbs of the *New Yorker* didn't like it either. He sent editor Harold Ross a memo saying, "It seems to me Eastman has got American humor down and broken its arm." Santayana received his copy with the usual warmth: "I don't understand a word of your book. Thus I am not able to share the happy experience that inspired you to write it."[25]

These were exceptions. Max was showered with praise by psychologists as usual, and better still by professional comedians. W. C. Fields thanked Max for his "wonderful, entertaining and interesting book," as did Al Jolson, Eddie Cantor, Fred Allen, Rube Goldberg, Jimmy Durante, and others.[26] Much later Eastman met the cartoonist Al Capp at a party, and he told Max that he had learned how to be funny by reading *Enjoyment of Laughter.* He was the fifth professional humorist to have profited from the book in this way, according to Max.[27]

Only one thing spoiled Eastman's pleasure. Despite rave reviews and heavy advertising by Simon and Schuster, the book sold only about 25,000 copies at first. This kept it on the best seller lists for a few weeks but did not make Eastman rich, nor his publishers either. They spent so much on promotion that they lost money on the early printings, though the book had a long life and turned a profit in the end. Max blamed the Stalinists for this disappointing sale. Unlikely as it seems, they were probably innocent. They found it difficult if not impossible to prevent a book with real popular appeal from succeeding. They hurt Max's political books because communism had influence in the small world of radical letters. But they had no control over the Book-of-the-Month Club, the *New York Times Book Review,* and other instruments of the mass market. Probably what *Enjoyment of Laughter* suffered from was that in the thirties non-fiction readers preferred do-it-yourself books such as *Life Begins at Forty* and Dale Carnegie's *How To Win*

Friends and Influence People. In this sort of atmosphere a serious book on humor, jokes notwithstanding, did well to sell 25,000 copies. The royalties were sufficient to free Max from lecturing for several years, and to make him better known. *Enjoyment of Laughter* gave him a reputation that would outlive his political fame.

* * *

In another area Stalinism probably did cost Eastman money. Ever since 1928 he had been working on a documentary film that he belived made sense politically and financially. The project began when he was approached by a young man named Herman Axelrod who had been collecting film on the Russian Revolution. He wanted Max to polish the film, write a commentary for it, and gather extra footage as needed. *Tsar to Lenin* cost a year of Max's life and various backers about $15,000. Then Max quarreled with Axelrod. As detailed in *Love and Revolution,* the story is a long one. The upshot is that Max became tangled in lawsuits that delayed release on the film until March 6, 1937.

It opened to packed houses and good reviews. The *New York Times* called it "the most complete, impartial, and intelligent film history of the Russian Revolution yet shown." Eastman won praise for signing off "without the usual 'documentary' postlude of the 'International' and an ecstatic glimpse of a tractor brigade. *"Tsar to Lenin* has chronicled only the first step of the revolt, but it has done it extremely well."[28] Yet the picture died at birth. It soon became known that any theater showing *Tsar to Lenin* would not be allowed to run Soviet films, which, thanks to Eisenstein and the vogue for things Russian, were big money-makers. That was the end of Max's film. A few copies were bought by history departments. Max deposited one in the Library of Congress. Axelrod sued him again, and to have done with it Max waived all rights to what should have become a film classic.

The slightly shortened print at the Library of Congress is still worth viewing. Max narrated it in the flat style of thirties newsreels. The background music sounds obtrusive to modern ears. Yet the film speaks for itself. It opens with shots of the Tsar at play, including a swimming scene that enables Max to say, "This is the first time the world has seen a king as he really is." The royal family attends a wedding. Other figures of pre-war Russia, including Prince Kropotkin, the anarchist leader, appear briefly as well. Then comes the war, scenes of combat, piles of corpses, and the first revolution that deposed the

Tsar. "Joy," Max says in an untypically lyrical moment, "was the sovereign of all Russia." After this we see Lenin, the October Revolution, civil war, and final victory of Bolshevism. Lenin and Trotsky are shown most often, but other red leaders appear too, including Krylenko, Rakovsky, and for a moment Stalin himself. At the end rare film clips show Big Bill Haywood puffing cheerfully on a cigarette, and Jack Reed attending public events.

Max was right to think of this unusual film as a potential gold mine. His mistake was in failing to realize how easily it could be suppressed. The only movie houses interested in exhibiting such a film were the very ones that showed Russian pictures. In the aggregate these were far more lucrative than a single documentary, no matter how absorbing. It was not paranoia this time either that led Max to think the Kremlin itself was responsible for killing his film. Shortly after it was released, Stalin gave a speech during which he called Eastman "a member of an international bandit gang" and "a notorious racketeer and gangster of the pen who lives by slandering the working class of the Soviet Union."[29] This was apparently the only time Stalin abused an American writer by name, a signal honor for Max that gratified both him and the *New York Times*.[30] Eastman thought it a direct result of *Tsar to Lenin* that gave offense by including only fifteen feet of film (out of some 2,000) on Stalin's part in the Revolution. Max claimed to have scoured the film libraries of Europe in hopes of finding additional material on Stalin to no avail. He had just not been that important in 1917.[31] Though this was scarcely Max's fault, it cost him his movie just the same. In Russia he would have lost his life, which thought may have been comforting.[32]

* * *

In 1937 Eastman had his celebrated fight with Ernest Hemingway, a matter not of words but of actual blows. Hemingway had been angry at Eastman ever since 1933 when Max reviewed his *Death in the Afternoon*. This was a fan's book on bullfighting, which Max hated, as he did all forms of violence. He called his review "Bull in the Afternoon," excoriating Hemingway's "juvenile romantic gushing and sentimentalizing of simple facts." Max was annoyed with Hemingway for insisting that tormenting an animal to the point where it could be skewered with minimum risk was an art form. Though Hemingway has proved

his manliness time and again, he still seemed uncertain of it. Doubts led
to overcompensation:

> Some circumstance seems to have laid upon Hemingway a continual
> sense of the obligation to put forward evidences of red-blooded mas-
> culinity. It must be made obvious not only in the swing of the big
> shoulders and the clothes he puts on, but in the stride of his prose
> style and the emotions he permits to come to the surface there. This
> trait of his character has been strong enough to form the nucleus of a
> new flavor in English literature, and it has moreover begotten a veri-
> table school of fiction-writers—creating a literary style, you might say,
> of wearing false hair on the chest.[33]

Hemingway says that his book is about life and death, Max wrote, but it
is really about killing, which Hemingway loves because "killing makes
him feel triumphant over death." This is a result, Max speculates, of
Hemingway's experience in the Great War and is more to be pitied
than censured.

Despite its Freudian overtones, this was a straightforward essay.
But Hemingway's then close friend Archibald MacLeish saw it differently. He wrote a hot letter to the *New Republic,* which first published
the review, charging that a line of Eastman's, "Hemingway lacks the
serene confidence that he *is* a full-sized man," was an accusation of sexual impotence. Stunned by this peculiar reading, Max insisted that he
never doubted Hemingway's manliness; it was Ernest who seemed un-
sure: "I have known Hemingway for years and always admired his genuine masculinity and cool courage. The first time I ever saw him he
had just been blown out of a bath-room by an exploding gas heater. He
arrived half-way down the hall with a smile on his face like a man on a
toboggan. That was before he had any literary reputation to hold onto
either." Max sincerely applauded Hemingway's talent: "Equally sincere,
however, and equally important to literature and social life is my conviction that Hemingway is gentle and sensitive and rather puritanical,
and that there is a lot of unreal bluster involved in his roaring about
whorehouses and bull's blood."[34] He wrote Hemingway directly, to say
that Ernest's virility was the furthest thing from his mind. But he stood
by his thesis: "I suppose it is fresh to psycho-analyze a man by way of
literary criticism, especially one whom you esteem as a friend, but I
think there is plenty of cruelty in the world without your helping it

along, and I am within my rights to say so with as much force as I can." [35]

MacLeish still felt that "whatever the intentions involved an injury has been done the finest living writer of English prose which no effort on your part or on the part of the *New Republic* will ever be able perfectly to repair." [36] Bewildered by this obtuseness, Eastman tried again: "I imagine that the idea, born of Freudian psychology—although to be found in Shakespeare, too—that anybody who 'protests too much' has brought with him out of childhood a *feeling*, not of confidence, but just the opposite, in the matter of which he protests, is far more generally current in the intellectual world than you realized, and that is why my remark seems as innocent of innuendo to most people as it was in my own mind." [37]

This would seem to end the matter. It was clear to everyone but Hemingway and MacLeish that Eastman admired Hemingway as a writer, did not like his cult of blood and violence, and believed that it was a result of unjustified fears created by the war. Though he did not say so at the time, this guess resulted from Max's having talked with Ernest about the war in 1922. Hemingway told Max that he was "scared to death" during combat, as, Max hastened to add, he would have been, too. After being wounded, Hemingway experienced such bouts of terror that he could not sleep in the dark for weeks. It was praiseworthy to Max that Hemingway mastered his fears. Too bad he overdid it.

What Max didn't know was that his review had enraged Hemingway, who was in a vile humor to begin with because *Death in the Afternoon* had been poorly received. Gertrude Stein and others had criticized it for the same reasons as Eastman. Max's essay, the last major review, was also the the last straw. When MacLeish detected a slur on Hemingway's virility, the latter quickly agreed. After hearing from Eastman, he wrote to Maxwell Perkins, their editor at Scribner's, that Eastman was jealous of him for being a real man and a better writer and had sent him a "kiss-ass letter," but Eastman was not yet "out of the woods." [38] Four years later, when they finally met, Hemingway was still angry, probably also drunk. He encountered Eastman in Maxwell Perkins's office on August 11, 1937, at a time when he was riding high, having been lionized on his return from Loyalist Spain, most recently in Hollywood where they really knew how to lionize.

Hemingway accused Max of having called him impotent, opening his shirt to reveal a hairy expanse. Max's joke about a literary style of "wearing false hair on your chest" had not been forgotten. Max's chest was inspected and found to be hairless. Everyone laughed, nervously we can be sure. Eastman picked up a copy of *Art and the Life of Action* intending to prove that Hemingway had misread his eassy. Hemingway shoved the book in his face. They grappled, falling to the floor. Perkins stopped the fight almost at once. Afterward each gave a victory statement to the press. In a final interview just before boarding ship for Spain, Hemingway drew a copy of *Art and the Life of Action* from his pocket and opened it to the offending passage: "In the center of the page was a black smudge which Mr. Hemingway said was 'Eastman's noseprint, where I slapped him in the face.' "[39]

New York papers could not agree on who won. The *World Telegram* and the *Post* accepted Max's version of the fight. The *Post*'s story was headlined, "Unimportance of Being Ernest Hemingway Shown, When Eastman Unbeards a Chest," and ended, "Mr. Eastman is planning an article to be entitled 'The Enjoyment of Thrashing Ernest.' "[40] Hemingway's version appeared in the *Herald Tribune* and the *Times*. According to him, Eastman had scratched at him, "clawing like a woman." Hemingway claimed to have used just enough force to subdue Eastman without hurting him, as Max was too old for him to punch. (Ten years older, Hemingway said. Actually, Max was sixteen years his senior.)[41] The affair was a two-day wonder in New York. Westbrook Pegler referred to Hemingway in his column as "one of the most talented of our fur-bearing authors." The *New Yorker* ran a cartoon showing a shirtless and hairy-chested young man being examined by a doctor who asks him, "Writer?"[42] A few weeks after the fight, Eastman visited Perkins, who told him: "I don't like to discuss the embarrassing thing that happened when you were here before, Max, but I do want to tell you that I think you acted magnificently. You were Arthurian; you couldn't let that pass without doing something, and you did just enough."[43] Though we only have Max's word for this, the quotation is probably exact. He was astonishingly honest. Whatever his faults, the ability to dissemble, still less to lie, was not among them. Then, too, people were getting tired of Hemingway, who was drinking a lot and throwing his weight around. It would have been natural for the gentlemanly Perkins to side with Max.*

---

* As no opinion polls were taken, it is hard to judge the immediate effect of this fight. Hemingway was at the peak of his career, widely read, influential, a friend of Loyalist

And that, presumably, was that. It wasn't though, because Eastman could not leave the incident behind him. He went over it repeatedly, in a later essay "The Great and Small in Ernest Hemingway," twice in the *Saturday Review,* again in *Love and Revolution,* and who knows how often in conversation.[44] Partly this was to ensure that his version went on record, mostly because the event was so unsettling. Max believed that he lacked physical courage and only the fear of showing fear made him act bravely, as in resisting the war effort and fighting with Hemingway.[45] He could not see that the important thing was not feeling fear, which everyone did, but overcoming it without overdoing it in the Hemingway manner. Max had no wish to be a coward or a bully either. Despite self-doubts, in this he succeeded admirably.

So far as Hemingway's biographer, Carlos Baker, was able to discover, Hemingway's last recorded statement about Max was a page of threats, written to himself in 1938, listing all the painful things he would do to Eastman if they ever met again—which they did in 1946, non-violently. Eastman's last statement on Hemingway (if we omit the final retelling of their fight in his memoirs) came just after the Nobel laureate killed himself. Though still bothered that Hemingway had, as he saw it, lied about their fight, Eastman concluded

> you can't ask everything of one man, and I find Ernest's triumph over fear, his scorn for the petty big city, big-celebrity life he might have lived in New York as a well-advertised literateur, his bold honesty in expressing his dissent from mollycoddle standards, and the superb style in which he often expressed it—I find these things a joy and an inspiration. I think sometimes in reading him of Walt Whitman's great lines: "This is no book—who touches this touches a man."[46]

Surely now the misunderstanding of 1933 was finally laid to rest.

The incident had a curious epilogue. When F. Scott Fitzgerald

Spain. Max was not nearly so famous and had the wrong political opinions. On the other hand, he was much older than Hemingway, which prevented Ernest from gaining much credit. If Hemingway won the fight, this was only to be expected. Defeat, on the other hand, would be humiliating. In either case Hemingway lost honor because of the difference in ages. Time did not improve Hemingway's case. Max's theory about his overcompensation gradually gained acceptance. Aaron Latham, who feels Hemingway has been misunderstood, writes that "more and more people began to see Hemingway's hemanism not as philosophy but as breast-beating. Or perhaps as 'insecurity'—that favorite 60s word. The once-lonely Max Eastman now had lots of company. Many believed the king had no hair." Aaron Latham, "A Farewell to Machismo," *New York Times Magazine* (October 16, 1977), p. 98.

learned of it, he wrote Maxwell Perkins for details and read the newspaper accounts. Fitzgerald had been one of the first writers to encourage Hemingway and was rewarded by a slighting reference to "poor Scott Fitzgerald" in *The Snows of Kilimanjaro*. Fitzgerald used the Eastman-Hemingway affair to exact a revenge so subtle it seems to have gone unrecognized until now. In *The Last Tycoon* (published posthumously in 1941) the main character, Stahr, becomes drunk and abusive and is flattened by a communist writer named Brimmer. The fight bears no obvious resemblance to the Eastman-Hemingway match. But Professor Neil R. Joy has demonstrated that the details, and even some of the dialogue, are based on accounts of the Eastman-Hemingway bout. Stahr represents Hemingway, and Brimmer, who wins decisively, Eastman when young.[47] In this way art improved upon life.

* * *

The Red Decade was the worst yet for Eastman as a poet. In 1936 he was dropped from the fifth edition of Louis Untermeyer's popular anthology *Modern American Poets*. As Untermeyer had Stalinist inclinations, Max decided that politics were behind this. Eastman may have been right, but it is equally likely that Untermeyer, who had never really cared for Max's poems, acted from conviction. Anyway, as new modern poets came along, old modern poets had to give way.[48] Max relieved his injured feelings with a poem:

OUR MAJOR POETS

(Composed after reading a recent Anthology of American Poetry.)

> *Our country has just fifty major poets—*
> *The words come from Olympus tipped with fire—*
> *And you can find them all in one fat volume*
> *Compiled by Jove and Louis Untermeyer.*
> *It is well known to every subtle critic*
> *That major poets do not much abound,*
> *And when they come, they come in numbers*
> *Convenient for anthologies and round.*
> *"But Louis," if you ask, "how do you know it?*
> *How can you with your fellow make so free?"*
> *"I am myself," he states, "a major poet.*
> *My songs are in the volume." Q.E.D.*[49]

This did not solve Max's problem, which was that by combining anti-Stalinism with anti-modernism he had offended nearly everyone.

E. E. Cummings who was far to the right, "more tory than you could imagine," John Dos Passos wrote, learned that anti-Stalinism alone would be harmful.[50] In 1931 Cummings published an anti-communist book on Russia called *Eimi* that sold only 1,381 copies. "When the book appeared, some of my 'best friends' crossed the street to avoid speaking to me," he told his biographer.[51]* For five years after that he was unable to find an American publisher and had to bring out his poems himself. Politics was not the whole story. *Eimi* was hard to read, even by Cummings's standards, the Worst Book of the Month, according to George Jean Nathan. Still, as Cummings was unquestionably modern, the boycott had to be related to his anti-Stalinism. Eastman, who had both the wrong politics and the wrong poetry, suffered accordingly.

Though it sold well for a book of poetry, Eastman's *Kinds of Love* (1931) received some harsh reviews. The *Nation* called his poems old-fashioned and derivative. The *New Republic* said they were infused with a tiresome "romantic, adolescent emotion."[52] The only person of real standing who cared much for Eastman's poetry was Edmund Wilson, who told Max that his lyrics had never been dealt with justly because "poetry and poetry criticism have gotten to be such a racket."[53] Most who attacked his poems, Wilson assured Max, were simply jealous.

This could not be said of Louise Bogan, herself a fine poet, who in 1939 reviewed a new edition of *Enjoyment of Poetry* together with an anthology of poems Max had prepared to go with it. As an anthologist, Max displayed his antique views on art and science. Max tended "to reject the truly dramatic poem in favor of the melodramatic, the metaphysical in favor of the 'fanciful,' the 'mystical' in favor of the ghostly, the satirical poem altogether." His science was out of date: "The cogwheels of the mechanistic universe have stopped turning: science has become humble before the intuitive thinker. All this makes Mr. Eastman rather cross."[54] Bogan was wounding and to the point. Eastman made a god of science while knowing little about it. This was not fatal, as few of his critics did either. What hurt him was that Eastman paid homage to the wrong kind of science. In his youth everyone's mind was

---

* This was a common experience in the thirties. When young Albert Halper had his first novel *Union Square* (1933), published and it got good reviews, all his left-wing friends hailed his talent and good fortune. When he was denounced in the communist press as a favorite of "reactionary liberals," they dropped him. Later he had an article published in the *New Masses,* whereupon they came back to him again. Albert Halper, *Good-by Union Square* (Chicago, 1970).

governed by Darwin. People saw the natural world as a place ruled by biological laws that explained all behavior, including man's. Eastman never overcame this way of thinking, so even his psychology, the one science he knew something about, owed more to the nineteenth century than to the twentieth. He never accepted the modern view of natural laws as being probable rather than absolute. By the 1930s science may not have become quite so humble before the intuitive thinker as Bogan imagined. It was less rigid than Max thought just the same. Max seemed not to care. What was good enough for Darwin was good enough for him.

* * *

Russia was always on Max's mind. The great terror which began in 1936 was for him the last straw. Early the next year he published an article, "The End of Socialism in Russia," renouncing the beliefs of two decades.[55] For years Max had attacked Stalinism while praising socialism. Now he felt that the one disproved the other. The means of socialism, state ownership of property, had become the end. All that socialism was supposed to accomplish had been sacrificed to it. Max was equally discouraged to find that, as Stalin's rule became more oppressive, support for it increased abroad. The very people on the liberal left who embraced what he called Stalin's phony socialism—Maxim Gorky, Romain Rolland, Waldo Frank, George Soule, Rockwell Kent, Malcolm Cowley, the Webbs, Harold Laski, and many others—had been against the real thing in Lenin's time. There were reasons for this that Eastman didn't care to explain and perhaps did not fully understand. Few intellectuals in the West favored violent revolutions, hence the fear of Lenin and Trotsky, hence also the admiration for Stalin, who seemed less dangerous. The worldwide depression and the rise of fascism in capitalist countries made people want an alternate model as Russia appeared to provide. But it was attractive only if not examined too closely, which even visitors to the Soviet Union tried to avoid doing. During the Third Period it was hard to admire Soviet Russia. In the age of the Popular Front it was much easier, as the search for allies compelled Stalinists everywhere to stop acting like revolutionaries.

The Popular Front happened to coincide with the great terror, which put an end not only to Bolshevism but to most Bolsheviks also. At first Stalin had concentrated on obvious enemies—oppositionists, stubborn peasants, independent engineers. But in 1934 the enemies list lengthened amazingly. The murder of Sergei Kirov, head of the Leningrad party and a close associate of Stalin, triggered reprisals that went on and on. Leningrad was purged to start with. Solzhenitsyn thinks that a quarter of the city wound up in Gulag. Yet, sympathizers took this bloodbath in stride. Edmund Wilson visited Russia from May to October in 1935 and recognized that it was a police state. The Society of Old Bolsheviks was abolished while he was there. Wilson repeated a story told him by an American friend who asked a Russian Communist if Voroshilov would replace Stalin should something happen to him. "Oh, no," was the reply. "Voroshilov is a Bolshevik."[56] Wilson found the cult of Stalin annoying, but was assured that Stalin disliked it, too, and allowed himself to be worshipped only because the ignorant masses required an ikon. Wilson barely managed to swallow this. He was troubled also by the systematic falsification of history. Zinoviev and Kamenev were being expunged from the record like Trotsky before them. "The atmosphere of fear and suspicion is really pretty oppressive," wrote Wilson. Yet, only a few pages earlier he had sensed "extraordinary heroism everywhere." In the Soviet Union "you are at the moral top of the world where the light never really goes out."[57] The will to believe surmounts all obstacles, though in Wilson's case not for long. He would soon break with Stalinism and write his masterful history of the revolutionary tradition.

Wilson's enthusiasm for the Soviets was typical; his early rejection was not. Nothing did more to turn Max against liberals than their denial or rationalization of the great terror. This is frequently defended on the ground that they meant well and did not know the truth. The full content of the terror may never be fully known, but even rough estimates are horrible enough. Robert Conquest estimates that Stalin was responsible for no fewer than twenty million Russian deaths between 1928 and 1950, with the bulk of these taking place in the 1930s.[58] Solzhenitsyn triples that figure. Whoever we believe, Stalin remains almost the greatest mass murderer in history, exceeding even Hitler in cruelty to his own. Before the Second World War people were not used to megadeaths and could not grasp the scale of these atrocities. Max, though better informed than most, thought Stalin had murdered only a quarter of a million persons as of 1940, thus missing the mark by at least a factor of forty. Slaughters of this magnitude could not be hidden completely. The river of humans flowing into Gulag was hardly visible to Westerners, but the show trials were meant to be seen. These strained the credulity of all but the most fanatic Stalinists. In 1936 Zinoviev and Kamenev confessed to having murdered Kirov on Trotsky's orders and were shot, as were their followers. Stalin then went after Bukharin, Rykov, and others. When party leaders balked at this, Stalin launched a general purge of the party and the army, too. The cream of the officer corps was destroyed, including Marshal Tukhachevsky and, it is believed, 57 out of 85 corps commanders and 110 out of 195 divisional commanders. Bukharin and most surviving heroes of the October Revolution perished in 1938. Krylenko and his whole family, including Eliena's three sisters, another brother, an aunt, a cousin, and five or six nieces and nephews, disappeared in the terror, which lasted until 1939.

Eastman's friend and hero Christian Rakovsky was executed, too, though not before naming Max as a fellow agent of the British secret service in March 1938. It was just a year since Stalin had called Max a "gangster of the pen." After Rakovsky's testimony, the *Daily Worker*'s headline was, "Max Eastman Is a British Agent." On the advice of his anarchist friend Carlo Tresca, Max sued the *Worker,* not for the money (he eventually received $1,500) but for publicity, which Tresca believed would make it impossible for Stalin to have Max assassinated. In the event it was Tresca who died. In 1943 he was shot to death two blocks from Eastman's residence in Greenwich Village. A fierce enemy of both Stalinism and fascism, he seems to have been killed by Italian-American gangsters as a favor to Mussolini.[59]

Most purge victims were outside Eastman's frame of reference— religious people of every faith, non-communist leftists, engineers, everyone involved in work accidents, those who did not meet quotas, those who falsified data to show that impossible quotas had been met, historians (an extraordinary number of whom led terrorist bands) to name a few categories. However, two groups that Max knew very well were purged. Every Bolshevik leader that Max esteemed was killed. Of the 700 (mostly young) writers who attended the Soviet's First Writers Congress in 1934, only fifty survived to make the Second Congress in 1954. Some died in the war but many others in Gulag.

As the terror worsened, Eastman wrote Calverton that it "has been to me a horrible month—'I've thought about nothing but these massacres, and yet more the massacres of honesty and political clear thinking effected by our famous 'liberals.'"[60] He meant especially the *Nation* and the *New Republic,* prominent journals of liberal thought except where Russia was concerned. As late as September 1938, after more than two years of butchery, the *Nation* was still explaining that the purges resulted from "an irresistible popular tide of anti-bureaucratic feeling."[61] This was the equal of Mike Gold's declaration in the *New Masses* that "Soviet justice must be . . . sound, as it comes from the same source as the Soviet cultural renaissance.' "[62] The *New Republic* believed that Zinoviev and Kamenev had actually conspired to murder Kirov. Both magazines tried to discredit the commission led by John Dewey that interviewed Trotsky in 1937 and found him not guilty of promoting treason, espionage, and the like in Russia. After the Bukharin trial in 1938 the two magazines admitted that Soviet justice did appear to lack respect for the rights of defendants. The Soviet system as a whole remained fundamentally sound in their eyes.

After the Radek-Piatakov trial Eastman wrote an angry letter to the *Nation*. Yuri Piatakov was a friend, and Leonid Serebriakov an even closer one. He had visited the Eastmans in Croton some years earlier and had told Max and Eliena (with whom he had a love affair) that in the end Stalin would kill them all. Serebriakov had an adored daughter for whose sake he returned to Russia and certain death. It was for her protection, Max believed, that Serebriakov confessed to various unlikely crimes. He had told Max that he would never turn his back to Stalin, that is, show cowardice. But in the end he, too, submitted to public humiliation, though more grudgingly than most defendants judging from the trial transcript. As a rule the prosecutor asserted his crimes, while Serebriakov merely admitted to them. At the end, when most defendants asked that their lives be spared, Serebriakov only requested the court to remember that he had "broken with the counter-revolutionary banditry of Trotsky and Trotskyism."[63] Without giving this personal history Eastman attacked both the *Nation* and the *New Republic*. The *Nation* had said the trials resulted from individual ambitions, and in any case the truth about them would not be known for a hundred years. It was possible the defendants were guilty as charged. Whatever the truth, Stalinist leaders must be doing something right or they would not still be enjoying the support of the working class. The *New Republic* had seen no reason to suppose that civil liberties had been violated and urged readers to keep an open mind.

Eastman's critique of the liberal weeklies, which the *Nation* would not print, was based on radical assumptions. He charged the *Nation* and the *New Republic* with practicing a "kind of half-hearted Menshevism." They supported Stalin precisely because he was a counter-revolutionary. Stalin himself was destroying the old Bolsheviks because they were a threat, or a potential threat, to his policy of betraying socialism. The issue that liberal magazines were avoiding was "whether the Stalinists in Russia, and to a degree throughout the world labor movement, shall be able with impunity to black jack, murder, slander, jail, exile, sabotage, break down morally, and otherwise destroy the defenders of the Bolshevik idea against a Bonapartist counter-revolution operating with the ideology of the Mensheviks." [64]

As Max saw it, the *New Republic* and *Nation* were edited by liberals who defended a dictatorship in Soviet Russia that they did not approve of and would fight against if it appeared in the United States. They betrayed their liberalism by accepting obviously fraudulent trials, and corrupted Marxism by "refusing to see the social and economic realities behind these political crimes." Liberals had to know that the confessions were false because no reasonable person could believe "that these palpable atrocity stories are true of a whole body of sturdy and highminded men, the loved and trusted leaders of a great party, *the best men of an epoch.*" [65] The magazines ignored other crimes of Stalin as well, such as a Soviet law making the entire family of an individual convicted of treason liable for his offense. That alone, he declared, could explain the phony confessions. Men admitted to what they had not done in hopes of saving their families from the Archipelago or worse.

By 1938 liberals were finding the purges harder to swallow. Apart from being ridiculous, the trials had two obvious weaknesses. Confessions were the only evidence, and they were full of holes, as anti-Stalinists repeatedly demonstrated.[66] Perhaps this explains why the *Nation* did finally print a letter from Max denouncing both the Soviets and the American Communist party. The latter had just adopted a new constitution renouncing proletarian seizure of power in favor of "preaching socialism to a democratic electorate. This seals the victory of Stalinism over the Bolshevik program—and was preceeded, naturally enough by the extermination of the old Bolsheviks." [67] Max then asked why, if the Communist party was now devoted to parliamentary democracy, did it not merge with the Socialists or some other left-wing organization? The answer was in the Constitution itself, which described measures to be taken against "spies, double-dealers, swindlers" and other undesirables. A truly democratic party, Max said, would have no need of such "journalistic billingsgate." The language of the party constitution was the same language used to defend Stalin's dictatorship:

> The defense of that dictatorship is thus revealed to be a constitutional function of this allegedly democratic party. And the method of defense is revealed to be the same as that adopted by Stalin: slander and misrepresentation in the place of argument and debate. This method succeeds in Russia only because free criticism is suppressed. That the Communists will proceed to such suppression in America if they win power is obvious from both the tone and meaning of this clause in the constitution.

A further clause, calling for the expulsion of "betrayers of party confidence," had the same intent. It showed that the Communist party was not an open political organization but had plans unknown to the general public. And this secret society took orders from a foreign dictator: "What the Stalin parties in general have done is to abandon the proletarian-insurrectionary aim of Lenin while retaining the conspiratorial habit, the centralized command, the jesuitical mores—in sum, the military tactics and the 'war psychology'—which were justified, if at all, only by that aim." This is precisely what Hitler and Mussolini had done also, showing how slight the difference between fascism and communism had become. Eastman concluded:

> In my opinion liberals who give support or tolerance to the Communist Party on the assumption that they are moving to the left are being decoyed by labels, and by a misunderstanding of recent history, into betraying civilization itself. They are aiding in propagation of the Totalitarian State of Mind, which should be the chief enemy.[68]

Eastman had now found his best voice. Previous attacks on Stalinism had always been weakened by the effort to remain revolutionary. Even his letter to the *Nation* a year earlier had been weighted down with the language and, to a degree, the ideology of the left opposition. His indictment of the *Nation* for "semi-Menshevism" was lost on most readers, and was a labored effort to adapt Soviet precedents to American conditions anyway. This phase was now behind him. But the 1938 letter, Eastman's most successful yet, a precursor of his political masterwork *Stalin's Russia,* had no effect. Long experience no doubt kept him from expecting favorable results. The Popular Front was too strong to be broken by facts about Russia. In any case, not Soviet practices but Soviet foreign policy counted most. In the late thirties it was chic to extol things Russian, drink vodka, wear a peasant blouse, admire the Five Year Plan. Feelings about Loyalist Spain ran deeper. Every year fascism became more alarming; every year the western will to resist seemed to lessen. Spain was widely regarded as the final testing ground. Hitler and Mussolini backed Franco and his rebels to the hilt. Western states, pretending to be neutral, gave no aid to the legal government. Only Russia helped it, earning the gratitude of millions outside Spain. Max was uninterested in this struggle and could not understand or sympathize with those who were.

Louis Fischer's autobiography, *Men and Politics,* explains the problem. He had written countless articles praising Soviet Russia for the *Nation* and other magazines. He lived in Moscow, had a Russian wife and a good idea of what went on. During his first years in Moscow, he was thrilled by the Five Year Plan and the "spectacle of creating and self-sacrifice." He was less thrilled by the GPU, not out of principle it seems but because official terrorism made everyone nervous and slowed production. Fischer regarded 1935, the year after the Kirov purge, as the highwater mark of democracy and prosperity in Russia. After that he began to lose faith in Soviet Russia, developing instead an equally obsessive affection for republican Spain. He joined one of the international brigades for a time until persuaded that he could do more good with a typewriter than a rifle. Even in Spain old habits persisted. He was against Catalonian nationalism because it obstructed the war effort, and against the anarchists because they appeared more interested in the social revolution than in fighting Franco. He suspected that GPU agents were murdering anarchist and Trotskyist leaders, but kept quiet about this as about the vastly greater slaughter in Russia.

Fischer returned in 1937 to find Moscow paralyzed with fear. Half of the 160 units in his apartment house had been raided by the GPU. American Communists were fleeing Russia. Most Polish, Hungarian, and German Communists had already vanished into Gulag. Again Fischer kept silent, not, he says, on account of his family, which would have been human and understandable, but for the sake of Spain. Criticism of the terror would weaken anti-fascism. The innocent in Russia had to die so that the innocent in Spain might live.

This was an extreme but not unrepresentative case. Fischer had better information about Russia than most Americans but behaved in the same way as those liberals who lacked it. Even in 1941, after he had broken with Stalinism, Fischer justified his earlier dishonesty on the ground that it served the interests first of socialism, then of Spain. When truth is held in such low regard, the possession of it does little good and may be harmful. Max failed to lie and so had to take the consequences:

> The warmth of emotion toward me among New York's liberals and radical-minded progressives sank to absolute zero. At Charlie Studin's cocktail parties—the nearest thing we had to a literary salon—I stalked about like the Masque of Death in Poe's horrible story. Eliena and I found it pleasanter to stay at home. Except for occasional evenings with our friends of the *Modern Monthly,* we spent the nights and days in Croton, hugging our fireside and our too private knowledge of a bitter truth." [69]

Things were not entirely bleak. Eastman's home became a stopping point for refugees from the Soviet Union. His love life was as varied and satisfying as ever. His finances were better than usual because of *Enjoyment of Laughter* and a radio show he hosted briefly called "The Word Game." On the strength of his salary from it, a banker on Martha's Vineyard loaned Max the money to buy a hilltop in Gay Head. There he built the house that would be home for the rest of his life. Just the same, isolation was unpleasant. Conservatives thought him a Communist still. To Stalinists and fellow travelers he was unclean. Max had not gotten along with moderate socialists since the war. Calverton was helpful but like most people did not understand what Eastman represented and what he had already accomplished.

Edmund Wilson was the exception. He first encountered *Marx, Lenin, and the Science of Revolution* in the spring of 1938 and found it to be "the best critical thing I've read on this philosophical aspect of Marxism." It would have been good, he wrote Eastman, "if people had read it a few years ago when everybody was going crazy about Marxism." [70] Yet, Wilson himself did not open the book until after his faith in the Soviets expired. Though a late convert, Wilson was a generous one. His mighty work, *To the Finland Station,* a history of the revolutionary tradition, acknowledged Eastman handsomely. A key chapter, first published in the Fall 1938 issue of *Partisan Review* as "The Myth of the Dialectic," made the debt plain by siding with Eastman against Sidney Hook:

> If you look up and piece together all that Marx and Engels wrote on the subject [philosophy], you do not get a very satisfactory picture. Max Eastman in his remarkable study, *Marx, Lenin, and the Science of Revolution,* has shown the discrepancies between the statements that Marx and Engels made at various times; Sidney Hook, in his extremely able but less acutely critical book, *Toward the Understanding of Karl Marx,* has tried to iron out the inconsistencies, to state with precision what has been left in the vague, and to formulate a presentable system.[71]

In this, Wilson implied, Hook failed. Parts of Wilson's essay were pure Eastmanism. Speaking of Marx and Engels, Wilson said: "From the moment that they had admitted the Dialectic into their semi-materialistic system, they had admitted an element of mysticism." And a little later: "They had actually carried along with them a good deal of the German idealism that they thought they were warring against."[72] And finally: "The Dialectic then is a religious myth, disencumbered of divine personality and tied up with the history of mankind."[73]

Wilson would always be scrupulous about his debt to Eastman, spelling it out years afterward in a private letter. In the course of correcting a long work on himself, Wilson stated: "Max Eastman was not my guide in my radical days. At the time I was most Marxist and pro-Soviet he was showing the fallacies of Marxism, attacking the Soviet regime, and even undermining the assumptions of Trotsky, whom he had at one time greatly admired. Eventually, when I had gone more deeply into Marxism, I came to see what he was driving at, and his writings influenced me the other way." When his friend Daniel Aaron published a history of radical letters, *Writers on the Left* (1961), Wilson again identified himself with Eastman: "The one important omission I feel is your failure to give attention to the later work of Max Eastman and myself, who seriously studied Marxism, extricated ourselves from the various official versions, and eventually produced a critique of it."[74]

Wilson's essay on the dialectic in 1938 was especially bad news for Trotskyists. They were finding the going hard enough as it was. Though often brilliant, they were few in number. They shared the Stalinist disadvantage of having linked their fortunes to an outside authority who dictated policy. This limited them, as it did Stalinists, but brought no corresponding gains, since Trotsky was powerless. Like Eastman, they had to defend socialism in principle while attacking its practical failures in Russia. This meant walking a narrow trail bounded

on one side by doubts about Marx and on the other by misgivings over
Lenin and Trotsky. An example of the problems this posed was an article in the Trotskyist *New International* in 1935 attacking Eastman's critique of Marxism. The essay had been commissioned by Trotsky himself, and the duty of writing it fell to James Burnham.

Using the pen name John West, Burnham tried to show that Eastman's Marx was a straw man.* Marx never believed in the inevitability
of the revolution, Burnham insisted. Accordingly, Eastman was right to
attack those who falsely claimed that Marx did. More than that, "to the
extent that his criticism is directed in essence not against Marx, but
against the non-revolutionary falsifiers of living Marxism, we must not
merely accept but drive home the lesson." [75] From a Trotskyist point of
view, this article was defective. It did not attack Eastmanism root and
branch. It criticized those who believed the revolution was inevitable,
foremost among whom was Trotsky himself. Little wonder that Burnham would chart an uncertain course in the future, ending up as a conservative, Christian, anti-communist. Even the *New International* would
change, though less drastically. It would accept before long ideas it had
always been criticizing Eastman for putting forward. Burnham himself
would admit after the Stalin-Hitler Pact that Eastman had been right all
along about the dialectic. [76] The trouble with being a Marxist was that
current history had a way of undermining philosophy.

William Phillips's effort to deal with Wilson was more successful
than Burnham's critique of Eastman. As an editor of *Partisan Review*
Phillips felt obliged to refute "The Myth of the Dialectic." He accused
Wilson of having reduced Marxism to "a colossal poem about history;
visionary, aggressive, shocking, irresponsible—and utterly Utopian." [77]
This last charge of Wilson's was the unkindest cut of all. To every
Marxist, of whatever party or sect, the crucial distinction between
Marxism and all other forms of socialism was that it alone could claim
to be scientific. It was what had drawn Eastman to Marx, and when he
discovered strains of mysticism he eliminated what gave offense, throwing out the baby with the bath, though for years he denied having done
so. Wilson was now doing the same, to Phillips's distress. Phillips admit-

---

* This was a common position, for a Marxist almost an inevitable one. In a grumpy
review of *To The Finland Station* Malcolm Cowley wrote that Wilson's "version of the
dialectic, apparently derived from a book by Max Eastman, is one that Marx and Engels
would have violently rejected." "From the Finland Station," *New Republic* (October 7,
1940), p. 478.

ted that the dialectic did verge on magic at times, as Hook had shown. But Phillips still believed that Marx's laws of history had been worked out on the basis of real political and economic facts. "Surely," Phillips wrote, "Mr. Wilson cannot hope to bury all this scientific work in the grave of the dialectic." He did, and would soon have company as other Marxists took the same course, Phillips included. Trotsky often remarked that he knew of no one who, after rejecting the dialectic, did not go on to reject Marxism itself. Eastman was the first of these in America, despite calling himself a Marxist long after he had revised Marx beyond recognition. He was followed by Hook, then Wilson, and then most prominent Trotskyists.

By 1939 Trotsky was defending himself against several lines of criticism, all pointing toward the same conclusion. One was that he personally had betrayed the revolution by destroying the Kronstadt rebels in 1921. Eastman, who did not notice the uprising when it happened, now saw it as the moment when Bolshevism's fatal weakness first became apparent. Boris Souvarine, Dwight Macdonald, and Victor Serge among others came to think so, too. Trotsky tried to brush them off by saying their information was second hand. This was untrue. Serge, for one, had been in Russia at the time and, though siding with the Communist party, had interviewed the Kronstadt survivors in prison and sympathized with their complaints regarding the suppression of democratic and civil liberties.[78] Trotsky defended the wholesale arrests and executions of the Kronstadt sailors on the usual ground that the end justified the means. But many people sick of the endless bloodshed in Russia no longer agreed. Kronstadt became part of the vocabulary of the anti-Bolshevik Left, standing not only for the betrayal of revolutionary idealism, but for the moment of truth when an individual realizes that he can no longer support communism in any form.

Trotsky compounded his difficulties after the Stalin-Hitler Pact in 1939 by insisting that his followers endorse the Soviet Union's invasions of Poland and Finland. Even though degenerate, Russia was still a workers' state. Its conquests were not imperialistic, since by definition socialist states were incapable of this. When the Soviet Union expanded, the area of capitalism shrank, which was progress no matter how accomplished. Once again Trotsky defeated himself, justifying Max's contention that this brilliant man was hopeless as a political leader. Trotsky's rationalizations destroyed the nascent Fourth International and alienated finally most of the intellectuals who had made

Trotskyism the leading American radical movement in terms of per capita brain power.

The reaction of Trotsky to these losses can be traced in a volume called *In Defense of Marxism*. It consists of statements and essays issued by Trotsky during the period when the Socialist Worker's party, as his American movement was called, broke apart. In these documents Trotsky was mainly concerned with his critics inside the Socialist Worker's party, especially Burnham, who announced in 1939 that the USSR was no longer a workers' state and thus not entitled to support, even critical support. Though Eastman was not a party to this internal debate, his name kept cropping up. Eastman had been Trotsky's first American follower and for over a decade the most distinguished and eloquent of his defenders. Trotsky saw his leftist critics as Eastman's children. Their rejection of the dialectic on pragmatic grounds was both typically American and in some sense Eastman's particular fault, according to Trotsky. In his "A Petty-Bourgeois Opposition in the Socialist Worker's Party" (December 15, 1939) Trotsky wrote:

> Pragmatism, a mixture of rationalism and empiricism, became the national philosophy of the United States. The theoretical methodology of Max Eastman is not fundamentally different from the methodology of Henry Ford—both regard living society from the point of view of an "engineer" (Eastman—platonically). Historically the present disdainful attitude toward the dialectic is explained simply by the fact that the grandfathers and great-grandmothers of Max Eastman and others did not need the dialectic in order to conquer territory and enrich themselves. But times have changed, the philosophy of pragmatism has entered a period of bankruptcy just as has American capitalism." [79]

This odd passage shows Trotsky at his rhetorical worst. The opposition, by virtue of opposing Trotsky, automatically becomes petty bourgeois. Eastman is compared to a great capitalist and accused of having wealthy forebears—a sure sign of petty bourgeois tendencies. The whole attack on Eastman is irrelevant in that he never belonged to the Socialist Workers party and was hateful to many members. So, too, is the statement that Eastman's conquering forebears did not need the dialectic to enrich themselves. In the whole history of the world, nobody's conquering ancestors required the dialectic for this purpose. And anyway, Eastman's family were honorably lacking in wealth and always had been.

Other remarks of a similar character followed. In "An Open Letter to James Burnham" (January 7, 1940), Trotsky wrote that he had been told that Burnham was saying he would not argue about the dialectic with Trotsky but only debate concrete issues. " 'I stopped arguing about religion long ago,' you added ironically. I once heard Max Eastman voice this same sentiment." [80] So much for that issue. On receiving Burnham's essay "Science and Style," Trotsky wrote that there was no science in it and "as far as 'style' is concerned, I frankly prefer Eastman." [81] Trotsky called his left opponents New Moralists and on February 29, 1940, wrote Joseph Hansen saying he had heard that they were discussing "my terrible crime concerning Eastman and Lenin's testament." Trotsky had disowned Eastman at that time for the best of reasons, expediency: "The transforming of this political necessity into an abstract moral question is only possible for petty-bourgeois fakers." And in any case, Eastman "published this document without consulting me and the others," thereby widening the split in the Politburo. [82]

Here Trotsky engaged in name-calling, invoked need as the higher law, lied (Eastman had gotten permission to release the Testament from Christian Rakovsky, who was very close to Trotsky), and exposed all those traits that were his undoing. As Serge put it in his memoirs, "Trotskyism was displaying symptoms of an outlook in harmony with that of the very Stalinism against which it had taken its stand, and by which it was being ground into powder." [83] Eastman was not saintlike by nature, nor even long-suffering. He could be as polemical as the next man, which in those days was very polemical indeed. Yet he never replied to Trotsky in kind. When Eastman criticized Trotsky, as happened later, he would be principled and fair. Max knew that a giant though fallen was a giant still.

* * *

Max's isolation came to a sudden end on August 24, 1939, when it was learned that Russia had signed a non-aggression pact with Germany, making straight the way to World War II. Max always said that he learned of this when invited off the street to join a party given by ex-friends in Greenwich Village who had not spoken to him for years. Eastman was seldom in New York during August, so the story may be apocryphal. But the point of it is true. No one remembered that Eastman had predicted years earlier that nazism and communism, being the same thing, would end up in bed together. His long vigil was re-

warded just the same. Stalin had sold out to Hitler for a bribe consisting of Eastern Poland and the Baltic states, plus a strip of Finland. This
was just what might be expected of the man Eastman had been writing
about, but bore little relation to the Stalin idolized by Popular Fronters.
The Front collapsed, aided by the joint nazi-communist invasion of
Poland and the Comintern's new line that France and Britain were imperialist monsters—unlike Germany, which ceased to figure in communist propaganda. For once history was on Eastman's side, and he
profited accordingly.

Though fondly remembered even today, the Popular Front suffered from two fatal defects. The first is that it was based on the absence of ideas. For the sake of anti-fascist unity, it abandoned the most
basic left-wing concepts—the class struggle, nationalization of the
means of production, expropriation of wealth. "Communism is twentieth century Americanism" was the meaningless slogan of Earl Browder, chairman of the party. The Popular Front had prejudices:
favoring workers, loyalist Spain, folk music; disliking employers,
Southerners, Trotskyists. These only masked a lack of substance. The
second flaw was the Popular Front's complete dependence on Moscow.
So long as Russia was the only country actively fighting fascism, especially in Spain, this did not matter. After the Pact, having to follow
Stalin's new line crippled the American party. Those with wills of their
own could see the Popular Front for what it was, a collection of futile
gestures.

The Pact led to many post-mortems from which little was learned.
Eugene Lyons gave the period its name in his book *The Red Decade*
(1941). This was a tiresome indictment making things seem worse than
they were. Even so, as Lyons had a passion for naming names, the book
is a Who's Who of the Popular Front and useful on that account. It
reminds us that distinction is no guarantee of wisdom. The liberal
weeklies remained self-righteous. Eastman wrote the *New Republic* to
say that former Communists and sympathizers should own up to their
misdeeds. They had been wrong to suppose you could serve both democracy and totalitarianism and should admit it. James T. Farrell rang
up a long list of charges against the *Nation* on similar grounds.[84] In
both cases the magazines proclaimed their virtue. Even when they were
wrong, which was seldom, it was for the right reasons both insisted. As
late as 1941 the *New Republic* was still defending its record in the thirties. That its views had paralleled Russia's much of the time was an un-
doubted fact. Did this imply fellow traveling? Nothing of the sort. It

was the "Communists [who] at that time adhered to the *New Republic* line."[85] At last the mystery of Comintern decision-making was solved. Stalin read the *New Republic*. Having learned nothing, the liberal weeklies promptly forgot everything. When Hitler invaded Russia, the Popular Front would rise again.

Not all who had been Communists or sympathizers in the thirties followed this course. Many got off the train of history for good. Few of these seem to have reflected on the experience publicly. Fewer still were apologetic. Granville Hicks was an exception. He would come back to the subject often in later years, but his first important effort was "Communism and the American Intellectuals," an essay that appeared in 1941. At the time there seemed many good reasons for supporting Communism, he recalled: the depression, the Communists' program of action, organization, doctrine, and their "working model—the USSR," the united front against fascism, the high quality of party members. These explained without excusing the communist and pro-communist intellectuals. "We were a good lot, but rather stupid," he confessed disarmingly.[86] Many scholars have agreed. Daniel Aaron concludes his book on literary leftists with these words. "We can regret," he says, "their inadequacies, and failures, their romanticism, their capacity for self-deception, their shrillness, their self-righteousness. It is less easy to scorn their efforts, however blundering and ineffective, to change the world."[87] Without wishing to scorn such attempts one may still ask if this doesn't miss the point. Good intentions are not at issue. Popular Fronters were seldom mendacious. Only a handful like Fischer consciously misled. At their worst, most only took care to avoid a confrontation with the truth about Russia. Still, can error be excused on the ground of blindness? Popular Fronters, had they the power, would indeed have changed the world. Soviet might would have increased and been further glorified. Spain would have gained a communist dictatorship instead of a fascist one. It is difficult to see how these would have benefited mankind. Popular Fronters desired peace and justice. To that end they applauded a regime steeped in blood and cruelty, an economic order resting on slavery, and a culture in which all worthwhile human values were sacrificed to the needs of the state. The discrepancy here was such that Popular Fronters had to fail and, of course, deserved to. That they meant well seems a poor excuse. There is hardly any point to having a history if we learn no more from it than this.

CHAPTER TEN

Politics

1940–1945

During the same year, after the disasters at Kerch (120,000 prisoners), at Kharkov (even more), and in the course of the big southern retreat to the Caucasus and the Volga, another very important wave of officers and soldiers was pumped through—those who refused to stand to the death and who retreated without permission, the men, whom, in the words of Stalin's immortal Order No. 227, the Motherland could not forgive for the shame they had caused her. This wave, however, never reached Gulag: after accelerated processing by divisional tribunals, it was, to a man, herded into punishment battalions, and was soaked up in the red sand of advanced positions, leaving not a trace. Thus was cemented the foundation of the Stalingrad victory, but it has found no place in the usual Russian history and exists only in the private history of the sewage system.

The Gulag Archipelago

The Stalin-Hitler Pact rehabilitated Eastman. He could never regain his old place on the Left. He was not young or heroic in the right way. Years of bitter feuding could not be erased. Yet Max's new position was in some ways better than the old. It had been based to a degree on exciting speeches and transient glamor. Now Max had the benefit of long experience, an expert knowledge of his subject, a couple of solid books, and historical vindication. In 1940 he capped this with two more books, his major statements on Marxism and the Soviet Union. *Stalin's Russia* may be the most important of Eastman's books, his memoirs excepted. Twenty-five years of living and thinking went into it, as he made plain by showing how his ideas had been shaped by events.

Eastman began by reviewing his political history, telling the story of his first skeptical encounters with Marxism while editing the *Masses,* and how he found in Lenin the answer to doubt. Leninism appeared to supply the practical, scientific element that Marxism lacked, hence *Marx, Lenin, and the Science of Revolution.* In 1940 he still stood by Part One of that book, which exposed the flaws in Marxism. But he now repudiated Part Two, which explained and endorsed the science of revolutionary engineering he attributed to Lenin. Time had shown him that the "criminal tyrannies of Stalinism" were directly related to failings in Leninism. As a practical method for seizing power, Leninism worked, but afterward it became utopian: "It trusted too much in education, too much in the reasonable and kind and tolerant and freedom-loving qualities of human nature. More accurately, perhaps, it trusted too much in the benign intentions of a dialectic universe." [1]

When young, Eastman felt that Lenin believed as he did, that the socialization of land and capital would "transform the instruments of production, which serve today mainly to enslave and exploit labor, into simple instruments of labor freely associating." [2] Education and socialization would create the just society. In retrospect Eastman saw a fatal defect in his view of things: "I thought that bourgeois democracy was something once and for all achieved, something we could afford to kick out from under us as we took the further step toward industrial democracy." [3] Now he regarded political democracy not as a step to transcend but as a foundation to build on. He had been repeatedly distressed by the failures of communism inside Russia and out, and now believed that the armed seizure of power, for whatever reason, by a well-organized minority would almost always result in a totalitarian state.

Having made this confession Eastman went on to repeat the arguments of his "The End of Socialism in Russia." It was even clearer to him in 1940 than in 1936 that Stalin had systematically destroyed all that was valuable in Soviet life—educational and family reforms, the freedom of women, and even birth control. Language itself was perverted in this effort, for "peasants have been starved by millions in the name of the workers' and peasants' republic." [4] And the republic was itself a dictatorship, whose power was maintained by jailing tens of thousands (in a footnote he added this should now read hundreds of thousands—we know that it ought to have read millions) of people. Eastman discussed wage differentials in the Soviet Union, which he found to be at least as great as under capitalism. American tourists ignored this,

Eastman believed, because in a poor country even the best paid were not well off by American standards. The fact remained that a manager might make up to a hundred times as much as a worker. The Stakhan-ovites, or shock workers, by themselves constituted a new privileged class, as did the leading collective farmers.

After a lengthy review of economic inequities, Eastman got to the best part of his book, a slashing analysis of the purge trials. Max was disturbed by the Western inability to understand why, if they weren't guilty, so many Bolsheviks confessed to treason. It was obvious to him that the confessions were false. The language used in them was not nat-ural to the confessors. They were clearly reciting scripts written by others. These betrayed little knowledge of Marxism, Leninism, or the history of the revolution. Moreover, while it was possible that one of Lenin's aides might have turned traitor, it was inconceivable that all could have. Eastman then discussed each aspect of the purges.

THE MEN

Eastman knew many of the leading victims personally, including Radek, Piatakov, Muralov, and the Georgian Budu Mdvani, "a big, broad-shouldered, powerful, jovial, prodigiously laughing, as-tonishingly handsome, veritable dynamo of a man, one of the well-loved friends of Lenin and Trotsky and everybody else who ever knew him, one of the gorgeous people of the earth, a 'prince' if there ever was one, and vastly amused to be confused with little titled princes of the same name. Now he is swept down too. They are all gone, all the great Bolshevik party men, the true leaders—either dead or in prison on their way to death."[5] Eastman had not liked Bukharin much, think-ing him unequal to his job as party theoretician. But Bukharin had been a sensitive man dedicated to socialism: "He served Stalin most of the time in a kind of bewildered despair, and his arrest added a night-mare touch to those trials, self-villifications and shootings of all in Rus-sia whom I trusted." Eastman did like Sosnovsky, chief feature writer for *Pravda* in Lenin's day, a brainy, fearless man: "He too is disgraced and dead now, although he never stood up in court and asked me to believe that he had become a depraved beast."[6]

These passages, together with the deliberate omission of Christian Rakovsky, whom of all the great Bolsheviks Eastman loved most and who had named him as a British agent, go a long way toward explaining the violent anti-communism of Eastman's later years. Most American writers who turned against Stalinism felt betrayed or deluded in some measure. Eastman was one of a handful with friends in Russia. More than that, he was almost the only one who had been in Russia when Lenin ruled and people were most hopeful. The purges swept away his friends, his in-laws, his heroes, everyone associated with the most thrilling adventure of his life—save for Litvinov the diplomat, who could not be spared. Most who hated Russian communism did so abstractly. Eastman had deep personal reasons, and they show.

THE POLITICAL SITUATION

Eastman's certainty of the victim's innocence was reinforced by his knowledge of Russian politics. He believed Stalin had destroyed nearly everything in Russia that Lenin constructed. Therefore Stalin had also to destroy the Old Bolsheviks who helped with the building. Eastman called Stalin a Menshevik, meaning by this not any general identification of Stalin's program with Menshevism as such, but rather Stalin's counter-revolutionary actions. Stalin was against the real revolution in Russia, and in Spain as well. His aid to the Spanish Republicans was conditional on their subordinating revolutionary programs to the war effort: "It is that policy of postponing the class issue and 'cooperating with the liberals' in a revolutionary situation upon which Lenin split with the Mensheviks in Russia, and thereby gave its essential meaning to the word 'Bolshevism,' and to the Bolshevik party its historic role and its triumph."[7] Stalin's blunders, the disaster of forced collectivization and the mistakes of the Five Year Plan, made him vulnerable. To avert a mass uprising, Stalin required a monolithic party loyal to him alone, and the elimination of all possible leaders of any stature—especially Trotsky, still his most dangerous adversary. The function of the treason trials was to break "once and for all the force of the October revolution." Thus the only mystery about the treason trials was why so many influential people outside Russia could not grasp these simple facts.

THE CONFESSIONS

They were unbelievable. It was absurd to think that dedicated Bolsheviks would plot to murder Stalin and his aides out of "sheer spitefulness," sabotage Soviet industry, conspire to overthrow socialism in Russia for personal gain, spread disease germs in the Red Army and worse. It was possible to accept such confessions as truthful only by assuming there was something inherently unnatural about Bolshevism. The acts confessed to, if real, amounted to "absolute and wanton treachery—to self, to friends, to principles, to party, to the working class and to humanity. Anyone who believed them must in sober judgment despair of and despise the human race." Fortunately this was not necessary. The confessions were false and resulted from the following: "the peculiar ethics of Bolshevism, which commits its adherents to a habit of class-loyal lying; the fact that the Bolshevik experiment had failed, and the equivocal way in which it failed; Stalin's penal code, which holds the immediate family of a political offender punishable for his crimes, whether aware of them or not; and finally, the passionately vindictive character of Stalin." [8]

PARTY LYING

Stalin, having decided to wipe out his potential enemies, was able to direct their confessions because the party had already subordinated truth to fidelity. Lenin and all the Bolsheviks held that lying and even death were preferable to disloyalty. Scorning bourgeois notions of honor and honesty, many Bolsheviks confessed and went to their deaths with a feeling that as loyal soldiers of the Party they were justified, and, so to speak redeemed" by this display of obedience.* Then, too, as W. G. Krivitsky had pointed out in *Stalin's Secret Service* (1939), torture was used to reduce victims to an infantile state, where they would say anything. Confession brought an end to torment, and a conviction that in death they were still serving the party. On the other hand, as Krivitsky also pointed out, for every one who confessed publicly a hundred were shot in private.

POLITICAL CONFUSION

Max felt that some who confessed might have had simpler motives. It was hard for a person to say that the cause to which he had given his whole life was a failure. And it was especially hard if you had a re-

---

* Arthur Koestler, who had been a Comintern agent, would make this point a central theme of his novel *Darkness at Noon* (1945).

ligious belief that history was on your side. There is no room in Marxism for failure. History marches forward to inevitable victory. Moreover, it was possible to argue that socialized production and other changes meant that the revolution was actually a success. Trotsky himself had shown a typically rigid mentality by offering as an alternative to Stalinism only another worker uprising like that which had produced it in the first place. Old Bolsheviks had only one choice, as Max saw it, "to pronounce their life work a failure, or to admit there was some hope for socialism and the workers in the regime, or after the regime, of Stalin." When to these complex pressures was added physical torture and threats to one's family, Max added, it was no great trick to see how the confessions were obtained.

STALIN'S REVENGE

A final question was why the victims were made to confess to such unlikely crimes. Max answered that Stalin's "passionately vindictive character" was reason enough. It did not satisfy him merely to have the accused shot. They had to plead guilty to the very traits Stalin possessed, "spitefulness" and a "thirst for power." They also had to take the blame for everything that went wrong in Russia. It was not Stalin's fault that poverty and injustice were widespread, but that of the "wreckers" in high places and low who willfully obstructed progress. Max had learned of Stalin's desire for revenge in 1929 when he was visited by Leonid Serebriakov. Max had reminded Serebriakov that it was dangerous for him to be seen with an enemy of the regime. Serebriakov answered that it made no difference because whatever he did Stalin would get him anyway: "If he lives long enough he will get every one of us who has ever injured him in speech or action. That is his principal aim in life." Serebriakov portrayed Stalin as "the most vindictive man on earth" and told Eastman a story used by Trotsky also. In a gathering of comrades the question arose as to what constituted a perfect day. Stalin said, "Mine is to plan an artistic revenge upon an enemy, carry it out to perfection and then go home and go peacefully to bed." [9]

In later chapters Eastman compared Stalin with Hitler, much to Hitler's advantage, since his crimes lay mostly in the future. Eastman reviewed the history of the Comintern, showing how it had been corrupted into serving as an arm of Russian foreign policy. He offered numerous instances of changes in direction, "crazy zigzags," Eastman called them, dictated by Soviet needs. He also wrote out for the first time an elaborate critique of Trotsky, who now seemed to embody most of what Eastman disliked in Stalin. He believed that Trotsky's original failure was in 1917. Until then he had criticized Lenin's organizational system in much the same terms as honest Socialists were doing in 1940. He attacked Lenin's idea of the vanguard party as, in his own words, "the replacement of the dictatorship over the proletariat, of the political rule of the class by organizational rule over the class." And more aptly still Trotsky had written that Lenin's "democratic centralism" meant in practice that "The apparatus of the party substitutes itself for the party, the Central Committee substitutes itself for the apparatus, and finally, the dictator substitutes himself for the central committee."[10] But in 1917 Trotsky surrendered to Lenin on this point, although Lenin also changed on another, embracing Trotsky's concept of the "permanent revolution." If only Trotsky were more flexible and self-reliant, Max continued, he would say that he was right and Lenin wrong on both counts. But instead, to defend himself against Stalinist charges of infidelity, he was trying to "out-Lenin Lenin."

Trotsky now dismissed the vanguard party issue out of hand. Where he had been against centralism in 1923, he today defended it. Eastman concluded from this that the only reason Trotsky had opposed centralism in 1923 was because he believed then that the rank and file was with him. Thus he favored party democracy only as a tactic. After defending Trotsky for fifteen years, Eastman had run out of patience. Trotsky stood condemned by his own words: "We learned from Marx that in the cause of socialism popular democracy must be abandoned for the dictatorship of the proletariat. We learned from Lenin that proletarian dictatorship must be abandoned for the dictatorship of the Party. We now learn from Trotsky that party dictatorship must be abandoned for the dictatorship of the Center. It is but one step, and that step inevitable, to the *Fuehrerprinzip*."[11] Trotsky had proven beyond a doubt that he was, in principle at least, as immoral as Stalin. It was Trotsky who wrote that the proletariat "must be free from the fictions of religion, 'democracy' and transcendental morality—the spiritual chains forged by the enemy to tame and enslave it. Only that which prepares the complete and final over-throw of imperialist bestiality is moral and nothing else. The welfare of the revolution—that is the supreme law."[12] To Eastman this was "more mad than Marxist."

Subsequently Eastman discussed the reasons why people became radical, drawing a line between "libertarian radicals," with whom he identified, and their enemies, the "totalitarian liberals," who were more numerous than outright Stalinists and thus more dangerous. He considered the future of socialism in light of what was now known about it. To him Stalinists were no longer betrayers of the Marxist revolution, "they are its outcome." Stalinism was "an inherent part of the process of nationalization in the only case in which it has been tried." As he saw it this put Socialists in a weak position. They had to fight the vulgarizers of left doctrine, the Stalinists who claimed that nationalization meant socialism. Worse still, they had to resist the nagging thought that perhaps this was true, that "Stalinism is socialism," the unforeseen consequence of the measures that were supposed to create a classless society.

Trotskyists ignored this, but even democratic Socialists seemed to Eastman cavalier on the point. Given the means, he prophesied, "they will sacrifice either democratic controls or the actual expropriation of the capitalists (and most probably the latter). In either case, as leaders toward a society of the free and equal based on state ownership, they remain, notwithstanding their better morals and more persuasive manners, as unconvincing as the Trotskyists."[13] Eastman correctly guessed that when they came to power, as in Western Europe after the war, democratic Socialists would fail to abolish private property. They would prove to be not socialists at all in the sense of actually intending to create a classless society. This made them the left wing of liberalism, which Eastman had always disdained as a political philosophy. Eastman now felt that, to be real, socialism had to be totalitarian. He scoffed at Clement Attlee, head of the British Labour party, for saying that socialism was needed to win the war. "When National Socialism joined hands with Socialism in One Country over the grave of Polish independence, the word "socialism" became, to say the least, a liability to any genuine movement of liberation."[14] Socialism as a word and a concept was finished.

The balance of *Stalin's Russia* concerned theoretical problems he had often dealt with before, the religious aspect of Marxism, wishful thinking on the part of true believers, and other matters of interest. At this point Eastman had abandoned socialism but not the motives that had led him to it. On the one hand, "the principles of freedom and individualism must be sacredly preserved"; on the other, "if life is to flourish in an age of machinery and mass production, there must also be a new cooperativeness, one involving a new degree of discipline and subordination to the collective purpose, and to that end more state control than would have been good sense in the time of Jefferson."[15] To escape the perils of socialism and totalitarian liberalism alike, he called vaguely for a new radicalism based on science and experience. This dim note scarcely mars an otherwise tremendous book.

* * *

Eastman's second big achievement in 1940 was *Marxism: Is It Science?* Like *Stalin's Russia* it includes much that he had written before, especially in *Marx, Lenin, and the Science of Revolution*. But it contained some new material and interesting reworkings of the old. Once again he demolished Hegel and the dialectic. He drew again his comparison between Marxism and Freudianism. He continued to admire Lenin's ability to dump Marx's metaphysics in the interest of practical politics. Eastman tried to define science more precisely than before so as to show how Marxism differed from it:

> Science, then, is distinguished from common sense by its degree of system and expertness; from magic and occult ritual, no matter how systemized and expert, by its concern for uncontrollable facts and the invariant relations among them; from charlatanism and pseudo science by its austere mental honesty and its skeptical equilibrium; from poetic literature by its loyalty to the generic and practical concept as against the particular and immediate perception, from religion and metaphysical belief by its refusal to allow interest or emotion to influence its judgment of fact.[16]

This was still not science as we understand it, but a big improvement over earlier efforts. As a result, his comparison of Marxists and anarchists became crisper. To Eastman, among the errors of Marxism was its unscientific attitude toward the goal of revolutionary action, the good society which it failed to define: "Just as the anarchists, in their preoccupation with the goal, fail to consider the facts and the method of procedure, so the Marxists, in the apotheosis of the facts and the method fail to consider the goal."[17] But if the goal is not clearly seen, a scientific means of reaching it cannot be worked out. So Bakunin was right to attack, as he put it, the "everlasting theoretical insanity" of Karl Marx. Eastman had grown more tolerant of anarchists than he had been in his Bolshevik days. He still felt that they too showed a want of science by failing to make clear the means by which their admirable vision was to be realized.

Eastman concluded *Marxism: Is It Science?* with a final attack on Trotsky and a rehash of his disagreements with Hook. This was in part redundant, as Hook had come around to Max's view on some issues. Though the language is Hook's, Max himself might have written this line: "Almost every variety of dialectic materialism current today is a bastard offspring, fathered by a politically-motivated metaphysical idealism upon the body of modern science."[18] Unlike Wilson, Hook did not admit any debt to Max. It is easy to see just the same.

These two big books were pastiches of new and old material. There probably was no real need for him to have published the books separately, given their overlap. A single volume, written from scratch to the degree possible, would have been more polished, better integrated, possibly more convincing. Even so, the books stand up. Eastman's critique of Marxism combines philosophical analysis with history. *Stalin's Russia* contained the best diagnosis then available of the Moscow trials and the confessions they produced. Time has confirmed Max's thesis for the most part. Solzhenitsyn, Robert Conquest, and others have provided more information without materially altering Eastman's analysis of these strange and horrible events. Adam Ulam in his absorbing biography portrays Stalin as somewhat less cynical than Max regarded him, and gives more weight to Stalin's fear of war in explaining the purges. All the same, Eastman's guesses were near the mark. Even his most controversial argument, that the failure of socialism in Russia justified abandoning socialism in principle, has not yet become obsolete. Democratic Socialists have always defended themselves by saying that because Russia (and later China, Cuba, and so on) was a totalitarian state did not mean that the idea of socialism was false. Local conditions are always invoked to explain why socialism went wrong in one country or another. Yet where Socialists are democratic, as in the West, there is little socialism, although much brave talk about it. And where they are truly socialistic, as in the communist nations, there is little democracy. In the more than forty years since Eastman first declared the thing to be impossible, not a single country has managed to be at once truly democratic and truly socialistic.

If there is to be little or no socialism where lies the hope of reform? Max was vague on this point because he wasn't sure. Later he decided that undiluted capitalism was the only basis for liberty. But recent history proves there is another, better way, though for ideological reasons Max refused to see it. Had he not become so conservative, he might have completed his argument in this way. Socialism remains a beautiful dream. In real life it has been proven unnecessary by the welfare states of Scandinavia. In combining some socialism with a great deal of private ownership, they have reached levels of prosperity, equity, and personal freedom that the founders of socialism thought only a revolution could achieve. These just societies are unexciting. The militant young of the world do not sing their praises. They are to be cherished all the same.

*   *   *

Despite their merits, Eastman's big books sold poorly. His general position was already well known. After the Stalin-Hitler Pact, interest in Marxism and the Soviets had declined sharply. Book reviewers underestimated *Stalin's Russia.* The *Nation* gave it a tepid notice of course, though it recognized, as Eastman still did not, that his argument was leading to this conclusion: "planning, socialist or otherwise, contains the seeds of totalitarianism." Michael Kapovich in a favorable review noted that Max had not faced up to his argument in another respect. He was able to see the amoralism of Trotsky and Stalin, but not that of Lenin. Philip Rahv, a Marxist still, dismissed Eastman for turning against socialism merely because it had gone wrong in Russia.[19] Lillian Symes, writing for Eastman's own *Modern Monthly,* claimed he attached too much weight to the dialectic, which few Westerners had ever been interested in.[20]

The main division between non-Marxist critics was over Eastman's argument that socialism had to be abandoned altogether and some new kind of radical politics devised. Those who like Eastman were moving from left to right agreed. John Chamberlain, a former Stalinist, thought with Max that free markets made free men and hoped for some mixture of Keynsian economics, syndicalism, Populism, and other elements that might appeal to Americans. Eugene Lyons, who with Max would end up on the *Reader's Digest,* said that democracy had to be the essential foundation of any good society.[21]

Liberal reviewers often liked the book, especially the Moscow trials section, the sharpest piece of detective work in it, but were unhappy with Max's dim prescription for future action. The *New York Times* said Eastman's final chapter was anti-climactic. His proposed movement seemed no more scientific than Lenin's, although "perhaps a utopian quality and an element of vagueness are essential ingredients of any comprehensive scheme for the salvation of mankind."[22] Harold Laski, a fellow-traveling Fabian and a lost soul to Eastman, reached the same conclusion in a surprisingly generous review—aided no doubt by the Stalin-Hitler Pact. He admitted many of Max's indictments, while modifying them with references to Russian backwardness and other excuses. Then he dismissed Eastman's proposals, which seemed to him slight and scattered: "Even the aphorisms of so attractive a mind as Mr. Eastman's do not constitute a philosophy."[23]

Marxism: Is It Science?, though a more difficult book than *Stalin's Russia*, was better received. Marxists thought poorly of it, as was to be expected. A curious review in the *Modern Quarterly* said that it came out at the wrong time because no one was interested in Marxism any longer, and then displayed great interest in defending Marxism against Eastman's charges.[24] J. D. Bernal, an English scientist well known for his efforts to apply the dialectic to research, disagreed with Eastman on all major points and insisted upon the usefulness of dialectical materialism.[25] These were the exceptions. Benjamin Stolberg, an old labor activist, wrote Max to say that he had once believed in dialectical materialism, but no longer: "And I do not doubt that your two books had a lot to do with it." John Dos Passos told Eastman that he had done more than anyone "to keep the subject [socialism] alive for Americans, to make some sense of it." Not knowing that he and Eastman would become conservative before long, he continued: "The danger is that we'll be thrown off the valuable part of Marx by the religious fanatics and the college professors who mainly verbalize on the subject." Rex Stout, the mystery writer, sent Eastman a note:

> It makes me almost apoplectic
> To hear a guy talk dialectic.
> But, evoluting from a beast, man
> Need go no higher than Max Eastman.

"Them's my sentiments upon finishing *Marxism: Is It Science?* It is neat, witty, lucid, effective and scholarly; and reading it is delightful mental exercise. Thank you warmly for sending it. My slogan: Take the R out of *Marxism*." Louis Hacker of Columbia called it a "brilliant analysis" and recommended it for "intelligent laymen." Even Santayana, who always disliked what Max sent him, was pleased.[26]

T. V. Smith called Max a great liberal and said the book was generous, progressive, and "potent enough to put the quietus on Marxian pretences of science and to beget immunity against its virus of the religion of disavowed power." The *Political Science Quarterly* observed that Marxism "could not have found a more able, critical expositor than Max Eastman." Selig Perlman began his review by saying, "Of all American intellectuals with an intimate contact with Marxian thought, Max Eastman represents the longest span of such mental experience as well as the most penetrating thinking and observation." He agreed with most of the book, though he still felt Max was overly impressed with Lenin. The *Times Literary Supplement* was also generous: "Mr. Eastman in this new volume handsomely repays the hard thought he asks for." So again was Harold Laski, who said the book was a "healthy and refreshing challenge to examine anew basic principles in a time when events have called all dogmas into question." [27]

Best of all was a giant essay (4,350 words) by Edmund Wilson in, of all places, the *New Republic*. For its issue of February 10, 1941, Wilson reviewed not only the two most recent works but Eastman's entire career. He traced it from the period 1913–22, when Max had been "one of the dominant figures of the intellectual life of New York" and a great influence on the impressionable young, of whom "an enormous number owe a special debt to Max Eastman." [28] But it seemed to Wilson that Max came back from Europe a different man. The once encouraging, appreciative editor appeared to be a "critic on the sidelines who girded and jeered and complained." *Enjoyment of Poetry* "had communicated the exhilaration of a lover of lyric verse." *The Literary Mind* "made itself disagreeable at the expense of precisely the oldest and most serious of those writers who were working to carry on the great tradition of literature." [29] It irritated everyone who was trying to defend Joyce and Eliot against the Philistines. *Marx, Lenin, and the Science of Revolution* was a relentless critique of Marxism with none of the "revolutionary ardor which had animated Marx and Lenin and which had taken Max Eastman himself to Russia." Eastman's polemics against Hook and others had a malicious tone. He appeared to be trying to undermine "their philosophical positions or the products of their artistic activity, by showing that they were suffering from adolescent fixations or infantile illusions of inferiority." Up to the middle thirties, Wilson thought, Eastman more and more resembled a bitter, querulous minority of one. Then came the purges and finally the Stalin-Hitler Pact:

Max Eastman, who had first published the Testament of Lenin and who had been warning people since 1925 against the tendencies that had now triumphed, was seen standing like a stout if slightly twisted lone pine. He began to reacquire credit; people quoted him with respect again. The young no longer shrank from contact as from a damned soul who had blasphemed the Kremlin. And Max himself seemed to muster new forces. *Stalin's Russia and the Crisis in Socialism* and *Marxism: Is It Science?* have presented what is, so far as I know, the most intelligent and searching as well as the best informed discussion of the implications of the Marxist movement and the development of the Revolution in Russia that has yet appeared in English.[30]

Eastman's big books of 1940 persuaded Wilson to reread some of the earlier works. *The Literary Mind,* for one, now looked quite different to him. He saw that Max had recognized important issues: "The end of the twenties was marked by a hullabaloo of aesthetic crankery, philosophical pedantry and academic moralizing; and Max Eastman was almost alone in his attempt to work out as an enlightened modern man the larger relations of art and science to one another, and of both to the society behind them." Even Max's poetry read better a second time. It was not perfectly crafted. Max never entirely escaped the "sentimental and amateurish verse" of the 1890s. Yet, "there is a lyric poet in Max Eastman, a personal voice, an original imagery, a temperament volatile and fugitive" that appeared in his best poems, especially those about birds or water. Max's writings on left politics were "the most valuable of the commentaries in English on this subject so inflammatory to prejudice."

Wilson compared Eastman with Max's own hero Mark Twain, saying that Eastman "brought to Moscow the Yankee skepticism and the humane common sense" of Twain's *Innocents Abroad,* and in that spirit never succumbed to Marxist jargon or its historical mythology. Rather, he stripped it of everything except "what is intelligible to American modes of thought and applicable to American actualities." Professional philosophers had disdained Marxism. It remained for Eastman, who had been trained in philosophy, to show the shortcomings which Marx, "in his preoccupation with politics, had never found the time to work out." And Wilson believed that Eastman had exposed the "theological delusions, carried over from the old religion by way of German idealistic philosophy, which were concealed by the scientific pretensions of Marx."[31] The difficulties of Marxism had led most American converts to swallow whole what they could not understand. But Eastman had made the effort, subjected Marxism to the scrutiny of a practical American mind, and produced the best critique, even though, as it came out when Marxism was fashionable, it received little serious attention. That Eastman persisted anyway in this thankless task Wilson attributed to his ministerial background. Because of it Max would go on preaching the truth whether anyone listened or not.

This role had its weaknesses, and Wilson spelled them out. Eastman was a poet who had not fully learned his trade, a revolutionist uncertain of victory, a philosopher without a chair, a journalist who let his magazine fall into the hands of interests that promoted everything he was most against. Worst of all, as Wilson saw it, was Eastman's scientism: "I do not know how it happened that Max Eastman became so obsessed by the idea of science: he has erected it into a totem about which it is as if he has talked too much because he has not known what clan he belonged to. So also the continual emphasis on what he calls 'living' may have compensated for his failure to cultivate intensively the several departments in which he has worked.

"Having said this, and it has already been said often, we must recognize that Max Eastman, after all, has justified his anomalous role of preacher-teacher-critic-poet."[32] And he did so not as a celebrity, the role for which he was best known, but, and Wilson italicized this, *as primarily a writer to be read.* Wilson remembered Max's *Liberator* articles as being "a little diffuse and lacking in bony structure. But the prose of these recent books has a clarity and terseness of form, an intellectual edge, which it would be hard to match elsewhere today in the American literature of ideas." Wilson was reminded by it of André Gide, "and the audience of intellectuals which has surely overrated Gide has underrated Max Eastman." Wilson ended: "Max Eastman has continued to perform for us the same function that he did in the first World War: that of the winter log that floats in the swimming-pool and prevents the concrete from cracking by itself taking the pressure of the ice."[33]

On reading this essay Max wrote Wilson that it "always makes you a little sick at heart when anything reminds you of the mess you've made of your life, and how you've slid and drifted along and never done or been any definite thing. However, I had been getting used to that in my autobiography [which he was writing at the time], and you seemed surprisingly tolerant of it. I am, anyway, enormously bucked up, if not perhaps a little dangerously swollen out, in my ego by your articles."[34] As Wilson recognized, Eastman's elevator was going up at last, taking him to some fine place in the minds, maybe even the hearts so long closed to him, of American intellectuals. This was a real possibility in 1941, perhaps even a certainty. He seemed destined to become the Lippmann of the Left—or some such honored, sage-like figure. Floyd Dell thought as much. In a warm review of *Stalin's Russia,* he said:

> History has been recently confirming some of the views he lately discovered and he will have more company henceforth than he had among radicals and liberal intellectuals just before the Hitler-Stalin pact. He will have the pleasure of fraternizing with some of the individuals whom he has been repudiating for their persistent hopefulness about Soviet Russia.[35]

* * *

The fates ruled otherwise. Though ambitious, Max could not stand success. The June 1941 issue of *Reader's Digest* carried an article by him entitled "Socialism Doesn't Gibe with Human Nature." It was the beginning of the end of his newly won reputation. Bad enough to have revived an ancient argument, one he himself had ridiculed years before, worse still to publish it in a super-patriotic, lowbrow stronghold of capitalism and bad taste.[36] Adding insult to injury was a glowing endorsement of the essay by Wendell Willkie, Republican candidate for President in 1940. Max then became a "roving editor" for the *Digest,* which paid him a handsome annual retainer for first claim on his articles. This assured him of a comfortable old age and much loss of respect. Few outside communist circles believed that the British Secret Service had given him $50,000 to do its dirty work, as was charged during the purge trials. But in joining the *Digest* Max had done something almost as wicked. The anti-war champion, Trotsky's defender and translator, the "Lone Rebel of Croton," had thrown in with the counter-revolution. It was as if all during the thirties he had been buying up worthless political securities, and then, just when they were about to jump in price, unloaded them. All the abuse taken, all the energy and passion poured into his critical writing, was to be wasted so far as reputation was concerned. The *Digest* was only interested in his name, and to a degree his clear, graceful style. Books like *Stalin's Russia* meant little to its readers, who liked their information in chewy, bite-sized morsels. His best work could never appear in the *Reader's Digest.* And the connection, plus his new opinions, was enormously damaging.

In going with it he lost the distinguished place he might have had on the liberal left. His future suffered, and his past, too, for the *Digest* connection justified, in a way, the false accusations of treason and venality made before. Where the Stalinists had failed, Max succeeded. He would rarely be taken seriously again in his lifetime by people whose opinions mattered.

Eastman's fall from grace was not quite so rapid as this suggests. The *Digest* connection might have been survivable. He was at least marginally respectable for another decade. But without knowing it, Max was preparing to embrace much of what he had always detested. One day the editor of the old *Masses* would be writing for the *National Review*. There are several ways of explaining this. Max belonged to a group of intellectuals who followed a similar course, moving from radicalism to conservative anti-communism in the forties. As John P. Diggins has shown, they had much in common. Bitter personal experience united them, for all had had encounters with communism in some form. Even the best of them had been corrupted by Bolshevik amorality. They would later stomach evil means, such as McCarthyism, for the sake of anti-Stalinist ends. Most were never truly liberal. "Before their break with the Left these writers chastised liberalism for its inability to make a social revolution; after their break, they condemned liberalism for its inability to prevent one."[37] On the *National Review* they would always be advocating liberalism in the East while ridiculing it in the West.

In Max's case there is a more personal explanation. Rejecting Marx did not obligate him to take up Adam Smith. There was a middle ground occupied by Edmund Wilson, the *Partisan Review* group, and others. But moderation was not Eastman's way. Though he admired the ancient Greeks for stressing proportion and restraint, and struggled in his daily life to equal them, it was uphill work. He did not steer a middle course so much as bounce off opposite walls. Fear was kept in check by over-reactions to it. Hating controversy and extreme positions he went to extremes and was controversial. In so doing he kept his mental balance but lost intellectual and political stature. It was a poor trade-off, though doubtless essential.

* * *

Max's decline began with a volley of denunciations in organs such as the socialist newspaper the *Call* and the *Progressive* magazine. Dwight

Macdonald dismissed Eastman in these terms: "the hero of the old *Masses* trial, the gay rebel, the original American Trotskyite . . . publishes an attack on socialism which Wendell Willkie implores every good American to read and which is the low-water mark to date in such affairs for vulgarity and just plain silliness."[38] This was pretty bad, but could have been worse. Macdonald was angry with Eastman for supporting American entry into World War II, placing him with a rather distinguished group of, as he saw it, backsliding pacifists including Sidney Hook, Louis Hacker, Dos Passos, and the former Marxist economist Lewis Corey. Being so partisan, Macdonald was not an entirely convincing critic of Eastman.

Moreover, Eastman's article itself was far from awful. Had it not appeared in the *Digest* with Willkie's endorsement, it would have attracted fewer sneers. In it Eastman did nothing more than draw a logical conclusion from his two big books of the year before: "The dream of Robert Owen, made plausible by the pseudo science of Karl Marx, and dynamic by the engineering genius of Lenin, is dead."[39] The error in socialism, Max wrote, was its failure to seriously consider human nature. Man was adaptable, which made change possible. But the degree to which he could be changed was limited by "a set of emotional impulses or instincts" that could be trained but not abolished. One of these was the pugnacious or aggressive instinct. Marxism was more compelling than Utopian socialism because it supplied targets for these aggressive impulses. But as socialism was more myth than science, its effect has been to "escape from reality" rather than to adjust to the real world. Contests between men, Eastman felt and had always felt, could not be abolished—only elevated and humanized. This process was less exciting than making a revolution, but more practical. Another failure of Marxism was to ignore the human tendency towards submission as well as dominance—what Erich Fromm would later call the "escape from freedom." It created possibilities for tyranny even within a socialist system that the faithful never properly allowed for. And, conversely, they assumed more self-reliance and peacefulness in mankind than the evidence warranted. Eastman now believed that private property was a major bulwark of freedom and equality. Marx had recognized this, but had not thought that those freedoms would disappear along with capitalism. Eastman finished by saying that Socialists used to believe that "primitive communism" showed that such an economic system was the right one for everybody. What did not occur to "us" was that in reverting to some aspects of savagery, people might also revert to that level of culture, as happened in Russia: "Socialism was amateur; we must learn to be expert."

His argument suffered, as did so much of Eastman's work in this vein, from obsolete science. John Dewey was critical of Eastman's reliance on the dubious instinct psychology of McDougall. He didn't feel the line between instinct and cultural conditioning could be drawn as sharply as Eastman thought. But he paid the article the compliment of treating it seriously and at length.[40] This was a comfort, but what really consoled Eastman was that Sol Levitas of the *New Leader* agreed to reprint the essay in full with its original title, "Socialism and Human Nature." Max was embarrassed by the *Digest* title, chosen without his knowledge, and by the Willkie endorsement, which he had not solicited and did not want. In a letter to the *New Leader* he apologized to his socialist friends for the *Digest* title, fearing that it might seem insulting.[41] But he stood by the contents, which were what really gave offense. Eastman was grateful to the *New Leader,* managed by ardently anti-Stalinist right-wing Socialists, for giving his essay respectability and himself a platform he would often speak from in coming years. The *New Leader* connection satisified his need to be associated with high-minded, low-budget magazines—a need that became all the more important in his later years when he was having trouble maintaining his tripartite life plan. He was homeless at the time, for the *Digest* would print very few of his political essays, and the *Modern Quarterly* was gone, having expired after the premature death of V. F. Calverton in 1940. Out of gratitude Eastman went so far as to help the *New Leader* raise money.

The *New Leader* printed a number of reactions to "Socialism and Human Nature," most of them brief. Several of these are of special interest because they addressed most of what to Socialists seemed the weak points in his essay. Eduard Heimann acknowledged Max's "brilliant and gallant" critique of Marx while disagreeing with it. He felt Eastman wanted to replace the economic reasoning of Marxism with a psychological interpretation. Heimann wanted better economic theory, a possibility Eastman did not consider. Marx erred on account of "his doctrinaire confidence in science, economic and social sciences" especially.[42] Eastman made the same mistake by proposing to substitute the psychology of 1900 for the economics of 1860. Heimann found in Eastman, as in Marx, an "uncritical, scientific dogmatism." Science could not be a guide to action because it was value-free. Man possessed a moral nature which had to be considered in any plan for his reformation. Eastman replied politely to many of his critics but was stung by Heimann's charge that he wished to replace dated economics with dated psychology—no doubt because it was true. He countered that Heimann, who was a refugee, had snubbed him for not being a professor. Heimann did not understand the robust American cultural tradition to which Eastman belonged. Heimann retaliated by calling Eastman a pragmatist, which he hotly denied—being almost alone in regarding himself as something else.[43]

Alfred Baker Lewis also frowned on Eastman's psychology. Socialism was important precisely because it recognized not merely that capitalism was unjust, but that it was "unable to satisfy the deepest psychological needs of man."[44] Eastman exaggerated the aggressive instinct and underestimated the extent to which tensions produced by the private ownership of property were causes of war and social violence. Capitalism made people feel insecure. Unemployment was both an economic and a psychological hardship. Real social security required social planning (which Eastman would not then have disputed). Eastman held that social ownership led to violence, but Lewis believed that the use of terror as a regular part of government was begun by Stalin during the economically conservative NEP era. The real failure of Bolshevism resulted from the one party system, not social ownership. A system of social ownership and democracy was "fully compatible with the most fundamental psychological urges of mankind, and certainly more fully compatible than either capitalist ownership or a one-party dictatorship, with or without private ownership."[45]

The most impassioned dissent from Max's views was written by the great anthropologist Ruth Benedict. She saw his essay as one of altogether too many statements declaring that heredity sharply limited human progress. This intellectual "failure of nerve," as Sidney Hook had called it, was commonplace in the 1940s when both communism and fascism persuaded many that attempts to improve the human condition were bound to fail. Benedict believed Eastman was saying that "no world will ever be very different from this one."[46] She agreed with Eastman that modern man had something in common with cave man. This was not warfare or the will to boss or be bossed but rather that man "took his ways of life into his own hands and his survival was no longer predicated upon adaptions written into his body but upon choice of expedients he had himself adopted." All human beings were plastic, capable of learning and making choices, and possessed "reason, foresight, and judgement." Human nature so defined did not dictate any particular world. Man could have the kind of world he wanted. Noting the variety of human cultures, she said that if people "have done a good job of social engineering they need not fear that aggressions inherited from Neanderthal Man will ever wreck their society." This was the most heartfelt rejoinder to Eastman's review of human nature. But, though eloquent, it was to him unconvincing. He no longer believed in social engineering or the liberal gospel of progress.

Taken together these are fair criticisms. Eastman's essay suffered from his habit of drawing exaggerated conclusions. That socialism had failed in Russia did not prove that it was alien to human nature. Democratic socialism had never been tried, so it was premature to say how it was related to human nature. It was perfectly clear that many social systems were compatible with human nature—including tyrannical ones such as those presided over by Stalin and Hitler. On the other hand, his critics generally ignored what was uncomfortable about Eastman's argument. It was a fact that socialism had failed to produce most of the benefits expected in the only country that had tried it. And it remains true that wherever Socialists have come to power through violence, tyranny results. Then, too, his critics often did not recognize that in rejecting socialism he had not yet rejected social democracy. As late as 1946 he was still calling himself a radical.

* * *

Though Eastman was no longer a Socialist, old habits did not die. It was business as usual so far as polemics were concerned. Thus in 1942, when James T. Farrell coupled him with Van Wyck Brooks, Eastman blew up. Brooks had just written a very odd book, *The Opinions of Oliver Allston* (1941), condemning science and practically all modern literature and most critics—including Eastman. In the *Partisan Review* Farrell wrote that "Brooks's diatribe against dead geniuses is really a means of attacking living writers: Max Eastman's personal war against Karl Marx seems to be a means of achieving the same end. Such attacks cannot disturb the bones of dead men: they can only injure the living. And herein, we observe one of the traits which the Philistine shows in all ages."[47] He further accused Eastman of attacking Marxism not because it was unscientific but because it was a fighting faith.

This was a clumsy attack arising mainly from prejudice. It should have been ignored, but as usual Max replied in kind. He said that Dwight Macdonald and Farrell took a "papal tone" toward him because they could not meet his arguments. Eastman's values had not changed as was alleged. Neither he nor such other ex-radicals as Louis Corey, Louis Hacker, Sidney Hook, and John Dos Passos had lost faith in democracy. The difference between Farrell and the former Marxists was that "we have remained loyal to the aim, you to the means."[48] The point was fairly made, but Eastman could not leave well enough alone. He had to add that this showed that "we" cared more for the workers than Farrell did because "we" were willing to sacrifice prestige for the greater good, whereas Farrell was more interested in his own "emotional and intellectual life which had been organized around the means."

Max resented being classed with Brooks, whose attack on science was as irritating to him as Brooks's critique of modernism was to Farrell. In his own review of *The Opinions of Oliver Allston,* Max described Brooks's fear of science as "decadence of a worse kind than the flight into unintelligibility."[49] It was, perhaps, this added insult that pushed him beyond the limits of fair play. Max declared that Farrell's distortions showed he was on a moral level with the Moscow trials and would shoot his enemies if given the power. He called on Farrell, who was still a Trotskyist, to stop associating with "near sighted cranks and crosspatches, the wounded veterans of an exploded theology."[50] This was overkill with a vengeance. Farrell, too, was anti-Stalinist, though an innocent reader of Eastman's polemic would never guess it. Shooting people like Eastman was definitely not part of Farrell's plan for the good society, as he made clear in answering Eastman's letter. But his tone was no better. He accused Eastman of changing not only his means but his opinions as well. Thus, in *Marxism: Is It Science?* Max said that Lenin did not understand human nature whereas in *Trotsky: Portrait of a Youth* Lenin is hailed as a master psychologist. This was true enough, for whatever it was worth. So also was Farrell's statement that Max always tried to dispose of his critics by calling them names—bigot, totalitarian, and the like. To show his contempt for this tactic he called Eastman a Philistine again, and damned his philosophy as a "compound of crude empiricism and shallow rationalism."[51] Farrell was not sorry to have put Eastman in the same camp as Brooks. Eastman's earlier attack on the great modernists had paved the way for Brooks's strictures.*

Eastman's rejection of Marx and Eliot were not the only, or even the main, reasons why he was detested by Macdonald and Farrell. They did not support American entry into World War II, and he did. This had been an agonizing decision for Max. He was still remembered for opposing the American declaration of war in 1917. It was one of the last pieces of his legend to survive. But as time went on the strain of keeping silent on the war was too great. As early as March 1940 it was evident that Max believed American intervention to be both inevitable and necessary. For the moment he accepted neutrality as a proper course on account of American unreadiness. But it was obvious that allowing events to take their course was not going to create a decent international order. "The best that can be hoped for—or indeed desired by those still interested in the colors of life—is a federation of patriotic nations exercising real police power through the world. That much however is a vital necessity, and to postpone working for it on the ground that a proletarian revolution is going to hand it to us on a silver platter with the 'dying of the state' is sheer mystical folly."[52] As this is what many independent Marxists believed, Eastman's statement was calculated to inflame them. Worse was to follow.

In May 1941 Eastman spoke to the issue plainly. He wrote a long letter calling for all-out aid to Britain, which the *New York Times* displayed prominently on the editorial page. It was addressed to "honest radicals and progressives" who were against fascism but also against involvement in another world war. "They are refusing out of loyalty to

---

* Farrell's abuse of Eastman was typical. His later apology was not. In 1950 Farrell contributed to a *Partisan Review* symposium "Religion and the Intellectuals" by quoting from *Artists in Uniform*. He also sent the editors a letter dated January 31, 1950 [copy in the Eastman MSS], saying that he was doing so to make amends for his response to Eastman's letter of eight years ago. "In my reply to Max Eastman I believe, that I was unwarrantedly sharp and showed inexcusable bad manners. On the basic questions which we were discussing, The Nature of Totalitarianism and of the War, I believe that he was more right and had more insight than I." After apologizing for his bad manners he went on: "Please let me add that all of us who are younger than Max Eastman owe him a great debt. At a time when it took great moral courage, Max Eastman wrote with frankness and honesty concerning the nature of totalitarianism." He sent a copy of this letter to Max with a note saying again that it was meant as a tribute. "Please let me add that it gives me great pleasure to make at least a small acknowledgment for the debt we all owe you. James T. Farrell to Max Eastman, January 31, 1950, Eastman MSS. This was a unique gesture in the history of radical letters.

an old dogma, to look a new reality in the eye."[53] Intellectuals were afraid of British trickery, but the real issue was whether democracy was to survive at all. If Hitler "conquers Europe this fatal myth—that tyranny means national power—will seize all uncritical minds, depriving them of their chief immunity to fascist propaganda. All men love power, and democracy must make visible its power or go down." Max still hoped, as he had during the last war, that out of conflict might come "a world union of democratic states capable of ensuring peace and civilized existence throughout the earth. In that direction lies the hope that, with free scope for thinking and experiment, a scientific social movement may yet solve the problems that confuse. In the other direction lies death to everything that radicals have ever fought for."

Eastman supported the present national policy of "vicarious belligerence" only because opinion polls showed that most Americans did. They wanted to aid Britain without going to war. To his mind this was half policy and half wishful thinking. It "is compelling us to suppress our civil liberties in time of formal peace. We are suppressing them too much already for the health of democracy, and yet not enough for wartime purposes. Democracy demands a clear division between peace and war. Only tyrants can afford to wage war without declaring it, and we are stepping in the same path of corruption when we become the arsenal for one side and yet pretend to be on peace terms with the other." Max wanted total aid to Britain and a declaration of war as soon as possible. Surely he was in the right here, and also in thinking it dangerous to follow a course of edging toward war and calling it peace.

Eastman's letter to the *Times* raised his stock among interventionists such as Solicitor General Anthony Biddle and Lewis Mumford, but not for long.[54] When war came, he did not follow the popular course of acclaiming the Soviets as gallant allies but continued to warn against them. A week after Pearl Harbor Max gave his first political lecture since 1934. He called it "Russia and the Fight for Democracy," and began by pointing out that Russia was still a totalitarian state, though "wearing the camouflage of democracy." For the sake of victory he supported lend-lease aid to Russia but did not want support of the Russian war effort to obscure or excuse the nature of communism. He urged that people guard against local fellow travelers and communist party members, whose prestige was bound to increase with that of Russia—as happened. He reminded listeners that Stalin did not want war in the first place and sold out to Hitler to avoid it. Stalin's record was worse than Hitler's, in that during the purges of the late thirties one million persons had been arrested in Russia and 300,000 executed.* The speech ended: "The fight for democracy on the international field is primarily a fight against Hitler. . . . But we must not permit the Stalinists, and their stooges, dupes and Fellow Travelers, to employ this opportunity to spread the power and the prestige and the mental habits of totalitarianism on the home front. I don't think that is asking too much of Anglo-Saxon common sense." [55]

There is no record of how this speech was first received on December 15, 1941. But when he gave it again in Montreal on January 12, 1942, he was constantly interrupted with boos, hisses, and cries of "shame." [56] Canadians, who had been fighting longer and suffering more, were even less willing than Americans to hear anyone speak ill of Russia. That was unfortunate, for Eastman was making a vital distinction usually ignored at the time. Russia was a necessary ally, but an undesirable one, too. Had this been kept in mind, there would have been less to cry about once the war was over. As always, because people did not want to hear the truth, Eastman was more determined to speak it. He repeated his warning in the *New Leader* five months later and in a lengthy article in the July 1943 *Reader's Digest.* [57] The editors tried to ease the blow by titling it "To Collaborate Successfully We Must Face the Facts about Russia." This was unnecessary, for conservative readers loved Max's hard-hitting essay. It drew more mail than any previous *Digest* article save one.

Unlike most of his political articles, which seemed always to come out at the wrong time, this one had some effect. A study of American attitudes toward the Soviet Union in World War II credits Eastman with opening a real debate. The tide of sympathy for Russia, rising since Pearl Harbor, was about to turn. Eastman's article appeared at just the right moment. Few moderates embraced his position completely, but his article stimulated thought about Russia and her postwar intentions, encouraging a more skeptical mood among opinion makers.[58] Eastman's remarks made the Popular Front unhappy. T.R.B., Washington columnist for the *New Republic,* mocked Eastman for showing "what a mistake communism is because the Russians are all hungry and have low living standards."[59] This was so absurd that T.R.B. did not trouble to refute it, leaving posterity to wonder why

* Max's guesses were still on the low side. According to Robert Conquest in the late thirties alone there were one million executions and perhaps eight million arrests.

hunger and low living standards did not discredit communism. The purest expression of that viewpoint came, as so often in those days, from Max Lerner. He was a staff member of the Popular Front's daily newspaper in New York, *PM,* and the "grand vizier in this country of double-talk on the Russian question," according to the *New Leader.*[60] "As I read Eastman," Lerner said in *PM,* "on Russian poverty and the subjection of the people, I kept thinking: if these poeple are slaves, why do slaves fight so well? Why do starving people form themselves not just into a nation with an army, but a nation in arms? Why do Russian children, as Maurice Hindus described them in *Mother Russia,* die for their country with a deep joy that would do honor to grown and mature men? Why do Russians have the sense that they are fashioning a new world, with new meanings—a sense we in America seem sadly to have lost?"[61] This was the mentality Eastman had been facing since the mid-thirties.

There was no use trying to tell such a person that Hitler didn't offer the Russian people much choice, or to suggest that even slaves might fight well if their lives were at stake. Eastman made the attempt anyway, rebutting Lerner in the *New Leader.*[62] Victor Serge wrote to say that his feelings about the Lerner piece were similar to Eastman's, only "plus brutal."[63] Even the *Partisan Review* unbent a little in appreciation. When the distinguished poet William Carlos Williams complained to it that neither Eastman nor John Dewey appreciated Russia, the magazine struck him down.* Noting that Williams was following the Stalinist line, it said that "insofar as they have helped to expose the real meaning of the Moscow trials and to show up the pretensions of the Stalinists to be something else than what they are, both Dewey and Eastman have rendered an invaluable service."[64]

It would take another volume to discuss the liberals' treatment of Soviet affairs during World War II. There was a tendency among those who had fellow-traveled before the war to do so again, forgetting, or covering over, or justifying the Moscow trials, the Stalin-Hitler Pact, and other unpleasant events. The *New Republic* was typical, cool toward Russia while the Pact was in effect, full of affection afterward.[65] For a

---

* Williams's biographer has explained this letter. It derived not only from the poet's affection for Russia but also his dislike of intellectuals. He singled out Eastman because his *Digest* article seemed exactly the kind of retrograde thing that might be expected of an intellectual. Reed Whittemore, *William Carlos Williams: Poet from New Jersey* (Boston, 1975).

time the mass media followed suit. Former Ambassador Joseph E. Davies's whitewash of Stalin's crimes, *Mission to Moscow* (1941), was a bestselling book and then a movie. The *Saturday Evening Post*'s chief authority on Soviet matters was Edgar Snow, an expert at finding virtues in both Russian and Chinese communism. A landmark in this vein was the March 29, 1943, issue of *Life* magazine, entirely devoted to stories on Russia. Though recognizing faults in the Soviet system, it was mostly congratulatory. An editorial set the tone:

> It is safe to say that no nation in history has ever done so much so fast. If Soviet leaders tell us that the control of information was necessary to get the job done, we can afford to take their word for it for the time being. We who know the power of free speech, and the necessity for it, may assume that if those leaders are sincere in their work of emancipating the Russian people they will swing around toward free speech—and we hope soon.[66]

The Stalin-Hitler Pact was explained away twice on the grounds of necessity in this issue, while the glories of collective farms were repeatedly acclaimed.

Max did what little he could to stem this flood of propaganda. In 1942 he pointed out that the frequent assertion that there was no disloyal Fifth Column in Russia thanks to the purges was untrue. He knew that the Volga Germans had been deported en masse from lands they occupied for centuries, and that political commissars had been restored to the Red Army, suggesting a lack of trust.[67] His case would have been stronger still had he known that the army high command had been all but wiped out by Stalin, which was hardly a gesture of confidence, still less a good way of preparing for war, one might well suppose. Worse than the lies, to Max's way of thinking, was the common practice of admitting the evils in Russia and then dismissing them. He felt the most startling example of this appeared in an information bulletin of the Federal Council of Churches in America dated December 18, 1943. It argued that as the churches did not condemn conscientious objectors, they should not condemn Communists either. As Max read it, the bulletin was saying that, because the churches did not attack conscientious objectors for standing by their moral principles, they should avoid taking issue with Communists for not having any. It was, Max said, "the lowest depth to which the Churches of Christ in America have ever sunk."[68]

Anti-communism was not yet the beginning and end of his political thought, however. During the war he was less partisan than the *New Leader* and appointed himself its conscience in recognition of this fact. After the editors printed a diatribe against the Congress party of India in 1942, Max wrote them that he was shocked at the "race-hatred" and "reckless bigotry" expressed by the author, who was furious with Indian nationalists for abstaining from the war. Max, too, wished that they had accepted Churchill's terms—independence after the war in return for support of the British effort now—but he also wished that the terms had been more generous. He reminded the *New Leader* that it was not enough merely to work for victory; all publications were doing that. The important thing was that when victory came, it amounted to more than military success. Max wanted it to be a victory for democracy as well.[69]

As late as April 1943 he thought there was still a chance of this happening. The national temper was greatly encouraging: "The contrast in this respect with World War I is startling. That disaster to mankind was widely greeted as a grand adventure. It started off, as all wars had, with fifes and glory-drums, with ringside shouts and exultation oratory. We who opposed it often felt more like wet blankets than dissenters; we were spoiling all the fun." It seemed to Max that people had learned something from past experience: "In short, the human race as a whole, for the first time in its history, is disillusioned of war for war's sake. It is united in wanting to bring the bloody long tale of suicidal folly to an end. It is ready to hear, on that subject, anything that anybody has to propose. Those who see no hope in these facts are blind indeed."[70]

The early forties were the best balanced and temperate years of Eastman's political life. His socialist years were behind him, but he had not yet gone over to the other side. Max was about as fair-minded as a strong-willed man could be, equally distant from the enthusiasms of his past and future. This enabled him to criticize the *New Leader* from a lofty if uncertain height. Its conservative socialist editors stood for the right things, he believed, though not always consistently. He thought the election of 1944 showed this and explained why afterward. For political reasons the *New Leader* constantly misrepresented Governor Dewey's statements, calling them false, phony, reactionary, and the like. Max believed that Dewey had actually been eloquent and correct on six major issues. Eastman agreed with Dewey that sixteen years in office was too long. There was a real danger that economic security might be obtained at the expense of political liberty. FDR's ill-health raised the prospect of having his undistinguished running mate, Harry S. Truman, become the next president. The President conducted foreign affairs in a high-handed manner. FDR was appeasing Stalin. Communist infiltration was a problem which if raised by Dewey in a non-election year would have won him the *New Leader*'s applause. Its anti-communism was what Eastman liked best in the *New Leader*. He was irritated that it had been put aside during the campaign: "In the light of its past, the *New Leader*'s statement that in 'playing up the red scare' Dewey was 'avoiding the real issues' can only honestly be described as stultifying."[71]

The editors rejected this counsel of perfection. They endorsed Roosevelt because the labor movement did so overwhelmingly. Not to have gone along would have alienated them from their real or potential audience. Anyway, Dewey was not sincere, only fishing for votes, as evidenced by his record: "He has never taken a hand in this anti-totalitarian struggle."[72] Max was not an editor and could afford to stand on principle, dispensing even-handed justice as it were. He wanted to see more scrupulousness than he had displayed as an editor, or would show again when his feelings rose. Max was in the eye of the hurricane, not home free as he thought.

During this period Eastman's old ability to distinguish between politics and personalities, never entirely lost, came back to him. He was sixty years old in 1943, and the friends of his golden youth were dying. This, together with his mellow mood, inspired generous reflections. He was especially touched by the murder of Carlo Tresca, whose heroism had been life-long and unspoiled. In a front-page obituary for the *New Leader,* Max called Tresca "the last of the great revolutionists who fought implacably with love instead of hate in their hearts." Though disagreeing with them politically, Max felt one could always get along with anarchists: "Common-sense had a chance with the anarchists; kindness had a chance, sympathy and justice." Tresca's death was shocking but fitting, too: "He had lived a violent life. He had loved danger. He had loved the fight. His last motion was to swing round and confront the long-expected enemy. He would have been surprised himself, and also a little injured in his pride, if he had died in bed."[73]

The funeral of Dolly Sloan prompted memories of both the Sloans, "dear and pleasant friends of my heart," and a graceful tribute to John, who was still alive though not present. Max and John had long been separated politically, but Max esteemed him still. "They have been good—and over and above that, John, through a gift of the gods, has been great. But their goodness and his greatness too, has had some edge to it. That is the rare thing. That is the thing to be grateful for, and to be joyful over. For nature will continue to bring forth these jewels, no matter what politics may do, so long as time lasts." [74]

Recalling Art Young was more painful, yet not entirely bitter. On a trip to Guatemala in 1944, "I thought of Art Young. Poor old mild-hearted Art Young, not tough enough to face the bitter facts, had died in the arms of 'the Comrades,' deceived and deceiving. Since 1939 when I first published my acknowledgment of the failure of the socialist experiment, Art had ceased even to send me his famous New Year's card, annulling with that negative token the friendship of a lifetime. Well, he died happy—he died with his dream. I would rather die with the truth, however sad." [75] That wish, at least, would be gratified.

Eastman's poise and optimism, the source of his mellowness, did not last long.[76] Communist gains in Eastern Europe and China chipped away at his composure. By 1945 he was applauding British moves in Greece as part of a hot exchange between himself and Dwight Macdonald. It began when Macdonald backed the Greek rebellion. Eastman responded by saying that as it was a tool of Stalinism, by favoring it Macdonald showed himself to be no friend of liberty. Macdonald was incensed at this, since he was in fact anti-Stalinist, though also something of a revolutionary still and thus drawn to the side of ambiguous movements. He accused Max of flabby writing and countered with this muscular description of Eastman:

> He represents a pitiable spectacle similar to that of persons in an advanced state of alcoholism, in which all emotional cerebral responses have atrophied and there remains only a reflexive reaction to alcohol. Eastman's drink is anti-Stalinism. His political ideal and ideas have eroded away leaving only an anti-Stalinist reflex.[77]

Neither Macdonald's facts nor his prose were as superior to Eastman's as he imagined. Macdonald held that the only issue was Britain's support of the Greek monarchy against the general will as expressed by the rebels. As he saw it, the line favored by Eastman and the *New Leader* of propping up reactionary regimes in Europe was "calculated to enable the Communists to pose as the real tribunes of the rebellious peo-

ple." There was truth in this, even so the rebellion was more than the
pure impulse of huddled masses yearning to breathe free. It was Com-
munist-led, and when in 1948 Yugoslavia broke with Russia and
stopped sending aid it collapsed.

Macdonald was vulnerable in another respect which Eastman was
happy to point out. At this time Macdonald appeared to favor proletarian revolution and democratic socialism. But in a previous issue of *Politics* he had said that he did not believe in elections. To Eastman this was
a crucial point, for his case on behalf of the Greek government was not
based on its character, which was deplorable, but on its promise to hold
free elections. Eastman quoted Macdonald on the issue of democracy.
"The trouble with elections," Macdonald had written, "is that they do
not measure the intensity with which people hold their views. Who is to
say that ten men and women who will die for beliefs are not as 'deserv-
ing' of realizing those beliefs as a hundred who will not do more than
mark a cross on a ballot." [78] This dangerous statement was related to his
drift toward anarchism and therefore clashed with earlier pronounce-
ments. As Macdonald's new position was not clear yet, Eastman could
fairly say that "the Macdonald type of 'working class government,' besides being non-proletarian and sneering at constitutionality, is committed to a 'democratic socialism' which does not believe in elections!" The
honors, such as they were, in this exchange had to be about even. Neither party knew much about Greece. Each made hits on the other.
Being sterile, the debate had no issue, as too often was the case.

Though wrong on some points, Macdonald rightly charged that
anti-communism was ruining Eastman's judgment. A few months after
their exchange Max co-authored an article in the *Digest* calling for unlimited aid to Nationalist China. As Eastman and his collaborator, an
American journalist, saw it, China was controlled by three groups, the
Communists, the Japanese, and Chiang Kai-shek's Kuomintang. This
last was said to champion national independence, political democracy,
and the people's welfare. [79] The only choice for China was between the
leadership of "democratic America or . . . totalitarian Russia." This
truth was being obscured by people such as Owen Lattimore, who were
still saying that Russia was a democracy and therefore China's future
was safe in its hands, Edgar Snow and others, who maintained that the
Chinese Communists were not really Communists, and in any case free
of Russian control, and those who argued that only the Chinese Communists, not the Nationalists, were fighting Japan. In order to save

China from becoming a puppet of Moscow like Yugoslavia, the United States must bolster Chiang Kai-shek, whose victory would save not only China but India and Iran as well from enslavement.

Here in a single article one finds almost every important error and prejudice that was to cripple Sino-American relations for years to come. Almost everything was wrong with it. The Kuomintang was not only undemocratic, which the authors admitted, but hopelessly corrupt, authoritarian, and incompetent. The "people's welfare" was the last thing on its mind. China did not have to choose between the United States and Russia. It was perfectly clear at the time not just to Edgar Snow but to most informed journalists that the Chinese Communists were genuinely independent, though of course genuinely communist as well, which not all wanted to admit. Snow, Lattimore, and the rest were not the molders of America's China policy. This article's attack on them foreshadowed the myth that America "lost China" partly because of evil journalists. Max's domino theory, that the fall of China meant the loss of Asia to communism, has yet to be proven. Eastman was not a founding member of the China Lobby, which kept America from having a sensible Far Eastern policy for many years, but he shared its delusions and soon its venom also. This unfortunate article, the worst Eastman had ever put his name to, was a sad omen. Max was losing touch with reality. Previously when he wrote on communism it was out of personal experience and continuing study. As time went on, he wrote mostly out of prejudice, dressing up his flimsy essays with thin layers of data gathered from obvious sources, such as the writings of Stalin and Mao, which he used over and over again. Even the style of his political writings, which Edmund Wilson admired so much in 1941, weakened. With loss of judgment went loss of taste. The mechanical formulas of the radical Right were becoming his stock in trade. It was a dismal end to a career in political journalism that only a few years earlier seemed so brilliant.

In 1945 Eastman wrote an essay for a *New Leader* pamphlet, "Morals and Politics." His theme was that, although Marxism had failed, people should not overreact to this, by, for instance, taking up religion. It would be hard "to avoid replacing one monomania with another—a mistake not uncommon in convalescent wards for crackpots." Liberals had failed morally in the 1930s because they were made to think it "naive, unrealistic—worst of all, unscientific—to demand that people who had set out to make the world in general just and humane should do justice and act humanely in specific instances." Civilization did need a "vision of the future," but he hoped that "the young and the courageous, the new generation in whom hope always resides, will not mix their projects for the improvement of social life with a contempt for those elementary wisdoms which have made social life possible." [80] A few years later the man who wrote this would be supporting Joseph McCarthy, so hard is it to "do justice and act humanely" where the passions are involved.

CHAPTER ELEVEN

Politics
and Literature
1942–1969

As the cold war worsened, so did Eastman's temper. As early as 1946 he was blaming the Truman administration for appeasing Russia and calling proposals to share nuclear information with the Soviets treasonable.[1] In a network radio debate with Harold Laski he predicted war with Russia. Eastman called for aid to anti-Communists everywhere in the world and demanded the publication of what he said were secret reports showing "Soviet depredations that are locked in the files of our pussyfooting State Department."[2] Like many anti-Communists, Eastman considered Truman to be hopelessly soft on Russia. Today it is the fashion, especially among revisionist diplomatic historians, to blame the cold war on Truman's hard line.[3] They point to the end of lend-lease aid to Russia, the failure to share atomic secrets, unwillingness to make a Russian loan, support of conservative governments, the Truman doctrine, sometimes even the Marshall Plan, as evidence of Truman's unreasonable suspicions. The hard line is supposed to have resulted from ideology, also from American desires to expand foreign trade. Nothing would have surprised Eastman more than this interpretation. To him the Truman administration was weak and confused, incapable of standing up to Russian aggression. Only a Stalinist would think its feeble policies were excessively belligerent.

Writing for the *Reader's Digest* and holding extreme opinions made Eastman extra sensitive. After a casual meeting with his old friend Carl

Sandburg, during which Sandburg said that he wished Eastman would stop writing for the *Digest* and start writing for himself, Eastman sent him a three-page letter of abuse. Sandburg had no right to patronize, considering the way anti-Communists were being smeared and slandered. Eastman was still fighting for the things he had believed in during his *Masses* years: "Another opinion of mine is that in hobnobbing with the totalitarian gang who are prostituting the name of Abraham Lincoln, not to memtion Jefferson and Tom Paine, for the purpose of introducing one-party tyranny into the United States, you are betraying and dishonoring the noblest work of your life."[4] Sandburg resisted the temptation to reply in kind. He answered that his advice to Max was well intended. He had read all of Eastman's books and owned two copies of *Enjoyment of Laughter.* Sandburg concluded: "You can well know I am in no 'smear campaign,' and if I banteringly mention to you that you are not living up to your best self, you can hand it right back to me to find I rate myself rather a useless worm."[5] This saintly forbearance was not typical. Unless they were fellow extremists, most people found Max's crotchety outbursts offensive.

As an anti-Communist, Eastman sometimes found himself in distinguished company. In 1948 he joined Norman Thomas, A. A. Berle, Oswald Garrison Villard, A. Philip Randolph, and sixty-five other liberals and Socialists in cabling British Foreign Minister Ernest Bevin the unsurprising news that Henry Wallace's soft approach to Russia was not endorsed by most Americans.[6] Often he acted alone. In 1948, during a hearing before the House Foreign Affairs Committee, then considering revisions to the UN Charter, Max declared that there could be no world peace so long as the Soviets controlled Russia. He asserted that they were at once manipulating the UN in the interests of world revolution and undermining it.[7] That this might be self-defeating seems not to have occurred to Max. He also called for an end to the great power veto in the Security Council, a common demand at that time. Few if any guessed that a day was coming when conditions would be reversed, and America, not Russia, would be wielding the veto. Later that year Eastman spoke to the national convention of the American Federation of Labor in similar terms. Stalin was out to conquer the world. American foreign policy was based on ignorance. Washington was losing China. Max urged the AFL not to kill the capitalist goose that was laying the golden eggs, an odd request inasmuch as the AFL's passion for violent revolution had always been non-existent.[8]

In 1949 Max spoke to Columbia University saying once again that the leaders of the free world were afraid to face the facts about communism. He attacked the recent State Department White Paper which said that the United States could not have saved Nationalist China. Much of his speech was a rehash of old themes—the twenty ways in which Stalin outdid Hitler, racial prejudice in the Soviet Union, and the like. But he now had better information on Stalin's slave labor empire, already known to Eastman as Gulag. And he made clear an important difference between himself and most of the radical Right. It was fascinated by hypothetical plans for military adventures, "preventive war," "rollback," and the like, even after Russia acquired nuclear weapons. Eastman saw the folly in this. He favored a tough but "non-military" offensive against Stalinism.[9] He also wanted the American Communist party outlawed, having demanded this for years. Eastman's libertarianism had never been absolute. In an article written before Pearl Harbor, he put survival ahead of free expression. A vigorous democracy, he wrote then, will "be ready to suspend its purity in order to defend its existence."[10]

One by one, Eastman discarded the symbols of his old political life. In 1948 he asked that his name be taken off the masthead of the *New Leader,* which in his angry letter to Sandburg he had called "the sole magazine in the country still fighting for freedom on all fronts." He could no longer give his name to a publication, however anticommunist, that supported, however timidly, left-wing ideas. He did not share the magazine's enthusiasm for social democracy in Europe or its view that wealth should be more equitably distributed at home. "I hate to withdraw from the *New Leader,* because it is necessary to my self-esteem that I serve some cause without pay and without any motive but a desire to defend and promote real values."[11] And he hated to injure the feelings of Sol (Samuel Morris) Levitas, who had given Max a platform after the *Modern Quarterly* expired. Levitas resisted this, but in the end Eastman's name was removed, though he went on contributing to the magazine. In 1952 Eastman resigned from the American Civil Liberties Union because it defended the rights of Communists, even though without much enthusiasm. The next year he resigned from the Federal Union, an organization headed by Clarence Streit that favored world government. He had believed in this since his school days but no longer considered it practical.

For some time Max remained within the pale because liberal and left-wing anti-Stalinists were equally harsh. In 1946 *Partisan Review* ran a famous editorial called "The 'Liberal' Fifth Column," charging the *Nation,* the *New Republic,* and PM, a liberal daily in New York, with betraying liberalism by justifying the crimes of Stalin. Quoting a *New Republic* editorial that said nothing was to be gained by getting tough with Russia, *Partisan Review* declared that with such statements the *New Republic* "was actually helping to herd Social Democrats into concentration camps in Germany, Poland, Rumania, Bulgaria, Hungary, Austria."[12] Two years later *Partisan Review* claimed that "the apparent sobriety and reasonableness of the official liberals and their opportunistic attempts to take a balanced view of a total evil [Stalinism] amount to nothing less than political muddle and cowardice, if not downright collaboration with the enemies of democracy and freedom."[13] Max himself might have said these things, and were it not for his anti-modernism and regard for Chiang Kai-shek, perhaps in *Partisan Review.*

In 1948 Dwight Macdonald devoted an entire issue of his remarkable magazine *Politics* to the USSR. In a long bibliographical essay he called *Marx, Lenin, and the Science of Revolution* "brilliant." *Artists in Uniform* showed "brilliantly and movingly the general meaning of the Stalinist cultural line" and provided "important information."[14] The next year Eastman cooperated with an ad hoc group of intellectuals against a Communist-inspired peace conference which met at the Waldorf Astoria hotel. This Conference of Scientific and Cultural Workers for World Peace brought together Popular Front intellectuals with like-minded Europeans, particularly East Europeans. In retaliation Sidney Hook organized a body called Americans for Intellectual Freedom. It infiltrated the conference, asking embarrassing questions, as when Macdonald demanded that the Soviet delegation tell what had become of Boris Pasternak and other silenced Russian writers. At a separate meeting nearby, Eastman called the roll of some thirty-three Russian writers whose fates were unknown.[15]

Americans for Intellectual Freedom became the American Committee for Cultural Freedom, a united front of anti-Stalinist intellectuals, ranging from democratic Socialists to conservative ex-radicals like Eastman. On March 29, 1952, it sponsored a meeting "In Defense of Free Culture" at the Waldorf-Astoria Hotel. The speakers included Eastman, Richard Rovere, Mary McCarthy, Sidney Hook, Lional Trilling, Arthur Koestler, Bertram Wolfe, and other distinguished anti-Stalinists. Six hundred people attended, and most became angry or incredulous when Max defended Senator Joseph McCarthy, who was then doing his worst.[16] This sealed Max's political doom, for few at the meeting believed that McCarthyism was the right way to defend a free culture. Eastman's reputation had been going downhill ever since the *Digest* article on socialism and human nature in 1941. When the cold war made anti-Stalinism respectable, Max gained the chance for a comeback, but lost it by going overboard. In the future no one would take him seriously except conservatives, which did not help him, since American intellectual life is dominated by liberals.

Max apparently did not realize what he had done at first. Strong language was the order of the day among intellectual anti-Stalinists. Diana Trilling in an essay on the Hiss case had written that the intelligent liberal "does not make the mistake of believing that just because the wrong people are looking for Soviet agents in the American government there are none. He does not deceive himself that whoever a McCarthy names is de facto an innocent liberal."[17] Irving Kristol went a step further. In *Commentary* he wrote that there "is one thing the American people know about Senator McCarthy: he, like them, is unequivocally anti-Communist. About the spokesmen of American liberalism, they feel they know no such thing. And with some justification."[18] This was Eastman's view also, but with a difference. Kristol stopped short of endorsing McCarthy while Max did not.

From sharing McCarthy's goal, which Trilling and Kristol and most people in the Committee for Cultural Freedom did, to endorsing his methods was a big step and made all the difference. Although Max had often written of the need for a right relation between means and ends, and hated Communists for ignoring it, he did not see that it applied here as well. He judged McCarthy by Russian standards and found his defects to be trivial compared with those of Stalin. He could not understand how a person could be anti-Communist and yet oppose McCarthy, whose principal sin was uncouthness. Writing to Peter Viereck, a conservative writer and poet, Max complained that Viereck was mistaken in attacking Senator McCarthy and in helping propagate the term "McCarthyism":

> The present Senatorial smear campaign against McCarthy is far more vicious and unprincipled that [sic] anything McCarthy has done. I regret his loose-jointed wild talk at the beginning as much as you do. . . . The worse thing he did, however, was to give his enemies, and ours, the opportunity to forge the word "McCarthyism"—a weapon

which they are employing to beat down and smash to death every bold effort to tell the truth about pro-communists and semi-procommunists (who are more dangerous) in the government. It's a mistake for you to help them with that weapon. We're in a political fight, not an ethical argument, and the thing to attack is our enemies, not our less scrupulous allies."[19]

The minor but uncharacteristic errors and awkwardnesses in this letter betray the agitation. Eastman's feelings had run away with him. Rational in other respects, he no longer made sense on the communist issue. His feeling of helplessness was justified to a considerable extent in the 1930s and early forties when pro-Soviet sentiments were powerful and Washington was leaning over backwards to get along with Russia. After the Truman Doctrine, the Berlin Airlift, and especially the Korean War, it was silly to claim that secret Communists were dictating government policy and had to be rooted out. The Korean War had finished off communism as a force in American life. Communists had been rooted out of trade unions, the mass media, and everywhere else of importance. Among intellectuals it was no longer chic to admire the Soviets. But Max's feelings, valid when they first arose, did not change. In his excitement over the hunt he failed to notice that the fox was dead. The campaign that denied re-election to Senator Millard Tydings of Maryland was to Max "one of the few notable victories our side has won." But Tydings was not a Communist or a sympathizer of any kind. The famous photograph showing him in the company of Earl Browder was a fake, political deception and slander at its filthiest. Max told Viereck that he and the *Saturday Review* and even the *New Leader* "go into battle like women in long dresses, more concerned with keeping your skirts clean than defeating the enemy." Max advocated getting into the dirt with McCarthy, and it stuck to him.

Eastman's oldest and most generous friends could not reach him on this. One of Edmund Wilson's great qualities was that he did not allow politics to stand in the way of friendship. But neither did he allow friendship to stand in the way of simple truths. In an otherwise genial letter he spoke to the issue by accusing Max's friend William Buckley of trying to "play Goebbels to McCarthy's Hitler," and called the senator from Wisconsin a "scoundrel who cares nothing about 'exposing Communists, graft, and corruption,' etc. and has done nothing about it."[20] Floyd Dell, now retired, tried hard to change Eastman's mind. Most of their correspondence was about poetry, but in 1954 a slighting remark of Dell's moved Eastman to a full defense of his position. He said again that he was still fighting the same good fight as of old. He dignified his position by associating it with Freidrich Hayek, Ludwig von Mises, James Burnham, William Henry Chamberlin, and others. "While you were working for the government," Max wrote unkindly, "persuading yourself that its measures of social reform were all you had ever meant by socialism, my colleagues in opinion" were giving serious thought to the great issues.[21]

Though perfectly entitled to, Floyd did not take offense. He hoped they could remain friends despite political differences, as in the civilized days of the old *Masses*. But it seemed to him that Max's mind was no longer open. Even when most infatuated with the Soviets, Max was never blind to their feelings. Today he seemed unaware of facts and events that might bear upon his views. Floyd did not admire Eastman's colleagues in opinion and hoped he did not confine his reading to them, as seems to have been the case. Later he speculated that Max might not be entirely comfortable with his newly acquired enthusiasm for capitalism. It always had its good points, Floyd pointed out, which radicals used to ignore, just as it had bad points which Max was ignoring today. He described Max's view of capitalism as utopian and wondered if Max's conservatism wasn't "somewhat jerry-built." Terming Max's connection with McCarthy "intellectually scandalous," he guessed that Max would someday have qualms about it: "At all counts, it is surely not the goal of your political history."[22] Floyd sweetened the pill, telling Max that "you are less neurotic and far more productive than I have been."

Coming from one writer to another, this was remarkably generous. There was some truth to it as well. Floyd's later years were less easy than Max's. He had once appeared destined to be the more successful. His first novel, the autobiographical *Moon-Calf* (1920), was a best seller. Other novels followed it throughout the 1920s. He also co-authored a Broadway hit *Little Accident*, which in 1944 was made into a Gary Cooper movie, *Casanova Brown*. But creative literature was not Floyd's best vein. *Moon-Calf* and its sequel, *The Briary-Bush* (1921), were based on Floyd's life. But it developed that he could not, as a novelist, write well about anything else. The later novels, even those drawn from his life, were progressively less interesting. In the depression he ceased being publishable and moved to Washington, where he was employed by the government from 1935 to 1947. At the time of his exchange with Eastman over McCarthyism, Dell was a forgotten man, living in obscurity and reduced circumstances, while Eastman was prosperous and still something of a celebrity. This makes Floyd's letters to Max all the more impressive for their lack of bitterness and envy.

Even so, they did not persuade. Max replied: "As to McCarthyism, I think McCarthy is a misbehaved and sloppy-minded person functioning in a place where the prime demand was for a well-behaved and extremely accurate and exact mind. But I think the idea that he is a 'menace' or that he has done any more harm to the prestige or reputation of innocent people than any thorough-going congressional investigation is a myth." It was "silly" to complain, as liberals did, that it took courage to stand up to McCarthy. What took courage was to issue sane statements about McCarthy as Max was doing. In any case, the main thing was that, while people argued over trifles like McCarthy, communism was "winning the world."[23]

Eastman's McCarthyism is the one real blot on his record. Though understandable in light of his political history, it remains unforgiveable. Even so, he avoided the worst excesses of the radical Right. He was never a militarist nor a defender of poison gas and similar weapons like Dos Passos. A supporter of the witchhunt, he did not practice it. Eastman never dropped long lists of names or conducted personal vendettas against Communists and fellow travelers. He once gave a deposition to the effect that Charlie Chaplin, despite his foolish politics, was not subversive. His McCarthyism resembled his Leninism in being principled and abstract. He was blind to the worst in McCarthy, as before to the worst in Lenin. So far as can be discovered, his political mistakes injured no one but himself. This does not excuse error, but puts it in perspective.

* * *

Eastman's loss of judgment is evident in *Reflections on the Failure of Socialism*, his last political book. It came out fifteen years after his big works of 1940 that Edmund Wilson had so admired. In that time the hard edge of his political prose had been worn away. *Reflections* is well written but lacks snap and brilliance. Like many of his books, it is a collection of essays, most originally having appeared in the *Digest*, the *New Leader*, the *Freeman*, and the *Saturday Evening Post*. By a happy accident Sidney Hook published his mature thoughts on Marxism that same year. The two books establish the final distinction between Hook and Eastman on the subject, a difference largely of temperament. Eastman had no sense of irony, and in later years especially inclined toward reductionism. Thus, in *Reflections* he declared baldly that Stalinism was the direct and inevitable consequence of Marx's "religion of immoralism":

> It was Marx and Engels who adopted "scorn and contempt" as the major key in which to attack the opponents of socialism, introducing a literature of vituperation that has few parallels in history. Even the political master-stroke of giving the land to the peasants "initially" in order to take it away from them when the power is secure came from the same source. The introduction of such unprincipled behavior into a movement toward the highest ends of man was entirely the work of Marx and Engels. Lenin added nothing to it but skill, and Stalin nothing but total instinctive indifference to the ends.[24]

Missing here are the careful distinctions of his earlier writings. Missing also was his earlier recognition of how Lenin had altered Marx to suit his own purposes. Now there is only a straight line from the character defects of Marx to the crimes of Stalin.

Hook, in contrast, had refined his ideas and clarified his style. His very readable book, *Marx and the Marxists,* offered both a history and a critique of Marxism that is hard to beat for vigor and precision. To Hook, communism was not the direct result of Marxism, but its opposite. Hook regarded Marx as essentially democratic and humane, though prone to error. One of Marx's mistakes was not to outline clearly the nature of his proposed socialist state, as Eastman had pointed out years before. Another was failing to realize that under socialism, democracy would become even more important than under capitalism because the state would then have a monopoloy of power. These two Marxist weaknesses, not fatal in their own right, became so in the hands of Lenin. To build socialism in an underdeveloped country, Lenin abandoned democracy, making the dictatorship of the proletariat—which Marx had expected would mean majority rule—a dictatorship over the proletariat, and everyone else. Communism is therefore a tragic and unintended perversion and repudiation of Marxism, not its outcome, as Eastman believed. Communists differ from Marxists in the following ways: "The Communists are neither historical nor economic determinists. Marxism in the Soviet Union functions strictly in the way Marx defined an ideology, i.e. as a 'false consciousness' which masks from the protagonists themselves the causes, ground, and motives of action." Stalinism to Hook is an ironic consequence of flaws in Marx's thought compounded by accidents of history. On the whole this seems a more satisfactory explanation than Eastman's. Unable to see the ironies in his own life and thought, he could not be expected to see them in others.

Though clear and sensible for the most part, *Reflections* is a weak book. Max thought best when addressing what was tangible, factual, or concrete. The more sharply focused an idea was the better he could handle it. One might say that Max was strongest when he was most scientific, not in the sense of invoking psychology or heredity, but when he addressed a specific problem and tried to work out its implications. He was at his worst when most abstract. The thinnest element of even his best political writing involved a tendency to blame Hegel for the crimes of Stalin. This resulted from pushing beyond what could be reasonably established—Hegel did, after all, influence Marx—to what was highly speculative. Eastman also imputed more power to ideas alone than they really deserve. This created the impression that dialectical materialism had more influence on Bolshevism than Russia's history and institutions, the character of Stalin, outside pressure on the Soviet Union, and other important factors. By the same token, when writing about capitalism as a believer, especially in *Reflections,* Eastman does not discuss the real American economy but some abstract mechanism bearing no relation to the way in which goods and services are actually produced.

Though never a utopian socialist, Eastman became, as Dell said, a utopian capitalist. His capitalism was not what one read about in *Business Week* or the *Wall Street Journal* but a collection of symbols labeled "the competitive market" and "the price system." As he knew nothing about such matters except what he had learned from Hayek and Von Mises, Eastman's capitalism was all theory and no fact. When writing about socialism, Eastman strained other people's idea though the cloth of his own knowledge and experience. In writing about capitalism, he merely brought up stale ideas he had swallowed whole. Worst of all, this book shows that Eastman's claim that he had not changed basic values—that, as he told Farrell, "we" remain loyal to the ends, you to the means—was false. He no longer cared deeply about economic justice, minority rights, racial prejudice, and the other causes of his youth and maturity.

Reflections had its fans. Calder Willingham, a well-known novelist and former Trotskyist, thanked Max for having proven to him that it was morally right to own property.[25] Eastman's conservative friends liked it, as did the *Wall Street Journal* and the *Saturday Evening Post.* William Z. Foster, a ghostly voice from the Communist party's militant past, attacked it in the *Daily Worker,* reminding the faithful few that Eastman had once been called a "gangster of the pen," though he did not say by whom, as Stalin was now in disrepute.[26] Liberal reviewers had no trouble locating the book's weak points. The *New York Times* said that Eastman's analysis bore little relation to the real world and would appeal only to those who agreed with him. Charles Frankel in the *Saturday Reveiw* thought Eastman correctly stressed consumer sovereignty, but wrongly assumed "that such sovereignty is in fact what is achieved when the operation of economic forces is left absolutely uncontrolled."[27]

Bertram Wolfe, a fellow refugee from Marxism, pointed out that Eastman admitted a free economy is in practice always a mixed economy, but would have made a better case if he had shown that this resulted not from rival ideologies but from practical necessity, as when depressions lead to social welfare measures. And Max ignored the extent to which business limited the free play of the market through price-fixing, tariffs, subsidies, and the like. Max had called Norway, of all places, "the closest imitation of an authoritarian state to be found this side of the iron curtain." What about Franco's Spain and Peron's Argentina? Wolf asked. Wolfe wanted to like the book, but could not praise what seemed designed to anger and therefore repel uncommitted readers.[28]

In changing sides Eastman largely abandoned not only the beliefs of a lifetime but the special knowledge related to them. Nothing in his experience prepared him to speak up for capitalism, and it should come as no surprise that he did so, by his previous standards, poorly. Journalistic polish was no substitute for expertise, still less for conviction. This is not to suggest dishonesty, or that Eastman didn't really believe that capitalism possessed the admirable traits he assigned it. All the same, his writings on capitalism lack feeling. Max was a rebel by nature, a capitalist only from necessity. The difference shows. Socialism had been the one grand passion of his political life, an affair of the mind and heart. With free enterprise he made a marriage of convenience.

* * *

As a conservative Max could no longer write political pieces for the *New Leader*. The monthly *Freeman* was conservative, but in 1954 it changed hands and after 1956 shrank in size and substance, losing its name writers, including Eastman. Thus Max welcomed the *National Review* at its inception. His association with it went back to 1951 when he reviewed *God and Man at Yale,* a fiery polemic by the then unknown William F. Buckley, Jr. This recent graduate meant to prove that atheism and collectivism were rampant at Yale. Max enjoyed the book for its cleverness and attacks on liberalism, while disagreeing with its message. As a devout atheist he naturally failed "to see why God can not take care of Himself at Yale, or even for that matter at Harvard."[29] Yale's policy of making religion an elective seemed to Max "dignified and wise" and possibly religious. He agreed that Yale students did seem to be afflicted with "creeping socialism," while ridiculing Buckley's solution, which involved alumni control of the university: "I don't think the thing to do is narrow the sphere of academic freedom." Apart from adding a few capitalist voices to the Economics department, Eastman would not, had he the power, change Yale. Though the review teased him a little, Buckley seemed not to mind. When he founded the *National Review* in 1955, Max was listed as an "Associate and Contributor."

Almost four years after he wrote it, Max's review of *God and Man at Yale* involved him in a small but revealing controversy. In 1955 Robert M. MacIver published *Academic Freedom in Our Time,* which expressed the conventionally beleaguered sentiments of liberal academicians at the end of the witchhunting era. In it he cited Max as an enemy of freedom for having praised Buckley's book. This angered Sidney Hook, now a friend of Max's, who was feeling somewhat beleaguered himself. Many of his fellow scholars for libertarian reasons took issue with his well-known objection to the employment of Communists as schoolteachers. Hook wrote Max to suggest that he answer MacIver in an open letter, pointing up the "lack of objectivity and elementary fairplay on the part of *ritualistic* liberals towards those who disagree with them. (Remember I am a liberal too.)" He continued, "for heaven's sake, Max, please leave free enterprise out of it! The issue concerns much more than free enterprise or the T.V.A."[30] Max took Hook's advice and protested against the falsification of his views, wondering why he alone was singled out by MacIver for "refutation and misrepresentation." MacIver replied stiffly that he took on Max because Eastman was the only person of "his standing" to admire *God and Man at Yale.* MacIver also had the feeling that Max thought Yale should do something about the faculty's liberal bias, which would be as much a violation of academic freedom as if the alumni took control.[31] This was the opposite of what Eastman had written and tells us much about the temper of the times. Embattled liberals could not be fair to Max, or even read him correctly.

Eastman was in familiar company on the *National Review,* whose contributors included other ex-radicals, including John Dos Passos, Will Herbert, Eugene Lyons, Freda Utley, John Chamberlain, and James Burnham. Max became fond of Buckley, a fellow sportsman, anti-communist, free-enterpriser, and writer of polemics. Even so Max found the *National Review* connection awkward. As a pagan and bohemian still, its mores were alien to him. In 1958 he asked Buckley to remove his name from the masthead. "It was an error in the first place to think that, because of political agreements, I could collaborate formally with a publication whose basic view of life and the universe I regard as primitive and superstitious," he wrote sternly, being never more ministerial than when denouncing religion. He objected to much that had been printed in the *National Review,* including "a snooty slap at Milovan Djilas," the brave enemy of Marshall Tito who "is in my opinion one of the major prophets, as well as moral heroes, of these sad times." Max was also angry at a recent dig at Pablo Casals, "whom I am celebrating in a forthcoming book as one of the few men of art who have stood inflexibly, with subtle intelligence, against every form of totalitarianism."[32]

Eastman could never bring himself to accept the conservative view that capitalism was the touchstone of all virtue. He continued to admire democratic radicals, whatever their economics. In 1952 he signed a letter of protest, along with Dos Passos, James T. Farrell, Allen Tate, Lionel Trilling, Albert Kazin, Edmund Wilson, and others, protesting the denial of a visa to the Italian novelist and former Communist Alberto Moravia. This was not the *National Review*'s way. Eastman liked the term "libertarian conservative," which he believed had been coined by John Chamberlain, but in 1958 he was obliged to tell Buckley, "I don't think your conservatism is consistently libertarian." It was time to remove his name from "the masthead of a magazine that voices so many opinions I violently and publicly disagree with." [33]

Eastman kept on writing for the *National Review* and arguing with Buckley, especially about religion. This was a familiar subject. Conservatives liked to say that theirs was a holy war against irreligion. To Eastman this was ridiculous, since communism was as much a religion as Christianity.[34] In 1962 he sent Buckley an essay protesting the magazine's association of anti-communism with Christianity. Inasmuch as two thirds of the world's population was not Christian, Max saw this as a self-defeating strategy. So was Barry Goldwater's identification of his program with God's will.[35] Buckley would not print the article on the ground that it implied a division of opinion among the editors that didn't exist, also that the *National Review* was putting something over on readers, and that signed pieces represented the view of all the editors, which they didn't. Buckley seems to have felt uneasy about this, since he claimed both that the editors didn't disagree and that they did. But he was clear on the relation between Christians and atheists. It was Eastman, not himself, Buckley pointed out, who was always bridling "at a common front with us." Buckley knew that atheists made very fine anti-Communists, "but I think atheists don't make altogether convincing conservatives." [36]

Neither was willing to let the question die. Buckley reviewed their exchange in his newspaper column. It was now apparent to him why Christians made better anti-Communists than atheists. Sure of an afterlife, they did not fear death: "Such men are less likely to panic when Khrushchev rattles his bombs and threatens the extermination of the world—unless he is given his way. . . . That is why I tell my impious friend Max—who as an individual I would trust to write our entire foreign policy, even while worrying, as I do for my own, for his eternal soul—that I consider it politically relevant, as a general rule, to ask whether our leaders are religious men." Max had a response to this astonishing theory, which he kept to himself: "but the atheistic Communists fight better than we do. Isn't it because their belief is more real?" [37]

In 1963 Buckley brought up the question again. He asked: "Can you be a conservative and despise God and feel contempt for those who beieve in Him?" Buckley did not think that he was reading Eastman out of the conservative movement. The problem was that Max could not get along with Christians, though they tolerated him! "The reason why Christian conservatives can associate with atheists is because we hold that, above all, faith is a gift and that, therefore, there is no accounting for the bad fortune that has beset those who do not believe, or the good fortune that has befallen those who do."[38] Max compounded his misfortune by failing to admit it. He kept voicing his non-belief, "and so the tension."

Though condescending in the manner of believers, Buckley was not unfair. He allowed Max his day in court. The following year *National Review* published Eastman's final statement on the subject. He was annoyed that a contributor had written that conservatives favored "an objective moral order." This was not what Eastman meant by freedom, supposedly the goal of conservatism:

> The content and purpose of freedom, to my mind, is to let men accept what appeals to them, and live their lives as they want to, so long as they do not encroach injuriously upon the lives of others. To advocate freedom, and then lay down the law as to how men "should" use it, is a contradiction in terms. It's a reversion, not to classic liberalism, but to pre-liberal ecclesiastical authoritarianism—or what is left of it. I don't strive to understand an objective moral order or move toward it, because I don't think any such objective moral order exists. To me all such talk is pedantic pulpiteering, and as a profession of belief in individual freedom it is insincere and untrustworthy.[39]

He still thought identifying anti-communism with Christianity was "parochial and self-defeating." He did not like the *National Review*'s habit of calling liberty a gift of God when it was actually "an extremely rare achievement of human will and intelligence." Buckley's argument that Christians fought better than atheists because of belief in an afterlife seemed to Max absurd. It was precisely because Communists believed so strongly in making life better here on earth that they were good fighters. Max did not answer the question in his title, "Am I a Conservative," but the inference was plain. He was not going to call himself a conservative if that meant "an emotional turning back on all subjects to Edmund Burke, and beyond Burke to the Middle Ages."

The two remained friends. "I think of Max often and with great and enduring affection," Buckley wrote recently.[40] Their principles continued to be far apart. Though conservative on given issues, Eastman was obviously not a conservative in Buckley's sense. His morals

were at odds with his politics, making him hard to place. After breaking with socialism, Max called himself a "democratic radical," then a
"scientific liberal," and after that a "libertarian conservative." None of
these labels fit. He was not a liberal as the term is now understood. A
believer in sexual freedom, the equality of women, birth control, and
saving the environment, he could never be comfortable on the Right.
Eastman finally returned to the liberalism of his youth, which defined
freedom negatively as the absence of constraint.

His last years saw Eastman mellow politically. His anti-communism
became more discriminating. He did not support the Vietnam war: "A
fiftieth part of what we spent on the irrelevant war in Viet Nam, if
spent on a prodigious campaign of world-wide educative propaganda
might convince mankind of the simple fact that communism must give
way to common sense," he wrote in 1968.[41] Eastman regained the ability to discuss politics without losing his temper. As prejudice declined,
so did dogmatism. Shortly before his death, Max told a young friend,
Jack A. Robbins, that he now believed he was mistaken in associating
liberty exclusively with free enterprise. *Reflections on the Failure of Socialism* no longer fully expressed his views. This was not a left turn but a
drift toward the center. Though slow to change, Eastman did not ignore events. History pushed him one way in the 1940s and '50s, another way in the '60s. Max did support Joseph McCarthy, at great and
doubtless permanent expense to his reputation. Even so, as Floyd Dell
said at the time, McCarthyism was not the end of his political history.
He lived to see a better day and take, if only in private, a better stand.

*   *   *

Though strongly held, Eastman's political opinions mattered less to
him after 1940 than his creative work. In a sense this was always true,
but in his radical days Max was always allowing politics to distract him
from his calling. This seldom happened afterward, perhaps because as
he grew old he could not afford the loss of time. Until near the end,
age did not impair his style. Politics excepted, some of Eastman's best
writing was done in his middle and later years.

In 1942 Eastman published two utterly different books: one, his
most ambitious poem, "Lot's Wife"; the other a book of essays he called
Heroes I Have Known. In these biographical sketches Max could use his
best voice. The essay was his natural form of expression, and he was
never more fluent than when writing about people he knew. Max pub-

lished two books of profiles in his life, *Heroes* and later *Great Companions*, which included many of the same essays. Though his profiles usually came out first in magazines, and were drawn on again in his memoirs, Eastman was right to publish them separately, as they show him in top form. *Heroes* was designed by Max to offset Carlyle's emphasis on conquering rulers. It celebrates great human qualities, such as the bravery of Carlo Tresca and the goodness of Art Young. Eastman admired Isadora Duncan without liking her. Along with everyone he knew, Max had been transported by her dancing. He thought her a great artist and moralist, but in person she made him uncomfortable: "I was repelled by her conversational and behavioral heroics," and her confusion of "gesticulation with gesture." Max wanted her to be "great and real, a classic in the mold of Walt Whitman, all the way through." Instead, she was theatrical and frequently irresponsible.* Max saw her a number of times in New York and once in Russia where, as usual, he was embarrassed "by the admirable force of character with which Isadora insisted on being half-baked." Much as she rubbed him the wrong way, Max would not deny her genius or importance:

> All the bare-legged girls, the sun-tanned, assured and natural girls with strong free steps wherever they go, owe more to Isadora Duncan than to any other person. And the boys that are unafraid of such girls and unafraid of their instincts—all who have escaped in any degree from the rigidity and prissiness of our once national religion of negation—owe a debt to Isadora Duncan's dancing. It is impossible, of course, to distinguish here the cause from the effect. She rode the wave of the revolt against puritanism; she rode it, and with her fame and Dionysian raptures drove it on. She *was*—perhaps it is simplest to say—the crest of the wave, an event not only in art, but the history of life.[42]

Heroes received mixed notices, though it is hard to see why.[43] The book's main flaw is ambivalence. His heroes had a disconcerting habit of developing faults the closer he got to them. It makes lovely reading just the same.

Lot's Wife was Eastman's most ambitious poem, and according to him his best. It was different in style from Eastman's other verse, not a

---

* This was especially the case where her dancers were concerned. Max knew several of them, but apparently they had not told him, or he thought it unwise to repeat, their chilling tales of neglect and abandonment. These can be found in Irma Duncan, *Duncan Dancers* (Middletown, Conn., 1966).

romantic lyric but a long narrative poem that takes liberties with the Biblical story. In Max's version Lot is a bully who runs his wife, family, and the town of Sodom with an iron hand. The town rebells, forcing Lot to abandon the city under the pretext that he is following God's instructions. Lot's wife refuses to leave, attacking his way of life, system of government, philosophy, and much else. She then tells her daughters that they should not dig a grave for her:

> But carve, please, on that pillar of white salt,
> Carve this, though only for the vulture's eyes:
> "Lot's wife, who for forty years has been dead,
> Here for one moment lived, here turned her head."[44]

As she expects, Lot kills her for this offense. After being dragged along by him, Lot's daughters lay plans to get him drunk and have intercourse with him, knowing he will then kill himself out of shame, and they will gain their freedom.

This reveals more than any of Eastman's poems, no doubt unintentionally. It is striking that of all the classic texts Eastman could have chosen as his subject he selected one that portrays a father negatively, develops an incest theme, and allows him to dispose of mother and father alike. Both the ideas and skills of his maturity are united in this dense and intricate poem, which is at once his most alusive and most powerful. It was Eastman's principal attempt not only to employ his fullest range as an artist, but, whether consciously or not, to escape the Oedipal situation.

Before publication Eastman showed the poem to Edmund Wilson, who made a number of criticisms.[45] These discouraged Max, even though Wilson later sweetened the pill by telling him that his translation of a Pushkin poem was the best Wilson had ever seen except for one by Vladimir Nabokov. Max took counsel with friends, who advised him that Wilson was wrong. *Lot's Wife* was perfect. In a note to himself Max dismissed Wilson: "It takes a poet to catch a poet."[46] Though it cheered Max to think this, Wilson, too, wrote poetry, and was a good judge of it, as Max would admit years afterward.

Lot's Wife was vitally important to Max because he saw it as his last chance at real artistic distinction. He had worked on it for years, trying to develop a different style. In a long letter to Wilson he described his poetry as "weak and too fluid," not related enough to the rest of him, his ideas and sense of humor. The poem was an effort to "get the

whole of myself pouring," to break out of the lyric mold that he thought
had enfeebled his art.[47] Friends applauded the work. Edna Millay sent
Max a telegram: "To this poem you have brought no only your talent
and equipment for poetry but also all the qualities which make your
writings in prose so very easy to keep on reading, so very hard to lay
down. Here you treat poetry as if it were as robust as prose." The book,
she concluded, was "striking and delightful" throughout. E. E. Cummings wrote, "your book delights me," and Mencken declared, "It is not
only amusing; it is full of waggish wisdom. To my barbaric mind, at
least, it makes such things as T. Eliot's 'Waste Land' sound childish."[48]
Granville Hicks, no longer a Stalinist but no friend of Eastman either,
agreed. It seemed to him "fresh and vigorous, a lot of fun to read, and
a shrewd commentary on the Biblical Story."[49]

The critics thought otherwise. *Lot's Wife* was not widely reviewed,
and the brief mentions of it were usually negative. The poem was
erotic, leading the *Nation* to call it a "vulgar performance" suited to a
Hearst newspaper. To the *New York Herald Tribune* it was a "juicy tidbit"
combining "vivid imagery, Biblical and Broadway, pungent humor, and
Byronic metrics with a juke-box flourish." The *Saturday Review* took the
same line. Ben Ray Redman found the poem "loud and vulgar. It is
also clever, often amusing, always glibly readable, coarsely effective in
many passages." But Redman refused to take it seriously. "According
to my judgment he rises to true poetry briefly in the hill scene above
burning Sodom, and in a few scattered lines, but the rest is verse of dubious value. . . ."[50]

Publicly Eastman behaved as if this cool reception did not matter.
In interviews he often mentioned *Lot's Wife* proudly. His true feelings
were quite different, as is shown by a note he wrote himself two years
after it came out. He had spent the previous evening looking over "my
futile and rather diffuse editorials in the old *Masses*." During the night
he dreamed that he was kneeling before the statue of some great man,
possibly Milton. He awoke sobbing, and when Eliena asked him what
was wrong, he said to her, "Eliena, I am sure I was meant to do something great." The next morning he described this scene on his typewriter, ending, "for that is not only my deepest but my most present
sorrow. I have wasted my talents."[51]

In aiming so high Max assured himself of failure, and not for the
first time. It was his habit to attempt the impossible. When by chance
he succeeded, as with his big books in 1940, he moved quickly to nullify

the advantage. Defeat and unpopularity made him melancholy. He seemed to think their opposites even worse. From the time he gave up the *Liberator,* Eastman's life was marked by one self-defeating act after another. Certain to gain enemies on account of politics, he acquired many more needlessly, going out of his way to give offense. And, as if to ensure frustration, Max sacrificed what he could do to what he couldn't. Since verse was his weakest suit, the reception of his poetry became the measure of achievement. Serious journalism was his strength, so naturally he disdained it. Throughout his life he suffered from depressions, usually self-induced. As a matter of principle Max was often happy just the same. Being cheerful was part of his religion.

*   *   *

Having failed, in terms of his ridiculous standards, as a poet, Eastman was left with but a single chance at greatness. Accordingly he returned to his autobiography, the last and best of Eastman's major creative efforts. The challenge was almost overwhelming. Nearly everyone agreed that Max's life was bigger than the sum of its parts, that he was, if not a great artist, great at the art of living. Everyone wanted, even demanded, that he write a brilliant autobiography. Easier said than done. For one thing he had to justify a career that often seemed scattered and unfocused, especially to himself. He had to meet the general expectation that the book would be worthy of the life it recorded. And he had to dredge up the painful memories of his unhappy youth. If honest, his memoirs would be brutally revealing.

So much depended on it that writing the book was a horror. Eastman once said that *Marxism: Is It Science?* was his hardest book to write. But he meant only that it was technically the most difficult. His memoirs were emotionally agonizing, so much so that for years it seemed doubtful they would ever appear. He signed a contract with his friends Dick Simon and Max Schuster and began work on the autobiography sometime in the late thirties. By 1939 he had written about 175,000 words, which no one seemed to like. Max believed that "a truly self-knowing autobiography is the great literary work this age of psychology is looking for."[52] To this end he dealt at length with his family background and early life. But when Simon and Schuster circulated this material, the readers agreed that Eastman's manuscript, still far from complete, was too long and boring. Simon told Eastman to bear in mind that his prospective audience included small-town intellectuals and literary clubwomen: "None of these people are interested in literary fights or in letters that father wrote to mother, but they are all potentially interested in a glamorous human being who has lived, and is continuing to live a full and exciting and unique life."[53] Simon and Schuster kept trying to sell Max on a brief version, heavy on the glamor. This was probably the right way to make a commercial success. It was the wrong way to change Eastman's mind. He explained, "I just can't write a book with that motive. I've got to write the book as it comes out of my heart and mind without any regard for popularity or sales, and I'm going to do that."[54] It was not that Eastman scorned money, he was too old for that. Actually he counted on having a best seller. But more than fortune he coveted glory and believed absolutely that compromise was not the way to gain it. His book would be pure and complete, running probably to 400,000 words—about the size of Steffens's celebrated autobiography.

Well-meaning friends tried to talk Max out of this, Margaret Halsey for one. She was a talented young woman whom Eastman had discovered. She did secretarial work for him, then he found her a job with Simon and Schuster. Subsequently she wrote a book of humor, *With Malice Toward Some,* which was a best seller in 1938, with a first printing of 125,000 copies—an astonishing sale for a new author, far greater than Max would ever enjoy. Halsey was typical of the intelligent liberal audience Max hoped to reach. And she shared the general opinion that his manuscript was too long and leisurely. Reading it, she was impatient for him to "get on to the heroic days of poetry and women and radicalism."[55] After a visit she wrote to apologize for having undermined "your confidence a little by my insistence on the days of maturity being the best part of the book. The suggestion seemed to fill you with a nervous insecurity that I'm afraid I'm responsible for. But what I think is that your main contribution to humanity—as far as this book is concerned—is your account of how you got into the radical movement and how it felt once you got there."[56] This was the common view, as Max discovered again when he gave up on Simon and Schuster. His editor at Scribner's, the legendary Maxwell Perkins, told Max that his approach would appeal to few readers. In light of this he was asking for too large an advance—ten thousand dollars, which would require an improbably large sale of 20,000 copies.[57] Though still certain the skeptics were wrong, Eastman beat a retreat. Rather than abandon the theory behind it, he stopped working on his book.

In 1947, having fiddled with it off and on, Eastman took up the manuscript again and resolved this time to see it through. In a note to himself, Max wrote, "often at night when my book was nearing publication, I would lie awake in a dripping sweat through dread of that event."[58] He was frightened that people would think he had described his sex life too graphically. He feared that Ida Rauh, with whom he was on bad terms, would be offended by his account of their relationship. For her part she failed to understand why he kept assuring her that everything was all right but would not show her what he had written: "Why not refer to our marriage (if you feel you must refer to it) as an experiment which did not result in a permanent relationship? Is it necessary to justify yourself to the public or to judge me? or blame me?"[59] Max kept looking to his friends for support. "It was extravagantly praised by strong-minded women and shy men," he said of it later. Fear and doubt notwithstanding, he clung to his original vision of the book. It would be distinguished for "its resolute and reckless inward-looking truthfulness" and the wealth of detail this required. When published by Harper and Brothers in 1948, it was 595 pages long, though it only went up to the early part of 1917.

Enjoyment of Living may not be Eastman's most important book. *Stalin's Russia* is his foremost political work, *Marxism: Is It Science?* his most finished statement of theory. But *Living* is, as literature, unquestionably the best, proof that he had the right idea all along. As always, he wove in previously published material, and in addition borrowed heavily from diaries, journals, letters, and family documents. The old and the new were stitched together so cleverly that few seams show. In a work of history the lack of documentation would be unfortunate. But Eastman was writing for aesthetic and emotional effect and properly kept the text moving along. It reads like a novel, being the tale of how a repressed youth from a family of ministers overcame the resulting afflictions to find love, life, and happiness in the great city. Though the plot is familiar, *Living* makes us forget this, showering the reader with details and delights. Its denseness and specificity, the very features editors objected to in the thirties, help make it work as literature and history. An example is the great attention paid to his mother. In 1939 Halsey thought this excessive because all that she wanted to know about Annis Ford Eastman was the degree to which mother radicalized Max, or made his radicalism possible. Today, thanks to the feminist movement, Mrs. Eastman seems important in her own right and Max justified in describing her so carefully.

Finally, the detail matters because it keeps the book from being just another self-absorbed chronicle. Most autobiographies fail not just because poorly written, though by comparison with *Living* most are, but because the writers, being egotists (why else write a book about one's self?), cannot keep from viewing everything in terms of their own feelings. Max had the customary self-regard, but in providing so much information enabled the reader to judge for himself on many points. Then, too, *Living* is shockingly honest. A truly confessional book, though including the odd small victory or minor triumph, it mainly concerns Max's struggle against debilitating and sometimes crippling emotional handicaps. It tells a real story, not just a true one but a dramatic tale with a beginning and an end. It concludes with Max at the age of 34 having just won his way through to love and health. "My life began in January, 1917," he had written in his journal. It is worth quoting him again as to what that meant:

> I had accomplished the feat of confiding in a friend; I had faced loneliness without melancholy; I had outlived that bashfulness which deprived me of the joys of adolescence; I had fallen wholeheartedly in love. After much preaching and philosophizing, and many academic vows of consecration to it, I had at last stepped forth into the enjoyment of living. It was possible for me now to use in a grown-up way whatever wisdoms I possessed.

Enjoyment of Living is just about everything that a great memoir should be. Finely written, it describes a fascinating life that took place in one of the richer and more exciting periods of American history. One cannot authenticate everything in the book. Part of it is impressionistic and subjective by design. Some vital documents have been lost or are not available to scholars. But on almost every major point for which there is hard evidence, Max's version of events checks out. His story is as factual as he could make it, and as unsparingly self-critical as anyone not prejudiced against him could wish.

Enjoyment of Living fails in only one respect, a crucial weakness in the life rather than the book. Dr. Gehring cured Max by treating his symptoms, not their source. Max resisted psychoanalysis on the ground that all he needed were applications of robust common sense. This

remedy was Eastman's stock-in-trade as an intellectual, but all problems
are not resolved by simple wisdoms, as he liked to think. Max did not
understand his contradictions and so could not explain them. As self-
analysis, *Enjoyment of Living* does not work. As self-description it is
splendid.

*   *   *

The book was not badly received. Robinson Jeffers wrote Max that it
was "probably the most honest piece of autobiography that I have ever
seen; honest and decent too." It was news to Upton Sinclair that Max
had been so full of uncertainties when young, as "you always managed
to impress me as an extraordinarily serene and well-balanced person."
Floyd Dell compared the book with Rousseau's *Confessions,* saying that
Max handled themes that usually appear only in fiction better than
most novelists.[60] Some reviewers were generous. The *Nation* unexpec-
tedly gave him high marks for humor, poetry, and even anti-Stalinism.
The book was full of surprises, if also "embarrassingly candid" confessions. Max's "seeming arrogance" was now found to be only shyness.
Indeed, Max's whole character appeared in a different light: "His
dogged pursuit of happiness in a tragic world makes him at times appear more coldly calculating than he really is. His childish clamoring
for attention, even now when he has behind him such splendid performances as may be found in many of his poems, especially his pioneering *Enjoyment of Poetry,* may well be due to the fact that both his mother
and his first wife were egregiously chary of praise."[61] Though missing
the point here, the reviewer did grasp some of Eastman's contradictions, and saw in him a "feminine gentleness and cattishness as well,
a high pride and deep humility which come out in this autobiography
and make him the contradictory, cantankerous, but always charming
personality that he is."

Richard Watts, Jr., a journalistic admirer of Chinese communism,
was not prepared to forgive what the *New Republic* considered Max's
political sins. He was glad that, though now conservative, Eastman was
still able to treat his radical past respectfully. But Watts made light of
Eastman's Marxist period, saying that Max "found it also an adventur-
ous fad, an outlet for his ego, and his appetite for intellectual excitement. It was something he cherished chiefly as a colorful chapter in
what he was determined to make a colorful life.[62] Here Watts was

reviewing not *Enjoyment of Living* but Max's later, as yet unwritten life, and showing his ignorance. Whatever its faults, *Marxism: Is It Science?* is not the work of a dilettante or a thrillseeker. Watts also disliked Max's account of his sex life or, rather, for the most part in this volume, his lack of one. More to the point, he took offense at Eastman's apparent contempt for writing as a profession, or "at least signs of scorn for letters as the enemy of rich, full, living." Max never seems to have appreciated the degree to which airing his conservative views on literature and his suspicion of journalism antagonized other writers. After politics it was the main reason intellectuals had for disapproving of him. When the Book-of-the-Month Club turned down *Enjoyment of Living,* Max replied that it was what he expected. "I never did stand in with the VIP's of modern literature. I just don't belong. It's my own fault I guess. I'm a black sheep that wandered away and fell into the chasm between literature and science." [63] Eastman would never face the truth here, probably owing to his enormous stubbornness, maybe also because it was too late.

Eastman was more complicated that he seemed, as *Enjoyment of Living* demonstrated. Most people did not care to see this. They wanted him safely tucked away in a pigeon hole marked "reactionary playboy nudist" or something of that sort. Granville Hicks was an exception. After the 1930s he was always fair to Max, and read the autobiography with a particularly clear eye: "As a piece of literary craftsmanship, it is beautifully sustained throughout its 600 pages, and it is an ardently honest attempt at self-revelation, though what one is to make of the self that is revealed remains a problem." [64] He appreciated the long, evocative sections on Max's boyhood. He was impressed that Eastman could write with affection and insight of his old associates, even those who became Stalinists such as William Z. Foster and Elizabeth Gurley Flynn. Despite caveats, Hicks wrote a penetrating review that was honest as well, and never more so than when he confessed that he had never understood Eastman and "after 600 pages I still don't." It was a pity that other reviewers did not follow his example.

The *New Leader* felt that Eastman was too hard on himself.

> Self deprecation did not square with militant radicalism, the flouting of convention, the writing of a score of books, a great deal of effective public speaking and journalism, the courage to stand by convictions and to form new ones when the old were made hollow. [65]

The *New Leader* had a few thousand readers; *Time* magazine had millions, who learned from it that "Max Eastman, once a violently articulate Socialist and now a *Reader's Digest* 'roving editor,' has written about enjoyment in a way that takes most of the joy out of it." Max's "candor will strike many readers as needless bad taste," said *Time,* a magazine of exquisite sensibility. Worse still, "there is endless talk of his sexual and mental characteristics—an often maudlin study which is not so much a matter of enjoyment as an involved, embarrassing account of the continuous trial and errors of an uncertain, mentally harried intellectual." [66]

Max did receive encouragement. The *Denver Post* called him the "reluctant dragon of American radicalism," which was not bad. Lewis Gannett in the *New York Herald Tribune* saw Max as a "belated Beecher" and his book as "a revealing chapter of Americana." The *Chicago Tribune* ran a poetic tribute to Eastman, modeled on Carl Sandburg's famous poem:

> *Poetry-enjoyer for America, Laugh-maker, Lover of Life, Player with Metaphors*
> *And the Nation's Stalin-Handler. Stormy, husky, brawling, Critic of the*
> *Big Shoulders.* [67]

John Sloan wrote Max to say that the critics were wrong: "The account of your boyhood and youth. Your interesting family life and school days are beautifully told. Your narrative of the high adventure of our days together in . . . *The Masses* is of course full of awakened memories for me. And is quite to my satisfaction." [68]

One friend even got Max to explain his title. Marion Townsend (Mrs. E. E. Cummings) was among the people who wondered why he called his book *Enjoyment of Living* since there was so much pain and depression in it. Eastman shot off a volley of excuses in reply. He thought up the title before writing the book. Happy days don't make a good story. These were pretty lame. He could, after all, have changed the title before going to press. One reason surely was that his two best-selling books each had "enjoyment" in the title. But perhaps the best reason, though buried in his letter among trivial points, was that he didn't mean enjoyment in the literal sense but "as an ethic rather than a victory achieved." [69] Happiness was part of his religion, but was not a gift of nature. He fought for it doggedly.

Most writers would have been pleased with the response to *En-*

joyment of Living. In the first six months it sold 7,637 copies and was reviewed in dozens of papers. But Max was crushed. It earned him in that period slightly less than $5,000 of the $8,000 advanced him by Harper and Brothers. And it was not reviewed as widely as he expected. Max had hoped for a great popular success that would make him financially independent, and for critical acclaim as well. That was why he had been ruthlessly honest in the book, recounting in full his neurotic difficulties and sexual failures. Yet to a degree it was Max's own fault that his labors went unrewarded.

To have gained a popular success, and probably a critical one as well, Eastman should have done two things. He ought to have followed advice and written a one-volume work, passing quickly over his youth and dwelling on the years of glory. The result would have been a poorer book with much better sales potential. Even more importantly, Eastman should have finished the book in 1940. This was entirely feasible, requiring only that he put aside *Stalin's Russia* and *Marxism: Is It Science?* Coming out in 1940 when events had justified his position, the book would have been saying the right things at the right time. It would have benefited from the large sales of *Enjoyment of Laughter* a few years earlier. It would not have had to bear the weight of political prejudice directed against Eastman by liberals in 1948.

Writing to himself in the summer of 1954, Max regretted the torment he had put himself through in writing a book that was not received as "I believed a great autobiography would be." His pains had been for nothing, the effort wasted. "Often now I am sorry I made it; the night sweats seem to have been wise and I foolish."[70] Eastman was certain that he had shot his last bolt. At 71 he was too old for a final masterpiece that would turn public opinion around. The second volume of his memoirs would never be finished, he was certain.

In terms of documented self-pity, the summer of 1954 was a very low point. Yet Eastman was still good-looking, still strong and vigorous, still having love affairs. He suffered from despair just the same. Sometimes he blamed himself for not achieving greatness. Other times it was the *Reader's Digest*'s fault. A week before the note to himself just quoted, Max wrote another sad document in the form of a letter to his dead sister Crystal on the anniversary of her birth. He began by reviewing his career with the *Digest.* When Max was hired by DeWitt Wallace as a roving editor, he was nearly 60 years old and broke. The money from *Enjoyment of Laughter* and from his radio show was gone. The big books on Russia and Marxism, though admired by critics, sold badly. He was faced once again with the need to lecture, something he no longer enjoyed. Then De Witt Wallace rescued him from the perils of poverty and lecturehood. Wallace offered Max an annual retainer of $10,000 in return for a first option on anything Eastman might write. For articles accepted by the *Digest* Max would get in addition the standard fee, which at first was about $1,200. Though they never had a written contract, Wallace honored this generous agreement for the rest of Max's life, and even beyond it by giving Max's widow a pension, though under no obligation.

At first the relation was a happy one. His enemies who claimed that Max sold out to the *Digest* were wrong. Max needed the money, but he craved the audience even more. The *Digest* was in some ways a natural home for him. It was anti-communist even during the war and would print attacks on Stalinism by Max that no other popular magazine wanted. It liked the human interest stories and biographical sketches that Max wrote so handily. And Wallace was a tremendously encouraging editor in the 1940s when Max was again alienated from his old constituency on the Left. He poured out a stream of letters praising Eastman's work, usually with checks enclosed. Thus, some months after Max's article on collaborating with Russia come out, Wallace wrote: "For having written the article of the year, you certainly deserve this extra payment." [71] Attached was a check for $3,000—what a working class family might earn in a year. Wallace also paid many of Eastman's expenses, including travel and secretarial costs.

After the war relations became more distant. A big reason was that Max didn't produce much. From 1941 until his death in 1969 Eastman contributed an average of only two articles a year, and in some years nothing at all. At first Wallace seems not to have minded, but with time came irritation. Perhaps this was because Max's name faded over the years. Then, too, he never again wrote anything for the *Digest* that attracted as much attention as his 1943 article on Russia. Max's failure to keep up with events in the communist world was limiting. But apparently the chief reason was low output. As early as 1952 Wallace was asking Max to "step up his quota." In 1955 he complained again that "I sometimes wonder, if I may say so, whether any Rover manifests as little persistent and apparent interest in producing for RD as you do." The next year he complained that at least thirty free-lancers had contributed more to the *Digest* than Max and said he would like to remove Eastman's name from the masthead.[72]

Max offered various excuses: he was getting old (true but irrelevant, as he remained fluent almost to the end); the *Digest* turned down a lot of his proposals. Anyway, he was not a professional journalist like other *Digest* contributors, but a "literary artist" and had been retained on that basis.[73] In 1959 Wallace suggested that in view of his unproductivity and generous stipend Max contribute his first article free to the *Digest* each year.[74] Here the correspondence ends, apparently because Wallace gave up trying to reform Max. But while Wallace cut back on the expense money, he continued to pay Eastman's retainer, even though Eastman continued to write very little for the *Digest*. After the first few years, during which Max earned his keep, the *Digest* connection was almost a philanthropic one. Wallace kept Eastman in comfort for more than a quarter century. This was a remarkably generous record, and though the *Digest* was rich and could afford to carry Eastman, the fact remains that many corporations are rich and few of them subsidize artists and intellectuals on a permanent basis. Max worried about the situation. It was in Wallace's power to cut Max off anytime he pleased. Wallace didn't, though, enabling Max to live as he pleased for the balance of his life.

Max sometimes complained of the limits imposed by the *Digest* formula. He explained to Peter Viereck that writing for the *Digest* was "a little like talking to children."[75] Everything had to be spelled out for the magazine's fourteen million readers, none of whom were intellectuals. In his letter to Crystal, Max regretted that his *Digest* articles had to be written "in the simplified and hasty-readable style, at once condensed and diluted, if that is possible—which such circulation requires."[76] But this was not the real issue. Simplicity was one of Eastman's hole cards, and he overplayed it at times throughout his life. He did not invent a whole new style for the *Digest*. It had been there all the time, cropping up in the weaker *Masses'* editorials and in his lectures, where informality had a way of becoming condescension. The *Digest* format brought out the worst in Eastman as a writer, and on some level he knew this. And yet, as Max also knew, the *Digest* never asked him to say anything he did not believe. Most writers were far worse off. And Max had consciously chosen this path rather than the "drearily dragged-out old age of a professional lecturer. But as time grows short and I see that I am not going to fulfill myself, it becomes harder and harder to do, thus taking more and more time, and giving me a feeling that I am trapped, I am beleaguered. Crystal, I would like to say, what do you think I should do?"

This was a rhetorical question, for Max had made his choice. When the *Digest* gave him a surplus income in the 1940s, he invested it in land rather than securities, acquiring some 90 acres on the Vineyard. They produced no revenue, so Max depended almost entirely on the *Digest* for actual cash. Max admitted in writing Crystal that this problem was his own fault. He could have put his *Digest* money into stocks and lived frugally off their modest dividends. This was not the whole story. There was another choice which Max refused to consider. He could have begun selling off his land as he grew older and it became more valuable. Yet, he parted with almost none of it. He loved his beautiful acres on Gay Head, and though he sometimes toyed with the idea of selling portions, he nearly always backed off in the end. So the *Digest* connection was priceless to him. It gave him leisure, comfort, and a gorgeous property that was his pride and joy and a consolation in his old age. Eastman realized this and was not ungrateful to the *Digest*. He often defended it against the sneers of friends and pointed out that it stood for principles he mostly believed in and distributed them to the whole free world. In seeming to criticize the *Digest* he was actually criticizing himself.

For most of his life Eastman had lived by his wits, giving no thought to the morrow. From the time of his college graduation until 1941 he was a free lance, supporting himself by lecturing, by raising funds to pay his salary as an editor, by translations, and by writings that seldom made much money. Except as an assistant at Columbia and for six months on the radio, he never had a regular job. When the *Digest* took him on, Eastman had nothing material to show for thirty years of service to letters and socialism but a small property on Martha's Vineyard and a few hundred dollars. Not surprisingly he spent his *Digest* money doing and buying things that had been denied him—land, travel, and minor luxuries. Eastman's letter to Crystal made plain his feeling of guilt. He admitted that he had never earned his retainer and that Wallace's demands on him were perfectly reasonable. The problem was that he had betrayed the promise of his youth and the high purposes to which he had been consecrated. He had wanted to save his pen for literature, to write great works of art, and to benefit humanity.

Now Max was earning his living at journalism, which he had always looked down upon. He had not, in the world's eyes, created a great work of art. He wasn't doing much for humanity either. When young, Eastman had set impossibly high standards for himself. His sorrow in old age was that he had not lived up to them. This was the last barrier that kept him from taking full pleasure in the enjoyment of living, and he never crossed it.

CHAPTER TWELVE

Eastman
in His Prime

The first impression was always of his good looks and vitality. Alfred Kazin remembered meeting the "Yankees" at V. F. Calverton's parties. They

> still looked as unscarred as Norman Thomas and Max Eastman—they looked indeed, as if they had personally enjoyed resistance to their stuffy beginnings as ministers or the sons of ministers; they looked as if they had fought down their own kind for the pleasure of fighting. With their open American faces and their frank American voices, with their lean figures and honest old American instincts, they looked dashing and splendid, undismayed by evil and not afraid to do good. They laughed a lot, even in argument.[1]

As readers of *Love and Revolution,* which understated them, know, once Max broke free of Victorian constraints he had many love affairs. Most of his love letters are not available to scholars, but those that remain in his papers at the Lilly Library indicate that he was a skillful and considerate lover who gave as well as received much sexual and romantic pleasure. He frequently had several affairs at once, but most seem not to have ended bitterly. There are a few hot letters of reproach in his collection. But there are also letters from former lovers with whom he remained on good terms. Some of his lovers became long-term friends. One was Rosalind Fuller, his sister-in-law through Crystal, with whom he had his first real affair in 1917. She achieved distinction as an actress but kept in touch. After his death, though she could not attend the memorial service, she wrote proudly: "I am an admirer and a lover of Max Eastman."[2]

Margaret Halsey, his former friend and secretary, remembered him as he was in the 1930s. "I was dazzled by Max Eastman's looks, by the charm and playful wit he could exert when he chose, by his poetry and by his prose style," she says in her autobiography. "Unlike most radical intellectuals, Eastman was as beautiful as an army with banners. Though a big man, he had a lithe, catlike walk and long before bright-colored clothes for men were an accepted thing, he wore cherry-red or pale blue slacks that made him seem, among the conventionally clad males, like some kind of messenger from Olympus."[3] Perhaps this explains why Max was able to go on having affairs into his seventies, and remained attractive to women nearly all his life, despite his reputation as a Don Juan—perhaps even because of it. As might be expected, Max's approach to women was not in the rugged, silent, he-man tradition of Hollywood movies. Crystal had noted when he was very young that Max had certain feminine qualities—sympathy, emotional responsiveness, tenderness—that together with his appearance and reputation help account for his success. Max was the kind of lover who wrote romantic letters and listened as well as talked. Even a brief encounter had to be associated with poetry, moonlight, and magic for full satisfaction. He might only stay for a night, but he would not care to think of it as a one-night stand. Max believed in sexual candor but he hated anything that suggested vulgarity in life and literature. No locker room humor for Max, and no scatology either. V. F. Calverton offended in both respects while working on an autobiographical novel near the end of his life. In a long critique Eastman told Calverton:

> I have a feeling that observing the prevalent trend of today's literature, in which the authors seem to try to out-do each other in depicting life of the dullest and most sordid kind and abusing their reader's sensitivity with the vulgarest possible language, you decided to go them one better.[4]

Calverton's manuscript was dull, sloppy, full of descriptions of "adolescent sex-curiosity, sex-discovery and sex-abuse." Eastman begged Calverton to go over it and "cut down all that sex stuff," and especially to "take out as many lavatories and unbuttoned pants as you possibly can." Sexual freedom to Max did not excuse bad taste. Though a rebel

against Victorian sexual codes, he remained faithful to nineteenth century manners. That was part of his charm.*

Max's sexual adventures were to some extent a healthy compensa-
tion for his repressed youth. He was at pains in his autobiography to
show them in this favorable light. But there was something obsessive
about Eastman's sexual interests. He could not always resist affairs that
gave pain to others, nor keep from boasting of his triumphs. There is
no way of knowing how much his unpopularity among intellectuals
arose from this. He could not help it that others might envy his sex life.
But Eastman made certain of it by advertising his exploits. When
young, Eastman had seemed modest about his private life, but it was
because he had much to be modest about. Later, when he broke loose,
the story was quite different. The lack of inhibitions was one thing, indiscretion another. Love affairs gave him pleasure and solace in times
of trouble. Flaunting them did him harm, too, more than he seems to
have realized.

Eastman did sense that his relations with women were not entirely
wholesome. He had no apology for the large number of his affairs, but
he did understand that his love of women was coupled with a fear of
intimacy. In a revealing letter (never sent), Max explained himself to a
woman who was bitter at having been dropped:

> Admittedly my sudden recoils against women who invade my life,
> even when I have invited them in, is abnormal—pathological, if you
> will. It has happened five times now, and I should have remembered
> and warned you. I did in fact come rather near it, for I told you quite
> early in our friendship that my tragedy is I am attracted by self-willed
> women, but being in a slower way self-willed myself, I can't in the
> long run love them.[5]

In this way Max had turned against Ida Rauh, against Florence Deshon
midway in their affair, and against Eliena before they were married.
Afterward he remained faithful to her only in his fashion. When they
were separated, he wrote her charming love letters. But apart or

---

* Society's definition of the sexually acceptable changed, but Max's did not. To my knowledge the only time I personally gave offense to him was when I sent Eastman a subscription to the *Realist.* It was a little Greenwich Village paper that was irreverrent and anti-
clerical. I thought he might find it amusing. As it appealed now and then to prurient interests, he did not: "I find the *Realist,* which you sent for my instruction, so horrible that I
blush to think my name is on their subscription list." Max Eastman to William L. O'Neill,
January 6, 1966.

together he was always chasing women, sometimes even bringing them as guests to Gay Head, where the Eastmans lived in a goldfish bowl as the town's most prominent residents.

Max wrote at length about Eliena's freedom from bourgeois convention and how she supported him in his amours. There was some truth to this. Eliena had a few affairs herself, one with Serebriakov, which Max described in *Love and Revolution,* and at least one other that he knew about and approved of.[6] Max welcomed these as evidence that freedom cut both ways. But Eliena's affairs were infrequent and discrete, his numerous and well publicized. Though he pretended differently, Max knew he hurt her and gave this secret knowledge away in describing her death. Eliena died of cancer in 1956. It was a hard death, eased only by taking place at home where Max and a nurse took care of her, so well he tells us that Eilena said to him: "In these two months you have repaid all that I ever did for you."[7] A bad conscience drove Max to put this in his book.

*   *   *

It would be unfair to leave Eliena on such a dim note. She was much more than yet another wronged wife. Everyone who knew her was impressed by her seemingly boundless energy, talent, warmth, and charm. Keeping house, even with hired help, was not easy, as they moved around so much, changing residences with the seasons. Max was fussy and needed a lot of attention. Even so, Eliena found time for her many personal interests. She wrote poetry in four languages and was a serious dancer and painter. Her pictures were given a number of shows, at the Bonstell Gallery on East 57th Street in New York among other places, and at least once in Paris. She studied dance and for years gave classes to the Indian children of Gay Head.

Most photographs fail to do her justice. Unlike Max, she was not photogenic. She smiled a lot and with her sturdy figure often looks more functional than decorative in snapshots. But Max did have one splendid photograph of her, a huge picture that hung over his desk both in Croton and Gay Head, showing Eliena running naked out of the surf, beaded with water, shot with sun, her dancer's body taut as a bowstring. Though not lacking in sex appeal, it was her virtues and talents that kept the Eastmans together. She was fiercely loyal to him, defending Max against his political enemies and indignant former girl friends. She remained with Max by choice, for she was attractive, talented, and admirable (the author has not found a scrap of paper or a living person that speaks ill of her) and could have married again or had a career if she wished. She needed Max, but he needed her, too, as became evident when she died, and he found life alone unbearable. They had much in common—Russia, artistic tastes, the Vineyard property, which was as important to Eliena as to Max. No outsider knows what really goes on in a marriage, even a relatively well-documented one like the Eastmans'. Max and Eliena did not have a perfect marriage—if such a thing exists. But in its way theirs worked out quite well.

Whatever Max's faults, a lack of respect for Eliena was not one of them. He often praised her dancing and painting. He did not want her to write, perhaps for fear of competition at home, maybe out of a sincere desire to see her make the best use of her abilities. In 1938 Maxwell Perkins asked Eliena to read V. F. Calverton's autobiographical novel in progress. On receiving her critique, Perkins wrote Max that Eliena's "letter to George Calverton is not only extraordinarily fine criticism, but it is full of energy and expressiveness." Perkins knew Eliena had led an interesting life, so he suggested to Max that, "while she might not want to write about it, she might want to write out of it." Max replied that Eliena's problem was that she had too many talents. She was good at cooking, gardening, dancing, and writing in all of her languages. But Max thought painting was her "most remarkable gift," and he told Perkins that he encouraged her in this above all.[8]

When she died on October 9, 1956, very bravely and with extraordinary tact and consideration for Max and her friends, there was a great outpouring of regret at the loss of this gay and gallant woman, whose qualities were esteemed by many people. Eastman received messages of sympathy from dozens of people, including the Cummings, the Hooks, Ruth Pickering Pinchot, Katharine Cornell, the Bertram Wolfes, even Charmion and Joseph Freeman. There were letters from her friends, Max's friends, and, most impressively, from his enemies or former enemies as well. No letter could have meant more to Eastman than that from Doris Stevens, their neighbor in Croton for many years: "Be comforted knowing that you helped Eliena to realize her many creative gifts."[9] So he had not failed as a husband after all.

* * *

Max did fail as a father, though in defense it must be said that the role was thrust upon him. Max did not want children, and Ida Rauh's pregnancy was one of his grievances against her. As a result Max had very little to do with his son Daniel. He excused himself by saying that a condition of the divorce was that Ida have sole custody. This alibi does not hold water after Daniel attained his majority in 1933. Yet it was not until twenty-three years later, following Eliena's death when Max was grief-stricken and lonely, that he and Daniel saw much of each other. Daniel was then in his forties and his character long since formed. Being abandoned by one's father is hardly the ideal start to life. Daniel had grown up to be charming, intelligent, and attractive, but frequently unhappy, too.

Daniel married twice, and both marriages failed. He underwent analysis and became himself a practicing psychologist (his second wife met him as a patient). Daniel continued to resent Max for having deserted him as a child, also no doubt for representing a level of achievement Daniel could not hope to equal. Thanks to Ida money was the least of his problems. He could afford to drift. In 1941, when he was 29 years old, Daniel had already been a newspaper reporter, science teacher, secretary of the International Committee for Political Prisoners, and an employee of the American Civil Liberties Union.[10] More jobs followed until he became a therapist. At the time of his death he had given that up to write a book.

That Max was disappointed in him did not keep Daniel from changing jobs. Daniel knew that Max hated his drinking, one reason probably why he drank. Max was extremely intolerant when it came to liquor. He liked a cocktail or two, but in correspondence with friends who were drinking too much Eastman was stern and unsympathetic. Drink was not a vice he could identify with. This may have been a carry-over from his Protestant background. Or it may have resulted from seeing what alcohol did to people he knew—Eugene O'Neill, Fitzgerald, Hemingway, Edna Millay, and so many others. Alfred Kazin thinks writers drink out of fear, that they have failed, or might fail, or are not making the best use of their talents.[11] Max was no stranger to the terror that came in the night, but physically he was self-protective rather than self-destructive. Nothing that Daniel might do, short of joining the Communist party, was better calculated to horrify his father than taking to drink.

Daniel punished Max by punishing himself. Where Max was disciplined and productive, Daniel was wayward. Max supported American entry into World War II, while Daniel was a conscientious objector.

Max moved to the right politically, but Daniel stayed on the left, ensuring that they would argue passionately. Ill health led Daniel to go on the wagon, but he fell off when Max died. An apparent heart attack caused Daniel's death within six months of his father's. Shakespeare says the evil that men do lives after them. In Max's case, though, not for long.[12]

His mother and sister excepted, Max did not work at maintaining family ties. When Crystal died, leaving two orphaned children, Max failed to take them in as expected. Instead, he found foster parents for them, selfishly putting his own needs first. This was unfeeling of him, and apparently resented. But, given his record as a father, it was the right thing to do, though small children could hardly know or understand that. In *Love and Revolution* Eastman seldom mentions his extended family. There are only a few letters in the Eastman papers at the Lilly Library from his brother Anstice, who was known as Peter. Of Peter's death in 1938, a time when Max was preoccupied with the Russian purge trials, Max says only: "I could not, in such a world, adequately grieve for my brother who died as we all hope to—suddenly of a brain hemorrhage, in mid-career as a brilliant surgeon, a father of three strong gifted sons."[13] Relatives visited him sometimes on the Vineyard. Samuel Eastman, one of Peter's sons, stayed with Max almost every summer weekend when he was a student at Harvard Law School after World War II. All the same, family ties did not bind Eastman very closely.

Eastman's behavior as husband and father especially fell short of what we expect from responsible people. There is no excuse for this, but maybe an explanation. Creative people generally, and writers in particular, are notoriously self-centered. Hemingway was a bad husband and capable of meanness. Fitzgerald could hardly take care of himself, still less his daughter. Theodore Dreiser's biographer calls him "on one plane a selfish, bullying, unreasonable, capricious, deceitful, evil old man."[14] Eugene O'Neill, though he hated his own father, treated his children even worse, cutting them completely out of his life. Upton Sinclair was at least as bad a father as Max. Some writers, Floyd Dell comes to mind, were good family men. This was unusual. By the standards of his peers Eastman doesn't look so bad. He drank little and was seldom malicious, bullying, devious, or intentionally cruel. He was ruthless when it came to protecting his work and his way of life. In this he resembled many writers. As a human being he was, perhaps, rather above their average.

* * *

Max was a better friend than relative. He prized loyalty and returned it with interest. His correspondence is laden with examples of his generosity in time and money to old friends and lovers. Sometimes this extended even to his enemies. In 1935 Albert Rhys Williams, who had been his friend in Russia but mendacious afterward, asked him for money: "Now that my book nearing completion, I am going East and will need a lot of money. Lucita is going to Hollywood and will need a lot of money too. How about helping out? It would be very nice if old Max would come across at the present juncture." [15] On the margin of this cheeky letter Max wrote, "sent $200.00," a large sum for him at the time. Eastman was often kind to virtual strangers. In the thirties he read some short stories by the then unknown Tess Slesinger, and, although they were barely if at all acquainted, he helped arrange for Simon and Schuster to publish her novel. [16] He was especially concerned with the fortunes of anti-Stalinists, particularly in the 1930s and early '40s when they most needed help. He read manuscripts, tried to find publishers, and sent them letters of encouragement. [17] He spent much time assisting left oppositionists. Though unable to get Trotsky into the United States, he did help Boris Souvarine, a refugee from Nazi-occupied France, make the crossing. And when Souvarine had trouble supporting himself, Max sent $500 and the promise of $300 a month until Souvarine was able to make money on his own. [18]

Max was remarkably cordial to young scholars. Not long before he died, Max wrote a friend that he was trying to protect himself, "mainly from dissertation writers who think I know something they can't find out . . . about past years. It's getting to be a pest!" [19] Yet, if he found these requests annoying, he gave no sign of it. In the 1930s, when Joseph Slater decided to do his Master's thesis on the old *Masses,* Eastman invited him to Croton and gave Slater a very good duck dinner. In the 1960s, when Wayne Cooper was editing a book of Claude McKay's writings, Max sent him originals, not copies, of his correspondence with McKay. Many such stories could be told by this author and by others who visited or corresponded with Eastman over the years.

Max felt most strongly about his oldest friends. In 1950, though

still angry at Louis Untermeyer for de-anthologizing him, Max sent
him a four-page letter begging him, for his own sake, not to put his
name to communist petitions and related "sucker lists."[20] Although no
one, except possibly Stalin and Mike Gold, had written worse things
about Max, he was delighted in 1947 to receive a friendly letter from
Joseph Freeman. He answered that he was certain Joe would not have
gone on "supporting tyranny and slave labor in the name of the working class," although many old friends from the *Masses-Liberator* period
were still doing so, Max wrote. "Excuse the fulmination, but I want you
to know what a joy it was to read your words. I find it a great deal more
painful to be denounced as a renegade by these former colleagues who
have betrayed—and, alas, also refuted, the revolution, than it was to be
prosecuted as a traitor to my country in the old days." Hearing from
Freeman was a "balm to my wounds."[21]

Eastman and Dos Passos, another former radical turned conservative anti-Communist, were in much the same position. In 1953 when
Max congratulated Dos Passos on his latest book, the latter responded:

> One of the bitterest things about growing older is the sense of soli-
> tude that hedges you about. Old friends harden into fanatics and
> stop liking you because they don't like the things you say. Sometimes
> I feel as if I were working down at the bottom of a well. . . . Anyway,
> it was damned heartwarming to know that somebody understood
> what I was trying to do.[22]

It was no fun to have turned conservative and been spurned by former
friends, and hardly surprising that as a result both Eastman and Dos
Passos cherished kind words from old acquaintances. In his later years
especially, Max was as quick to give as he was to receive assurances of
good will. He tried to retain friends and mend fences, to stay on speaking terms with people of opposing beliefs—Stalinists excepted.

Nothing in Eastman's career as a friend was more creditable than
his long connection with Claude McKay, the black poet from Jamaica.
McKay gave some of his poems to the *Liberator* and became warm
friends with Max and Crystal, whom he adored. In 1920, when Dell
turned to writing novels, McKay replaced him on the *Liberator* staff,
becoming Eastman's closest collaborator. They had, despite radically
different backgrounds, much in common. Both were poets of the old
school. Both were leftists who early became anti-Stalinists. McKay admired Max for his style: "Eastman had a lazy manner and there was a

general idea (which apparently pleased him) that he was more of a playboy than a worker. But he was really a very hard and meticulous worker. I know of no other writer who works so sternly and carefully, rewriting, chiseling and polishing his phrases."[23]

Eastman, for his part, liked McKay's poetry and his company also. Max was as free from prejudice as a white man brought up in the racist America of his formative years could be. As noted earlier, one of his very first editorials in the *Masses* had been a protest against lynchings. He advocated black power half a century before the fact. Not all blacks agreed with McKay that Eastman was entirely unprejudiced. Bruce Nugent, an artist and writer who knew them both, admired Max as an early supporter of racial equality. But he never felt that Max regarded blacks as actually equal to himself. There are several ways of looking at this. Possibly Max did have a touch of racism he was unaware of. Or perhaps Nugent was oversensitive. Eastman was both vain and shy, which led people of all races and sexes to consider him distant or arrogant when he was often only uncomfortable.[24]

The long friendship of Eastman and McKay survived great strains, race being the least of them. The main problem was that McKay needed a lot of help, and this dependent relationship was hard for a proud, quick-tempered man to bear. There was little reason to suppose at first that the relation would be so one-sided. McKay pulled his weight on the *Liberator,* and in 1922 his book of poetry, *Harlem Shadows,* was a critical success. Soon he was in Russia being lionized. His early infatuation with Bolshevism did not last. McKay came to identify with Eastman and the left opposition, providing moral support that meant a great deal to Eastman. They agreed on literature, too. When Eastman sent him a copy of *The Literary Mind,* McKay congratulated him for attacking the "ultra-modernists" and said that, if it were not for their domination of literature, Max would be the poetry editor of a major magazine.[25]

In the great depression McKay's finances, never very sound to begin with, collapsed entirely. By 1933 he was living in Morocco without any money and begging Eastman for help.[26] Max helped raise the funds to bring Claude home, but he remained hard up, so much so that even gifts of underwear were appreciated.[27] In the late thirties McKay finally got a job on the WPA Writer's Project, but then was fired, he told Eastman, by a Stalinist supervisor who was angry at a McKay article attacking the Popular Front and blaming the fall of republican Spain on its Moroccan policy.[28] From this time on, McKay was constantly in need. It was practically a national scandal that so gifted a writer could not make a living at his trade. Max kept helping him, though it was often uphill work. Their correspondence is full of begging letters, but sometimes McKay sickened of this role and sometimes Max had to resort to subterfuges, such as giving a mutual friend money to pass on to McKay so he would not know the source.

Now and then Claude lashed out at Max, no doubt because so much in Eastman's debt. In 1942 McKay tried for a job with the Office of War Information and asked Eastman for a letter of recommendation to its head Elmer Davis. It was sent to McKay, and he read it as disparaging his administrative abilities:

> It is easy to kick people around, when they are in trouble. A man may be ever so much a son-of-a bitch, while he is up and in [sic] everybody fawns on him—it's when you're down that you learn about your faults.[29]

Eastman replied to this with soft words, for he knew how desperate Claude was. On learning the next year that McKay had suffered a stroke and lost his job in a shipyard, Eastman sent him another check.[30]

In 1944 McKay finally exhausted that well of saintly self-control which Eastman seems to have reserved for him alone. He joined the Catholic Church. On learning of his intentions, Max implored him not to become a Catholic. It would be like going Stalinist, Max said, and would actually please the Stalinists very much. McKay replied that this was a natural step for him as he had always been religious.[31] To Max Christianity was distasteful, but Catholicism especially so for being, to his mind, authoritarian and anti-scientific. The word Catholic meant the Spanish Inquisition, the attack on Galileo, and more recently, the fight against birth control—always a favorite cause of Eastman's. Max was not prepared to make allowances for McKay's position. Catholics had taken McKay in when he was sick and destitute, finding him a job with the Catholic Youth Organization. Dorothy Day's Catholic Worker movement gave him a way to reconcile his left-wing politics with the still basically conservative church that he was prepared to join. The Catholic Workers were, and are, tolerated anarchists and pacifists who operated houses of refuge for derelicts.

McKay's religion and politics were now equally alien to Eastman. In one letter McKay condemned American and British imperialism.

Max responded that Claude was repeating communist propaganda. He believed a "little ignorant-minded neurotic like Dorothy Day" was doing Claude's thinking. Eastman remembered her only as the young girl who used to assist Floyd Dell on the old *Masses* and knew nothing of her work among the indigent or her politics, which were undefiled by allegiance to any nation or party. Claude naturally blistered Max with a defense of Dorothy Day and the Catholic left. He denounced the *New Leader* as neo-reactionary and aligned himself with Henry Wallace, to Max a limb of Satan.[32] So ended their friendship.

Despite everything, Max always respected Claude's talent, and after death his memory. A volume of McKay's poems was brought out posthumously with an introduction by John Dewey and an affectionate biographical sketch by Eastman. In it Max wrote of Claude's courage and said that "his place in world literature is unique and is assured."[33] During their long association each was unfair to the other at times, but Max had loved Claude as much as he could any man. Where McKay is concerned, Eastman should not be remembered for the last bitter letters, rather for his many years as McKay's constant friend and supporter. When Claude was starving in Morocco, one of the people Max obtained money from to bring him back to New York was Oswald Garrison Villard, to whom Max wrote: "He is in my opinion unquestionably the most gifted poet and writer that the Negro race has produced. He is a dear friend of mine too, and I can't bear to think of his genius flickering out over there in destitution."[34] McKay brought out the best in Eastman almost to the end.

* * *

In habits, tastes, values, and manners Eastman was consistent. Once his adult character was established—that is, by 1917 at the latest—it was set for life. Freedom was what he esteemed above all, which accounts for much that was both attractive and disagreeable about him. It was the touchstone of Eastman's political and private lives equally, and applied even to his marriage. Though married for most of his adult life, he was against matrimony in principle and to a degree in practice as well. When he did marry, it was done casually and, on the face of it, for reasons of convenience. He married Ida Rauh before a Justice of the Peace, supposedly to make traveling easier. He married Eliena Krylenko so that she could get out of Russia. Not only was there no service, but she wasn't even present at the registry office where the knot was tied. In 1958 when he married Yvette Szekely, it was because she wouldn't live with him otherwise. He wanted her to give up her job in New York and move into his home on Gay Head. Yvette pointed out that she could hardly be expected to change her whole life on the basis of what might be only his whim. So, gracelessly as usual, Max got married again, before a Justice of the Peace as usual, and without wedding rings, which was usual, too.

When his friends Doris Stevens and Dudley Field Malone were wed just after the First World War, Max prepared some remarks. He had the warmest feelings for both of them. Doris Stevens was his neighbor and a militant suffragist who had picketed the White House, been imprisoned, gone on hunger strikes, and been force-fed as a result. Her book, *Jailed for Freedom,* is a feminist classic. Malone was a successful lawyer and Democratic politician who represented the *Masses'* editors when the passions of war were most intense, and romatically gave up his position as Collector of the Port of New York to protest the maltreatment of Doris and her friends. At their wedding Max said, in fun of course, but in truth as well, that he felt less enthusiastic about weddings than funerals, especially when a beautiful girl like Doris was involved:

> There is something about that condition of moral bondage and legal beatitude which the scientists describe with so much poetic appropriateness as Durable Monogamous Wedlock—a word that I can never quite distinguish in my association centers with padlock—there is something about it that I cannot greet with quite the same patriotic enthusiasm with which I greeted the news that Doris had been arrested. I ask myself what is the use of being jailed for freedom if you get right out again and marry your lawyer? [35]

More than a third of a century later, Max wrote out his objections to marriage in detail. Yvette and some friends were kidding him about his famous hostility, so he made a speech against marriage, which he summarized on his typewriter the next day. There were five things he disliked about marriage, as against living with Yvette, which he favored. First was the ceremony—he hated public performances. Second was its official character, which meant "the interference of the State in my private life." Third was the "public fuss." Max believed that news of who he was living with should be gossiped about, like other private matters, rather than formally proclaimed. Next was the "vow of fidelity," which needed no explanation. Lastly, he opposed "the barbarous custom of applying the man's name to the woman. Against that my revolt is absolute and fanatical. Why should a man who loves a woman as herself, want to express it by pasting his name on her—an act of childish egotism, indifference to poetry and execrable bad taste."[36]

Yet, Eastman was married three times and divorced only once. His marriage to Eliena lasted more than thirty years. Marriage, for all that it threatened his personal and sexual freedom, was not just expedient, as he liked to pretend. Max needed a wife for more than practical reasons. He could and did hire housekeepers to make his meals and pack his bags. He had no trouble, even when elderly, in finding sexual partners. For all his independence Max was no different from other people in wanting someone to whom he could reveal weakness, who would stand by him whether he was right or wrong, and be his consolation in all seasons. Although he professed to hate it, marriage was necessary to him. His denunciations of it are wonderful, but not entirely convincing.

Max's feminism, on the other hand, was life-long and genuine. Women's rights was the first cause he ever spoke for, and he was true to it always. This is not at all inconsistent with his treatment of Eliena, nor with his conventional view that his wives should look after him and pursue their interests in ways compatible with his. The gap between principle and practice is a big one. Few people live up to their highest ideals. Max was quite ordinary in this respect. At the same time he was a true feminist in the sense of believing absolutely in equal rights, also in liking women. Max was closer to women than men as a rule. He had male friends, but in later life none were as close to him, sex apart, as his wives, some of his lovers, and certain women with whom he had purely social relations. If promiscuity was one of Max's less admirable traits, his respect for women as persons was its opposite. He valued their achievements, listened to their criticism of his work, and treated them much as he did men. As a husband Max fell short of feminist standards, but he lived up to them in his regard for women as a sex. His normal mode of address to women was slightly formal and gallant, in the fashion of his youth. This did not make his esteem for them any less real.

* * *

Age did not lessen his contradictions, nor his sense of failure. He remained ambivalent about writing and writers. Once the painter Thomas Hart Benton, an old friend, asked, "Max, why does the literary crowd dislike you so much?" Eastman thought about this and decided it was because "I've always had a tendency to shun the company of people who think of themselves as 'writers.' It's a part of my high regard for Mark Twain who mastered three other professions before he started writing—the last man in the world you'd think of as a 'litterateur.' "[37] This was, in the first instance, untrue—he knew a good many writers socially—and in the second curious to say the least. A man who had been a poet, critic, and novelist, with more than half a century of experience in the world of letters, ought, one might suppose, to have become used to the idea of being literary. Max never did.

At the same time as he appeared to disdain "writers" and the "litterateur," Eastman had incredible literary ambitions. It was because he had not equaled Milton that he felt a failure. Despite his achievements, and a need to write that kept him at it almost to his death, Max could be self-deprecating. Once this author told Eastman about a friend of Max's who had blocked publication of a doctoral dissertation on himself drawn largely from his own papers because the dissertation, though flattering, defined him as a minor writer. To this Eastman responded, "well, you always know that, but you never like to admit it."

Max declined to accept the kind of writing he did best as a worthy end in itself. Only art and science were self-justifying. Hence his depression when his poems were not acclaimed; hence also Max's insistence that his greatest accomplishments were scientific. In 1956 he was excited to learn he would be listed in the *Directory of American Men of Science*. He wrote the publisher that his theory of metaphor in *Enjoyment of Poetry* was "one of my three contributions to science," the other two being *Enjoyment of Laughter* and *Marxism: Is It Science?*"[38] Even so, Max knew in his heart that he was not a scientist. In a file of uncompleted poems there is one that was supposed to be his epitaph. The last line reads: "I am not science, and I am not song."[39] Max's delusion, proclaimed in many books, that he was an artist and a scientist hurt him greatly, but the secret fear that he was neither hurt him most of all.

* * *

These private self-estimates are important because they correct the impression that Max was egotistical, obtuse about himself, and superficial. When he appeared to be self-serving it was usually in reaction to deep fears that, though grounded in reality, went far beyond it. In *Love and*

Revolution he lamented the years wasted on the *Masses* and the *Liberator*, on radicalism in general. He wrote notes to himself saying he had wasted his talents. Max's real problem was not egotism, but the lack of it.

Eastman compensated for feelings of failure and inadequacy by having affairs and living beautifully. Early in their friendship Claude McKay wrote Max after visiting him in Croton: "I was glad to see how you live—so unaffectedly free—not striving to be like the masses like some radicals, but just yourself. I love your life—more than your poetry, more than your personality."[40] Max was an engaging conversationalist, so much so that in the twenties Heywood Broun named Max to his All-American Talking Team, a group that included such formidable talkers as Clarence Darrow, George Jean Nathan, Alice Roosevelt Longworth, Dorothy Parker, and Alexander Woollcott.[41] Max had a fund of stories, accumulated and polished over the years, that he told with splendid effect at the small gatherings he favored, and at which he was naturally the center of attention. He did not like big parties, seldom gave them, and in his later years went to bed early at the expense of formal entertainments. He was a good host and at his dinner parties liked the food, wine, furnishings, and service to be perfect. But it was part of his charm that everything did not have to revolve around him all the time. He listened well, a rare quality in talkers. And if his practiced story-telling was an act, his interest in other people seemed entirely genuine. He had a gift for making unknown young people feel as if they mattered. He gave his attention not as if extending courtesy but in a manner suggesting real interest. Eastman's peers sometimes complained of his vanity and arrogance. These traits were not evident in his dealings with the young.

Max had certain child-like qualities (Daniel Aaron called him a "wise child"). One was his ability to take intense pleasure in the moment, eating, drinking, smoking, swimming, or whatever with gusto and appreciation. Another, less agreeable trait, was his occasional petulance. But fits of temper seldom lasted long, and Eastman did not hold grudges—except when deeply injured. Despite long experience and numerous attacks on him, Max was surprisingly open and unguarded. In this, too, he seemed childlike in a most appealing way. Visitors were always remarking upon how much younger than his years Max seemed, even when very old. There were three reasons for this, temperament apart. The first was his good looks, which remained until the last year or so of his life. The second was his physical condition, good into his eighties. Vigor was his third asset. Charles Neider, who met Eastman when Max was 74, found it striking: "He was tremendously alive and increased one's own vitality."[42] Though much younger than Max, Neider was pressed to keep up with him on the long walks they took together in the canyons near the Huntington Hartford Foundation where they were both residents. Neider is a good witness also to Max's sense of humor. They had gone sailing off Southern California with Max's nephew Peter one day, and when the water got rough Max ordered Peter to turn around because "Charles and I aren't having fun!" Afterward Neider teased Max about the "admiral" side of his character: "No one laughed harder than he. He knew the human comedy, as well as his role in it." Generally one saw the best side of Max on water or at his country homes. Though his reputation was made in New York, Max, as he had told his grandfather when very small, belonged in the country. Margaret Halsey once suggested that they meet at Croton, "because you look better there. In New York [you are] always gloomy and you look like Atlas with a bedsore."[43]

Though bohemian in some respects, Max loved his creature comforts. He did not stand when he could sit, or sit when he could sprawl. Usually short of cash, even as a *Digest* roving editor, Max hired as much help as he needed anyway. And while not a fashion plate, Max dressed well in comfortable clothes, soft collars before they became common, warm sweaters, and smooth-textured shirts. Loving books and recordings of concert music, he spent a lot, in relation to his income, on them. No doubt it was his love of the good things that McKay had in mind when he admired Max for "not striving to be like the masses like some radicals." Max, even when most revolutionary, never believed that working class life could be enhanced by lessening his own.

Eastman was passionately addicted to nude bathing, both for the pleasure of it and as a symbol of his break with Protestantism and Victorian taboos. The Greenwich Village rebels of his youth regarded it as proof of liberation, as to a degree it was. And it still seemed unconventional, even threatening to some in his old age. It was one thing for youngsters to disrobe at rock festivals, quite another to have an old person do so as a way of life. Max found this amusing. He respected custom by swimming mostly at private or secluded beaches where nudity was allowed. But he was not afraid of public opinion. Max once took the author to a fairly busy beach on the Vineyard, bringing along trunks out of deference to my feelings or those of the multitude. But there was no place to change easily and Max caught his feet in the trunks. Finally he threw them down in disgust and marched naked into the water through, as it seemed to my astonished eyes, clouds of women and children. Some of his friends were embarrassed by such events, but to others the pleasure of nude bathing was a revelation. When she was middle-aged, Ruth Pickering Pinchot visited Max and Eliena and worked up the nerve to go nude bathing with them. To her surprise she loved it and wrote them a touching letter of thanks afterward, saying how much fun it had been, and how sad it made her to realize that so many people went through a lifetime with parts of their bodies forever hidden from the sun.[44]

The pattern of Eastman's days on the Vineyard was idyllic. His comfortable house sat on top of a hill. From it he could see, as he wrote in his memoirs:

> The whole of Vineyard Sound . . . the Elizabeth islands with Buzzards Bay behind them, Menemsha Bight and its little harbor village to which artists and poets flock like deer to a saltlick—Menemsha Praecox we sometimes call it. All that on the north side, a lagoon the size of a small lake to the east, and to the south a freshwater pond the Indians named Squibnocket, some dunes and the ocean beach, and then the entire Atlantic ocean with the little wild island called No-man's Land afloat in it.[45]

And all around him was his own land, ensuring his privacy, protecting his view, and making him, through its steady appreciation, a rich man—on paper at least. It was bare to begin with, but the Eastmans planted it heavily and in time the hill became green and beautiful.

In this gorgeous place Max had a fixed routine. He started the day with breakfast in bed. On arising, he did exercises appropriate to his age and condition while listening to music. Then he would work in his study, or sometimes in an outbuilding he used for writing. When he finished working, between one and two in the afternoon, a picnic lunch would be waiting, and he would take it with him to the beach. Max would have a drink or two with friends before dinner and was in bed by ten. His year was marked off in the same regular way. He spent about half of it in Gay Head. Spring and fall would see him in his apartment in Greenwich Village. In winter he moved to some warm place. Barbados was his favorite in the last years.

This style of life was sustained on a moderate income, which, however, he employed shrewdly. Max did not have a good head for financial matters in the sense of being an astute investor or brilliant evader of taxes. His Vineyard properties which became so valuable were acquired through sheer love of them. Realtors on the island considered him an outstanding businessman, which he often laughed about. Max knew that it was his passion for land, not for land values, that had made his fortune. He built a summer house out of sight of his own home, and the rental income from it covered his property taxes. In the same manner he acquired a second apartment in New York, and the rent from it supported his first one. The *Digest* paid some, in the early years most, of his expenses for travel and secretaries.

On an income that did not exceed $20,000 a year, Max lived like a millionaire, better in some ways, for he had no business to run, no investments to look after, no labor force to supervise. Max did worry about money toward the end of his life when his income did not go as far as it used to. This was his own fault for being reluctant to sell any of his precious acres. Max lived in beauty and comfort to the end of his days. And for almost all of them he enjoyed good health, which he safeguarded by drinking and smoking little, avoiding chills, getting plenty of rest, bathing every day, and exercising as much as he could. He ate too much; in old age it was his only vice. But despite his expanded waistline he was never fat. Old age and declining powers made him melancholy at times. This was to be expected. On the whole, few men had less to be sad about. Eastman mastered the art of living early on, and it was a talent that never failed him.

* CHAPTER THIRTEEN *

Last Years

1949–1969

After, as he saw it, the failure of *Enjoyment of Living,* Eastman did not put ambition behind him or give up writing. The *Digest* expected something from him now and again, if only as a token. More than that, writing was basic to Eastman's self-esteem. When young, he had wanted to write for the love of letters alone, but he had become a professional journalist despite himself and remained one to the end.

In addition to casual work, Eastman translated a book of popular science written by a chemist named Jacob Rosin called *The Road to Abundance* (1953).[1] Though Max carefully pointed out in the introduction that the ideas were all Rosin's, he agreed with them and was willing to be listed as a co-author at Rosin's request. This remarkable little volume, which required much effort on Max's part, anticipated both the ecological movement of the 1960s and the energy crisis of the 1970s. Rosin's first argument was that agriculture as practiced in most parts of the world, and even in the United States, was wasteful and inefficient. He wanted to see mankind freed from bondage to the plant by means of chemically synthesized foodstuffs utilizing cheap solar energy.

Rosin also called for freedom from the mine, getting away from the present policy of exploiting limited supplies of high grade ores. He envisioned a new technology permitting the use of abundant low-grade raw materials. Rosin wanted to save the environment by totally recycling waste products. Industrial waste was not only uneconomic in his view, but dangerous to health as well. He was scandalized by the misuse of "our most precious raw materials." Most fuels were burned needlessly, he argued, citing studies that showed two-thirds of the energy from coal, oil, and natural gas was wasted in stack gases, exhaust gases, and radiated heat. Even what was used put carbon dioxide into the atmosphere. This was waste also, since all CO_2 should be saved and transformed into carbon or carbohydrates. Total recycling could stretch out coal reserves for thousands of years.

Floyd Dell said that this "scientific utopia" was much more attractive and natural than the capitalist utopia Eastman was writing about elsewhere.[2] But the book was not widely reviewed, and most critics missed the point, at least the one that today seems most important. The *San Francisco Chronicle* said that *The Road to Abundance* refuted Cassandras who held that raw materials were vanishing. Both the *New York Times* and the *New Yorker* saw it as just another optimistic look at the future.[3] The book did claim that science could work wonders, as Eastman had always believed. And Rosin predicted further advances as a result of scientific research and development. But though seen by some reviewers as a rebuke to pessimists, the book reads today like an environmentalist tract. Its subject was not so much better living through chemistry as that doing so would require an entirely different industrial system based on recycling, zero pollution, and the use of commonplace rather than scarce raw materials. When it came out, readers were predisposed to see Eastman and Rosin only as participants in the national celebration of technology and affluence. Now the book seems a little masterpiece of prophecy, anticipating nearly all the priorities regarding energy and the environment that are so urgent now. Like many wise books, it was too far in advance of its time and so failed. That Max took such a large hand in it remains to his credit just the same. It reflected the deep concern of his later years that prosperity not be gained at the expense of those things—clean air and water, natural beauty, elbow room—that made life worth living.

The next year Max published *Poems of Five Decades,* his last major effort as a poet. By this time Max could not hope to enhance his artistic reputation. But he still wanted to be known as a poet, and to put his best work in order before he died. So this volume includes what he regarded as the flower of his poetry, and an introduction that both apologized for and in a way justified his approach. He said again that poetry writing had been "incidental" to him, that he only wrote it when moved by some emotion. Calling himself a poet of the "intermittent school," he said of such a person:

He will never rise to the heights of his art; he will never quite decide
what his personality is and make a cult of it as great artists usually do;
he will be clumsy sometimes in his highest and best flights because he
is out of practice. But he will always be sincerely filled to overflowing
with the thing he is trying to pour into a poem.[4]

The collection included "Lot's Wife," which he had revised. His indignation at Edmund Wilson for having found fault with it had now
changed to gratitude. Eastman wrote Wilson that he was making the
changes suggested by Wilson almost a dozen years before: "My metrical
carelessnesses particularly astound me when I study it over now." Wilson was magnanimous. After publication he read the book "with pleasure: The best still stand up, and it's obvious here that you have much
improved" "Lot's Wife."[5] Wilson was always kind to Max, even when
most critical. People could not understand why. One of Wilson's biog-
raphers suggests disapprovingly that Wilson went on taking Max
seriously long after this was warranted because of Eastman's link with
Trotsky.[6] This seems unlikely. Wilson did not care for everyone associated with Trotsky and Trotskyism, nor did Trotskyists hold Max in
high regard except as a translator. Genuine admiration apart, the most
plausible explanation is suggested by a postscript Wilson once wrote to
an article on Stravinsky:

> In youth, we admire the heroes, the affirmers, the "lords of life."
> Later on when we have had some experience of the difficulty of prac-
> ticing an art, of surviving to grow old in its practice, when we have
> seen how many entrants drop out, we must honor any entrant who
> finishes."[7]

Max could be appreciated both ways. When young he had been a "lord
of life." In old age, though no longer an affirmer, Max was running
still.

It was in this spirit that his final volume of poetry was received.
Poems of Five Decades was reviewed warmly if not widely. Oliver St. John
Gogarty, a friend and fellow poet, wrote that Max was a poet of "very
great stature." Merrill Root, another friend, gave the book a nice
write-up in the *New Leader*. *The Saturday Review* was complimentary
also. Its critic, who had disliked "Lot's Wife" when first published, now
compared Eastman with Mark Van Doren and Stephen Vincent Benét,
who were all "fine poets . . . who have won success and even critical

favor without plunging into dark thickets of thought, swamps of ambivalence, and brambles of ambiguity." [8]

In 1954 Max made his last attack on modernism, this time in the
plastic arts. He wrote an essay for the *Freeman* called "Non-Communicative Art," quoting his friend Bernard Berenson on the "confusion, struttings, blustering, solemn puerilities" that characterized modern art. He reviewed his essay of a quarter century earlier, "The Cult
of Unintelligibility," most of which he felt could be applied to modern
sculpture and painting.[9] Max distributed copies of this piece widely
with encouraging results. Letters and blurbs poured in from Norman
Angell, Pablo Casals, Berenson of course, Gilbert Murray, Roger Baldwin, Rockwell Kent, and others who, it might reasonably be supposed,
would not normally agree on anything. Carl Sandburg responded typically when he wrote Eastman that "Max and me is brudders yet." Norman Thomas called it a worthy successor to "The Cult of Unintelligibility."[10] Max had tapped a deep well of resentment and dismay
to little purpose. His views were widely shared except where it mattered, in the art world.

Eliena's death in 1956 caused Eastman great sorrow and misery.
No lover could take her place as confidante, companion, and best
friend. Charles Neider, who met Eastman at the Hartford Foundation
in Southern California the next year, was struck by Max's unhappiness.
When Upton Sinclair, who lived near the foundation, invited Max to
visit, he declined, saying, "I cling to my desk as the main support."[11]
Writing helped Eastman, but not enough. In 1958, about a year and a
half after Eliena died, Max married again. Max had known Yvette
Szekely for a long time, though she was much younger than he. After
his return from California Max invited Yvette to visit him on the Vineyard. The visit was a success, and afterward Max asked her to live with
him. This conformed with his romantic view of life and his frequently
expressed distaste for matrimony. As we saw, Yvette disagreed, and
marriage was the outcome. Max gave in to convention reluctantly as
usual. Their union prospered just the same. Few widowers of Max's
age (he was then 75) are privileged to marry again, fewer still to
younger, attractive women. Yvette became Max's helpmeet and friend.
Thus, to the extent old age permitted, his last years were as happy and
comfortable as those that had gone before.

* * *

Eastman lived to see himself become a figure in written history, and was concerned that his role as participant, observer, and commentator on great events be properly recorded. He was helpful and courteous when approached by inquiring scholars. Despite his politics, which few if any of them shared, Eastman did not have much reason to complain of the results. The encyclopedic *Socialism and American Life* (1952) cited him seventeen times. Isaac Deutscher, Trotsky's biographer, was fair to Eastman, though himself a Marxist. In 1956 while working on the second volume, *Prophet Unarmed: Trotsky 1921–1929* (1958), Deutscher asked Max for information, assuring him: "As to your *Since Lenin Died* I have had it on my shelves for years and have repeatedly quoted it in my *Stalin* in a way which leaves the reader with no doubt that I treat it as a reliable and trustworthy account of the events."[12] Max also appeared as a useful source in Theodore Draper's *The Roots of American Communism* (1957), and in Daniel Aaron's *Writers on the Left* (1961), which included a biographical sketch of the "Lone Rebel of Croton."

Mostly, however, Max hoped to mark out his place in history through his own writings. His memoirs were crucial, but also important were his two volumes of biographical essays, which were written in the first person. In them Max described great or interesting people largely out of his own experience with them. *Great Companions,* the second of his biographical works, resembles the first in form and content and included some of the same essays, notably those on his mother, Dewey, and Freud.[13] Freud really did not qualify as a companion, for Max had only met him once. But Max had been one of the first to popularize Freud, to his later regret no doubt, and had given much thought to psychoanalysis. Eastman had employed Freudian concepts in *Marx, Lenin, and the Science of Revolution* without, it appears, ever quite believing them. Before long he came to feel that Freud had worked a good deal of mythology into his science and had not escaped the tendency of mental healing to run off into magic. Eastman was irritated that even in conversation Freud insisted upon the infallibility of his system.

Eastman did not regard Freud as a scientist. Freud jumped to conclusions, was not well read in the field of psychology as a whole, did not like or practice rigorous experiments, refused to verify his ideas empirically, and did not accept the opinions of others. He had, Eastman wrote, an "intensely emotional and recklessly inventive mind." Eastman compared Freud not with Newton or Darwin, as was usual, but with Paracelsus, who contributed to science even though infatuated with magic. Eastman noted that Freud believed cocaine was a miracle drug and used it freely for years (as did many physicians at that time, which Max failed to point out). During the ten most creative years of his life Freud was addicted to the crank ideas of a Berlin savant who believed that all life's problems could be solved by proper application of the ratio between the numbers 28 and 23. So much for psychoanalysis as a science.

On the other hand, Eastman defended Freud against what used to be the common charge that Freud regarded sexual disorders as causes of neurosis because of his own abnormal sexual impulses. To the contrary, Eastman declared, Freud was a "prude and a puritan," and, worst of all, "a fanatical monogamist." However, Freud was absolutely right, Eastman believed, in describing himself as an intellectual conquistador. This was what made him great: "Freud played the major part in making psychology dynamic, bringing the wish into it, the instinctive drive, in place of the old unlifelike tale of stimulus and reaction, association and disassociation." Freud had also discovered that repression led to hysteria and neurosis. His place as one of the giants of knowledge was secure.

Among Eastman's most heartfelt essays was "My Friendship with Edna Millay." Strangely enough, it was marked by discretion. In the essay he claimed not to have fallen in love with Edna, unlike Dell and Edmund Wilson and nearly all the men who knew her as a young woman. This may have been true, but Max was attracted to her all the same, though he neglected to say so. In one of his notes to himself, he described an erotic though unconsummated physical encounter with Edna, part of which took place underwater. And he hinted at an affair with her in France while on his way to Russia. Whether they had relations or not, it's clear Max loved Edna's poems more than herself. He lashed out at critics who denigrated her poetry.* He believed her "Epitaph for the Race of Man" was unequalled in the whole of American lit-

---

*Wrongly in one case, he later decided. In the essay he dismissed Allen Tate as "one who can rarely say clearly even in a prose essay what he is driving at." Five years later, Max wrote a friend that "Allen Tate really has a legitimate gripe against me . . . for I insulted his intellect in my portrait of Edna Millay in *Great Companions.* It was honestly a shameless insult for I knew nothing about his intellect; I had only read one essay; I was merely following where the argument led, as Socrates used to recommend, a dangerous habit when it leads smack into the self-esteem of another person. (I've tried to atone for it by quoting him respectfully in *Love and Revolution.*)" Max Eastman to Joseph Slater, October 22, 1964.

erature for scope, intellectual grasp and eloquence. It was a commentary on their limitations that the New Critics (a school of criticism based on close textual analysis) could not comment intelligently "about this great poem, its epic wealth of imagery, its perfected dreadfulness, the virile courage of the mind that dared at last to speak it out." Edna had as "clear, hard, alert and logical a mind as I have encountered in man or woman." There is little doubt that Edna was the poet Max longed to be. He praised her unstintingly anyway. Envy, so common among writers, was not one of his faults.

Great Companions attracted many reviews, but, because it was such a personal book, and at points vain and self-serving (in the portrait of Einstein we find Max lecturing the great scientist on causal determinism), critics reacted to it personally. Thus, while Lewis Gannett liked some of the essays, he complained that "the focus is too often blurred; after all, Mr. Eastman's primary interest today, as he avows in his foreword, is in Max Eastman." The *New Yorker* was patronizing as usual. So was the *Times Literary Supplement.*[14] The *Spectator* found Eastman's personality unattractive and obtrusive, while admitting that he was good company. "It is as the greatest of his own companions that he often forfeits our esteem because of virtues underlined and willful self-celebration."[15]

By contrast the *New York Times* reviewer was charmed. He admired Max's "sturdy common sense, for the author is a naturally skeptical American who has often stayed to scoff at shrines where he has come to pray. A variety of readers may find these memoirs as engaging and instructive as this reviewer did." The *Saturday Review* was happy with the book also on account of Eastman's "acute sense of atmosphere, his dexterity at grasping ideas, and his knack of projecting his people alive on the page."[16] People who disliked Eastman were not going to like *Great Companions.* Even so it contains examples of some of his best writing, and his most sympathetic too.

* * *

Great Companions proved to be a harbinger of *Love and Revolution,* the final volume of his memoirs. This was probably not clear at the time he assembled his essays. He had been crushed by the relative failure of *Enjoyment of Living.* Writing it had been the most painful act of his creative life. The book's poor reception devastated Max. Years later thinking about it still made him gloomy. He kept telling friends that he could not go on with the second volume as planned. But Edmund Wilson, Dell, Daniel Aaron, and others urged him to return to it, and in the early sixties he did. Like the first volume, *Love and Revolution* was long in gestation and great in size, an elephant of a book that would have been even larger had Max gotten his way. Jason Epstein of Random House talked him into compressing what Max originally thought of as two books into one. Even so, the text alone ran to 650 and one-half pages.

Love and Revolution suffers by comparison with *Enjoyment of Living*. This is not a consequence of bad writing. Max was still in command of his talents and wove old yarns into new cloth as skillfully as ever. The trouble lies in the story itself. *Enjoyment of Living* naturally assumed the shape of a novel, with the added benefit of a happy ending. *Love and Revolution,* which covers Eastman's life up to 1941, lacks these advantages. As theater it runs downhill. Beginning with the *Masses,* it ends with the *Reader's Digest.* That it covers the most genuinely heroic period of his life is not much help.

To start with, we see Eastman in all his glory, surrounded by worshipful admirers. But this high tone, though it takes up almost half the book, cannot be sustained. Thereafter the reader sees Max taking the road to alienation. Until he left for Russia in 1922, Eastman seemed glamorous, romantic, and brave in all the right ways. Thereafter he continues to be these things, but in the wrong ways. During the Jazz Age, when everyone is going to speakeasies and reading T. S. Eliot, Eastman is chastising Stalin and revising Marx. In the Red Decade, when everyone moves left, Eastman does the opposite. That he was right and his critics usually wrong does not make his fight against Stalinism any more exciting. Max was great in the thirties, but in an unpopular manner. As a cavalier of the Left, Max had been thrilling; as its conscience he was a pain. No one likes to be nagged, especially when in error. And no one likes to be reminded of it afterward. *Enjoyment of Living* resembled fiction; *Love and Revolution* was too much like real life.

Finally, though readers could not know this, it is a less candid book than the first volume. There are no lies in it, but rather sins of omission forced by the design of *Enjoyment of Living.* That book ended with Max achieving happiness and mental health. This obliged Max in the second volume to minimize depressions and feelings of failure. His ability to enjoy life was not something gained once and for all. Every so often it had to be renewed. Had he explained this, *Love and Revolution* would have been more interesting, and he would have appeared less shallow. But the need to protect *Enjoyment of Living* intervened. Thus, where it had been great, *Love and Revolution* was merely very good.

Two men who were prejudiced in favor of *Love and Revolution* had this to say of it. James T. Farrell wrote a friend that "it is a contribution of value. It will begin to make more significant and important the years we have known and the longer span of years Max Eastman has known. This book has every prospect of being a lasting work in the body of American literature, and the record of American life." And Lewis Feuer, a distinguished scholar who knew Max, called the book "the most honest autobiography that has ever been done by an American writer. He was the greatest editor of radical magazines we have ever had, and he was the first American to go through the fullness of the Marxist experience and to cope with its short-comings. The originality of his analysis has yet to be appreciated." [17]

These careful judgments have aged well but were far from typical when made. Even as late as 1964 it was still not easy for Max to get a fair hearing. It was the custom among intellectuals to sneer at Eastman, or to dismiss him entirely. This dated back to 1950, when Edmund Wilson published his essays of the forties as *Classics and Commercials*. His "Max Eastman in 1941" was but one of 68 items in the collection and yet was repeatedly singled out for attack by reviewers. One critic said that it was "a misguided effort to make Eastman appear to be a prophet without honor in his own country." Irving Howe was annoyed that Wilson had not revised his estimate downward: "To praise Max Eastman as an intellectual iconoclast without so much as mentioning his recent phase as Marx-baiter for the *Reader's Digest* carries generosity beyond the point friendship might require." Irving Kristol, then an editor of *Commentary,* detected in Wilson a "laxity of intellect" which explained why in *"Classics and Commercials,* he has high praise for Max Eastman's very superficial books on Marxist theory." [18]

Though opinions had not changed since then, *Love and Revolution* received some of the most thoughtful reviews of anything he had written, far better ones than *Enjoyment of Living,* though it was the superior book. Time was working in Max's favor. A new generation of critics had grown up who disagreed with his politics but were not personally affronted by them. Their reviews were not malicious, with one important exception. Though young, the *New York Review of Books* was already an influential journal of literary and, at that time, political opin-

ion. It assigned George Lichtheim to review Eastman's book. He was a
European authority on Marxism who, on the evidence, knew little
about American history and less about Eastman's other books. The
result was a snobbish review that praised Eastman only to bury him.
Lichtheim described Max as the "Frank Harris of Socialism, an inspired
amateur from the moment a girl friend explained Marx to him in three
easy lessons."[19] As Harris was a shady literary journalist whose memoirs were pornographic, the comparison was not to Max's advantage.

One of the chief weaknesses of *Love and Revolution,* though an un-
avoidable one, was that in order to cover a lot of ground Eastman had
to oversimplify his ideas. This was not a problem with *Enjoyment of Living* because in it the story was the thing. But *Love and Revolution* covers
the period of his intellectual maturation, when his most important political books were written. In simplifying his intellectual accomplishments during the 1920s and 1930s, as he had to, Eastman inadvertently
diminished them. Unless the reviewer had read at least one of Eastman's major political books, which was seldom the case, he could not
judge the quality of Eastman's thought. It also helped if the critic knew
a good deal about both Russian and American history in the twenties
and thirties, which again many did not.

Out of ignorance Lichtheim dismissed Max's ideas, and even his
trials under the Espionage Acts as publicity stunts. An editor of the
New York Review apologized in advance for Lichtheim's excesses. Perhaps they would help sales anyway, she speculated. Eastman was not
satisfied with this. He assumed Lichtheim's intent had been to keep
young people especially from reading the book and feared Lichtheim
had succeeded: "I am sad to see you do this, not only because it concerns me and my book, but because in a civilized society such unre-
strained effluvia of political and personal hate posing as intellectual
and literary criticism ought not to be published at all."[20] The letter was
not meant for publication. At the age of 81 Max was through with
polemics, and a good thing, too.

Other reviewers were negative without being destructive. Hilton
Kramer, art critic of the *New York Times,* began by saying that American
radicalism in the twentieth century had been rich in personalities but
poor in ideas. It had produced no first-rate thinker, no coherent body
of thought, and had emphasized rhetoric and reportage at the expense
of fundamentals. It bequeathed to the present "not an intellectual tradition but a collection of case histories," of which Eastman's was among

the more dismaying.[21] Kramer deplored Eastman's opinions on art, his "philistine pieties, facile appeal to 'science' and genteel romantic rhetoric." He was disappointed at Max's fall from political grace. Kramer's essay was important because unlike most major art critics he is not an unqualified admirer of modernism. Eastman's anti-modernism did not prejudice Kramer against him in advance as so often happened. In Kramer's view Eastman simply did not understand modernism and so could not write about it usefully. This seems fair enough.

Norman Podhoretz, editor of *Commentary,* was more interested in the book than Kramer, but equally depressed by it. He had wondered how a young artist could come "eventually to symbolize philistinism and middle-brow vulgarity," how a young Socialist became conservative, how in old age a man like Eastman could stand for everything he repudiated as a youth.[22] Podhoretz didn't like Eastman's discursive, self-indulgent style. Max wrote, Podhoretz said, like a man who "still thinks of himself in some curious way as an adored darling endowed with an unfailing charm that can be counted on to cover for anything." But though he disliked Eastman, Podhoretz thought his book was fascinating anyway. Eastman was one of the last survivors of the pre-modernist cultural ethos, and what had happened to him said much about that vanished culture itself. His Greenwich Village was modern in the sense of being anti-Victorian and anti-bourgeois, but it was not yet modernist. Pound, Eliot, Joyce, Picasso, and the rest had yet to touch it. What Podhoretz called the "brow" issue raised by modernism lay in the future. The only distinctions were between the serious and the commercial, or between gentility and outspokenness. Otherwise, everyone was drawn together in a general protest against oppression. Eastman had been most comfortable in this environment, where everybody was at once liberal, socialist, pacifist, and feminist. The First World War (and Bolshevism, Podhoretz might have added) destroyed that world, and Max was never as comfortable again. This is a sharp assessment of Eastman's background. Intellectually he remained fixed in the pre-war Village, what Max himself had called "the comparative paradise that prevailed in America at the turn of the century."

Podhoretz then traced Max's intellectual decline, which he attributed to Eastman's failure to realize that modernism was to culture what the Russian Revolution was to the history of society. It shocked Podhoretz that when F. Scott Fitzgerald read "The Wasteland" to him Max failed to appreciate it. As he saw it, Eastman "was punished as a

writer for his arrogant dismissal of the literary revolution by falling victim to the very decline in the standards of the calling that the modernists had come to arrest." Having failed to comprehend the modernist
revolution in art, Max succumbed easily to the retrograde low-browism
of the *Reader's Digest*. There was something to this, as to Kramer's stric-
ture on the point. Max's impassioned and imperious rejection of modernism excused literary people from the need to take him seriously.
But Podhoretz was wrong to suppose that rejecting modernism corrupted Eastman's style, or that going on the *Digest* represented a loss of
ability. Max wrote as well after joining the *Digest* as he ever had. *Enjoyment of Living* is the best evidence of this, and so is *Great Companions*.[23] Eastman's *Digest* pieces show the loss of nothing save political
judgment. The weaknesses in them were not new. As Max had admitted in the *Liberator,* there was always a minister in the back of his
mind, and he loved a pulpit.

The *National Review* echoed Podhoretz, feeling that Eastman was
formed by, and most at home in, the radical culture of America in the
early years of the twentieth century. The magazine had always seen
Max as anachronistic, regarding him as more a Greenwich Village indi-
vidualist than a really dedicated conservative. But the *National Review*
liked him and so did its reviewer. William Schlamm pointed out that
Max was a "happy pagan," whose only God was science and who "preserved and carried the optimistic scientism of the nineteenth century
into the tragic religious wars of the twentieth. And he broke with Communism because Communism was a religion."[24] This was on the mark.
Eastman was a pagan, and saw himself as such—though with a reserva-
tion. This came out in an exchange with Santayana. The great philosopher believed that Max's essay on him (which appears in *Great Companions*) erred on major points because "you do not understand that I
am a *pagan*. Perhaps you don't care for Greek and Roman classics. That
seems to blind you to normality. America is not normal, not natural,
but forced, Protestant." Max promptly straightened him out.

> You are quite wrong in thinking that I don't understand you are a
> pagan. It was as a pagan that you meant so much to me in my early
> life. A sentence from one of your books: "The Greeks were able to
> think straight about morals," has come to my mind as often in the
> forty or fifty years since I read it as any other sentence I can remem-
> ber. My own feeling is that I am more pagan than you and that is why
> I find it hard to reconcile myself with your Catholicism. However,

this may be because I am by birth and early environment at least, a Protestant. My paganism bears that flavor as your's does the glaze of Catholicism."[25]

Newsweek accused Max of intellectual fickleness.[26] On the contrary, Eastman's greatest weakness was not flightyness but its opposite. He was always being reproached as a turncoat because having been a Socialist he turned to capitalism. But that was one of the rare times in his life when he exchanged one major conviction for another. His most important beliefs on love, life, literature, ethics, and the function of politics were lifelong and unshakeable. It was intellectual tenacity that distinguished Eastman's career, and hurt it as well. He was, if anything, more of a dogmatist than a dilettante. If Eastman had been more supple he would have been more popular. Some reviews were favorable. *Time* magazine, as if to make up for its sleazy treatment of *Enjoyment of Living*, summarized *Love and Revolution* at some length, calling it "long, racy, candid, and vain. It has the egalitarian earnestness of a Tom Paine, the lighthearted sexual adventurousness of a Casanova, the self-preoccupation of a Cellini. The book is also an important document, because Eastman, who observed the early Bolsheviks closely in Russia, was pre-maturely anti-Communist."[27] Arthur Schlesinger, Jr., gave the book a good notice in the *New York Times*.[28]

The *New Republic* carried an especially acute review by Joseph Featherstone. He too noticed that despite emotional ups and downs there was a hard core in Max, a "small, shrewd, sacred crystal of self which women and movements have never been permitted to touch."[29] Unlike most critics Featherstone recognized Max's special achievement during the period 1913–1922 when he was at the center of intellectual life in New York. At that time "it still seemed possible to unite artistic and social revolutions under one banner, and by and large this is what Eastman succeeded in doing." The *Masses* combined scientific socialism with cultural radicalism. Everyone who was anyone wrote for it. "With its handsome layouts and the editorial standards set by Eastman's own clear and epigrammatic prose, it became a model of imaginative journalism." Featherstone found Eastman's material on Trotsky absorbing. Eastman's Marxism "no less than Trotsky's, was sometimes abstract and lacking in economic and social analysis." Despite this, *Marxism: Is It Science?* "is still one of the keenest critical studies of Marxist philosophy ever written."

Featherstone disliked Eastman's chapters on the thirties when he "was endlessly, needlessly, defensive and self-justifying." A self-pitying tone entered Eastman's writing then, Featherstone believed. "It was the tone of a man speaking alone to a huge, empty theater." "*The Literary Mind* attacked obscurantism in modern art and was misunderstood because it was such a crabby book." Featherstone admired Eastman's verve, marveled at the many people he had met and described so well, and the big events he was involved in. The critic felt "awe at the man's comprehensive, tough intellect," and "dismay at some of the uses he has put it to." Like many reviewers Featherstone could have done without the information on Eastman's sex life. Featherstone believed that Max was saying politics ought to be kept in perspective. "Into perspective, but not clean out of sight. We can accept Max Eastman's warning: politics is a limited activity, and it can never satisfy people completely. But we need not share his despair of politics; there still remains the political problem of creating" a better world where private values can flourish.

Featherstone had done his homework, hence his penetrating essay. One of Eastman's problems was that his memoirs could not be fairly judged in isolation. Though they make a vital contribution both to autobiography as an American form and to our knowledge of American history, they are not analytical in the manner, say, of *The Education of Henry Adams*. It is unreasonable to expect that busy people will have time to read four or five books in preparation for reviewing one. Yet to measure Eastman as an intellectual one must know his best books. By 1965 hardly anyone did. Featherstone was a happy exception. Few journals had been more unfair to Eastman that the *New Republic*. Yet it also printed the most thoughtful and wide ranging evaluations of his work to appear in Eastman's lifetime, Edmund Wilson's "Max Eastman in 1941" and Joseph L. Featherstone's review of *Love and Revolution*. They evened the balance.

Let us give the last word here to Eastman's friend Joseph Slater, who wrote of Max with affection and, as a literary scholar, out of a close acquaintance with his work. Slater reminded readers that the book was leisurely by design. It is "discursive, gossipy, unbuttoned, it's full of name-dropping and anecdote, as reminiscence ought to be." He admired the descriptions of Trotsky, Radek, Bukharin, Bill Haywood, and others. But Slater disagreed with Max's own view that events had pushed him in the wrong direction. "History has been kinder to him than he thinks. His five volumes of poetry got written, and the best of it will be read again when fashions change. In carrying out the endless polemical tasks of politics he became one of the best essayists of his time, a fellow townsman in yet another way of Mark Twain." Eastman's memoirs are "rich and dramatic enough to compensate him—and history—for the fiction that did not get written."[30]

* * *

Love and Revolution was Eastman's last big creative effort. Five years of life remained to him after it came out and he went on writing for most of them, if less intensely than before. Until near the end his health was pretty good, except that from time to time he suffered pains that were diagnosed as sciatica. Though immobilizing, these bouts were irregular, and he could work and even swim between them sometimes. He took considerable pleasure in the reception of *Love and Revolution.* It was warmer than he had probably expected, considering what happened to *Enjoyment of Living.* Yet, the second volume sold even more poorly than the first. Only 4,557 copies were purchased, earning Max $3,822. He cherished letters of praise from friends, especially from Sidney Hook, who wrote him that it was a magnificent record of a magnificent life: "It has many virtues but I value it above all for its story of superb courage—The courage to stand alone when necessary. Would that it were more widespread today."[31] Max was amused by a *New Yorker* cartoon showing a married couple watching their hippy son go out the door. The husband comforts the wife thus: "Don't worry too much about it. Look at Max Eastman. He wound up on *Reader's Digest.*"[32]

In 1966 he was cheered by the publication of *Echoes of Revolt,* an anthology taken from the old *Masses* that was dedicated to him by its editor, William L. O'Neill.[33] Eastman had worked closely with O'Neill, especially by correcting the errors in O'Neill's introduction (it was his maiden voyage), and contributed an afterword drawn from *Enjoyment of Living.* Thanks to Ivan Dee of Quadrangle Books, who spared no expense, the book was gorgeous. Lavish illustrations made it, visually at least, worthy of the magazine it honored. *Echoes* was exceptionally well reviewed. Eastman's pleasure at this, and his eagerness to see all the reviews, however slight, gives the lie to his statements that his years on the *Masses* were wasted. The book received such good reviews not because of the editorial notes, or Max's afterword, or even Irving Howe's warm foreword, but because after fifty years so much of the material remained fresh and lively. Some of the magazine's soft spots were included deliberately, especially the poetry. Despite them, reviewers were impressed by how well the material stood up, and by the splendid moment in American history the book celebrated. Granville Hicks put it nicely when he called his review, "Something Wonderful Happened."[34]

A few people could not resist using the book as an excuse to chastise Eastman and others for abandoning radicalism. One of these reviews by a young leftist in the *Nation* irritated O'Neill, who sent the editors a letter of protest.[35] Remembering the times Oswald Garrison Villard had reproved him in the old days, Max found this amusing. He wrote Joseph Slater that O'Neill "was quite incensed at that review of his *Masses* anthology in the *Nation*," though Eastman could not see why. "Being disapproved of by the *Nation* never bothered the *Masses* much!"[36]

Max worked on two more projects in his last years. One was a book of essays dealing with the great teachers of ethics—Buddha, Confucius, Plato, and even Jesus among others. He called the book *Seven Kinds of Goodness*, and its concluding essay, "The Cardinal Virtues," summed up the moral principles by which he had tried to live.[37] The book was handsomely produced and pleasingly written. Indeed parts of it were as graceful as anything Max had done. But it was not advertised and to Eastman's regret attracted little notice. The other project was a kind of historical curiosity. In the 1930s Max had nearly finished a translation of Trotsky's *The Young Lenin* when the manuscript disappeared, stolen by Communists, he always assumed. In the 1960s it mysteriously turned up in the Houghton Library of Harvard University, home of the Trotsky papers. Max agreed to finish his translation and then learned that he had actually signed a contract for the book with Doubleday in the thirties. Both parties honored this ancient document, and Max would have completed the book, had death not intervened. His translation was edited and annotated by Maurice Friedberg and appeared in 1972, some thirty-five years late.[38]

Eastman's last public act was an interview given to the *New York Times* just before his final trip to Barbados. It showed how Eastman had mellowed. His intemperate years were behind him, so he could look at current events with something like the composure of his youth. Max was now rather sorry for the new generation of militant radicals. Ten years earlier they would have made him angry. He told Alden Whitman that the new leftists were bound to fail because they had no class base and no workable ideology, unlike the Socialists of his younger days, who had working class ties and in Marxism what was then a viable philosophy. Of the militant blacks, he declared with equal sureness: "they are bound to raise hell, but they can't make a revolution." [39]

Eastman did not live to see his predictions borne out. He died in Barbados on March 25, 1969, of a cerebral hemorrhage. It was how his mother and brother Peter had died, "as we all hope to," Max had written in *Love and Revolution*. His death was not as quick as Peter's. He lingered unconscious for a week after the stroke. But considering the alternatives it was an easy way to go. In death, as in life, Eastman's luck did not desert him. There were many nice statements made about Max after his death, but he had already written his own best obituary. *Seven Kinds of Goodness* ends with this passage:

> A man who knows himself and knows the world, whatever his attitude to the mystery of the universe, needs no God and no Sunday-school teacher to tell him to be good. If he preserves, together with mindfulness, courage, sympathy, temperance, justice and the art of inquiry, the gift nature gave him of growth, he will live well, and with good luck will live happily; and when his time comes to fall to the ground with the sparrow, he will know that he has made a jewel of the accident of his being. [40]

* * *

The *New York Times* obituary was long and fair. It summed up his career accurately and described his tastes and personality, noting his skill at swimming and tennis, his gift for story-telling. It pointed out Max's two sides, the part of him that was warm, impulsive, if sometimes egotistical and self-indulgent also, and the cool, analytical side that produced *Stalin's Russia* and *Marxism: Is It Science?*" [41]

This book has frequently made note of Eastman's failings. But at the end he was memorialized, as a fine person should be, for the good things in his life and character. At a moving service on May 19, 1969, in the Williams Club in New York City, Roger Baldwin, who had known and disagreed with Max for over half a century, spoke of the "gentle, shy, sweet side of Max." Leon Edel, his neighbor on the Vineyard for many years, sent a personal tribute that was read at the service. It says in part:

Whatever one made of his politics, one knew that love had filled him all his life—love of justice, of his fellow humans, of the animal life about which he wrote with such charm, and above all a love of poetry. Max had a poet's nature; he wrote many deeply felt poems; and he lived a poet's life. There was a time when he wanted to remake the world; but I think in later years he felt strongly that the struggle of our time was not to remake it—technology was doing that with violence—but to preserve it. He wanted to preserve the beauty and dignity of man and woman, the simplicities of sea and sky, the rural charm, the simple joy of living. It was no accident that the word "enjoyment" kept creeping into his book titles—enjoyment of laughter, of poetry, of living. He had in him a great fund of beautiful innocence.

Edel concluded with this sentence: "It might seem fatuous to speak of him as the last of our romantics: but there are no others left who knew the real meaning of the word 'joy,' and who left that feeling in the hearts of those who knew him."[42]

Max had given pain to others in his lifetime, as we all do. But he had given much pleasure as well. And to people who love his books he will go on doing so. The worst thing to be said of Max he said himself, fearing that he had never done or been any particular thing, and writing, "I am not Science, and I am not Song." This was not the important truth about him. Those who cared for Max will agree with his first biographer that he was like "Sherwood Anderson's gnarled apple which had the sweetest taste."[43]

Notes

CHAPTER ONE

1. Max Eastman, *Enjoyment of Living* (New York, 1948), p. xiii.
2. *Ibid.*, p. 53.
3. Max Eastman, *Great Companions* (New York, 1959), p. 299.
4. Max Eastman, "Mark Twain's Elmira: The Influence of a Great Preacher and His Parish," in *Heroes I Have Known* (New York, 1942), p. 116.
5. *Ibid.*, p. 118.
6. *Ibid.*, p. 119.
7. Julia Beecher to Max Eastman, January 13, 1901, Eastman MSS.
8. Quoted in Justin M. Kaplan, *Mr. Clemens and Mark Twain* (New York, 1966), p. 89.
9. *Ibid.*, p. 161.
10. Max Eastman to Morgan Lewis Eastman, January 20, 1895, Vineyard MSS.
11. William Mann Irvine to Max Eastman, April 11, 1913, Eastman MSS.
12. *Enjoyment of Living,* p. 122.
13. Ralph Erskine to Max Eastman, May 9, 1938, Vineyard MSS.
14. Anstice Eastman to Max Eastman, September 3, 1900, Anstice Ford Eastman MSS.
15. *Enjoyment of Living,* p. 196.
16. Annis Ford Eastman to Anstice Eastman, July 24, 1903, Anstice Ford Eastman MSS.
17. Annis Ford Eastman to Mr. Vail, January 10, 1905, Eastman MSS.
18. *Enjoyment of Living,* p. 492.
19. Max Eastman, "The New Art of Healing," *Atlantic Monthly* (May, 1908), pp. 644–50.
20. "The Reminiscences of John Spargo," pp. 174–75, Columbia Oral History Collection. Claude McKay, *A Long Way from Home* (New York, 1937), p. 29.
21. Max Eastman, "Patriotism, A Primitive Ideal," *International Journal of Ethics* (July, 1906), pp. 472–86.

22. From an unpublished typescript, "Part I: My Political History," p. 3., Vineyard MSS.
23. *Ibid.*, p. 4.
24. Caroline Ware, *Greenwich Village* (Boston, 1935).
25. From Eastman's handwritten lecture notes on "Modern Philosophy," Vineyard MSS.
26. Max Eastman, "Margins," *Masses* (January, 1916), p. 11.
27. Max Eastman, "The Poet's Mind," *North American Review* (March, 1908), pp. 417, 422, 423, 425.
28. *Great Companions, op. cit.,* p. 293.
29. Typescript entitled "Feminism—Cooper Union," Vineyard MSS.
30. Max Eastman, "The Unlimited Franchise," *Atlantic Monthly* (July, 1911), p. 48.
31. *Ibid.*, p. 49.
32. Max Eastman, "Values of the Vote," an address given before the Men's League for Woman Suffrage of New York, March 21, 1912, and published by the League, p. 4.
33. Max Eastman, "Woman Suffrage and Sentiment," a pamphlet distributed by the NAWSA.
34. Newspaper clipping of an address given by Eastman in Springfield, Massachusetts, February, 1913, Eastman MSS.
35. *Enjoyment of Living*, p. 347.
36. *Ibid.*, p. 357.
37. Typescript, "From Crystal's Notebook while at Vassar and After," entry dated June 9, 1902, Vineyard MSS.
38. Max Eastman, *Love and Revolution: My Journey Through an Epoch* (New York, 1964), p. 9.
39. *Enjoyment of Living*, pp. 360–61.
40. *Ibid.*, p. 380.
41. Max Eastman, "Leif Ericson," *Twentieth Century Magazine* (April, 1912), pp. 544–45.
42. Henry F. May, *The End of American Innocence* (New York, 1959).
43. The best anecdotes concerning Greenwich Village in this period have been brought together in Alan Churchill, *The Improper Bohemians* (New York, 1959). A gushy contemporary equivalent is Anna Alice Chapin, *Greenwich Village* (New York, 1917).
44. *Enjoyment of Living*, p. 523.

CHAPTER TWO

1. His autobiography is *Art Young: His Life and Times* (New York, 1939).
2. Floyd Dell, *Homecoming* (New York, 1933), p. 252.
3. Max Eastman, "Knowledge and Revolution," *Masses* (December, 1912), p. 5.
4. See Van Wyck Brooks, *John Sloan: A Painter's Life* (New York, 1955).

5. *Enjoyment of Living,* p. 399.
6. James Hopper, "The Job," *Masses* (March, 1913).
7. See Granville Hicks, *John Reed: The Making of a Revolutionary* (New York, 1936).
8. John Reed, *A Day in Bohemia: Or Life Among the Artists* (New York, 1913), p. 15.
9. Carlotta Russell Lowell and Max Eastman, "The *Masses* and The Negro," *Masses* (May, 1915), p. 6.
10. Max Eastman, "Niggers and Night Riders," *Masses* (January, 1913), p. 6.
11. Max Eastman to William L. O'Neill, January 6, 1966.
12. John Sloan, "A Slight Attack of Third Dimentia Brought on by Excessive Study of the Much Talked of Cubist Pictures in the International Exhibition at New York," *Masses* (April, 1913), p. 12. The quotation is from Richard Fitzgerald, *Art and Politics: Cartoonists of the* Masses *and* Liberator (Westbrook, Conn., 1973), p. 32. This is a useful guide to the art work of both magazines, but full of undigested political opinions.
13. Harvey Swados, "Echoes of Revolt," *Massachusetts Review* (Spring, 1967), p. 383.
14. See George Thomas Tanselle, "Faun at the Barricades: The Life and Work of Floyd Dell" (Ph.D. dissertation, Northwestern University, 1959).
15. *Ibid.,* p. 142.
16. Irving Howe, "To the *Masses* With Love and Envy," in William L. O'Neill, ed., *Echoes of Revolt: The* Masses, *1911 to 1917* (Chicago, 1966), p. 5.
17. Swados, *op. cit.,* p. 383.
18. Oswald Garrison Villard to Max Eastman, April 28, 1913, Villard MSS.
19. See, for example, "Socialists Up for Libel," *New York Times* (July 22, 1913), p. 2. "Harsh Words for the Newspapers," *New York Times* (March 6, 1914), p. 20. This describes a mass meeting at Cooper Union in support of the *Masses* at which 1,200 people heard Lincoln Steffens, Amos Pinchot, Charlotte Perkins Gilman, and other notables denounce the AP and the press.
20. "Confiscate Issue of Masses," *New York Times* (September 1, 1916), p. 20.
21. George Bernard Shaw to Max Eastman, July 13, 1914, Eastman MSS. George Santayana to Max Eastman, July 18, 1917. Eastman MSS. Expresses the same opinion.
22. Max Eastman to Upton Sinclair, March 28 [1916?], Sinclair MSS.
23. Max Eastman to Louise Bryant, May 24, 1932, Reed MSS.
24. Max Eastman to Norman Thomas, May 28, 1917. Quoted in J. Dennis McGreen, "Norman Thomas and the Search for an All-Inclusive Socialist Party," (Ph.D. dissertation, Rutgers University, 1975).
25. Max Eastman to William L. O'Neill, n.d., probably 1966.
26. Max Eastman, "A Sermon on Reverence," *Masses* (February, 1916), p. 21.
27. "Are We Indecent?" *Masses* (February, 1916), p. 24.
28. "Bar Magazine the *Masses,*" *New York Times* (December 12, 1915), Sec. III, p. 3.
29. Floyd Dell to Arthur Davison Ficke, March 23, 1914, quoted in Tanselle, *op. cit.*

30. Floyd Dell, *Homecoming*, p. 281.
31. Reed Whittemore, *William Carlos Williams: Poet from Jersey* (Boston, 1975), p. 178.
32. Frederick J. Hoffman, *The Twenties: American Writers in the Postwar Decade* (New York, 1955), p. 350.
33. Max Eastman, "Class War in Colorado," *Masses* (June, 1914), p. 8.
34. *Enjoyment of Living*, p. 554.
35. Joseph Slater, "The Social Policies of the *Masses*" (Master's thesis, Columbia University, 1939).
36. Max Eastman, "Concerning an Idealism," *Masses* (July, 1913), p. 5.
37. Untitled socialist speech, Vineyard MSS.
38. Max Eastman, "The Anarchist's Almanac," *Masses* (March, 1914), p. 6.
39. Max Eastman, "Anarchy and Rockefeller," *Masses* (August, 1913), p. 5.
40. Max Eastman, "Knowledge and Revolution," *Masses* (January, 1913), p. 5.
41. Slater, *op. cit.*, p. 50.
42. This is mentioned in Hutchins Hapgood, "The Socialists and the Social Movement," unidentified newspaper clipping, Reed MSS.
43. Max Eastman, "Socialist Doubt," *Masses* (April, 1917), p. 5.
44. Max Eastman, "Towards Liberty: The Method of Progress," *Masses* (September, 1916), p. 29, and same title (October, 1916), p. 24.
45. Max Eastman, "Gettes and Gists," *Masses* (April, 1913), p. 6.
46. Max Eastman, "Confession of a Suffrage Orator," *Masses* (November, 1915), p. 9. "Talk on Feminism Stirs Great Crowd," *New York Times* (February 18, 1914), p. 2.
47. Untitled address, Vineyard MSS.
48. Everett P. Wheeler, Letter to the Editor, *New York Times* (December 28, 1913), Sec. 11, p. 14.
49. Max Eastman, "The Woman Rebel," *Masses* (May, 1914), p. 5.
50. Max Eastman to Margaret Sanger, January 11, 1916, Margaret Sanger Papers, Library of Congress. The incident is described in David M. Kennedy, *Birth Control in America* (New Haven, 1970), pp. 70–80.
51. Max Eastman, "Revolutionary Birth-Control," *Masses* (July, 1915), p. 21.
52. Author's Questionnaire for *Love and Revolution*, Vineyard MSS.
53. Max Eastman, *Enjoyment of Poetry* (New York, 1913), p. v.
54. *Enjoyment of Living*, p. 433.
55. Walter Lippmann to Max Eastman, April 24, 1913; Walter Weyl to Max Eastman, April 15, 1913; Bliss Perry to Max Eastman, May 25, 1913, Eastman MSS.
56. *North American Review* (June, 1913), p. 859. *New York Times* (November 30, 1913), p. 666.
57. Maxwell Perkins to Max Eastman, May 14, 1943, Eastman MSS.
58. Vida D. Scudder, "The Muse and the 'Causes,'" *Survey* (July 13, 1913), pp. 489–90.
59. Helen Bullis, "Poetry of Today," *New York Times* (July 13, 1913), p. 397.
60. *Enjoyment of Living*, p. 436.

CHAPTER THREE

1. Max Eastman, "Exploring the Soul and Healing the Body," *Everybody's Magazine* (June, 1915), pp. 741–55. "Mr.-er-er oh! What's His Name? Ever Say That?" (July, 1915), pp. 90–103. For an excellent history that discusses Eastman's encounter with psychoanalysis, see Nathan G. Hale, Jr., *Freud and the Americans: The Beginnings of Psychoanalysis in the United States* (New York, 1971).

2. Frederick J. Hoffman, *Freudianism and the Literary Mind* (Baton Rouge, 1957), p. 52. Edmund Wilson, *The Twenties* (New York, 1975), p. 230.

3. Ms. Fuller went on to become a successful actress in Britain. They exchanged notes and letters for many years. There are thirty-nine items in her file at the Lilly Library, the last dated 1956. Max used her real name in his description of their sexual romp; this seemed to please her.

4. Max Eastman, *Love and Revolution: My Journey Through an Epoch* (New York, 1964), p. 22.

5. Max Eastman, "Is Socialism Lost?", *Masses* (October, 1914), p. 6.

6. Max Eastman, "Let the War Go On," *Masses* (October, 1914), p. 6. "War for War's Sake," *Masses* (September, 1914), pp. 5–6.

7. Max Eastman, "The Uninteresting War," *Masses* (September, 1915), pp. 5–8.

8. Max Eastman, *Journalism vs. Art* (New York, 1916), p. 68.

9. *Ibid.*, p. 68.

10. In an off-the-record conversation with me.

11. In Max Eastman, *Understanding Germany* (New York, 1915).

12. Ed., "The Old Order Changeth?", *New York Times* (November 25, 1915), p. 12. Max's address had been given three days earlier at Cooper Union under the auspices of the Women's Peace Party, to which Crystal belonged.

13. Anon., *New York Times Book Review* (December 17, 1916), p. 556.

14. Francis Hackett, "Patronizing the War," *New Republic* (January 13, 1917), p. 301. Ruth Pickering, whom Max used to fall in love with every summer, came to his defense. Letter to the Editor, *New Republic* (January 27, 1917), p. 354.

15. Arturo Giovannitti, "Militant Pacifism," *Masses* (May, 1917), p. 354.

16. Undated clipping in the Eastman MSS from the *New York Tribune*.

17. Max Eastman, "War and the Struggle for Liberty," Vineyard MSS.

18. Max Eastman, "War Psychology and International Socialism," *Masses* (August, 1916), p. 28.

19. Max Eastman, untitled typescript, Vineyard MSS.

20. Max Eastman, "The *Masses* at the White House," *Masses* (July, 1916), p. 16.

21. Max Eastman, "To Socialist Party Critics," *Masses* (February, 1917), p. 24.

22. Max Eastman, "Advertising Democracy," *Masses* (June, 1917), pp. 5–8.

23. Max Eastman, typescript, "Detroit, Sunday, April 1, 1917. Mass Meeting." Vineyard MSS.

24. For a full account of this reign of terror, see Horace C. Peterson and Gilbert C. Fite, *Opponents of War, 1917–1918* (Madison, Wisc., 1957).

25. "Speech of Max Eastman, Madison Square Garden, August 1," Vineyard MSS. See also "Swelter for Peace," *New York Times* (August 2, 1917), p. 2.
26. Floyd Dell, *Homecoming* (New York, 1933), pp. 292–93.
27. "The *Masses* Again Barred from Mails," *New York Times* (September 15, 1917), p. 20.
28. "Woodrow Wilson to Max Eastman," *Masses* (November–December, 1917), p. 2.
29. Max Eastman, "Syndicalist-Socialist Russia," *Masses* (August, 1917), p. 5.
30. Max Eastman, "It Is True," *Masses* (August, 1917), p. 6.
31. Max Eastman, "The Pro-War Socialists," *Masses* (September, 1917), pp. 17–18. For an especially brilliant contemporary analysis of the war and the intellectuals, see Lillian Schlissel, ed., *The World of Randolph Bourne* (New York, 1965), pp. 147–203.

CHAPTER FOUR

1. *Enjoyment of Living*, p. 586.
2. Quoted in Daniel Aaron, *Writers on the Left* (New York, 1961), p. 83.
3. Robert Hallowell to Crystal Eastman, May 17, 1918, Eastman MSS.
4. Their friendship is described in Max Eastman, *Heroes I Have Known* (New York, 1942).
5. "Eastman Denies Rift with Miss Deshon," *New York Times* (February 6, 1922), p. 3.
6. Quoted in *Love and Revolution*, p. 281.
7. His relations with the Duncan girls are touched on in Irma Duncan, *Duncan Dancers* (Middletown, Conn., 1966).
8. Max Eastman, *Colors of Life* (New York, 1918), p. 13.
9. Harriet Monroe, "A Radical-Conservative," *Poetry* (March, 1919), p. 326.
10. Max Eastman, "Science and Free Verse," *Seven Arts* (February, 1917), p. 426.
11. W. F., "Editorial Note," *Seven Arts* (February, 1917), pp. 430, 431.
12. Vachel Lindsay to Max Eastman (December 29, 1918), Eastman MSS. Floyd Dell, *Liberator* (December, 1918), p. 44.
13. O. W. Firkin, *Nation* (January 4, 1919), p. 21. Louis Untermeyer, "Whitman, Poe and Max Eastman," *Dial* (December 28, 1918), p. 612.
14. Arturo Giovannitti to Max Eastman, n.d., but before *Colors of Life* was published, Eastman MSS. His reply to Untermeyer is a letter to the editor, *Dial* (February 8, 1919), p. 146. Untermeyer's response is another letter to the editor, *Dial* (February 22, 1919), p. 202.
15. Max Eastman, *The Sense of Humor* (New York, 1921), p. viii.
16. G. Stanley Hall to Max Eastman, January 31, 1922; John Dewey to Max Eastman, December 7, 1921, Eastman MSS.
17. Max Eastman, "Editorial," *Liberator* (March, 1918), p. 3.
18. *Ibid.*, p. 5.

19. Max Eastman, "Wilson and the World's Future," *Liberator* (May, 1918), p. 19.
20. Max Eastman, "Wilson's Style," *Liberator* (March, 1921), p. 24.
21. Quoted in *Love and Revolution,* p. 109.
22. John Reed to Max Eastman, n.d., Reed MSS.
23. "Hard To Get Jury for *Masses* Trial," *New York Times* (April 16, 1918), p. 8.
24. Floyd Dell, "The Story of the Trial," *Liberator* (June, 1918), p. 8.
25. *Ibid.,* p. 7.
26. Quoted in *Love and Revolution,* p. 97.
27. Art Young, "Art Young on Trial for His Life," *Liberator* (June, 1918), p. 11.
28. "Speeches of Max Eastman and Morris Hillquit at the *Masses* dinner, May 9," *Liberator* (June, 1918), p. 19.
29. *Ibid.,* p. 21.
30. Morris Hillquit, *Loose Leaves from a Busy Life* (New York, 1934), p. 229.
31. "Socialists Name Eastman," *New York Times* (June 20, 1918), p. 11. "Name Nearing for Congress," *New York Times* (June 27, 1918), p. 4. Eastman did not run and was replaced by one Leonora Byrne.
32. John Reed, "The Second *Masses* Trial," *Liberator* (December, 1918), p. 37.
33. Louis B. Davidson to Max Eastman, August 8, 1939, Eastman MSS.
34. "Max Eastman's Address to the Jury in the Second *Masses* Trial" (New York, 1918), p. 11.
35. Sherman Rogers, "New York Bolsheviks Divided but Both Groups Work Night and Day Spreading Propaganda," *New York World* (June 4, 1919), p. 4.
36. *"Masses* Defendents Free," *New York Times* (January 11, 1919), p. 22.
37. "Speeches of Max Eastman and Morris Hillquit," *op. cit.,* p. 19.
38. Eugene V. Debs to Max Eastman, November 18, 1918, Eastman MSS. Eastman reprinted his account with some alterations as "Greek Drama in Cleveland: The Trial of Eugene Debs," in *Heroes I Have Known* (New York, 1942).
39. "Reds in Garden Urge Revolution and Soviets Here," *New York Times* (June 21, 1919), p. 1.
40. Editorial, "The Red Night at the Garden," *New York Times* (June 23, 1919), p. 12.
41. *Love and Revolution,* pp. 151–56, describes this incident in detail.

CHAPTER FIVE

1. Editorial, *Liberator* (October, 1918), p. 25.
2. Max Eastman, The Chicago Conventions," *Liberator* (October, 1919), p. 5. Two useful histories are James Weinstein, *The Decline of Socialism in America, 1912–1925* (New York, 1967), and Theodore Draper, *The Roots of American Communism* (New York, 1957).

3. *Ibid.,* p. 15.
4. *Ibid.,* p. 16.
5. Quoted in Weinstein, *op. cit.,* p. 24.
6. Editorial, "Hillquit Excommunicates the Soviets," *Liberator* (November, 1920), pp. 22–25. Editorial, "Hillquit Repeats His Error," *Liberator* (January, 1921), pp. 20–24.
7. Quoted in Max Eastman, "Dogmatism Again," *Liberator* (May, 1921), p. 7.
8. *Ibid.*
9. Editorial, "An Opinion on Tactics," *Liberator* (October, 1921), p. 5. For a good account of communism's bizarre adventures in the 1920s, see Daniel Bell, "Marxian Socialism in the United States" in Volume 1 of *Socialism and American Life,* pp. 334–45.
10. "An Opinion on Tactics," p. 6.
11. Romain Rolland to Max Eastman, April 17, 1919, Eastman MSS.
12. Editorial, "The Clarté Movement," *Liberator* (April, 1920), p. 41.
13. *Ibid.,* p. 42.
14. Quoted in Max Eastman, "Clarifying the Light," *Liberator* (June, 1921), p. 5. Lunacharsky was the Soviet Minister of Education.
15. *Ibid.,* p. 7.
16. Editorial, "Addendum," *Liberator* (July 1921), 5.
17. Freeman recalled this in a letter to Floyd Dell on July 2, 1951. It is cited in James Gilbert, *Writers and Partisans* (New York, 1968), p. 74.
18. Quoted in *Love and Revolution,* p. 239.
19. Max Eastman, "Inspiration or Leadership," *Liberator* (August, 1921), p. 9.
20. Floyd Dell, "Explanations and Apologies," *Liberator* (June, 1922), p. 26.
21. Max Eastman, "Bolshevik Problems," *Liberator* (April, 1918), pp. 8–9.
22. Editorial, "A Statesman of the New Order," *Liberator* (September, 1918), p. 10.
23. Editorial, "A Statesman of the New Order," *Liberator* (October, 1918), p. 31.
24. *Love and Revolution,* p. 130. Max Eastman, "To Nicolai Lenin," *Liberator* (November, 1918), p. 17.
25. Editorial, "About Dogmatism," *Liberator* (November, 1920), p. 8.
26. "Editorials," *Liberator* (May, 1920), p. 6.
27. "Editorials," *Liberator* (August, 1920), p. 5.
28. Max Eastman, "The New International," *Liberator* (July, 1919), p. 26.
29. "Editorials," *Liberator* (May, 1919), p. 6.
30. Editorial, "Free Speech Again," *Liberator* (September, 1918), p. 7.
31. Editorial, "The Free Press," *Liberator* (May, 1921), p. 5.
32. *The Gulag Archipelago,* p. 28.
33. Max Eastman, "Examples of Americanism," *Liberator* (February, 1920), p. 13.
34. *Ibid.,* pp. 13–14.
35. William E. Bohn, "Poet as Man of Action: Close-up of Max Eastman," *New Leader* (July, 10, 1948), p. 7.
36. Editorial, "Bob Minor and the Bolsheviki," *Liberator* (March, 1919), p. 6.

Minor's three articles appeared in the *New York World* on February 4, 6, and 7.

37. Typescript, untitled socialist speech, n.d., Vineyard MSS.

38. Robert Minor, "I Change My Mind a Little," *Liberator* (October, 1920), pp. 5–15. The *World* had altered his original stories, he claimed, making his critique of the Soviets seem more sweeping than it was. Robert Minor to Max Eastman, April 20, 1919, Eastman MSS. Minor wavered between friendship and criticism before settling down to Stalinism. For discussions of this, see Christopher Lasch, *The American Liberal and the Russian Revolution* (New York, 1962), and Benjamin Gitlow, *The Whole of Their Lives* (New York, 1948).

39. Editorial, "Robert Lansing Explains Bolshevism," *Liberator* (March, 1920), p. 43.

40. Bertrand Russell, "Democracy and Revolution," *Liberator* (May, 1920), pp. 10–14, and (June, 1920), pp. 23–25.

41. Bertrand Russell, "Soviet Russia—1920," *Nation* (July, 31, 1920), p. 126, and (August 7, 1920), pp. 152–54.

42. Bertrand Russell, "Bolshevik Theory," *New Republic* (September, 3, 1920), p. 241. The other two parts of this essay appeared in the issues of September 15, pp. 267–69, and November 17, pp. 296–98.

43. Editorial, "Nietzsche, Plato, and Bertrand Russell," *Liberator* (September, 1920), p. 6.

44. Editorial, "Red Aristocrats," *New York Times* (September 5, 1920), Sec. 11, p. 2.

45. *Ibid.*

46. "Editorials," *Liberator* (August, 1921), p. 5.

47. Walter Lippmann and Charles Merz, "A Test of the News," *New Republic* (August 4, 1920), pp. 10–11.

48. This view is sustained in Richard O'Connor and Dale L. Walker, *The Lost Revolutionary* (New York, 1967).

49. Louise Bryant, "Last Days with John Reed," *Liberator* (February, 1921), p. 11.

50. Max Eastman, "John Reed," a speech given at the John Reed Memorial Meeting, New York, October 25, 1920, Vineyard MSS.

51. John Reed, "The Dead and the Living," *Liberator* (February, 1921), p. 20.

52. "Mylius Says He Only 'Borrowed' $4,000." *New York Times* (December 2, 1921), p. 10. "Max Eastman Replies to E. F. Mylius Letter," *New York Times* (December 3, 1921), p. 24.

53. "Man Who Libeled George V Robs Paper," *New York Times* (December 1, 1921), p. 11.

CHAPTER SIX

1. Some useful histories are Adam B. Ulam, *The Bolsheviks* (New York, 1965); G. F. Hudson, *Fifty Years of Communism* (New York, 1968); and the classic Bertram Wolfe, *Three Who Made a Revolution* (New York, 1948).

2. Georges Haupt and Jean Jacques Marie, *Makers of the Russian Revolution* (Ithaca, 1974), p. 398.

3. *Love and Revolution*, p. 317.

4. Max Eastman, "A Permanent Revolution," *Liberator* (December, 1923), p. 11.

5. Max Eastman, "The Wisdom of Lenin," *Liberator* (June, 1924, p. 8.

6. Max Eastman, "The Wisdom of Lenin," *Liberator* (July, 1924), p. 26.

7. Max Eastman, *Since Lenin Died* (Westport, Conn., 1973), p. 59. This is a reprint of the original edition brought out by Boni & Liveright in 1925.

8. *Ibid.*, p. 102.

9. *Ibid.*, p. 103.

10. Issac Deutscher, *The Prophet Unarmed* (London, 1959), p. 16.

11. Eden Paul to Max Eastman, May 5, 1925, Eastman MSS.

12. C. M. Roebuck, "Since Eastman Lied," *Worker's Monthly* (June, 1925), p. 369.

13. *Love and Revolution*, pp. 446–47.

14. Lincoln Steffens to Max Eastman, June 16, 1925, Eastman MSS.

15. Steffens to Ella Winter, December 31, 1931, in Ella Winter and Granville Hicks, eds., *The Letters of Lincoln Steffens* (New York, 1938).

16. Christopher Lasch, *The New Radicalism in America,* (1889–1963) (New York, 1965), p. 280.

17. Anon., "The Worship of Lenin," *The Nation and Athenaeum* (July 11, 1925), p. 1. J. Donald Adams, "Lenin Betrayed by His Party," *New York Times Book Review* (July 12, 1925), p. 1.

18. "Says Lenin Distrusted Red Triumvirate," *New York Times* (May 1, 1925), p. 5. Editorial, "Dictatorial Dictators," *ibid.*, p. 18.

19. Henry Alsberg, "Son of the Prophet," *New York Herald Tribune Books* (August 16, 1925), p. 4.

20. Eastman described their San Francisco affair in *Love and Revolution,* pp. 178–79, without mentioning her name. She spoke of his having "brought" her to New York in an undated letter to him in the Eastman MSS.

21. Genevieve Taggard, ed., *May Days* (New York, 1925), p. 12.

22. Genevieve Taggard to Max Eastman, n.d., Eastman MSS.

23. Max Eastman to Horace Liveright, n.d. (probably September, 1925), Eastman MSS.

24. Max Eastman to Genevieve Taggard, September 15, 1925, Eastman MSS. Like many Communists and fellow travelers, Taggard had very devout parents. As a student at Berkeley she rebelled against them, being attracted first to bohemianism, later to communism. She was as devout in her way as her parents in theirs.

25. Genevieve Taggard to Max Eastman, n.d., Eastman MSS.

26. Babette Deutsch, *New York Herald Tribune Books* (January 31, 1926), p. 3; *Nation* (December 30, 1925), p. 761; *Saturday Review* (May 8, 1925), p. 160; *Outlook* (January 6, 1926), p. 6.

27. Mike Gold, "May Days and Revolutionary Art," *Modern Quarterly* (February–April 1925), p. 160.

28. Max Eastman, *Leon Trotsky: Portrait of a Youth* (New York, 1925), p. 180; *Bookman* (August, 1925), p. 712; *Dial* (October, 1925), p. 353; *New York Herald Tribune Books* (June 28, 1925), p. 8. John Maynard Keynes to Max Eastman, December 22, 1926, Eastman MSS.

29. Max Eastman, "Lenin Testament at Last Revealed," *New York Times* (October 18, 1926), p. 5.

30. Walter Duranty, "Trotsky Admits Defeat, Bows to Stalin Group as the Real Red Chiefs," *New York Times* (October 18, 1926), p. 1.

31. Editorial, "Peasant and Proletarion," *New York Times* (October 19, 1926), p. 28. Walter Duranty, "Red Loyalty Stops Split at Moscow," *New York Times* (October 23, 1926), p. 6.

32. Gustavus Tuckerman, ed., *Duranty Reports Russia* (New York, 1934), p. 120. This is a collection of Duranty's dispatches.

33. *Ibid.*, p. 174. This story was dated January 18, 1931.

34. *Ibid.*, p. 190, dated June 31, 1931.

35. *Ibid.*, p. 211, dated June 23, 1937.

36. Walter Duranty, *I Write as I Please* (New York, 1935), p. 302.

37. John P. Diggins, "Getting Hegel out of History: Max Eastman's Quarrel with Marxism," *American Historical Review* (February, 1974), p. 44.

38. Max Eastman, *Marx, Lenin, and the Science of Revolution* (New York, 1928), p. 92.

39. *Ibid.*, p. 113.

40. *Ibid.*, p. 114.

41. *Ibid.*, p. 122.

42. John P. Diggins, *Up from Communism: Conservative Odysseys in American Intellectual History* (New York, 1975), p. 39.

43. *Ibid.*, p. 40.

44. Samuel D. Schmalhausen, "These Tragic Comedians," *Modern Quarterly* (November–February, 1927), p. 218.

45. Oscar H. Swede to Max Eastman, October 1, 1927, Eastman MSS.

46. Lincoln Steffens to Max Eastman, January 7, 1927, Eastman MSS.

47. Bertram D. Wolfe, "Eastman Revises Marx–And Corrects Lenin," *The Communist* (December, 1927), p. 403. The Scott Nearing review is an otherwise unidentified clipping in the Eastman papers.

48. Walter Duranty, "Soviet Opens War on Bureaucratism," *New York Times* (March 28, 1928), p. 7.

49. H. G. Wells to Max Eastman, n.d., Eastman MSS.

50. John Strachey, in the English *New Leader* (December 10, 1926), p. 11.

51. HJL, *Manchester Guardian* (December 11, 1926). *Economist* (May 3, 1927).

52. Malcomb McComb, *Journal of Philosophy* (August 16, 1928), p. 471. Robert W. Bruere, *Survey* (May 1, 1928), p. 183.

53. Henry Raymond Mussey, "How To Change Things," *Nation* (August 15, 1928), p. 159. T. V. Smith, *International Journal of Ethics* (July, 1928), p.

480. James Harvey Robinson to Max Eastman, February 7, 1933, Eastman MSS.

54. Simeon Strunsky, *New York Times Book Review* (April 1, 1928), p. 4.

55. Max Eastman, *The Real Situation in Russia* (New York, 1928), p. viii.

CHAPTER SEVEN

1. *Love and Revolution*, p. 467.
2. Eliena Eastman to Max Eastman, October 4, 1926, Eliena Eastman MSS.
3. "Eastman Views America," *New York Times* (April 9, 1927), p. 15. "Tells How Trotsky Fought at Exile," *New York Times* (March 1, 1928), p. 7.
4. *Love and Revolution*, p. 491.
5. F. Scott Fitzgerald to Max Eastman, n.d., Eastman MSS.
6. Oswald Garrison Villard to Max Eastman, December 25, 1927; Mabel Dodge to Max Eastman, n.d., Eastman MSS. Anon., "Max Eastman's *Venture* and Other Works of Fiction," *New York Times Book Review* (December 11, 1927), p. 9. Sinclair Lewis disliked the book. Sinclair Lewis to Max Eastman, January 2, 1928, Eastman MSS.
7. Walter Rideout, *The Radical Novel in the United States* (Cambridge, 1956), pp. 119–20.
8. Freda Kirchwey, "Crystal Eastman," *Nation* (August 8, 1928), p. 123.
9. Max Eastman to Oswald Garrison Villard, January 12, 1928, Villard MSS. Villard to Eastman, January 17, 1928, Villard MSS.
10. Max Eastman, "The Last Words of Adolphe Joffe," *Nation* (February 1, 1928), pp. 132–34.
11. Editorial, "Russia's Thermidor," *Nation* (February 1, 1928), p. 113.
12. Albert Rhys Williams, Joseph Freeman, Kenneth Durant, to Oswald Garrison Villard, January 30, 1928, Villard MSS. Max Eastman to Villard, February 3, 1928, Villard MSS.
13. Max Eastman, ed. and trans., *The Real Situation in Russia by Leon Trotsky* (New York, 1928), pp. xii–xiii.
14. Albert Rhys Williams, "The Real Situation in Russia," *Nation* (November 14, 1928), p. 516.
15. *Ibid.*, p. 517.
16. *Ibid.*, p. 518.
17. "Max Eastman Replies," *Nation* (December 26, 1928), p. 715. Max Eastman, "To the Editor," *Nation* (February 27, 1929), p. 257.
18. Arthur Ruhl, "Trotsky's Side of the Question," *New York Herald Tribune Books* (August 19, 1929), p. 2.
19. Anon., "Trotsky Quotes Lenin's Gospel," *New York Times Book Review* (July 29, 1928), p. 1. J. B. S. Hardman, *The New Republic* (November 7, 1928), p. 332.
20. "The Reminiscences of Max Shachtman," Columbia Oral History Collection, p. 174.
21. *The Gulag Archipelago*, p. 374.
22. Eugene Lyons, *Assignment in Utopia* (New York, 1937), pp. 116, 118.

23. Louise Bryant, *Six Red Months in Russia* (New York, 1918), pp. 151, 155.

24. Walter Duranty, "Death for 22 Asked in Soviet Don Trial," *New York Times* (June 30, 1928), p. 25.

25. "Editorial," *Nation* (July 18, 1928), p. 53.

26. Max Eastman to Leon Trotsky, n.d., Trotsky MSS.

27. Max Eastman to Leon Trotsky, July 9, 1929, Trotsky MSS.

28. Max Shachtman, "The Revolutionary Optimist," *New International* (August, 1941), p. 169.

29. Sidney Hook, "Marxism, Metaphysics, and Modern Science," *Modern Quarterly* (May–August, 1928), p. 388.

30. Max Eastman, "As to Sidney Hook's Morals," *Modern Quarterly* (November–February, 1928–29), pp. 85–87.

31. Sidney Hook, "As to Max Eastman's Mentality," *Modern Quarterly* (November–February, 1928–29), p. 88.

32. Lewis Mumford, "To the Editor," *Modern Quarterly* (Winter, 1930–31), pp. vii–viii.

33. John P. Diggins, "Getting Hegel out of History: Max Eastman's Quarrel with Marxism," *American Historical Review* (February, 1974), p. 59.

34. Edna St. Vincent Millay to Max Eastman, February 6, 1929, Eastman MSS.

35. Arturo Giovannitti to Max Eastman, September 24, 1929, Eastman MSS.

36. Eliena Eastman to Max Eastman, February 8, 1929, Eliena Eastman MSS.

37. Max Eastman to Eliena Eastman, February 18, 1930, Eliena Eastman MSS.

38. Max Eastman, *The Literary Mind: Its Place in an Age of Science* (New York, 1931), p. 3.

39. *Ibid.*, p. 9.

40. *Ibid.*, p. 16.

41. Fred H. Higgenson, ed., *Anna Livia Plurabelle: The Making of a Chapter* (Minneapolis, 1960), p. 13.

42. *The Literary Mind*, p. 158.

43. *Ibid.*, pp. 170, 216.

44. *Ibid.*, p. 288.

45. Austin Clark, *"The Literary Mind," Spectator* (February 27, 1932), p. 296.

46. Bernard Berenson to Max Eastman, August 30, 1933; H. G. Wells to Max Eastman, July 7, 1932; Sinclair Lewis to Max Eastman, December 21, 1931, Eastman MSS.

47. Clive Bell to Max Eastman, August 25, 1932, Eastman MSS.

48. Haakon Chevalier to Max Eastman, June 4, 1932, Eastman MSS.

49. George Santayana to Max Eastman, June 4, 1932, Eastman MSS.

50. G. W. Stonier, "A Scientific Critic," *New Statesman and Nation* (February 20, 1932), p. 238. Henry Hazlitt, "Science and Poetry," *Nation* (December 9, 1931), p. 646.

51. John Chamberlain, "Max Eastman's Blast against Modern Literature," *New York Times Book Review* (November 21, 1931), p. 329.

52. I. A. Richards, *The Criterion* (October, 1932), p. 151.

53. Leon Whipple, "Letters and Life," *Survey* (February 1, 1933), p. 497.

54. Robert M. Coates, *New Yorker* (December 5, 1931), pp. 111–12.

55. Frederick J. Hoffman, *The Twenties: American Writing in the Postwar Decade* (New York, 1955), p. 246.
56. Murray Krieger, *The New Apologists for Poetry* (Minneapolis, 1956), pp. 191, 193.
57. Van Wyck Brooks, *Opinions of Oliver Allston* (New York, 1941), p. 153.
58. Alan Tate, *On the Limits of Poetry* (New York, 1948), p. 117.
59. Alfred Kazin, *On Native Grounds* (New York, 1956), p. 315. It was first published in 1942.
60. Max Eastman, *Art and the Life of Action* (New York, 1934), p. 61.
61. *Ibid.*, p. 70.
62. *Ibid.*, p. 75.
63. Selden Rodman, *Common Sense* (December, 1934), p. 27. V. F. Calverton, *Modern Monthly* (December, 1934), pp. 632–33. Ernest Sutherland Bates, "A Magician with Language," *New York Herald Tribune Books* (December 16, 1934), p. 5. Henry Seidel Canby, "Art for Life's Sake," *Saturday Review* (June 9, 1934), p. 255. George Santayana to Max Eastman, April 30, 1935, Eastman MSS. See also Raymond Mortimer, "Books in General," *New Statesman and Nation* (March 23, 1935), pp. 420–21. Anon., "Art and Action, *Times Literary Supplement* (May 9, 1934).
64. Granville Hicks, "The Vigorous Abandon of Max Eastman's Mind," *New Masses* (November 6, 1934), pp. 22–23.
65. Obed Brooks, "Eastman's Puritanism," *Partisan Review* (April–May, 1935), p. 86.
66. Babette Deutsch, *"Art and the Life of Action,"* *Nation* (December 12, 1934), p. 688. For a nicely balanced review, see I. E., *The Journal of Philosophy* (February 14, 1935), p. 104.

CHAPTER EIGHT

1. William Rose Benét, *Saturday Review of Literature* (April 11, 1931). Genevieve Taggard, *New York Herald Tribune Books* (May 3, 1931).
2. Max Eastman, "The Doctrinal Crisis in Socialism," *Modern Quarterly* (Winter, 1930–31), pp. 428, 429.
3. Arthur W. Calhoun, "The Doctrinal Crisis in Eastmanism," *Modern Quarterly* (Winter, 1930–31), p. 437.
4. Albert Parry, a Russian historian, thinks Eastman's translation of Trotsky's *History of the Russian Revolution* is better "than that work deserves." Albert Parry to William L. O'Neill, September 19, 1975. The first of its three volumes was translated by Boris Shishkin for the *Saturday Evening Post.* Trotsky didn't like the result, and it was arranged for Eastman to translate the other two. Shishkin did not receive credit in the book version and was still bitter about this years later. "The Reminiscences of Boris Shishkin," p. 431, Columbia Oral History Collection.
5. Trotsky on Max Eastman," *New International* (November, 1934), p. 125.

6. Quoted in Max Eastman, "Excommunication and Exorcism as Critical Methods," *Modern Monthly* (May, 1933), pp. 211, 212.

7. See, for example, Max Eastman to Oswald Garrison Villard, June 7, 1933, Villard MSS.

8. Sidney Hook, *Modern Monthly* (May, 1933), p. 248.

9. *Ibid.*, p. 249.

10. Max Eastman, "To the Editor," *Modern Quarterly* (June, 1933), p. 320.

11. "A Note from Sidney Hook," *Modern Monthly* (July, 1933), pp. 350–51.

12. Max Eastman, "To the Editor," *Modern Monthly* (August, 1933), p. 448. Sidney Hook, "To the Editor," *Modern Monthly* (September, 1933), p. 511.

13. John Dewey to Max Eastman, November 8, 1933, Eastman MSS.

14. Max Eastman, *Art and the Life of Action* (New York, 1934), pp. 126–27.

15. Max Eastman, *The Last Stand of Dialectical Materialism* (New York, 1934).

16. Alfred Kazin, *Starting out in the Thirties* (Boston, 1965), p. 72.

17. John Dewey to Max Eastman, April 17, 1934, Eastman MSS.

18. Theodore B. Brameld, "The Last Stand of Dialectical Materialism," *Modern Monthly* (September, 1934), p. 498.

19. *Ibid.*, p. 500.

20. Irving Howe, "The New York Intellectuals," *Commentary* (October, 1968), p. 33.

21. Max Eastman, "Religion and the Bolsheviks," first given on March 16, 1930, Vineyard MSS.

22. *Ibid.*, p. 115.

23. Max Eastman, "Present Trends in Russia," p. 18. This was a pamphlet circulated by the Foreign Policy Association and consisting of talks by Eastman and two others on March 29, 1930.

24. Untitled lecture, Vineyard MSS.

25. Kendall E. Bailes, "The Politics of Technology: Stalin and Technocratic Thinking among Soviet Engineers," *American Historical Review* (April, 1974), pp. 445–69.

26. *The Gulag Archipelago,* p. 382.

27. Editorial, "The Week," *New Republic* (November 26, 1930), pp. 28–29. Editorial, "The Week," *New Republic* (December 17, 1930), p. 122. Louis Fischer, "Servants of the Soviets," *Nation* (November 24, 1930), pp. 577–79.

28. Max Eastman, "Am I a Technocrat?", *Common Sense* (May 11, 1933), p. 16.

29. Max Eastman, "Discrimination about Russia," *Modern Monthly* (September, 1934), p. 479.

30. *Ibid.*, p. 480.

31. *Ibid.*, p. 482.

32. *Ibid.*, p. 485.

33. For a sketch of Calverton's life, see Daniel Aaron, *Writers on the Left* (New York, 1961), pp. 322–32.

34. Max Eastman to V. F. Calverton, July 11, 1933; June 26, 1934; August 25, 1934, Calverton MSS.

35. Max Eastman to V. F. Calverton, October 28, 1933, Calverton MSS.

36. Beals thought this was unfair, as he opposed Stalinists and Trotskyists alike. "I am kicked off the board for believing the same things you do." Carleton Beals to V. F. Calverton, April 11, 1937, Calverton MSS.

37. Max Eastman, "Artists in Uniform," *Modern Monthly* (August, 1933), p. 399.

38. *Ibid.*, p. 403.

39. Max Shachtman to Max Eastman, October 8, 1935, Eastman MSS.

40. Joshua Kunitz, "Choose Your Uniform," *New Masses* (August, 1933), p. 14.

41. Max Eastman, "How Art Became a Class Weapon," *Modern Monthly* (October, 1933), pp. 56–57.

42. Quoted in Joshua Kunitz, "Max Eastman's Hot Unnecessary Tears," *New Masses* (September, 1933), p. 13.

43. Quoted in Max Eastman, "Stalin's Literary Inquisition," *Modern Monthly* (November, 1933), p. 625.

44. *Ibid.*, p. 630.

45. Joshua Kunitz, "A Note on Max Eastman," *New Masses* (May 8, 1934), p. 24.

46. Boris Pilnyak, "In Reference to Myself," *Partisan Review* (June–July, 1934), p. 20.

47. Leon Dennen, "Bunk by a Bohemian," *Partisan Review* (June–July, 1934), p. 23.

48. A. Stork, "Mr. Calverton and His Friends," *International Literature*, no. 3 (1934), p. 97.

49. Daniel Bell, "Marxian Socialism in the United States," *Socialism and American Life* (Princeton, 1952), vol. 1, p. 355.

50. Selden Rodman, *Common Sense* (June, 1934), p. 27.

51. Harold Strauss, "Literature under Red Banner," *New York Times Book Review* (May 19, 1934), p. 2.

52. William Harlan Hale, "Radicalism in Straight-Jackets," *Saturday Review* (June 9, 1934), p. 738.

53. *Spectator* (November 23, 1934), p. 38. See also the *New Statesman and Nation* (November 17, 1934), pp. 724–26.

54. Carl Becker, "The Writer in Soviet Russia," *Nation* (May 30, 1934), p. 624.

55. *Ibid.*, p. 625.

56. Babette Deutsch, "Dictatorship and the Artist," *New York Herald Tribune Books* (June 3, 1934), p. 6.

57. Lincoln Steffens, "Swatting Flies in Russia," *New Republic* (June 20, 1934), pp. 161–62.

58. Max Eastman to V. F. Calverton, June 29, 1934, Calverton MSS.

59. Quoted in Justin Kaplan, *Lincoln Steffens* (New York, 1974), p. 321.

60. *Ibid.*, p. 324.

61. Max Eastman, "To the Editor," *New Republic* (August 1, 1934), p. 322.

62. Matthew Josephson, "The Literary Life in Russia," *New Republic* (June 6, 1934), p. 90.

63. Lincoln Steffens, "To the Editor," *New Republic* (August 1, 1934), p. 322.

CHAPTER NINE

1. Joseph Freeman, "Greenwich Village Types," *New Masses* (May, 1933), p. 20.
2. Bob Brown, "Them Asses," *American Mercury* (December, 1933), p. 411.
3. Max Eastman, "Bunk about Bohemia," *Modern Monthly* (May, 1934), p. 207.
4. Alfred Kazin, *Starting Out in the Thirties* (Boston, 1965), p. 69.
5. Sherwood Anderson to Max Eastman, May 6, 1933, Eastman MSS.
6. Max Eastman to Theodore Dreiser, April 23, 1933; Theodore Dreiser to Max Eastman, April 26, 1933, Eastman MSS.
7. Max Eastman to Theodore Dreiser, May 1, 1933, Eastman MSS.
8. Peter A. Bogdanov to Theodore Dreiser, May 3, 1933, in Robert H. Elias, ed., *The Letters of Theodore Dreiser* (Philadelphia, 1959), p. 630.
9. Theodore Dreiser to Max Eastman, May 26, 1933, Eastman MSS.
10. Henry Hart, ed., *American Writers Congress* (New York, 1935), p. 17.
11. *The Gulag Archipelago,* p. xii.
12. *American Writers Congress,* p. 54.
13. *Ibid.,* p. 95.
14. Quoted in Eric Bentley, ed., *Thirty Years of Treason* (New York, 1971), p. 232.
15. Granville Hicks, *John Reed: The Making of a Revolutionary* (New York, 1936), p. 93.
16. *Ibid.,* pp. 319–20.
17. Max Eastman, "John Reed and the Russian Revolution," *Modern Monthly* (December, 1935), pp. 14–21.
18. Angelica Balabanoff, "John Reed's Last Days," *Modern Monthly* (January, 1937), pp. 3–6.
19. Granville Hicks, "To the Editor," *Modern Monthly* (December, 1936), pp. 29–30.
20. Andrew Kopkind, *New York Times Book Review* (December 2, 1975), p. 5.
21. Mabel Dodge Luhan to Max Eastman, May 10, 1938, Eastman MSS.
22. Max Eastman to Mabel Dodge, n.d., Eastman MSS.
23. Edmund Wilson to Babette Deutsch, December 10, 1936, in Edmund Wilson, *Letters on Literature and Politics, 1912–1972* (New York, 1977), p. 283. The review in question was of *The Works of Pushkin,* a 902-page book translated by Ms. Deutsch and her husband Avrahm Yarmolinsky. See Max Eastman, "Pushkin and His English Translators," *New Republic* (December 9, 1936), pp. 187–90. Max was annoyed that the translators had failed to understand and appreciate Pushkin's robust sex life, which, of course, Max privately felt resembled his own.
24. *Enjoyment of Living,* p. 614. Some reviews are Irwin Edman, "A Poet on the Art of Enjoying Laughter," *New York Herald Tribune Books* (December 6, 1936), p. 2; Leonard Bacon, "What Makes Us Laugh," *Saturday Review of Literature* (November 14, 1936), p. 10; Charles Poore, "A Hilarious Primer to Laughter," *New York Times Book Review* (November 15, 1936), p. 2; I.E.,

Journal of Philosophy (March 18, 1937), pp. 165–66; Joseph Wood Krutch, "Good Jokes and Bad," *Nation* (November 21, 1936), pp. 607–8; Anon., "The Trade in Jokes," *Times Literary Supplement* (April 17, 1937), p. 637, a cold review.

25. Louis Kronenberger, "Allegiance to the Gag," *New Republic* (January 13, 1937), p. 336. Quoted in James Thurber, *The Years with Ross* (Boston, 1959), p. 48. George Santayana to Max Eastman, November 20, 1936, Eastman MSS.

26. W. C. Fields to Max Eastman, November 20, 1936, Eastman MSS.

27. Max Eastman, note dated December 14, 1959, Vineyard MSS.

28. Frank S. Nugent, *New York Times* (March 9, 1937), p. 27.

29. Harold Denny, "Stalin Calls Halt to Fulsome Praise," *New York Times* (March 29, 1937), p. 10.

30. Editorial, "Russians Must Be Rough," *New York Times* (March 30, 1937), p. 10.

31. Max Eastman, Letter to the Editor, *New York Times* (April 5, 1937), p. 18. Max Eastman, "Reply to the Stalinists," *New York Times* (March 21, 1937), Sec. XI, p. 3, defends the objectivity of his film.

32. Max's view that the Stalinist boycott had ruined his film commercially was endorsed by a columnist for the *Times*. B. R. Crisler, "Gossip of the Films," *New York Times* (June 13, 1937), Sec. XI, p. 4.

33. Max Eastman, "Bull in the Afternoon," reprinted in *Art and the Life of Action* (New York, 1934), p. 87.

34. Max Eastman to the editor of the *New Republic,* June 15, 1933, Eastman MSS.

35. Max Eastman to Ernest Hemingway, June 15, 1933, Eastman MSS.

36. Archibald MacLeish to Max Eastman, June 20, 1933, Eastman MSS.

37. Max Eastman to Archibald MacLeish, July 3, 1933, Eastman MSS.

38. Quoted in Carlos Baker, *Ernest Hemingway: A Life Story* (New York, 1969), p. 242.

39. "Hemingway off to Spain," *New York Times* (August 15, 1937), p. 31.

40. *New York Post,* August 13, 1937, Eastman MSS.

41. *New York Herald Tribune,* August 14, 1937, and the *New York Times,* August 14 and August 15, Eastman MSS.

42. *New Yorker* (September 4, 1937), p. 10.

43. Max Eastman, note to himself, September 3, 1937, Eastman MSS.

44. The essay is in *Great Companions* (New York, 1959). The two *Saturday Review* pieces are in the April 4, 1959, and March 24, 1962, issues. See also *Love and Revolution,* pp. 589–92.

45. Eastman discussed this with me on August 6, 1963.

46. Max Eastman, "Thoughts about Hemingway," *Saturday Review* (March 24, 1962), p. 54.

47. The absorbing detective work which this reconstruction is based on appears in the unpublished Neil R. Joy, *"The Last Tycoon,* and Max Eastman: A Political Reading." The author is not quite as certain as Professor Joy

that Brimmer is modeled on Eastman, but Joy does show conclusively that the Brimmer-Stahr fight is based on Eastman's encounter with Hemingway.

48. When working on his autobiography a few years later Untermeyer sent Eastman a warm note that assumed their friendship was still intact. Louis Untermeyer to Max Eastman, September 18, 1938.

49. Max Eastman, "Our Major Poets," *Modern Quarterly* (Fall, 1938), p. 56.

50. John Dos Passos to Steward Mitchell, January 22, 1937, in Townsend Ludington, ed., *The Fourteenth Chronicle* (Boston, 1973), p. 504.

51. Charles Norman, *E. E. Cummings* (New York, 1964).

52. *Nation* (July 8, 1931), p. 46. *New Republic* (August 12, 1931), p. 349.

53. Edmund Wilson to Max Eastman, February 1, 1939, Eastman MSS.

54. Louise Bogan, "Verse," *New Yorker* (October 28, 1939), p. 80.

55. Max Eastman, "The End of Socialism in Russia." It appeared first in *Harper's* and was reprinted as a pamphlet by Little, Brown in 1937.

56. Edmund Wilson, *Travels in Two Democracies* (New York, 1936), p. 213.

57. *Ibid.*, p. 321.

58. Robert Conquest, *The Great Terror: Stalin's Purge of the Thirties* (New York, 1968).

59. Paul S. Meskil, "Meet the New Godfather," *New York Magazine* (February 28, 1977), pp. 28–32. According to this article, Tresca's assassin was Carmine Galante, now putative head of the Mafia. Max was not alone in suing the *Daily Worker* for libel; Trotskyists did so as well. "Leftist Libel," *Time* (May 23, 1938), p. 47.

60. Max Eastman to V. F. Calverton, April 3, 1937, Calverton MSS.

61. Quoted in Frank A. Warren, *Liberals and Communism* (Bloomington, Indiana, 1966), p. 167.

62. *Ibid.*, p. 169.

63. *The Case of the Anti-Soviet Trotskyite Center* (Moscow, 1937), p. 556. Serebriakov and twelve other defendants were shot immediately. Radek and others perished later.

64. Max Eastman, "An Open Letter to the *Nation:* A Letter the Nation Did Not Print," *Modern Monthly* (April, 1937), p. 5.

65. *Ibid.*, p. 6.

66. See the following pamphlets emanating from the American Socialist party: Anon., "Letter of an Old Bolshevik: The Key to the Moscow Trials" (New York, 1937); Friedrich Adler, "The Witchcraft Trial in Moscow" (New York, 1937); Francis Heisler, "The First Two Moscow Trials" (Chicago, 1937); especially impressive is Max Shachtman, "Behind the Moscow Trials" (New York, 1936).

67. Max Eastman, "The Communist Constitution," *Nation* (June 4, 1938), p. 655.

68. *Ibid.*, p. 655.

69. *Love and Revolution*, p. 610.

70. Edmund Wilson to Max Eastman, October 5, 1938, Eastman MSS.

71. Edmund Wilson, "The Myth of the Marxist Dialectic," *Partisan Review* (Fall, 1938), pp. 66–81. The quotations here are from the essay as it appeared in *To the Finland Station* (Garden City, 1940), p. 182.

72. *Ibid.*, p. 189.

73. *Ibid.*, p. 194.

74. Edmund Wilson to John E. Austin, 1957, and Edmund Wilson to Daniel Aaron, 1961, in Wilson, *Letters, op. cit.*, pp. 359, 441.

75. John West, "Max Eastman's Straw Man," *New International* (December, 1935), p. 225.

76. John P. Diggins, *Up from Communism* (New York, 1975), p. 186.

77. William Phillips, "The Devil Theory of the Dialectic," *Partisan Review* (Fall, 1938), p. 82.

78. The debate over Kronstadt has often been discussed. See, for example, James Gilbert, *Writers and Partisans* (New York, 1968); Victor Serge, *Memoirs of a Revolutionary* (London, 1963); Isaac Deutscher, *The Prophet Outcast* (London, 1963).

79. Leon Trotsky, *In Defense of Marxism (Against the Petty-Bourgeois Opposition)* (New York, 1965), p. 44. This curious volume is a collection of documents written by Trotsky in 1939 and 1940 but seemingly not collected until much later. It lists Max Eastman as the translator with no other explanation, and includes an introductory essay written by Joseph Hansen and William F. Warde, apparently in the mid-1960s, passionately attacking the backsliders of 1939.

80. *Ibid.*, p. 72.

81. *Ibid.*, p. 156.

82. *Ibid.*, p. 160.

83. Victor Serge, *Memoirs of a Revolutionary* (London, 1963), p. 349.

84. The letters and responses to them are discussed in Frank A. Warren, *Liberals and Communism* (Bloomington, Indiana, 1966), pp. 213–14. Eastman's letter was in the October 25, 1939, issue of the *New Republic;* Farrell's in the September 30, 1939, *Nation.*

85. Editors, "Mr. Stolberg's Glue," *New Republic* (February 1941), p. 261.

86. Granville Hicks, "Communism and the American Intellectuals," in Irving DeWitt Talmadge, ed., *Whose Revolution: A Study of the Future Course of Liberalism in the United States* (New York, 1941).

87. Daniel Aaron, *Writers on the Left* (New York, 1961), p. 396.

CHAPTER TEN

1. Max Eastman, *Stalin's Russia and the Crisis in Socialism* (New York, 1940), p. 9.

2. *Ibid.*, p. 9.

3. *Ibid.*, p. 10.

4. *Ibid.*, p. 30.

5. *Ibid.*, p. 56–57.

6. *Ibid.*, p. 58.

7. *Ibid.*, p. 61.

8. *Ibid.*, pp. 66–67.

9. *Ibid.*, p. 77.

10. *Ibid.*, p. 120.

11. *Ibid.*, p. 125.

12. *Ibid.*, p. 126.

13. *Ibid.*, p. 156.

14. *Ibid.*, p. 156.

15. *Ibid.*, p. 195.

16. Max Eastman, *Marxism: Is It Science?* (New York, 1940), p. 172.

17. *Ibid.*, p. 203.

18. Sidney Hook, *Reason, Social Myth and Democracy* (New York, 1940), p. 224.

19. Abram L. Harris, "The Crisis in Marxism," *Nation* (June 8, 1940), p. 714. Michael Karpovich, "Stalin and His Policies," *Yale Review* (June, 1940), p. 818. Philip Rahv, "What Is Living and What Is Dead?", *Partisan Review* (Summer, 1940), p. 180.

20. Lillian Symes, *Modern Quarterly* (Winter, 1939), p. 86.

21. John Chamberlain, "Up from Marxism," *Common Sense* (April, 1940), pp. 25–26. Eugene Lyons, "The Light That Failed," *Saturday Review* (March 16, 1940), p. 7.

22. Michael T. Florinsky, "Max Eastman's Critical Examination of Stalin's Russia," *New York Times Book Review* (March 17, 1940), p. 19.

23. Harold J. Laski, "Critic of Stalin," *New Statesman and Nation* (September 14, 1940), p. 263. The same point appears also in Philip Burnham, "Postscript and Introduction," *Commonweal* (March 22, 1940), pp. 476–77.

24. Rubin Gotesky, *Modern Quarterly*, 11, no. 7 (n.d.), pp. 96–98.

25. J. D. Bernal, "Is Marxism Science?", *Nature* (August 30, 1941), pp. 237–39.

26. Benjamin Stolberg to Max Eastman, October 22, 1940; John Dos Passos to Max Eastman, November 14, 1940; Rex Stout to Max Eastman, December 9, 1940; Louis Hacker to W. W. Norton, November 15, 1940; George Santayana to Max Eastman, December 31, 1940, Eastman MSS.

27. T. V. Smith, *Ethics* (April, 1941), pp. 335–36. Joseph Carwell, *Political Science Quarterly* (June, 1941), p. 291. Selig Perlman, *American Political Science Review* (October, 1941), p. 971. Anon., "Marx's Parlour Game," *Times Literary Supplement* (April 26, 1941), p. 198. Harold J. Laski, "Marxism Dissected," *New Statesman and Nation* (April 26, 1941), p. 442.

28. Wilson loyally stood by this assessment when he reprinted his essays of the 1940s. Accordingly this and subsequent quotations are from "Max Eastman in 1941," in Edmund Wilson, *Classics and Commercials* (New York, 1950), p. 58.

29. *Ibid.*, p. 59.

30. *Ibid.*, pp. 61–62.

31. *Ibid.*, p. 65.

32. *Ibid.*, p. 67.

33. *Ibid.*, p. 69.

34. Max Eastman to Edmund Wilson, February 17, 1941, Eastman MSS.
35. Floyd Dell, "Out of Love with Utopia," *New York Herald Tribune Books* (March 10, 1940), p. 6.
36. He had made fun of the human nature argument in an editorial in the *Liberator*, "Robert Lansing Explains Bolshevism" (March, 1920), p. 43.
37. John P. Diggins, *Up From Communism* (New York, 1975), p. 441–42.
38. Eastman quoted from these attacks in *Love and Revolution*, p. 638. Dwight Macdonald's statement is "Kulturbolschewismus Is Here," *Partisan Review* (November–December, 1941), pp. 442–43. A predictable sneer was the editorial, "Max Eastman's New Faith," *New International* (June, 1941), p. 101.
39. Max Eastman, "Socialism Doesn't Gibe with Human Nature," *Reader's Digest* (June, 1941), p. 44.
40. John Dewey to Max Eastman, March 21, 1941, Eastman MSS.
41. Max Eastman, Letter to the Editor, *New Leader* (June 28, 1941), p. 8. His essay appeared in the issues of January 24 and 31, 1942.
42. Eduard Heimann, "Eastman and Marx Err Because of 'Doctrinaire Faith in Science,'" *New Leader* (March 7, 1942), p. 4.
43. "Max Eastman Poses New 'Human' Problems for Socialist Thinkers in Second Reply to Critics," *New Leader* (November 28, 1942), p. 5. The final Heimann-Eastman exchange consisted of letters to the editor in the *New Leader* (December 5, 1942), p. 8.
44. Alfred Baker Lewis, "Socialism and Human Nature," *New Leader* (May 2, 1945), p. 8.
45. *Ibid.*, p. 8. The commentators generally agreed that Eastman's conclusions were partially right but overstated. Many also agreed that his psychology was out of date. See, for example, Reinhold Niebuhr in the February 7, 1942, issue: Jacques Barzun, February 14, 1942; August Classens, March 14, 1942.
46. Ruth Benedict, "Human Nature Is Not a Trap," *Partisan Review* (January–February, 1943), p. 161.
47. James T. Farrell, "On the Brooks-MacLeish Thesis," *Partisan Review* (January–February, 1942), p. 45.
48. "Max Eastman to James T. Farrell," *Partisan Review* (March–April, 1942), p. 204.
49. Max Eastman, "The Library," *American Mercury* (March, 1942), p. 369.
50. "Max Eastman to James T. Farrell," *op. cit.*, p. 205.
51. "Reply by Mr. Farrell," *Partisan Review* (January–February 1942), p. 212.
52. Max Eastman, "Radicals Quit Utopia, Face War Problems," *New Leader* (March 9, 1940), p. 7.
53. Max Eastman, "To the Editor," *New York Times* (May 11, 1941), Sec. E., p. 10.
54. Francis Biddle to Max Eastman, May 14, 1941; Lewis Mumford to Max Eastman, May 12, 1941, Eastman MSS.
55. Max Eastman, "Russia and the Fight for Democracy," Vineyard MSS.
56. "Max Eastman Address on Soviet Gets Turbulent Reception Here," unidentified Montreal newspaper clipping, Vineyard MSS.

57. Max Eastman, "Help Russia, But Keep Your Head," *New Leader* (June 13, 1943), p. 5; "To Collaborate Successfully We Must Face the Facts about Russia," *Reader's Digest* (July, 1943), pp. 1–14.

58. Ralph B. Levering, *American Opinion and the Russian Alliance 1939–45* (Chapel Hill, 1976), p. 148.

59. T.R.B., "Political Indigestion," *New Republic* (August 9, 1943), p. 195.

60. Editorial Note, *New Leader* (July 3, 1943), p. 1.

61. Max Lerner, "Answering Max Eastman," *PM* (July 1, 1943), p. 2.

62. "Max Eastman Comments on *PM* 'Double Talk' on Russia," *New Leader* (July 24, 1943), p. 5.

63. Victor Serge to Max Eastman, August 6, 1943, Eastman MSS.

64. William Carlos Williams, "A Fault of Learning: A Communication," *Partisan Review* (September–October, 1943), pp. 466–68. Eds., "The Politics of W. C. Williams," same issue, p. 470.

65. See, for example, the issue of November 17, 1941, in which the *New Republic* surveyed Russian life. Roger Baldwin, "The Question of Liberty," managed to find some. John Scott, "Administrators at Work" was pure Stalinism. It bragged that thanks to the purges no one was disloyal in Russia when Hitler invaded, an absolute lie.

66. Editorial, "The U.S.S.R.," *Life* (March 29, 1943), p. 20.

67. Max Eastman, "Help Russia, But Keep Your Head," *op. cit.*, p. 5.

68. Max Eastman, "Morals and Politics," *New Leader* (March 18, 1944), p. 10.

69. Max Eastman, Letter to the Editor, *New Leader* (August 22, 1942), p. 8.

70. Max Eastman, "In My Opinion," *New Leader* (April 17, 1943), p. 1.

71. Max Eastman, "A Case of Campaign Oratory," *New Leader* (November, 25, 1944), p. 4.

72. Editors, "A Reply to Max Eastman," *New Leader* (April 17, 1943), p. 5.

73. Max Eastman, "Carlo Tresca—The Death of a Rebel," *New Leader* (January 16, 1943), p. 1.

74. Max Eastman, "For Dolly Sloan," *New Leader* (May 15, 1943), p. 4.

75. Max Eastman, "Emotions on a Trip to New Orleans," *New Leader* (September 30, 1944), p. 8.

76. The early forties were not entirely tranquil. Eastman was politically active, writing letters and trying to influence men and events. But though frustrated at times, he remained hopeful until near the end of the war. On activities I have not listed here, see John P. Diggins, *Up from Communism* (New York, 1975), pp. 201–18.

77. Dwight Macdonald, "Eastmania," *Politics* (February, 1945), p. 59. Eastman's offending article was "A Cerebral Revolution Busts Loose! A Literary Marxist Shows His Hand," *New Leader* (January 13, 1945), p. 6.

78. Quoted in "Rebuttal by Max Eastman," *Politics* (April, 1945), p. 126.

79. Max Eastman and J. B. Powell, "The Fate of the World Is at Stake in China," *Reader's Digest* (June, 1945), p. 13.

80. Max Eastman in *Morals and Politics* (New York, 1945), p. 21. The other contributors were John Chamberlain, John Dewey, and Sidney Hook.

CHAPTER ELEVEN

1. Max Eastman, "Behind Soviet Foreign Policy," *American Mercury* (September, 1946), pp. 261–69.
2. Max Eastman, "Are We Headed for War with Russia?", The Town Hall, Inc., New York, September 19, 1946, p. 7. Transcript of the radio debate.
3. The historical literature on this subject is vast. The father of cold war "revisionist" history is William Appleman Williams, whose *The Tragedy of American Diplomacy,* rev. ed. (New York, 1962), has had many children. A useful review essay on the revisionists and their critics is Warren F. Kimball, "The Cold War Warmed Over," *American Historical Review* (October, 1974), pp. 1119–36.
4. Max Eastman to Carl Sandburg, January 30, 1946, Eastman MSS. The reference here is to Sandburg's six-volume biography of Lincoln published between 1926 and 1939.
5. Carl Sandburg to Max Eastman, March 5, 1946, Eastman MSS.
6. "Liberals Attack Wallace Policy," *New York Times* (January 23, 1947), p. 14.
7. The *New York World-Telegram* made Eastman's testimony its lead story for the day, "World Peace Must Await End of Soviet Regime" (May 8, 1948), p. 1.
8. This speech was front page news. "Our China Policy is a Mess, Max Eastman Tells AFL Meeting," *New York Times* (November 19, 1948), p. 1.
9. Max Eastman, "Russia's Foreign Policy and How To Meet It," typescript, Vineyard MSS.
10. Max Eastman, "The Dilemma of Free Speech," *Modern Quarterly,* XI, no. 7, p. 62.
11. Max Eastman to Sol Levitas, April 11, 1948, Eastman MSS.
12. "The 'Liberal' Fifth Column," *Partisan Review,* no. 3 (1946), pp. 279–80.
13. Philip Rahv, "Disillusionment and Partial Answers," *Partisan Review,* no. 5 (1948), pp. 519–29.
14. Dwight Macdonald, "Theory," *Politics* (Spring, 1948), p. 117.
15. Joseph P. Lash, "Weekend at the Waldorf," *New Republic* (April 18, 1949), pp. 10–14.
16. Daniel James, "The Debate on Cultural Freedom," *New Leader* (April 7, 1952), pp. 3–4.
17. Diana Trilling, "A Memorandum on the Hiss Case," *Partisan Review,* no. 3 (1950), pp. 484–500.
18. Irving Crystal, " 'Civil Liberties,' 1952—A Study in Confusion," *Commentary* (March, 1952), p. 229.
19. Max Eastman to Peter Viereck, September 28, 1951, Eastman MSS.
20. Edmund Wilson to Max Eastman, November 19, 1954, Eastman MSS. Wilson treated John Dos Passos, who was more extreme than Eastman, in the same way. See his letter of March 18, 1964, in Edmund Wilson, "Letters to Dos Passos," *New York Review of Books* (March 3, 1977), p. 17.
21. Max Eastman to Floyd Dell, May 14, 1954, Eastman MSS. For a longer ac-

count of Eastman's correspondence with Dell, see John P. Diggins, *Up from Communism* (New York, 1975).

22. Floyd Dell to Max Eastman, July 10, 1954, Eastman MSS.

23. Max Eastman to Floyd Dell, September 16, 1954, Eastman MSS.

24. Max Eastman, *Reflections on the Failure of Socialism* (New York, 1955), pp. 85–86.

25. Calder Willingham to Max Eastman, April 2, 1955, Eastman MSS. Willingham was so overcome by this revelation that he wrote to influential friends—James T. Farrell, Adlai Stevenson, Herman Wouk—praising the book.

26. Reviewed by William Henry Chamberlin in the *Wall Street Journal* (March 31, 1955), p. 9. Editorials in the *Wall Street Journal* (March 31, 1955), p. 8, and the *Saturday Evening Post* (May 21, 1955), pp. 10–.

27. William Barrett, "One Man's Pilgrimage," *New York Times Book Review* (April 3, 1955), p. 14. Charles Frankel, "Sorry Socialism," *Saturday Review* (August 13, 1955), p. 10.

28. Bertram D. Wolfe, "Case for a Liberal Economy," *New York Herald Tribune Books* (June 5, 1955), p. 6. See also Robert Ludlow, "From Marxism to Free Enterprise," *Commonweal* (April 8, 1955), p. 20.

29. Max Eastman, "Buckley versus Yale," *American Mercury* (December, 1951), p. 23.

30. Sidney Hook to Max Eastman, October 12, 1955, Eastman MSS. Hook gave his own view in "The Grounds on Which Our Educators Stand," *New York Times Book Review* (October 30, 1955), pp. 6–.

31. Max Eastman, Robert M. MacIver, Letters to the Editor, *Saturday Review* (March 10, 1956), p. 23. There was a similar exchange in the *New York Times Book Review* (December 11, 1955), p. 36, (January 1, 1956), p. 36.

32. Max Eastman to William F. Buckley, Jr., November 28, 1958, Vineyard MSS.

33. *Ibid.*

34. Max Eastman, "The Religion of Immoralism," *Freeman* (June 1, 1953), pp. 622–24.

35. Max Eastman, "A Question to the National Review," unpublished manuscript, Vineyard MSS.

36. William F. Buckley, Jr., to Max Eastman, April 24, 1962, Vineyard MSS.

37. William F. Buckley, Jr., "On the Right" (August 25, 1962). Eastman's reply was scribbled on the margin of his copy, Vineyard MSS.

38. William F. Buckley, Jr., "Notes toward an Empirical Definition of Conservatism," *Teacher's College Record* (October, 1963), p. 32.

39. Max Eastman, "Am I a Conservative?," *National Review* (January 28, 1964), p. 57.

40. William F. Buckley, Jr., to William L. O'Neill, October 23, 1975.

41. This was written in a note appended to an unpublished collection of essays, Max Eastman, "Communism, Socialism, and Democracy," p. 9, Vineyard MSS.

42. Max Eastman, *Heroes I Have Known: Twelve Who Led Great Lives* (New York, 1942), p. 86. In addition to Duncan, they are Annis Ford Eastman, Carlo Tresca, Eugene Debs, Thomas K. Beecher, Anatole France, Charles Chaplin, John Reed, Leon Trotsky, Sigmund Freud, and John Dewey.

43. See, for example, *Commonweal* (July 31, 1942), p. 354; *New Republic* (May 18, 1942), p. 677; *New York Herald Tribune Books* (April 26, 1942), p. 2; *New York Times Book Review* (May 3, 1942), p. 13; *Saturday Review* (May 23, 1942), p. 5.

44. Max Eastman, *Lot's Wife* (New York, 1942). It is printed again in Eastman's *Poems of Five Decades* (New York, 1954), from which this quotation is taken, p. 206.

45. Edmund Wilson to Max Eastman, August 27, 1942, Eastman MSS.

46. Max Eastman to himself, n.d., Eastman MSS. Wilson praised Eastman's translation of "October" in a letter dated November 15, 1942, Houghton Library.

47. Max Eastman to Edmund Wilson, August 31, 1942, Eastman MSS.

48. Edna St. Vincent Millay to Max Eastman, October 13, 1942; E. E. Cummings to Max Eastman, September 27, 1942; H. L. Mencken to Max Eastman, November 27, 1942, Eastman MSS.

49. Granville Hicks to Miss Hardman, September 25, 1942, Eastman MSS.

50. Anon., *Nation* (October 25, 1942), p. 714. Ruth Lechlitner, "Genesis Brought up to Date," *New York Herald Tribune Books* (November 22, 1942), p. 26. Ben Ray Redman, "Genesis with a Difference," *Saturday Review* (January 16, 1943), p. 18.

51. Max Eastman to himself, September 11, 1944, Eastman MSS.

52. Max Eastman, "What I Feel Like Writing at This Moment," July 2, 1954, Vineyard MSS.

53. Richard Simon to Max Eastman, December 5, 1938, Eastman MSS.

54. Max Eastman to M. Lincoln Schuster, April 7, 1939, Eastman MSS.

55. Margaret Halsey to Max Eastman, May 4, 1939, Eastman MSS.

56. Margaret Halsey to Max Eastman, May 30, 1939, Eastman MSS.

57. Maxwell Perkins to Max Eastman, July 26, 1939, Eastman MSS.

58. Max Eastman, "What I Feel Like Writing," *op. cit.*

59. Ida Rauh to Max Eastman, October 22, 1947, Eastman MSS.

60. Robinson Jeffers to Max Eastman, June 1, 1948; Upton Sinclair to Max Eastman, April 19, 1948; Floyd Dell to Max Eastman, n.d., Eastman MSS. See also letters from Boardman Robinson, Herbert Bayard Swope, Carl Van Doren, and others to whom Eastman had sent copies of the book.

61. McAlister Coleman, "Max Eastman: An Upper-Case History," *Nation* (May 1, 1948), p. 479.

62. Richard Watts, Jr., "Enjoyment of Eastman," *New Republic* (April 12, 1948), p. 18.

63. Max Eastman to Harry Scherman, January 3, 1948, Eastman MSS.

64. Granville Hicks, "Sorrows of Eastman," *Saturday Review* (April 17, 1948), p. 21.

65. J. Donald Adams, "Individual and Masses," *New Leader* (April 17, 1948), p. 10.

66. Anon., "Enormous Trifle," *Time* (April 19, 1948), p. 106. Orville Prescott agreed, "Books of the Times" (April 2, 1948). Charles W. Lawrence, *Cleveland Plain Dealer* (April 7, 1948), took issue with Prescott.

67. Alex Murphee, *Denver Post* (April, 1948); Lewis Gannett, *New York Herald Tribune* (April 11, 1948). John Abbott Clark, *Chicago Tribune* (April 11, 1948).

68. John Sloan to Max Eastman, April 28, 1948, Eastman MSS.

69. Max Eastman to Marion Townsend, April 11, 1948, Eastman MSS.

70. Max Eastman, "What I Feel Like Writing," *op. cit.*

71. DeWitt Wallace to Max Eastman, December 7, 1943, Eastman MSS.

72. DeWitt Wallace to Max Eastman, December 13, 1952; November 14, 1955; June 18, 1956; Eastman MSS.

73. Max Eastman to DeWitt Wallace, December 13, 1952, and November 26, 1955, Eastman MSS.

74. DeWitt Wallace to Max Eastman, January 29, 1959, Eastman MSS.

75. Max Eastman to Peter Viereck, September 28, 1951, Eastman MSS.

76. Max Eastman to Crystal Eastman, June 25, 1954, Vineyard MSS.

CHAPTER TWELVE

1. Alfred Kazin *Starting Out in the Thirties* (Boston, 1965), p. 67. Where it is not documented, the material in this chapter is derived from my conversations with Max, in the summers of 1963 and 1965 especially, and from talking with people who knew him in the last third of his life.

2. Rosalind Fuller, M.B.E., to Richard G. Green, May 12, 1969, Vineyard MSS.

3. Margaret Halsey, *No Laughing Matter: The Autobiography of a Wasp* (Philadelphia, 1977), pp. 74–75.

4. Max Eastman to V. F. Calverton, November 7, 1938, Eastman MSS.

5. Max Eastman to a lady, 1954, Eastman MSS.

6. "I haven't a single quiver of anything but joy in . . . your being with him." Max Eastman to Eliena Eastman, February 13, 1932, Eastman MSS.

7. *Love and Revolution,* p. 649.

8. Maxwell Perkins to Max Eastman, November 22, 1938; Max Eastman to Maxwell Perkins, November 30, 1938, Eastman MSS.

9. Doris Stevens to Max Eastman, October 19, 1956, Eastman MSS.

10. He wrote an article for the *New Republic* that year (Daniel Eastman, "The Minneapolis 'Sedition' Trial" [October 20, 1941], pp. 503–4), and was credited by the magazine with this list of jobs.

11. Alfred Kazin, "The Giant Killer: Drink and the American Writer," *Commentary* (March, 1976), p. 50.

12. The Eastman papers say almost nothing about Daniel. For information on

him I relied largely on Mariejo Eastman, his widow, from whom Daniel was separated at the time of his death. His friend Karl Meyer feels this assessment is too negative and minimizes his good qualities and achievements. Meyer, who also writes, says that Daniel's unpublished book manuscript was finished before he died and "is a not bad piece of work." Karl E. Meyer to William L. O'Neill, April 12, 1976.

13. *Love and Revolution,* p. 624.
14. W. A. Swanberg, *Dreiser* (New York, 1965), p. 493.
15. Albert Rhys Williams to Max Eastman, October 21, 1935, Eastman MSS.
16. Tess Slesinger to Max Eastman, n.d., Eastman MSS. A letter of thanks. Her novel The *Dispossessed* won critical acclaim. She then became a screenwriter in Hollywood and died at the age of forty.
17. For example, see Max Eastman to George Moreby Acklow, n.d., Eastman MSS, in which Max urges E. P. Dutton to publish, as it did, Ben Gitlow's *I Confess* (1940).
18. Max Eastman to Boris Souvarine, November 1, 1943, Eastman MSS. There is no evidence of how much Eastman eventually gave Souvarine, or if it was repaid.
19. Max Eastman to David Randall, August 3, 1967, Eastman MSS.
20. Max Eastman to Louis Untermeyer, July 24, 1950, Eastman MSS.
21. Max Eastman to Joseph Freeman, 1947, Eastman MSS.
22. John Dos Passos to Max Eastman, December 25, 1953, in Townsend Ludington, ed., *The Fourteenth Chronicle* (Boston, 1973), p. 605.
23. Claude McKay, *A Long Way from Home* (New York, 1937), p. 29.
24. Nugent made his statement in a taped interview with Wayne Cooper on October 2, 1975.
25. Claude McKay to Max Eastman, April 25, 1932, McKay MSS. Many of the letters between Eastman and McKay are reprinted in Wayne Cooper, ed., *The Passion of Claude McKay: Selected Prose and Poems* (New York 1973).
26. Claude McKay to Max Eastman, July 23, 1933, McKay MSS. On October 20, 1933, and again on October 30, 1933, McKay wrote asking for loans.
27. Claude McKay to Max Eastman, November 10, 1934, McKay MSS.
28. Claude McKay to Max Eastman, March 2, 1939, McKay MSS.
29. *The Passion of Claude McKay, op. cit.,* p. 302.
30. Max Eastman to Claude McKay, August 21, 1942, and September 3, 1943, McKay MSS.
31. Max Eastman to Claude McKay, June 7, 1944, McKay MSS. Claude McKay to Max Eastman, June 30, 1944, McKay MSS.
32. Claude McKay to Max Eastman, August 28, 1946: Max Eastman to Claude McKay, September 9, 1946; Claude McKay to Max Eastman, September 16, 1946, Claude McKay MSS.
33. Claude McKay, *Selected Poems* (New York, 1953), p. 112.
34. Max Eastman to Oswald Garrison Villard, June 30, 1933, Villard MSS.
35. Max Eastman, untitled speech, Vineyard MSS.
36. Max Eastman, "My Feelings about Marriage," Vineyard MSS.
37. Max Eastman to Joseph Slater, March 17, 1948.

38. Max Eastman to Jacques Cattell, April 16, 1956, Eastman MSS.
39. Max Eastman, untitled poem, Vineyard MSS.
40. Quoted in Wayne Cooper, ed., *The Passion of Claude McKay,* p. 11.
41. Richard O'Connor, *Heywood Broun: A Biography* (New York, 1975), p. 83.
42. Charles Neider, "Max Eastman," *Saturday Review* (May 17, 1969), p. 6.
43. Margaret Halsey to Max Eastman, March 22, 1939, Eastman MSS.
44. Ruth Pickering Pinchot to Max and Eliena Eastman. August, 1946, Eastman MSS.
45. *Love and Revolution,* p. 620.

CHAPTER THIRTEEN

1. Jacob Rosin and Max Eastman, *The Road to Abundance* (New York, 1953).
2. Floyd Dell to Max Eastman, July 10, 1954, Eastman MSS.
3. J. H. Jackson, *San Francisco Chronicle* (June 18, 1953). Waldemar Kaempffert, "The Plentiful Tomorrow," *New York Times Book Review* (July 5, 1953), p. 7. Anon., *New Yorker* (June 13, 1953), pp. 118–19.
4. Max Eastman, *Poems of Five Decades* (New York, 1954), p. xii.
5. Max Eastman to Edmund Wilson, May 1, 1954; Edmund Wilson to Max Eastman, November 19, 1954, Eastman MSS.
6. Leonard Kriegel, *Edmund Wilson* (Carbondale, Illinois, 1971), p. 44.
7. Quoted in Paul Sherman, *Edmund Wilson: A Study of Literary Vocation in Our Time* (Urbana, Illinois, 1965), p. 2.
8. Oliver St. John Gogarty, "A Poet in Love with Nature," *New York Times Book Review* (October 17, 1954), p. 40. E. Merrill Root, "The Poetry of Max Eastman," *New Leader* (November 8, 1954), pp. 25–26. Ben Ray Redman, "A Nest of Singing Birds," *Saturday Review* (October 23, 1954), p. 39.
9. Max Eastman, "Non-Communicative Art," *Freeman* (May 3, 1954), pp. 571–74.
10. Carl Sandburg to Max Eastman, May 5, 1954, Eastman MSS. Norman Thomas, Letter to the Editor, *Freeman* (June 14, 1954), p. 652.
11. Max Eastman to Upton Sinclair, March 31, 1957, Sinclair MSS.
12. Isaac Deutscher to Max Eastman, May 25, 1956, Eastman MSS.
13. Max Eastman, *Great Companions: Critical Memoirs of Some Famous Friends* (New York, 1959). The subjects are E. W. Scripps, Albert Einstein, Ernest Hemingway, Edna St. Vincent Millay, George Santayana, Pablo Casals, Trotsky, Freud, and Bertrand Russell.
14. Lewis Gannett, *New York Herald Tribune Book Review* (April 12, 1959), p. 11. Anon., *New Yorker* (April 24, 1959), p. 179. Anon., "How To Make Friends and Button-Hole People" *Times Literary Supplement* (April 1, 1960), p. 210.
15. Arthur Boyars, "Unconscionable Max," *Spectator* (April 8, 1960), p. 517.
16. Milton Hindus, *New York Times Book Review* (April 26, 1959), p. 22. Harry T. Moore, "Galvanic Glimpses," *Saturday Review* (May 2, 1959), p. 40.
17. James T. Farrell to Bennett Cerf, December 10, 1964; Lewis S. Feuer to Mimi Matsner, December 30, 1964, Vineyard MSS.

18. Milton Rugoff, "A Literary Journalist," *New York Herald Tribune Book Review* (November 26, 1950), p. 8. Irving Howe," "The Value of Taste," *Partisan Review,* no. 1, (1951), p. 127. Irving Kristol, "American Humanist," *Commentary* (November, 1950), p. 499.

19. George Lichtheim, "The Romance of Max Eastman," *New York Review of Books* (January 14, 1965), p. 8.

20. Max Eastman to Barbara Epstein, December 23, 1964, Vineyard MSS.

21. Hilton Kramer, "Politics without Pain," *Commentary* (July, 1965), p. 92.

22. Norman Podhoretz, "Out of the Brambles into the Corn Field," *Book Week* (January 24, 1965), p. 5.

23. Further proof that Eastman's mental powers did not fail with age is his exchange with Sidney Hook over pragmatism in the *New Leader.* They led the magazine to consider changing its name to the *Epistemological Leader.* Eastman offered a sophisticated analysis of pragmatism that explained why he didn't agree with it. His objections were narrowly technical. In the largest sense Eastman was pragmatic, and to the degree that he had a philosophy it was the instrumentalism he had learned from Dewey. See Max Eastman, "Marx, Dewey, and Hook," *New Leader* (February 10, 1958), pp. 16–18, and Sidney Hook, "Marx, Dewey and Eastman," same issue, pp. 18–19.

24. William S. Schlamm, "Eastman's Loves and Revolutions," *National Review* (January 16, 1965), p. 66.

25. George Santayana to Max Eastman, January 1, 1952; Max Eastman to George Santayana, February 21, 1952, Eastman MSS.

26. Anon., "Traveling Man," *Newsweek* (January 4, 1965), p. 62.

27. Anon., "The Cheerful Radical," *Time* (January 8, 1965), p. 67.

28. Arthur M. Schlesinger, Jr., *New York Times Book Review* (January 3, 1965), p. 7.

29. Joseph L. Featherstone "An Exile from Socialism," *New Republic* (January 16, 1965), p. 19.

30. Joseph Slater, "On Coming Home to Poetry," *Saturday Review* (February 6, 1965), p. 19.

31. Sidney Hook to Max Eastman, n.d., Vineyard MSS.

32. *New Yorker* (August 14, 1965), p. 32.

33. William L. O'Neill, ed., *Echoes of Revolt: The* Masses, *1911 to 1917* (Chicago, 1966).

34. Granville Hicks, "Something Wonderfu Happened," *Saturday Review* (December 10, 1966), p. 41.

35. The review was Michael B. Folsom, "The Masses: Working Class Dreams," *Nation* (February 27, 1967), pp. 177–79. In many respects it was a thoughtful essay.

36. Max Eastman to Joseph Slater, March 17, 1967.

37. Max Eastman, *Seven Kinds of Goodness* (New York, 1967).

38. Leon Trotsky, *The Young Lenin* (New York, 1972), translated by Max Eastman, edited and annotated by Maurice Friedberg.

39. Alden Whitman, "Max Eastman Is 'Sorry' for Today's Rebels," *New York Times* (January 9, 1969), p. 33.
40. *Seven Kinds of Goodness*, pp. 148–49.
41. *New York Times* (March 27, 1969), p. 50.
42. Leon Edel, untitled statement, sent with cover letter to Richard G. Green, May 12, 1969, Vineyard MSS.
43. Milton Cantor, *Max Eastman* (New York, 1970), p. 173.

Index